International Trials and Reconciliation

Transitional justice is a burgeoning field of scholarly inquiry. Yet while the transitional justice literature is replete with claims about the benefits of criminal trials, too often these claims lack an empirical basis and hence remain unproven. While there has been much discussion about whether criminal trials can aid reconciliation, the extent to which they actually do so in practice remains under-explored. This book investigates the relationship between criminal trials and reconciliation, through a particular focus on the International Criminal Tribunal for the former Yugoslavia (ICTY).

Using detailed empirical data – in the form of qualitative interviews and observations from five years of fieldwork – to assess and analyze the ICTY's impact on reconciliation in Bosnia-Hercegovina, Croatia and Kosovo, *International Trials and Reconciliation: Assessing the Impact of the International Criminal Tribunal for the Former Yugoslavia* argues that reconciliation is not a realistic aim for a criminal court. They are, Janine Natalya Clark argues, only one part of a rich tapestry of justice, which must also include non-retributive transitional justice processes and mechanisms.

Challenging many of the common yet untested assumptions about the benefits of criminal trials, this innovative and extremely timely monograph will be invaluable for those with interests in the theory and practice of transitional justice.

Janine Natalya Clark is based in the Politics Department, University of Sheffield.

Transitional Justice
Series Editor: Kieran McEvoy
Queen's University Belfast

The study of justice in transition has emerged as one of the most diverse and intellectually exciting developments in the social sciences. From its origins in human rights activism and comparative political science, the field is increasingly characterised by its geographic and disciplinary breadth. This series aims to publish the most innovative scholarship from a range of disciplines working on transitional justice related topics, including law, sociology, criminology, psychology, anthropology, political science, development studies and international relations.

Titles in this series:

Families of the Missing
A Test for Contemporary Approaches to Transitional Justice
Simon Robins (2013)

Transitional Justice Theories
Edited by Susanne Buckley Zistel, Teresa Koloma Beck, Christian Braun,
Friederike Mieth (2014)

Truth, Denial and Transition
The Contested Past in Northern Ireland
Cheryl Lawther (2014)

Transitional Justice and the Arab Spring
Edited by Kirsten Fisher and Robert Stewart (2014)

The Art of Post-Dictatorship
Ethics and Aesthetics in Transitional Argentina
Vikki Bell (2014)

International Trials and Reconciliation
Assessing the Impact of the International Criminal Tribunal for
the Former Yugoslavia
Janine Clark (2014)

Forthcoming titles in the series:

The Concept of the Civilian
Legal Recognition, Adjudication and the Trials of International Criminal Justice
Claire Garbett

The Judiciary and the Politics of Transition
Police Brutality Cases in Chile, Northern Ireland and South Africa
Marny Requa

The Trouble with Truth
Dealing with the Past in Northern Ireland
Kieran McEvoy

Transitional Justice, Peace and Democracy
After Conflict
Elin Skaar, Camila Gianella and Trine Eide

'Janine Natalya Clark dispels the myth that international criminal courts can serve as a beacon for reconciliation in countries ripped apart by ethnic cleansing and genocide. Clark's findings remind us that the pursuit of justice, as important as it may be, should never be viewed as some kind of panacea for righting past wrongs or as a magic bullet for healing victims and war-torn societies. To do so, Clark rightly argues, belittles the suffering of victims and distorts the enormity of the task of rebuilding shattering communities. This is an important book that diplomats, court staff and justice activists should take seriously.'

Eric Stover, Faculty Director, Human Rights Center,
University of California, Berkeley School of Law and author of
The Witnesses: War Crimes and the Pursuit of Justice in The Hague

'This book, based on extensive research, is an important reminder to all involved in international and criminal courts, that justice done with fear or with favour, or to further some political compromise, will never conduce to peace because victims see through it. Courts must do the justice job for which they are qualified, namely to convict mass murderers as quickly and fairly as possible and punish them as retribution for their atrocities as a deterrent to future perpetrators. Judges should forget about writing history – they are not qualified – or producing reconciliation, which criminal justice cannot do, other than as a precondition. The evidence shows the importance of more honest outreach programmes: people must understand not only the work of global justice, but also its human limits.'

Geoffrey Robertson QC, author of *Crimes Against Humanity*

International Trials and Reconciliation

Assessing the Impact of the International Criminal Tribunal for the Former Yugoslavia

Janine Natalya Clark

Routledge
Taylor & Francis Group
a GlassHouse Book

First published 2014
by Routledge
2 Park Square, Milton Park, Abingdon, Oxon, OX14 4RN

and by Routledge
711 Third Avenue, New York, NY 10017

a GlassHouse Book

Routledge is an imprint of the Taylor & Francis Group, an informa business

© 2014 Janine Natalya Clark

British Library Cataloguing in Publication Data
A catalogue record for this book is available from the British Library

Library of Congress Cataloging-in-Publication Data
Clark, Janine N. (Janine Natalya), author.
International trials and reconciliation : assessing the impact of the
international criminal tribunal for the former Yugoslavia / Janine Natalya
Clark.
pages cm. – (Transitional justice)
Includes bibliographical references and index.
ISBN 978-0-415-71778-6 (hardback) – ISBN 978-1-315-87111-0 (ebk)
1. International Tribunal for the Prosecution of Persons Responsible for
Serious Violations of International Humanitarian Law Committed in the
Territory of the Former Yugoslavia since 1991. 2. Yugoslav War Crime
Trials, Hague, Netherlands, 1994- I. Title.
KZ1203.C53 2014
341.6'90268–dc23
2014010329

ISBN: 978-0-415-71778-6 (hbk)
ISBN: 978-1-315-87111-0 (ebk)

Typeset in Galliard
by Cenveo Publisher Services

MIX
Paper from
responsible sources
FSC
www.fsc.org   FSC® C013604   Printed and bound by CPI Group (UK) Ltd, Croydon, CR0 4YY

In memory of all of the victims of the wars
in the former Yugoslavia

Contents

Contents

List of figures

Acknowledgements

This book is the product of a long journey, based on fieldwork which I first began in 2008. It would not have been possible without the hundreds of people who have helped me along the way by giving up their time to speak to me and to share their personal stories. Their kindness and generosity was deeply humbling, their courage and strength inspiring. While it is impossible to mention all of them by name, their voices and experiences run through this book, which is dedicated to all of the victims of the wars in the former Yugoslavia. In Bosnia-Hercegovina (BiH), I would particularly like to thank the following people: Edin Ramulić, Sejda Karabašić, Sudbin Musić, Mirsad Duratović, Nusreta Sivac, Emsuda Mujagić, Mehmed Begić, Hiba Ramić, Sakib Mehmetović, Zahid Ahmić, Zikret Ahmić, Hajrudin Pezar, Hatidža Mehmedović, Munira Subašič, Kada Hotić, Hajra Ćatić, Hasan Nuhanović, Nefisa Medošević, Lilit Umroyan, Bosa Miletić, Slavko Klisura, Fadila Memiševic, Adam Boys, Derek Chappell, Matias Hellman, Bakira Hasečić, Goran Bubalo and Nerin Dizdar.

In Croatia, special thanks must go to Dr Liljana Gehreke, Dr Charles Tauber, Marija Molnar, Liljana Pekić, members of the veterans' association Croatian War Invalids of the Homeland War (HVIDR) in both Vukovar and Knin, Ankica Mikić, Manda Patko, Suzana Lazarević, Veselinka Kastratović, Mladen Stojanović, Miren Špek, Dragutin Glasanović, Vlado Ilković, Danijel Rehak, Nenad Marić, Tomo Aračić, Tanja Kale, Lada Blagaić and Ljubo Manojlović.

In Kosovo, I am especially grateful to William Ortiz, Jonathan Browning, Miodrag Milićević, Kirsten Joppe, Katarina Grbesa, Judith Brand, Rexhep Selimi, Hyrie Veliu, Nenad Maksimović, the 'bridge watchers' in north Mitrovica/ë, Mehmetali Perolli, Gens Strezi, Engjëll Berisha and Suphije Tafarshiku.

Thank you also to staff at the International Criminal Tribunal for the former Yugoslavia (ICTY) for taking the time out of their extremely busy schedules to speak and to share their thoughts with me when I visited the Tribunal in February 2008. Liam McDowall and his team in the Outreach Unit were particularly generous with their time.

I must also thank the Leverhulme Trust for funding my first two fieldtrips (in 2008 and 2009) to BiH, as part of a Leverhulme Early Career Fellowship (2007–2009). Thank you also to my editors at Routledge, Dr Colin Perrin and Rebekah Jenkins, who have been wonderful and incredibly efficient. Finally, I would like to thank my Mother, Marion Clark, for all her love and support during the process of writing this book.

Abbreviations

ABiH	Bosnian Army
AFRC	Armed Forces Revolutionary Council
AU	African Union
BiH	Bosnia-Hercegovina
CDF	Civil Defence Forces
CDRSSE	Centre for Democracy and Reconciliation in Southeast Europe
CWWPP	Coalition for Work with Psychotrauma and Peace
DPA	Dayton Peace Accords
DRC	Democratic Republic of Congo
EC	European Commission
ECCC	Extraordinary Chambers in the Courts of Cambodia
EEC	European Economic Community
EU	European Union
EULEX	European Union Rule of Law Mission in Kosovo
HDLSKL	Croatian Association of Camp Inmates of Serbian Concentration Camps
HDZ	Croatian Democratic Union
HLC	Humanitarian Law Centre
HRHB	Croatian Republic of Herceg-Bosna
HV	Croatian Army
HVO	Bosnian Croat Army
HZHB	Croatian Community of Herceg-Bosna
ICC	International Criminal Court
ICG	International Crisis Group
ICJ	International criminal justice
ICMP	International Commission for Missing Persons
ICRC	International Committee of the Red Cross
ICTR	International Criminal Tribunal for Rwanda
ICTY	International Criminal Tribunal for the former Yugoslavia
IDP	Internally displaced person
IJR	Institute for Justice and Reconciliation

JCE	Joint Criminal Enterprise
JHP	Joint History Project
JNA	Yugoslav National Army
KLA	Kosovo Liberation Army
KM	Bosnian Marks
KPA	Kosovo Property Agency
KVM	Kosovo Verification Mission
LRA	Lord's Resistance Army
LTTE	Liberation Tigers of Tamil Eelam
MRGI	Minority Rights Group International
MUP	Ministry of Internal Affairs
NATO	North Atlantic Treaty Organization
NDZ	Independent State of Croatia
NGOs	Non-governmental organizations
OSCE	Organization for Security and Co-operation in Europe
OTP	Office of the Prosecutor
RDC	Research and Documentation Centre
RECOM	Regional Commission for Establishing the Facts about War Crimes and Other Gross Violations of Human Rights Committed on the Territory of the former Yugoslavia
RPF	Rwandan Patriotic Front
RS	Republika Srpska
RSK	Republic of Serbian Krajina
RUF	Revolutionary United Front
SCSL	Special Court for Sierra Leone
SENSE	South East News Service Europe
SOC	Serbian Orthodox Church
SRS	Serbian Radical Party
TJ	Transitional Justice
TO	Territorial Defence
TRC	Truth and Reconciliation Commission
UN	United Nations
UNDP	United Nations Development Programme
UNHCR	United Nations High Commissioner for Refugees
UNMIK	United Nations Mission in Kosovo
UPC	Union of Congolese Patriots
UPDF	United People's Defence Force
US	United States
VJ	Yugoslav Army
VRS	Army of the Republika Srpska
WWII	World War Two

Introduction

Speaking in Kampala in May 2010, the United Nations (UN) Secretary-General declared that, 'The old era of impunity is over. In its place, slowly but surely, we are witnessing the birth of a new Age of Accountability' (Ban 2010). While the first of these claims seems premature and overly definitive, the second draws attention to the fact that the cloak of impunity which once protected powerful leaders from criminal prosecution is no longer as thick and fibrous as it once was. In places at least, the fabric has become extremely thin and threadbare. The trial of the former Serbian President Slobodan Milošević, the ongoing trial of the former Bosnian Serb leader Radovan Karadžić, the trial and conviction of Rwanda's former Prime Minister, Jean Kambanda, and the criminal proceedings and guilty verdict against the former Liberian President, Charles Taylor, are all part of a veritable 'justice cascade' (Sikkink and Walling 2007: 433) which began during the early 1990s. Following the creation of the International Criminal Tribunal for the former Yugoslavia (ICTY) and the International Criminal Tribunal for Rwanda (ICTR) in 1993 and 1994 respectively, the number of international courts[1] has steadily increased, culminating in the establishment of the International Criminal Court (ICC) – the first ever permanent international penal court.

These courts are a defining feature of the 'new Age of Accountability' and their existence has inevitably spawned a rich and extensive body of literature. Yet, while scholars continue to debate the merits, benefits and costs of international courts, 'these debates are fuelled largely by normative conceptions of how such mechanisms should work, with very little analysis of whether they actually do work' (Millar 2010: 477). Fundamentally, extant literature on transitional justice (TJ) in general and on international criminal courts in particular has often neglected the crucial issue of impact. In short, 'Too often, public debate about the accomplishments of international tribunals has been driven by untested assumptions' (Orentlichter 2008: 10). What do criminal trials *actually* achieve? What are their *effects* on the ground? A number of scholars have attempted to

---

1 This research uses the term international courts to include hybrid courts.

answer these key questions, with a particular focus on the ICTY (see, for example, Delpla 2007; Khan 2014; Mannergren Selimović 2010; Meernik 2005; Nettelfield 2010; Obradović-Wochnik 2014; Orentlicher 2008, 2010; Stover and Weinstein 2004a; Subotić 2009).[2] This inter-disciplinary research seeks to build on this body of literature by addressing a crucial dimension of impact that remains critically under-investigated.

Why this book?

H lives in Ahmići, a mixed Bosniak (Bosnian Muslim) and Bosnian Croat village in central Bosnia-Hercegovina (BiH). In April 1993, during the Bosnian war, the Bosnian Croat Army (HVO) attacked Ahmići, killing 116 of its Bosniak inhabitants. H's parents, brother and three sisters were among the dead. The remains of his father and brother were found 14 years later, buried under an apple tree on H's land. He suspects that his nearest neighbours, a Bosnian Croat family, always knew where his father and brother were buried and deliberately withheld this information. H returned to Ahmići in 2001 but has minimal contact with Croats in the village. His trust has gone.

Kravica is a Serb village in the municipality of Bratunac, in eastern BiH. In January 1993, the Bosnian Army (ABiH) launched an attack on the village and V's only son was one of the victims. Her husband died after the war ended. While she enjoyed good relations with Bosnian Muslims before the war, the loss of her son changed everything. She is sure that Bosnian Muslim women who lost their sons feel exactly the same way.

D lived through the three-month siege of Vukovar, a town in eastern Croatia whose name will forever be synonymous with overwhelming destruction. She was raped and both her husband and father were killed. She nevertheless decided to return to Vukovar, which for her will always be home. She greets her Serb neighbours, but she no longer has any Serb friends. Relations have changed since the war in 1991.

Gjakovë/Đakovica, in western Kosovo, is one of the areas that bore the brunt of the war between Serbian forces and the Kosovo Liberation Army (KLA) during the late 1990s. Today, M is alone; her husband and four sons were killed. She visits their graves every day. Her home is full of photographs and memories. She has no contact with Serbs and never wants any. All of the Serbs in Gjakovë/Đakovica left when the war ended, with the exception of the five (mainly elderly) Serb women who live in the grounds of the local Serbian Orthodox Church (SOC). The church is surrounded by high walls and an Albanian policeman is on guard 24 hours.

During my years of fieldwork in the former Yugoslavia, I have heard many powerful stories of loss and suffering, of pain and tragedy. These stories, in turn,

---

2　There is also a small body of anthropological literature exploring the impact of different TJ processes (see, for example, Kelsall 2005; Shaw 2007; Wilson 2003).

have left me with many questions: how do war victims continue to live alongside those whom they no longer trust; can peaceful coexistence develop into something deeper; and, above all, is reconciliation ever truly possible in communities profoundly affected and scarred by war and bloodshed? In any post-conflict society, reconciliation poses enormous challenges; and the more I have learnt from my own fieldwork experiences regarding the multiplicity of potential obstacles to reconciliation, the more I have become fascinated and intrigued by the claim that international criminal courts can contribute to reconciliation.

In his aforementioned speech in Kampala, Ban Ki-Moon emphasized that, 'the time has passed when we might speak of peace versus justice, or think of them as somehow opposed to each other' (Ban 2010). His words both reflect and highlight the fact that since the early 1990s, the relationship between justice and peace has been significantly re-theorized. Contrary to the long-accepted idea that post-conflict societies must choose between justice and peace,[3] the 'peace through law' premise essentially holds that there can be no peace without justice (Fara-Andrianarijaona 2013: 16). The UN Security Council, for example, mandated the ICTY and ICTR to, *inter alia*, contribute to 'the restoration and maintenance of peace' (UN 1993b, 1994).[4] It is in the context of these developments that certain scholars and commentators have sought to argue that international courts can aid reconciliation (see, for example, Adami 2007; Akhavan 1998; Cassese 1998; Crocker 2002; Jallow 2008; Kerr 2007; Kritz 1996; May 2010; Scharf and Williams 2003). In September 2013, for example, after the Appeals Chamber of the Special Court for Sierra Leone (SCSL) upheld the conviction of the former Liberian President, Charles Taylor, the United States (US) Secretary of State, John Kerry, declared that: 'In holding Charles Taylor accountable for war crimes and crimes against humanity, the Appeals Chamber... has brought a measure of justice to the people of Sierra Leone, and helped to cement the foundation on which reconciliation can proceed' (Kerry 2013).

Not only is there a fundamental dearth of empirical evidence to support claims that courts can promote reconciliation, but the very issue of whether they do in fact aid the process remains crucially under-explored. The purpose of this research, therefore, is precisely to address this particular impact gap. Focusing on the ICTY, it seeks to establish whether the Tribunal has contributed to inter-ethnic reconciliation in the former Yugoslavia.[5] While it is important to acknowledge

3 Explaining why post-apartheid South Africa opted for a truth and reconciliation commission (TRC) rather than extensive criminal trials, for example, the TRC's former chairman, Archbishop Desmond Tutu, has underlined that, 'We have had to balance the requirements of justice, accountability, stability, peace and reconciliation. We could very well have had retributive justice, and had a South Africa lying in ashes – a truly Pyrrhic victory if ever there was one' (1999: 27).
4 The ICTR's mandate also refers to reconciliation.
5 As this research is about international courts, it does not focus on local courts in the former Yugoslavia which are now conducting their own war crimes trials. These trials are significant in their own right and an important topic for future research.

that reconciliation is not an official part of the Tribunal's mandate, this does not mean that this research has created a straw man. Rather, this book is specifically a response to claims that the ICTY *is* aiding reconciliation; and as will be seen in Chapter 1, these claims have come from, *inter alia*, certain prominent figures within the Tribunal itself.

The ICTY is the centre-piece of this book for three key reasons. Firstly, the ICTY is the oldest of all the international courts which currently exist; on 27 May 2013, it marked the twentieth anniversary of its creation. It has also issued the most indictments (161) and conducted the most trials. Hence, it has arguably had the most opportunities to aid reconciliation. Secondly, at a time when the Tribunal is approaching the end of its mandate, there is growing debate about and reflection on its legacy and achievements. In an address before the UN Security Council on 12 June 2013, for example, the ICTY Prosecutor declared that: 'Never before has so much been said and written about our cases, our legacy and our contribution to reconciliation in the region' (Brammertz 2013b). This book's focus on the ICTY thus gives it a particular timeliness and relevance. Thirdly, as a specialist on the former Yugoslavia, I have always had a special interest in the ICTY. This interest co-exists with the desire to draw much-needed attention to some of the post-war problems which continue to affect societies in the former Yugoslavia. As one scholar underlines, 'The Balkans may have been out of the headlines for the past few years, but the challenges to peacebuilding there remain' (Pickering 2007: 170).

Many excellent books on the ICTY have already been written (see, for example, Gow, Kerr and Pajić 2014; Nettelfield 2010; Steinberg 2011; Stover 2007; Stover and Weinstein 2004a; Subotić 2009). Nevertheless, this research is unique for several reasons. The first is that while scholars have discussed whether criminal trials *can* aid reconciliation (see, for example, Akhavan 1998; Amstutz 2005; Fatić 2000; Humphrey 2003; Kamatali 2003; Kerr 2005; Sarkin 2001), very few have engaged with this question empirically. Those who have, for their part, have omitted to sufficiently address the critical issue of how we actually measure the impact of criminal trials on reconciliation (Meernik, Nichols and King 2010; Orentlicher 2010; Stover and Weinstein 2004a). This research, in contrast, develops and utilizes a three-pronged measurement model for assessing the ICTY's impact on reconciliation. As part of this, it operationalizes the concept of reconciliation – '...one of the most contested concepts in the scholarly debate on transitional justice, and arguably also the most difficult to measure empirically' (Skaar 2012: 54) – in the form of a 'Reconciliation Matrix'.

The second factor that makes this research original is its comparative approach. Thoms, Ron and Paris note that, 'Among the minority of studies that do investigate TJ impacts, many are single-case studies of individual countries rather than structured cross-case comparisons, making general policy-relevant conclusions difficult to draw' (2010: 335). Existing research on the ICTY, which overwhelmingly focuses on BiH, is a case in point. To comprehensively analyze whether the ICTY's trials have contributed to reconciliation, however, it is not sufficient to confine the impact assessment to BiH alone. Accordingly, this research broadens the focus to include Croatia and Kosovo. Scholarly literature on the ICTY has massively neglected Kosovo; the latter has received more attention in the context of the work of the Special Court for Kosovo (see, for example, Carolan 2008; Dickinson 2003). While Croatia is less overlooked (see, for example, Peskin 2008; Peskin and Boduszyński 2003; Subotić 2009; Vukušić 2014), the issue of whether and to what extent the Tribunal's work has contributed to reconciliation in Croatia has barely been empirically explored. Stover and Weinstein's *My Neighbor, My Enemy* (2004a), a stellar edited volume which asks, *inter alia*, what role courts play in social reconstruction and reconciliation, includes the Croatian town of Vukovar as a case study. Based on fieldwork that was conducted more than ten years ago, however, the book is now somewhat dated; it does not specifically measure the impact of the ICTY's trials on reconciliation in Croatia; and when the book was published in 2004, only the so-called 'Vukovar Three' (discussed in Chapter 6) had stood trial. Since then, the ICTY has undertaken and completed its most important and highly publicized trial in relation to Croatia – the trial of Ante Gotovina – and no analysis of the ICTY's impact on reconciliation would be complete without the inclusion of this particular case.

Some readers may question why this research focuses only on BiH, Croatia and Kosovo and does not include Serbia as a case study. The explanation is simple: Serbia did not directly experience war until 1999, when the North Atlantic Treaty Organization (NATO) bombed targets throughout the country in response to atrocities by the Serbian military and police in Kosovo. With the exception of Kosovo (which until 1999 was part of Serbian territory), moreover, there was no serious ethnic conflict in Serbia. Hence, inter-ethnic reconciliation is not an issue in Serbia in the way that it is in BiH, Croatia and Kosovo.

The third claim to originality that this research can make is an empirical one. Too many existing discussions and claims regarding the relationship between courts and reconciliation lack empirical substance. Writing on the SCSL, for example, Tejan-Cole claims that, 'Prosecutions give peace processes an added impetus but they must not be pursued simply for the sake of locking up a few bad guys; they must contribute to reconciliation and nation-building...' (2009: 243). Problematically, he provides no evidence of whether and how prosecutions do in fact contribute to reconciliation. For their part, Kerr and Mobekk reflect on the relationship between courts, peace and reconciliation. In the absence of empirical data, however, their discussion is largely theoretical and speculative. Apropos of the ICTY and ICTR, for example, they argue that, 'In both cases, reconciliation may not only be an unrealistic goal, but one which is extremely difficult to measure' (2007: 48). Reconciliation is of course immensely difficult to measure; but this does not mean that we should make no attempts to do so or to develop ways of empirically testing our theoretical claims (van der Merwe, Baxter and Chapman 2009: 4).

The few existing attempts to empirically assess the ICTY's impact on peace and reconciliation have often relied on quantitative methods (see, for example, Meernik 2005; Meernik, Nichols and King 2010); and such methods often yield limited results. Meernik, Nichols and King, for example, list a range of ways in which criminal trials can potentially aid human rights and peace (2010: 315–316). Also acknowledging, however, that, '...we cannot test the precise causal logic behind our hypotheses', they thus explain that: 'Our analysis, like others...focuses on the hypothesized ultimate benefits of transitional justice' (Meernik, Nichols and King 2010: 316). In contradistinction, this research is qualitative and ethnographic, and based on over 350 semi-structured interviews conducted over a five-year period (see below). It thus adds crucial empirical richness and detail to many existing debates regarding the relationship between courts and reconciliation. Weinstein underlines that, '...we have not been successful at promoting a research agenda that values the study of effectiveness [of TJ mechanisms]. Anecdotes abound, assumptions remain untouched by lack of evidence...' (2011: 1). It is precisely such anecdotes and unsupported assumptions about the relationship between trials and reconciliation which this book will test and challenge.

The arguments

Using the three-pronged measurement model that is developed in Chapter 2, this research analyzes whether the ICTY's trials have contributed to inter-ethnic reconciliation by examining: (i) popular perceptions of the Tribunal and whether local communities associate its work with justice; (ii) truth acceptance and the extent to which the ICTY's work has narrowed the gap between competing ethnic truths; and (iii) the nature of everyday inter-ethnic relations on the ground. Embracing the argument that, 'Reconciliation must begin at the level of the individual – neighbor to neighbor, then house to house, and finally, community to community' (Halpern and Weinstein 2004: 306), this research is specifically concerned with reconciliation at the individual and community level. Making a clear distinction between coexistence and reconciliation, and adopting a relatively 'thick' definition of reconciliation as the repair and restoration of relationships and the rebuilding of trust, it argues that the ICTY has not contributed to inter-ethnic reconciliation in BiH, Croatia or Kosovo.

Widespread popular dissatisfaction and disappointment with the Tribunal exist. From complaints that the ICTY has prosecuted too few people and imposes unduly light sentences, to allegations that its trials are biased and politically-motivated, all sides have their own particular grievances. Hence, the 'justice' that the ICTY dispenses is deeply contested, and disputed justice cannot be the basis for reconciliation. Indeed, some of the Tribunal's most controversial judgements have helped to entrench rather than to bridge ethnic divides. The ICTY's unpopularity, in turn, means that the facts and truths that it has established have failed to penetrate and gain local acceptance. Highlighting the reality that 'truth' and identity are fundamentally intertwined (Andrieu 2009: 11), it is often the case that communities overwhelmingly continue to cling on to their own ethnic truths, only accepting the ICTY's work when it supports their particular war narratives. The persistence of rival narratives emphasizing 'our' victimhood and 'their' culpability is a serious impediment to inter-ethnic reconciliation, and the

ICTY's trials have often helped to harden these narratives rather than to facilitate a reciprocal process of 'narrative incorporation' (Dwyer 2003: 96). Hence, the Tribunal's claim that its work limits the scope for denial (ICTY n.d.) is both naïve and fundamentally flawed.

If the ICTY has not contributed to reconciliation by delivering justice and establishing the truth, this does not necessarily mean that it has not done so in other ways; and thus it is important to examine everyday inter-ethnic relations in BiH, Croatia and Kosovo. These relations are generally peaceful (although less so in Kosovo), and coexistence largely exists. Rather than attributing this to the ICTY's work, however, it is argued that it is primarily domestic factors – including an overwhelming popular desire for peace, the exigencies of everyday life and simple pragmatism – which have made coexistence possible. Nevertheless, coexistence is distinct from reconciliation and in order to specifically measure whether the latter exists, this research uses the Reconciliation Matrix developed in Chapter 2. Assessed against the four key criteria of human security, deep contact, trust and mutual acceptance, it is submitted that there is no inter-ethnic reconciliation in BiH, Croatia or Kosovo.

There is no doubt that the ICTY could and should have done more to reach out to local communities in the former Yugoslavia. Lack of information and crucial knowledge gaps have helped to fuel popular grievances and hostility towards the Tribunal. The need for early and sustained grassroots-focused outreach work is thus one of the key themes running through this book. Greater investment in outreach could have helped to improve the ICTY's image in the former Yugoslavia, but would it have made a fundamental difference in terms of the Tribunal's impact on reconciliation? It seems unlikely. This research is deeply sceptical about whether *any* international court[6] can aid reconciliation and argues that there are generic factors common to all international courts and the difficult environments in which they operate that render the justice–reconciliation nexus problematic. While further studies are needed using different case studies, this research asserts that reconciliation is not a realistic goal for international courts – and hence it should be neither part of their mandates nor something that we expect them to achieve. As Moghalu points out, 'There is no empirical proof of any situation…where trials in and of themselves created reconciliation' (2009: 90). In April 2013, I participated as a panellist in a thematic debate on justice and reconciliation at the UN General Assembly in New York. While many of the member-state representatives expressed strong support for the idea that international justice facilitates reconciliation, Rwanda's Minister of Justice and Attorney General, Tharcisse Karugarama, was far more cynical. In a powerful speech which drew on the experiences of his own country, he declared that, '…international criminal justice is in a crisis of credibility

---

6 Although this book is specifically about international criminal courts, it is questionable whether domestic courts are any better equipped to contribute to reconciliation in post-conflict societies (see, for example, Clark 2010a).

with regard to fostering national reconciliation in post conflict situations' (Karugarama 2013). This research shares this viewpoint and argues that a 'crisis of credibility' exists precisely because international courts are not well-equipped to facilitate such a complex and challenging process as post-conflict reconciliation.

Reconciliation calls for a multi-layered approach which does not over-rely on criminal trials alone, and restorative justice should form part of this approach. An important complement to criminal trials, restorative justice – which includes truth and reconciliation commissions (TRCs), reparations and memorials – is not about punishing perpetrators, but rather about addressing the needs of all those affected by crime, and above all the needs of victims. The fact, therefore, that many victims in the former Yugoslavia have been left feeling disappointed with the ICTY highlights a potentially important role for restorative justice – and the Coalition for a Regional Commission for Establishing the Facts about War Crimes and Other Gross Violations of Human Rights Committed on the Territory of the former Yugoslavia (RECOM), discussed in Chapter 8, highlights this. The impact of restorative justice processes, and in particular TRCs, however, also remains under-explored. According to Wiebelhaus-Brahm, 'Generally, existing studies insufficiently measure potential truth commission effects…As a result, the global spread of truth commissions is based largely on faith in the power of truth-seeking rather than solid empirical evidence' (2010: 7). Ultimately, therefore, this research advocates a holistic approach to reconciliation which extends beyond the use of TJ processes. The immense challenges that reconciliation presents in deeply-divided post-conflict societies call for creativity, imagination and innovation, rather than simply a mechanistic recourse to courts and TRCs.

Fieldwork and methodology

In order to assess whether the ICTY's trials have assisted inter-ethnic reconciliation in BiH, Croatia and Kosovo, this research uses a specifically bottom-up methodology focused on ordinary people – and in particular, victims. The rationale for doing so is three-fold. Firstly, decisions about TJ and assessments of its impact 'are too often made without consulting the population affected' (Lambourne 2009: 28). This is deeply problematic because ethnic conflict and war crimes primarily affect the lives of ordinary people. The views of local communities – and specifically war victims – should therefore be at the centre of any analysis of TJ impact. As Klarin argues apropos of the ICTY, 'More than the Judges, Prosecutors, Defence Counsel or journalists, it is the victims who have the right to judge whether the Tribunal has been a success or failure' (2004: 557).

Secondly, victims have a fundamental part to play in any reconciliation process (Kontsevaia 2013: 24). Hence, in order to gauge whether reconciliation exists and whether the ICTY can take any credit for this, victims must be a central focus (Dancy 2010: 376; Hodžić 2010: 114; Weinstein and Stover 2004: 11). This research accordingly privileges victims' perspectives and experiences, thereby both endorsing and reflecting the argument that, 'any understanding of reconciliation profits from beginning with an examination of the beliefs, values, attitudes, and behaviors of ordinary people' (Gibson 2009: 175).

Thirdly, and closely linked to the previous point, ethnic conflict and war crimes destroy the lives of individuals and devastate communities. Accordingly, it is at the grassroots level that the repair of relationships – the essence of reconciliation – is especially important (Halpern and Weinstein 2004: 305). It is also at the grassroots level that some of the most significant tests for peace and reconciliation exist (Halpern and Weinstein 2004: 304). None of this is to suggest that the elite level is unimportant; the actions and behaviour of politicians and those in power obviously matter. This research, however, is based on the premise that we can gain the most authentic picture of inter-ethnic relations and the deepest insights into the complexities and nuances of these relations by primarily focusing on the view from below.

This research therefore utilizes a largely ethnographic approach, which according to Shaw is 'the most appropriate approach if we want to examine how transitional justice mechanisms actually work in practice for ordinary people' (2005: 5). It is crucial not only to explore the views and concerns of ordinary people, but also to search for insights into their daily lives (Pickering 2007: 188). During fieldwork in BiH, Croatia and Kosovo, I therefore endeavoured wherever possible to live among the individuals and communities that I was researching;[7] I participated in community life as much as possible by, *inter alia*, going to church, visiting local markets and frequenting popular cafes where there were always opportunities to meet and talk to people; and I took part in a number of local events as a participant observer. On 11 May 2008, for example, I participated in a monthly protest in the city of Tuzla in north-eastern BiH, arranged by internally-displaced women from Srebrenica to draw attention to the unresolved fate of their missing loved-ones (see Clark 2010b). On 26 July 2008, I joined a small rally in Prijedor in north-west BiH, organized by a group of local Serbs and the SOC in support of the (at that time) recently-arrested former Bosnian Serb leader, Radovan Karadžić (see Clark 2010c). On 5 August 2011, I travelled to Knin, in western Croatia, for the annual 'Day of Victory, Thanksgiving and the Croatian Defenders', a national holiday celebrating Croatia's victory in Operation 'Storm' in August 1995; and in November 2011, I took part in the extensive commemorations to mark the twentieth anniversary of the fall of Vukovar on 18 November 1991 (see Clark 2013a).

This research, however, is primarily based on qualitative interview data, and specifically on 372 semi-structured interviews. Over the course of ten fieldwork visits to the former Yugoslavia between 2008 and 2013, amounting to approximately ten months in total, I interviewed 210 people in BiH, 86 people in Croatia and 76 people in Kosovo.[8] Table 0.1 gives a summary of the entire interview sample.

---

7 This was not always straightforward in mixed communities (see Clark 2012a).
8 To protect the identity of interviewees, no names are used in this book.

Table 0.1 Total interview sample (= 372)

Location	Ethnicity	Sex
BiH – 210	Bosniak – 98	Men – 244
Croatia – 86	Bosnian Serb – 51	Women – 128
Kosovo – 76	Bosnian Croat – 41	
	Croat – 47	
	Croatian Serb – 38	
	Kosovo Albanian – 33	
	Kosovo Serb – 33	
	Other* – 31	

*N.B. The 'other' category consists largely of internationals

Table 0.2 Total BiH sample (= 210)

Sex	Ethnicity	Age	Social Profile
Men – 135	Bosniak – 98	Under 35 – 38	Non-elite – 157
Women – 75	Bosnian Serb – 51	35–50 – 69	Elite – 53
	Bosnian Croat – 41	Over 50 – 60	
	Other – 20	Over 60 – 43	

Fieldwork in BiH

Between 2008 and 2013, I made four fieldwork trips to BiH, amounting to just over six months in total. Of the 210 interviewees (see Table 0.2), 157 were 'ordinary people', including pensioners, students, taxi drivers, housewives, security guards, secretaries and shop assistants. These 157 individuals – many of whom could also be described as victims (see Table 0.3) – are the focus of the three chapters on BiH. The remaining 53 individuals within the BiH sample included religious actors,[9] officials, representatives of European and international bodies, as well as leaders of non-governmental organizations (NGOs) who did not fit the profile of ordinary people (including a lawyer, a medical doctor and a psychologist). These 'elite' interviewees primarily provided crucial background information and contextual details.

I deliberately concentrated on areas which have been a strong focus of the Tribunal's work – in particular Ahmići, Prijedor and Srebrenica – and my fieldwork in these locations generated some of the richest data. I also visited/returned to certain areas specifically to gauge local reactions to particular ICTY verdicts. On 29 May 2013, for example, one of the Tribunal's three Trial Chambers sentenced six high-ranking Bosnian Croats to prison terms of between ten and

---

9 This research began as a Leverhulme Early Career Fellowship (2007–2009) focused on judicial and religious paths to peace-building in BiH (on the issue of religious peace-building in BiH, see Clark 2010c).

Table 0.3 BiH non-elite sample (= 157)

Sex	Ethnicity	Age	War Experiences*
Men – 96	Bosniak – 83	Under 35 – 28	Displacement – 96
Women – 61	Bosnian Serb – 41	35–50 – 47	Loss of close family
	Bosnian Croat – 33	Over 50 – 44	members – 58
		Over 60 – 38	Camps/torture – 35
			Combatants – 30
			Rape –10

*N.B. The fourth column lists only some of the most common war experiences, and these experiences were overlapping rather than mutually exclusive. Some internally displaced interviewees, for example, had also lost close family members during the war. The numbers in the 'War Experiences' column therefore add up to more than 157.

25 years for crimes against humanity, violations of the laws or customs of war and grave breaches of the Geneva Conventions committed as part of a joint criminal enterprise or JCE.[10] This was an extremely significant judgement against the most senior members of the Bosnian Croat leadership and the HVO, and I was therefore keen to hear what Bosnian Croats had to say about it. Hence, in August 2013, in addition to returning to Stolac, I also visited (for the first time) Grude, the former *de facto* seat of the Croatian Republic of Herceg-Bosna (HRHB), and nearby Široki Brijeg. Both towns, located in the heart of Hercegovina, are ethnically Croat and have a reputation as strong nationalist areas. On the issue of the ICTY, however, interviewees in Grude and Široki Brijeg were no more hard-line than any of the other Bosnian Croats whom I have interviewed; they voiced the same criticisms and complaints. Earlier in the year, in March 2013, a month after the Appeals Chamber controversially acquitted the former chief of the Yugoslav Army (VJ) General Staff, Momčilo Perišić, I returned to Srebrenica to speak to local people – and specifically Bosnian Muslims and some of the Mothers of Srebrenica – about the verdict. I also returned to Prijedor, which I had not visited since 2008, just a couple of days after the ICTY issued its trial verdict against Mićo Stanišić, the former Minister of the Interior of Republika Srpska (RS), and Stojan Župljanin, the former chief of the Regional Security Services Centre of Banja Luka, on 27 March 2013. Both men were found guilty of crimes committed, *inter alia*, in Prijedor municipality. I also wanted to conduct second interviews with some of the people whom I had previously interviewed five years earlier, in order to examine whether intermediate events – most notably the arrest of the former Bosnian Serb commander Ratko Mladić – had altered their views of the Tribunal. I was able to re-interview four people in Srebrenica and two in Prijedor.

This research, however, is not confined only to those parts of BiH which have received the most attention from the ICTY. During my fieldwork in the country

10 A JCE exists when 'a plurality of persons participates in the realization of a common criminal objective' (Prosecutor v. Gotovina, Čermak and Markač 2011: §1953).

between 2008 and 2013, I conducted interviews in 32 different locations across BiH.[11] Firstly, although the interview data cannot be described as representative, I wanted to generate a sample as rich and comprehensive as possible, and to address the problem of 'forgotten victims' by drawing attention to places which the ICTY has largely overlooked, such as Bratunac in eastern BiH. Secondly, I was interested to find out whether there is a link between people's attitudes towards the ICTY and how informed they are about it, and to do this I selected both areas that have been a key focus of the Tribunal's work and those that have not. I had initially assumed that interviewees in places such as Prijedor and Srebrenica would be more informed about the ICTY than interviewees in towns and cities such as Goražde, Mostar and Tuzla, but this was not necessarily the case. The vast majority of interviewees, regardless of where they lived, were poorly informed about the Tribunal. The most obvious difference was that interviewees in areas that have been a focal point of the ICTY's work were more likely to express deeply critical views of the Tribunal, whereas interviewees in other areas were more likely to express simple indifference. Thirdly, I was keen to find out whether a correlation exists between a person's level of suffering during the war and his/her attitudes towards the Tribunal. Hence, I interviewed people in places where both some of the worst and some of the fewest war crimes and atrocities occurred. What quickly emerged is that those interviewees who greatly suffered during the war often had very high initial expectations of the ICTY. In particular, they expected it to prosecute *all* war criminals and to severely punish them with long prison sentences. Inevitably, (unrealistically) high expectations generate deep disappointments, and the latter have in turn helped to cloud people's perceptions of the Tribunal. In contrast, interviewees who had endured lower levels of suffering tended to have similarly lower expectations, and this helps to explain why some of them primarily expressed indifference towards the Tribunal.

In BiH, as in Croatia and Kosovo, I used a combination of snowball, purposive and opportunistic sampling strategies. Snowball sampling was particularly useful when I first entered the field, as a way of establishing contacts, but increasingly I relied more on purposive sampling in order to find particular groups of interviewees, such as war veterans, camp survivors and individuals who had lost close family members. Opportunistic sampling simply means taking advantage of any new interviewing opportunities as they arose. I always used an interview guide with a series of questions, *inter alia*, about the ICTY, inter-ethnic relations and reconciliation. However, I did not rigidly adhere to this; I wanted the interviews to be informal and free-flowing, and thus to give

11 Ahmići, Banja Luka, Bratunac, Brčko, Čapljina, Čelebići, Dobrinja (eastern Sarajevo), Foča, Fojnica, Goražde, Gornji Vakuf-Uskoplje, Grude, Iljaš, Ilidža, Konjic, Kozarac, Kravica, Ljubiški, Mostar, Potočari, Prijedor, Prozor, Sanski Most, Sarajevo, Široki Brijeg, Srebrenica, Stolac, Trnopolje, Tuzla, Višegrad, Vitez and Zenica.

interviewees the freedom and opportunity to say what was important to them. Most interviews lasted approximately one hour, although some were shorter and some were considerably longer; and as relatively few interviewees spoke English, I conducted the majority of the interviews in the local languages (Bosnian/Croatian/Serbian). Occasionally I interviewed people in their own homes, but in most cases I interviewed them in public places. Interviews were recorded, except in those cases where interviewees did not consent to this, and transcribed using a combination of open and closed coding in order to identify key themes.

Fieldwork in Croatia

The war in Croatia was never a big news story and the country's wartime president never attracted the same level of media attention as his Serbian counterpart, Slobodan Milošević. On the contrary, '...Croatia and its wartime leader, Franjo Tuđman, were usually relegated to the inside pages of Western newspapers' (Peskin 2008: 93). In a similar vein, existing scholarly research on the ICTY has tended to neglect Croatia. Certainly, the number of ICTY trials relating to Croatia is comparatively small. This should not, however, detract from the latter's importance as a case study. The war in Croatia, all too often eclipsed by the bloodier and more protracted war in neighbouring BiH, tore apart the existing social fabric and inflicted deep wounds. In the words of one Balkans specialist, 'Apart from Bosnia, no state in Eastern Europe had suffered such material destruction and loss of life to win its independence...' (Tanner 2010: 301). In Croatia, thus, both the need for reconciliation and the challenges that it poses are significant.

Among the various war crimes committed in Croatia on both sides, two in particular stand out – the massacre of at least 200 sick and wounded individuals (predominantly Croats) at Ovčara, near Vukovar, in November 1991; and the expulsion of thousands of Serbs from Knin and the Krajina area in western Croatia during Operation Storm in August 1995. Vukovar and the Krajina area have therefore been an important focus of the ICTY's work vis-à-vis Croatia. Furthermore, the trials of, and judgements against, the so-called 'Vukovar Three' and the Croatian generals Ante Gotovina and Mladen Markač, discussed in Chapter 6, have not only generated the most controversy and publicity in Croatia, but have also had the greatest impact on popular opinion regarding the ICTY. Accordingly, my fieldwork in Croatia – during which I interviewed a total of 86 people (see Table 0.4) – centred on Vukovar and Knin.

In July and August 2011, I undertook six weeks of fieldwork in Vukovar (including Borovo Naselje and the nearby Serb village of Borovo Selo), during which I carried out semi-structured interviews with 54 people. I interviewed a further four people when I returned to the area in November 2011 on the occasion of the twentieth anniversary of the fall of Vukovar (see Clark 2013a).

As in BiH, I purposively focused on ordinary people, and interviewees included market traders, pensioners, taxi drivers and shop assistants. Almost all of them had lived through the devastating three-month siege of Vukovar in 1991; 20 of them had fought in the war (17 of them as Croatian 'defenders' or *branitelji*); and many of them could be categorized as victims (see Table 0.5). In order to enrich the data and to explore more specialist opinions on particular issues, I also conducted 13 'elite' interviews with, *inter alia*, the leaders of three NGOs in Vukovar (namely the Coalition for Work with Psychotrauma and Peace or CWWPP, the European House and the Centre for Peace, Legal Advice and Psychosocial Assistance); three legal experts from the Centre for Peace, Non-Violence and Human Rights in Osijek; a war crimes analyst at *Documenta*, a Zagreb-based NGO working on TJ issues; and a communications officer at the ICTY's outreach office in Zagreb.

In April 2012, I returned to Croatia for two weeks to undertake fieldwork in Knin. I interviewed a total of 20 people, including Croatian ex-combatants, Serb returnees and Croat settlers from BiH who fled to Croatia during the Bosnian war. While the majority of these interviews took place in Knin, I also completed two interviews in nearby Benkovac (a town which also bore the brunt of Operation Storm) and five interviews in the Serb returnee village of Golubić. Seventeen of the interviewees were ordinary people and the remaining three included a senior figure within the UN High Commissioner for Refugees (UNHCR) in Knin. In March 2013, *en-route* to BiH, I made a second, five-day visit to Knin to speak to people regarding the acquittal of the Croatian generals Gotovina and Markač. During this time, I carried out a further eight interviews. As in BiH, only a minority of the interviewees in Croatia spoke English, and hence I interviewed the majority in Croatian and Serbian. Tables 0.4 and 0.5 below summarize the interview data for Croatia.

Fieldwork in Kosovo

During the course of two field visits to Kosovo – a five-week trip in July and August 2012 and a ten-day trip in January 2013 – I interviewed a total of 76 people (see Table 0.6). In order to explore a broad range of viewpoints and to include in the sample people from both heavily-affected and lightly-affected war

Table 0.4 Total sample for Croatia (= 86)

Sex	Ethnicity	Age	Social Category
Men – 57	Croat – 47	Under 35 – 6	Non-elite – 70
Women – 29	Croatian Serb – 38	35–50 – 27	Elite – 16
	Other – 1	Over 50 – 28	
		Over 60 – 25	

Table 0.5 Non-elite sample for Croatia (= 70)

Sex	Ethnicity	Age	War Experiences
Men – 49	Croat – 38	Under 35 – 4	Displacement – 40
Women – 21	Croatian Serb – 32	35–50 – 22	Combatants – 26
		Over 50 – 23	Loss of close family
		Over 60 – 21	members – 16
			Camps/torture – 11
			Rape – 1

Table 0.6 Total sample for Kosovo (= 76)

Sex	Ethnicity	Age	Social Profile
Men – 52	Kosovo Albanian – 33	Under 35 – 14	Non-elite – 66
Women – 24	Kosovo Serb – 33	35–50 – 31	Elite – 10
	Other – 10	Over 50 – 18	
		Over 60 – 13	

areas, I travelled to 15 different locations throughout Kosovo.[12] However, I prioritized the west and the north of Kosovo. The west experienced some of the most intense fighting during the war in Kosovo; the KLA was mainly based in this area and the ICTY's Kosovo-related trials have largely concentrated on war crimes committed in the west of the country.[13] To give expression to the significance of this particular part of Kosovo, I conducted 22 interviews in western Kosovo (primarily in Gjakovë/Đakovica, but also in Pejë/Peć, Istog/k and Goraždevac/Gorazhdevc). Although it has not been a focus of the ICTY's work, the north of Kosovo is also a crucial area for the purposes of this research. It is the most volatile part of Kosovo and the future stability of the country is inextricably bound up with the Gordian knot of the north. My fieldwork centred mainly on the divided city of Mitrovica/ë, the compact northern part of which is predominantly Serb[14] while the much larger southern part is exclusively Albanian. This flashpoint city remains extremely tense and, like western Kosovo, presents particular challenges in terms of reconciliation. According to a poll by the UN Development

12 Gjakovë/Đakovica, Gjilan/Gnjilane, Goraždevac/Gorazhdevc, Gračanica/Graçanicë, Istog/k, Leposavić/q, north Mitrovica/ë, Pejë/Peć, Prishtinë/Priština, Raçak/Račak, south Mitrovicë/a, Štrpce/Shtërpcë, Vushtrri/Vučitrn, Zubin Potok and Zvečan/Zveçan. Every place name in Kosovo has both an Albanian and a Serbian spelling. In places where there is an Albanian majority, I use the Albanian spelling first, followed by the Serbian spelling (e.g. Prishtinë/Priština). In places where Kosovo Serbs are a majority, in contrast, the Serbian spelling precedes the Albanian spelling (e.g. north Mitrovica/ë).

13 Although I refer to Kosovo as a country, it must be emphasized that certain states – including Greece, Serbia and Spain – still do not recognize Kosovo's 2008 declaration of independence.

14 There are some Kosovo Albanians who live in the north. A small number reside in north Mitrovica/ë itself, including in the ethnically-mixed Bosnjačka Mahala/Lagja e Boshnjakëve area.

Table 0.7 Non-elite sample for Kosovo (= 66)

Sex	Ethnicity	Age	War Experiences
Men – 47	Kosovo Albanian – 33	Under 35 – 10	Displacement – 39
Women – 19	Kosovo Serb – 33	35–50 – 26	Loss of close family
		Over 50 – 17	members – 25
		Over 60 – 13	Combatants – 20

Programme (UNDP) in November 2010, for example, 53.8 per cent of Kosovo Albanians and 61.5 per cent of Kosovo Serbs said that they felt very unsafe crossing the River Ibër/Ibar which divides the city (UNDP 2011: 45). In total, I conducted 20 interviews in northern Kosovo (including 11 in north Mitrovica/ë) and nine interviews in south Mitrovicë/a.

Once again, the primary aim was to examine the perspectives and experiences of ordinary people – and in particular of victims and those who directly participated in the war in Kosovo (see Table 0.7). These are the individuals whose lives were fundamentally affected by the conflict and whose views are therefore critical for analyzing the ICTY's impact on reconciliation. Interviewees included former members of the KLA, policemen who patrol the particularly volatile areas linking north Mitrovica/ë and south Mitrovica/ë, market traders and Serb 'bridge-watchers'.[15] Although Kosovo is an ethnically-mixed society,[16] this research focuses on the two main ethnicities, Kosovo Albanians and Kosovo Serbs. Both historically and today, all of the problems in Kosovo have centred on these two groups and the inter-ethnic relations between them. However, I was also keen to explore the perspectives of some of the many internationals who are based in Kosovo. As many of them have been living and working in Kosovo for several years, they are a rich source of information. I therefore interviewed ten internationals, including members of the European Rule of Law Mission in Kosovo (EULEX), the UN Mission in Kosovo (UNMIK) and the Organization for Security and Co-operation in Europe (OSCE). These interviews mainly took place in Prishtinë/Priština.

I conducted almost all of the interviews in Bosnian/Serbian and English. Although I do not speak Albanian, other than a few words, most Kosovo Albanians over the age of 30–35 speak Serbian. However, due to the sensitive political situation in Kosovo (specifically regarding northern Kosovo) and the fact that there are ongoing inter-ethnic problems in certain areas, it was more prudent to ask Kosovo Albanians if they spoke Bosnian rather than Serbian. Bosnian and Serbian are, for all intents and purposes, one and the same

---

15 The 'bridge-watchers' are groups of Kosovo Serb men who watch the main bridge in Mitrovica/ë for any signs of trouble or danger from the Albanian side.
16 Kosovo's population, for example, includes Roma, Ashkali, Egyptian and Gorani minorities.

language.[17] The main difference between the two is that the Bosnian language uses the ijekavian dialect whereas the Serbian language, as spoken in Serbia, uses the ekavian dialect.[18] Hence, when interviewing Kosovo Albanians, I spoke in the ijekavian dialect, which for them was far more acceptable; but when interviewing Kosovo Serbs, I used the ekavian dialect. In the case of the three Albanian interviewees who spoke neither English nor Bosnian/Serbian, I used a professional Albanian translator.

Readers will have noticed from the seven data tables that there is a substantial gender imbalance in this research (which was not deliberate) in favour of men.[19] This imbalance is particularly pronounced in the Kosovo non-elite sample, where only 28.78 per cent of interviewees were female. This significant under-representation of women (and in particular of Kosovo Albanian women) – which again was not deliberate – stems from three particular factors. The first is that in addition to using snowball and purposive sampling techniques, I also relied heavily on opportunistic sampling in Kosovo; and while in the field, I simply had far more opportunities to meet and interview men than women, especially on the Albanian side. In the small Kosovo Albanian town of Vushtrri/Vučitrn, for example, the local cafes I visited were almost entirely full of men. The second factor is that I used a purposive sampling strategy to identify and locate, *inter alia*, ex-combatants from the KLA, and the latter consisted mainly – although by no means exclusively – of men. My goal of interviewing former KLA fighters thus further slanted the interview sample towards men; among the 15 interviewees who had fought in the KLA, only one was female. Thirdly, prior to entering the field, contacts within the former Yugoslavia had warned me that because the situation in Kosovo remains tense, particularly in the north, I might struggle to find people willing to be interviewed. While this was not entirely true, it was often the case that men were more ready to speak than women; the latter often claimed that they had nothing to say and did not follow politics.

In addition to my interviews in BiH, Croatia and Kosovo, I also conducted 12 semi-structured interviews at the ICTY in February 2008. The Tribunal consists of the Office of the Prosecutor (OTP), the Chambers and the Registry, and

---

17 Bosnian, Croatian and Serbian are mutually comprehensible 'languages' and the differences between them are minor.

18 As the difference between the two names suggests, many words in the ijekavian dialect have an extra 'ij'; for example, *mlijeko* (milk) rather than *mleko*.

19 This gender imbalance primarily reflects a combination of practical factors. In particular, I generally had greater access to men than women in the field. When I visited veterans' organizations and camp survivors' associations, for example, I overwhelmingly encountered men. It was also frequently the case that men were more ready to give interviews than women (perhaps a reflection in part of the fact that societies in the Balkans remain strongly patriarchal). In the central Bosnian village of Ahmići, for example, Bosniak women often declined to speak to me; some simply did not wish to be interviewed and others claimed that they had previously given many interviews to local journalists and were tired of telling their stories.

I purposively selected interviewees from each of these three organs. Interviewees therefore included the spokesperson for the Prosecutor, the *Chef de Cabinet*, the Tribunal's then Registrar and the head of the Outreach Unit.[20] All of these interviews were conducted in English and lasted approximately one hour.

Layout of the book

This book is divided into eight chapters. Chapter 1 sets the scene and provides key background information about the wars in the former Yugoslavia and the creation of the ICTY. A rich and comprehensive literature analyzing the break-up of Yugoslavia and the wars of secession already exists,[21] and hence the purpose of this first chapter is simply to provide readers with a concise and general overview of these events – in a way that does justice to their complexity and preserves the inter-linkages between them. The second part of the chapter outlines the various developments which preceded the adoption of UN Security Council Resolution 827 and the establishment of the ICTY in 1993. The final part of the chapter examines the origins of the posited linkage between international criminal courts and reconciliation. It analyzes UN Security Council Resolutions related to the ICTY and ICTR and explores the significance of the Tribunals' creation under Chapter VII of the UN Charter. It also demonstrates that certain figures (although not all) within the ICTY itself have fostered the idea that a positive nexus exists between criminal trials and reconciliation.

Chapter 2 is a crucial theoretical and conceptual chapter which lays the foundations for the empirical chapters. It extensively engages with the fundamental issues of how to define reconciliation and how to operationalize the concept in order to measure it. To the latter end, it constructs a 'Reconciliation Matrix'. The final part of the chapter develops a measurement model for assessing whether the ICTY has contributed to inter-ethnic reconciliation in BiH, Croatia and Kosovo. The three key prongs of this model, which has a broader applicability beyond the ICTY, are justice, truth and the nature of inter-ethnic relations.

Chapters 3, 4 and 5 apply this measurement model to the first case study, BiH. Chapter 3, which focuses on justice, analyzes whether and to what extent ordinary people in BiH associate the ICTY's work with justice; it identifies some of the main grievances that Bosniaks, Bosnian Serbs and Bosnian Croats have with the Tribunal; and it reflects on whether a greater use of outreach activities aimed at filling in crucial knowledge gaps could have helped to alleviate popular dissatisfaction with the ICTY. Chapter 4 centres on the second prong of the measurement model, truth. Specifically, it examines whether the facts established in the ICTY's courtrooms are widely accepted on the ground and demonstrates that

---

20 I also interviewed a former deputy Prosecutor via telephone in January 2008.
21 See, for example, Cohen 1998; Hayden 2000; Judah 2000; Malcolm 2002; Owen 1996; Ramet 2002; Rogel 1998; Silber and Little 1996; Woodward 1995.

the penetrability of these facts is actually very limited. A major reason for this is that Tribunal truths must co-exist with competing ethnic truths which have an inherent filter mechanism. This means that, typically, only those facts and judgements which support a group's own meta narrative are accepted, while those which do not are filtered out and reinterpreted or denied. In this way, the ICTY's work has contributed to embedding rather than overcoming ethnic divides. Chapter 5 focuses on inter-ethnic relations in BiH and uses the Reconciliation Matrix developed in Chapter 2 to assess whether reconciliation exists among individuals and within ethnically-mixed communities – and if it does, whether the ICTY can take some of the credit for this.

Chapter 6 utilizes the measurement model to explore whether the Tribunal has assisted inter-ethnic reconciliation in Croatia (and specifically in Vukovar and Knin), and Chapter 7 applies the model to the case of Kosovo. That this research devotes one chapter each to Croatia and Kosovo yet three chapters to BiH is simply in keeping with, and reflects, the fact that the ICTY's work has primarily centred on BiH. All of the book's empirical chapters, however, strongly point to the same conclusion: that the ICTY's trials have not in any way contributed to reconciliation.

This necessarily raises the question of whether any court can foster reconciliation. The final chapter explores this issue through a comparative analysis drawing on the experiences of the SCSL, the Extraordinary Chambers of Cambodia (ECCC) and the ICC. Building on the findings of Chapters 3 to 7, Chapter 8 seeks to demonstrate that courts are not well-suited to the task of aiding reconciliation. By extension, it emphasizes the importance of restorative justice as a critical complement to criminal courts, and examines the potential utility of a regional TRC in the former Yugoslavia. Ultimately arguing, however, that we cannot rely on TJ alone to facilitate reconciliation, particularly as the impact of TJ processes remains empirically under-explored, it considers other possible paths to reconciliation, focusing specifically on the media and education.

Finally, the conclusion summarizes the main findings of this research and reflects on its practical and policy significance by highlighting and discussing four crucial lessons to be learnt from it. It also identifies some key areas for future research.

Chapter 1

The Violent Death of Yugoslavia and the Rebirth of International Criminal Justice

Every year, thousands of tourists would flock to Yugoslavia. A desirable destination for holiday-makers, it similarly offered its citizens a good standard of living and socio-economic security. Due to the turbulent history of the South Slavs, the legacy of the internecine civil war that took place in Yugoslavia during World War Two (WWII) and the fact that not all republics were equally committed to the Yugoslav state, President Tito ruled the country with a strong fist and was instrumental to the successful functioning of the Socialist Federal Republic of Yugoslavia. Doder reflects that, following Tito's death in May 1980, 'The glue that held the federation together was gone' (1993: 14). While this is partly true, it is arguable that the disintegration of Yugoslavia was already inevitable – with or without Tito at the helm. In the post-Cold War world, in which the triumph of liberal democracy was declared as 'the end of history' (Fukuyama 1992), Yugoslavia was an anachronism – an unwieldy socialist edifice with bloated bureaucracies and outmoded structures of governance. Furthermore, following the end of the Cold War, when Yugoslavia fundamentally lost its geopolitical and strategic importance in the eyes of the West (Doder 1993: 4; Zimmermann 1995: 2), there was little international interest in countering the various centrifugal forces that ultimately tore the Federation apart.

Yugoslavia unravels

During the 1980s, serious problems were already developing in Yugoslavia. Firstly, it was experiencing a growing economic crisis and falling further into crippling international debt. By 1986, it owed $21 billion (Stephen 2004: 36–37); and four years later, 'things were so desperate that state banks had "frozen" all hard currency...' (Stewart 2007: 116–117). The country's financial difficulties became a source of contention among the six republics, by accelerating unequal economic development. In particular, the wealthier republics, Slovenia and Croatia, did not wish to be dragged into the country's mounting economic problems and grew ever more resentful of having to subsidize the least developed republics, BiH and Macedonia (LeBor 2002: 130).

Secondly, Tito's death in 1980 created a power vacuum in Yugoslavia which paved the way for a destructive resurgence of ethnic nationalisms. At the epicentre of this nationalist revival was Slobodan Milošević, whose notoriety began in April 1987 when he visited Kosovo – at that time an autonomous province of Serbia. Relations between Kosovo's Albanians and Serbs had become increasingly tense, and Milošević – then the head of the Communist Party of Serbia – openly took up the cause of the Kosovo Serbs by pledging to defend and protect them. This marked the start of Milošević's meteoric rise to power, and two years later he was President of Serbia. Yet, it was not only determination that enabled his success. It was also his sheer ruthlessness. During the Eighth Session of the Serbian Communist Party Central Committee on 22 September 1987, he carefully engineered the ousting of Dragiša Pavlović, the head of the Belgrade Communist Party, and thereby indirectly attacked his former mentor, Serbian President Ivan Stambolić. Although Stambolić was not the primary target of Milošević's manoeuvrings during the Eighth Session, 'his [Stambolić's] reputation suffered a big blow as it became apparent the power balance had tipped toward his former protégé' (Vladisavljević 2008: 69). With Stambolić critically weakened, Milošević could now concentrate on carving out his own path to power. Unleashing his so-called 'anti-bureaucratic revolution', he replaced the leaderships of Vojvodina (also an autonomous province of Serbia), Kosovo and Montenegro with Milošević loyalists. This meant that, 'Milošević now controlled Montenegro and Serbia, and could pick four of the Yugoslav presidency members, one short of having total power' (Stephen 2004: 51). These developments generated significant unease in other Yugoslav republics, ultimately leading the Slovene delegation to walk out of the Fourteenth Congress of the Yugoslav Communist Party on 23 January 1990. The Congress was never to reconvene. While Milošević always professed his commitment to Yugoslavia, his actions and the disquiet they created in other republics were a fundamental cause of its disintegration.

Thirdly, the fact that Yugoslavia's past remained unresolved crucially facilitated the rise of competing ethnic nationalisms. Under Tito's leadership, the legacy of the numerous atrocities committed on Yugoslav soil during WWII, most notably at the hands of the fascist Ustaše, was never discussed or addressed. People were simply expected to draw a line under the war in the name of Tito's 'brotherhood and unity'. However, the past cannot be buried so easily; 'It makes intuitive sense that people's memories of traumatic events...will continue to affect the social fabric in some perhaps intangible but nevertheless important way' (Sorabji 2006: 1). So it was in Yugoslavia. Embedded into the social fabric was a repository of suppressed memories, anger and bitterness which leaders such as Milošević and his Croatian counterpart, President Franjo Tuđman, manipulated for their own ends. It was not 'ancient hatreds' that destroyed Yugoslavia. To cite Oberschall, 'The emotion that poisons ethnic relations is fear...' (2000: 990); and the fear that insidiously poisoned Yugoslavia was inextricably linked to the latter's past. Hence, it is almost impossible to envisage how Yugoslavia, particularly in view of its complex ethnic make-up, could have disintegrated peacefully.

Bloodshed and war crimes in the former Yugoslavia

The wars in Slovenia and Croatia

On 25 June 1991, Slovenia declared independence. It had legitimate political and economic reasons for wanting to leave Yugoslavia and its population was largely ethnically homogeneous; but it seceded without any regard for the rest of Yugoslavia. According to Warren Zimmermann, the last US ambassador to Yugoslavia, the Slovenes thus 'bear considerable responsibility for the bloodbath that followed their secession' (1995: 7) – a bloodbath which they themselves did not have to experience. The war in Slovenia, fought between the Yugoslav National Army (JNA)[1] and the Slovene territorial defence forces, was a 'clean' combat which did not give rise to the brutality and war crimes that were later seen elsewhere in the former Yugoslavia. The absence of a strong ethnic component also facilitated a speedy resolution of the conflict. After ten days of fighting, the parties came together – under the auspices of the European Economic Community (EEC) and the Conference on Security and Co-operation in Europe – to sign the Brioni Accord on 7 July 1991. Shortly thereafter, the JNA withdrew from Slovenia.

Croatia also declared independence on 25 June 1991. Unlike Slovenia, however, Croatia had a significant Serb minority, totalling approximately 12 per cent of its population. This crucial ethnic factor meant that Croatia would pay a far higher price for its independence. Inter-ethnic relations between Croats and the Serb minority seriously deteriorated following the election victory of the right-wing Croatian Democratic Union (HDZ) in April 1990 and the election of its leader, Franjo Tuđman, as the new President of Croatia. For Serbs, the prospect of the nationalist HDZ winning the elections generated deep concern; and once in power, Tuđman and the HDZ merely fuelled Serbs' legitimate fears. In December 1990, the Croatian parliament adopted a new constitution which downgraded Serbs from the status of a constituent people to a national minority – and thereby eroded many of their rights. In January 1992, the Badinter Commission[2] thus opined that it would be premature for the EEC to recognize Croatia's independence at that time, on the grounds that the new Croatian constitution did not include sufficient guarantees for minorities (an opinion which the EEC nevertheless chose to ignore). Large numbers of Serbs, for example, lost their jobs, particularly those working in the police (Glenny 1996: 13). Compounding matters, Milošević and Serbian nationalists cynically exploited the situation to reinforce a sense of impending threat among Croatia's Serbs.

---

1 Gallagher notes that in the space of a year, the formerly multi-ethnic JNA 'had changed out of all recognition…During 1991, almost all Slovene and Croatian officers had been forced to quit, regardless of their loyalty' (2003: 74).

2 The Badinter Commission was created by the EEC in August 1991 to give its opinions on major legal questions arising from the break-up of Yugoslavia.

Relentless Serbian propaganda disseminated the terrifying message that if Croatia were to leave Yugoslavia, history would repeat itself and Serbs would find themselves living in another Independent State of Croatia (NDZ), only this time with Tuđman rather than Ante Pavelić at the helm (Bass 2000: 209).[3]

In Croatia, the centre of resistance to the idea of Croatian independence was Knin. In early 1990, the psychiatrist Jovan Rašković and a group of Serb nationalists founded the Serbian Democratic Party. The latter grew in strength following the HDZ's victory in the April elections, and in July 1990 Rašković announced that a referendum would be held at the end of August regarding the future of Croatia's Serbs. This growing unrest in Knin was a major concern to Tuđman. Not only was the situation likely to escalate and spread, but Knin was enormously important economically; 'Whoever controlled Knin controlled the roads and railways linking Zagreb to the coast' (LeBor 2002: 142). Tuđman thus needed to gain control of the situation and on 17 August 1990, he sent two helicopters to Knin containing members of his newly-created special unit of the police. While the plan was for the police to secure the town hall and police station in Knin, the JNA intercepted the helicopter and it had to turn back. According to Tanner, 'Although no one died, the bungled assault on Knin marked the beginning of the Yugoslav wars' (2010: 233). The local mayor immediately declared a war situation and barricades were erected; this was the start of the Serbs' 'log revolution'. Despite Tuđman's appeals, Serbs went ahead with their referendum and on 25 August 1990, the head of the recently-created Serb National Council, Milan Babić, pronounced the establishment of the Serb Autonomous Republic of Krajina. A year later, the Serb leadership in Croatia would declare the formation of a new state, the Republic of Serbian Krajina (RSK).

If the war in Croatia began in Knin, the most intense fighting occurred in eastern Slavonia, most notably in the town of Vukovar. Inter-ethnic relations in Vukovar began to change in 1990; tensions mounted, Serb homes and businesses were attacked and Serbs began to disappear (Dabić and Lukić 1997: 21–23). Serb interviewees claimed that they were increasingly victimized in a bid to force them to flee. In the spring of 1991, this volatile situation dangerously escalated. Serbian paramilitary groups began to arrive in Vukovar; Josip Reichl-Kir, the head of the Croatian police in Osijek and a man who had tirelessly sought to calm the situation, was killed by a Croat extremist in the village of New Tenja; and events in Borovo Selo, a Serb village close to Vukovar, 'were to herald the beginning of armed clashes in the area' (Prosecutor v. Mrkšić, Radić and Šljivančanin 2007: §26). On 1 May 1991, Serb irregulars in Borovo Selo shot at and apprehended two Croat policemen in a patrol car. The next day, the head of the police in nearby Vinkovci sent 20 of his men into Borovo Selo to investigate the incident;

3 Ante Pavelić was the leader of the fascist Ustaše movement, established in 1929 with the aim of liberating Croatia from alien rule. His three-point plan was to expel one-third of Serbs from Croatia, to kill one-third and to convert the remaining third to Roman Catholicism.

'But they were unable to fight their way through and it was left to the army to divide the two warring sides' (Glenny 1996: 76). Twelve Croat policemen and three Serb civilians were killed in Borovo Selo that day. As a result of these bloody developments, the Federal Presidency authorized the JNA to intervene to stop the fighting between local Serbs and Croats. Far from acting as a neutral force, however, the JNA quickly took the side of the Serbs.

The JNA massively outnumbered the Croatian combatants and hence should have easily defeated them. However, the latter were highly motivated, while the JNA was 'an uninspired force' with an ever-increasing daily desertion rate (Stewart 2007: 158). Struggling to break the Croat defence, the JNA's siege of Vukovar dragged on for three long months, while the town's inhabitants – Croats and Serbs alike – huddled in their freezing basements waiting for the relentless shelling to stop. When the siege finally ended on 18 November 1991, 'Vukovar looked like Stalingrad in 1943' (Thompson 1992: 297). Serb paramilitaries prowled the streets, all of the town's Croats were expelled, many were interned in camps (see Rehak 2008) and at least 200 people were taken from the local hospital to nearby Ovčara and killed (Prosecutor v. Mrkšić, Radić and Šljivančanin 2007: §494).

Following the fall of Vukovar, the Croatian government formally called upon the UN to establish a war crimes tribunal. Peskin argues that, 'from the vantage point of November 1991, the Croatian government viewed a tribunal as providing leverage in its dual goals of gaining recognition [as an independent state] and isolating Serbia' (2008: 99). Croatia's request, however, garnered little international support at this time. The termination of hostilities was already in sight, and on 3 January 1992 the UN Special Envoy, Cyrus Vance, successfully negotiated a ceasefire between the two sides. The fact that Serbs still held a quarter of Croatia's territory inevitably meant that the final phase of the war was yet to come, but in the meantime the world's attention shifted to neighbouring BiH.

The war in BiH

When Slovenia and Croatia seceded from Yugoslavia, this left BiH in an extremely difficult position. If it remained within a rump Yugoslavia, it would be dominated by Milošević's Serbia; but if it declared its own independence, Bosnian Serbs – who wished to remain part of Yugoslavia – would never accept this.[4] Independence, in short, meant war. If the Bosniak leadership was thus caught between a rock and a hard place, Glenny maintains that, 'The death sentence for Bosnia-Hercegovina was passed in the middle of December 1991 when Germany announced that it would recognize Slovenia and Croatia unconditionally on 15 January 1992' (1996: 163). Partly for historical reasons dating back to WWII,

---

4 According to the last pre-war census in 1991, Bosnian Serbs accounted for 31.4 per cent of BiH's population. Bosnian Muslims and Bosnian Croats constituted 43.7 per cent and 17.3 per cent respectively (Cohen 1993: 139).

Germany strongly supported Croatia's declaration of independence. Its enthusiasm, however, was not universally shared. During a meeting of the EEC's foreign ministers in Brussels in December 1991, Germany found itself in a minority; but as the discussions continued, positions changed. According to the BBC's former war correspondent, Martin Bell,

> Late at night Germany's long-serving Foreign Minister, Hans-Dietrich Genscher, reminded his British counterpart, Douglas Hurd, of the German helpfulness over Maastricht.[5] Seeking instructions, Hurd passed on this politically freighted reminder to Downing Street. In the early hours of the morning of 17 December 1991, the British agreed to the recognition of Croatia and all twelve countries swung into line (2012: 3).

Those who had previously questioned the wisdom of recognizing Croatia's independence now seemingly set aside their qualms for the sake of European unity (Gallagher 2003: 73). In fact, the EEC's decision to recognize Croatia's independence not only undermined the work of the aforementioned Badinter Commission, but also backed BiH into a corner. In December 1991, BiH sought recognition from EEC states, a request that was denied. The following month, the Badinter Commission found that BiH did not meet all of the necessary criteria for recognition. It nevertheless left the door open, opining that this decision could be reassessed if BiH were to hold a referendum on independence under international supervision. It is questionable whether the Badinter Commission was right to suggest a referendum at this time (Burg and Shoup 1999: 126), but BiH duly held a referendum on 29 February and 1 March 1992. The turnout was 63.4 per cent and 92.68 per cent voted for independence (Gallagher 2003: 85). On 21 December 1991, however, the Bosnian Serb assembly had announced the creation of the Serb Republic of BiH (the precursor to the RS), which declared its independence from BiH on 9 January 1992. Bosnian Serbs therefore boycotted the referendum, and 'within hours of the result, barricades manned by armed Serbs went up in the capital and elsewhere, provoking the first demonstrations by unarmed civilians' (Vulliamy 1994: 75). Undeterred, BiH declared independence on 6 April 1992. For the next three years, this erstwhile microcosm of Yugoslavia would be a bloody battleground and the scene of violence and brutality on a scale not seen in Europe since WWII.

There were three main, overlapping stages in the Bosnian war. In the first stage, from 1992 until 1993, the ABiH and the HVO jointly fought against the Bosnian Serb Army (VRS). During this period of the conflict, the VRS, under the command of Ratko Mladić, made enormous military gains, while the UN arms

---

5 Lesova and Turner recall that, 'Britain famously refused to sign the Maastricht treaty, which paved the way to the creation of the euro, until it had negotiated an opt-out clause' (2011).

embargo imposed on the former Yugoslavia in September 1991 prevented a level playing field and severely disadvantaged the Bosnian Muslims. It was also during this first stage of the conflict that Serb-run camps in the municipality of Prijedor were discovered (Vulliamy 1994: 102). Shocking images from these camps made it increasingly difficult for the international community to simply stand on the sidelines and do nothing.

During the second stage of the war, from late 1992 to 1994, the military alliance between the ABiH and the HVO broke down and the two armies turned on each other. In November 1991, the Bosnian Croat leadership had announced the creation of the Croatian Community of Herceg-Bosna (HZHB), which subsequently became the HRHB. Although Herceg-Bosna was never internationally recognized, the ICTY has found that it was established with the purpose of ultimately seceding from BiH and uniting with neighbouring Croatia (Prosecutor v. Kordić and Čerkez 2001: §491).[6] Hence, its very existence, under the leadership of Mate Boban, necessarily placed a heavy strain on the alliance between Bosnian Muslims and Bosnian Croats, exposing the fact that the two sides were fighting for different objectives. Ironically, the Vance-Owen plan in 1993, negotiated by the UN Special Envoy to BiH, Cyrus Vance, and Lord David Owen, the European Community representative, further increased the strain. The Vance-Owen plan proposed to divide BiH into ten cantons, each of which would have a Serb, Croat or Bosniak majority. While this was never accepted, due to opposition from the Bosnian Serb leadership, the HVO quickly sought to gain control of those areas which the plan had designated as Croat (Vulliamy 1994: 261). It was thus a tragic irony that, 'the maps delineating the cantons triggered a fresh outbreak of fighting in central Bosnia as the Bosnian Croats attempted to grab the lands marked as Croat cantons' (LeBor 2002: 232). The most intense fighting occurred in central BiH and in the Lašva Valley area, culminating in the massacre of 116 Bosnian Muslims in the village of Ahmići on 16 April 1993 (see Clark 2012b).

During the third phase of the war, from 1994 to 1995, the situation on the ground fundamentally changed again. Fighting between Bosnian Muslims and Bosnian Croats ended, and under the Washington Agreement signed in March 1994 the two sides restored their military alliance against the VRS. This would eventually pay enormous dividends. Before that could happen, however, thousands more people would die while the international community stood by. In 1992, the UN had declared Bihać, Goražde, Sarajevo, Srebrenica, Tuzla and Žepa as 'safe areas'. In reality, they were anything but safe; while the then UN Secretary-General, Boutros Boutros-Ghali, had requested 34,000 troops to protect these areas, 'the United States and other countries balked at sending their own troops. A second proposal, sarcastically referred to as "safe areas lite" by UN

---

6 Bosnian Croat interviewees, however, always denied this. According to them, the HRHB was created with the sole purpose of protecting the rights of Croats in BiH.

officials, was adopted and only 7,600 peacekeepers were sent to the six new safe areas' (Rohde 2012: xx). So it was that when the VRS overran Srebrenica on 11 July 1995, the lightly-armed Dutch peacekeepers were massively outnumbered. Over the following days, between 7,000 and 8,000 Bosnian Muslim men and boys were massacred, victims of a genocide which many Bosnian Serbs continue to deny. The NATO air strikes which could have pushed back the advancing VRS and thus prevented the slaughter never materialized. It was only a month later, after the VRS shelled a central market in Sarajevo on 28 August 1995, killing 37 people, that NATO planes intensively bombed Bosnian Serb positions. Due to a combination of factors, the tide of war now began to turn.

On 5 August 1995, in the final phase of Croatia's war of secession, the Croatian Army (HV) launched Operation Storm, in order to retake the quarter of the country's territory which it had lost to the Serbs in 1991. Commanded by Ante Gotovina, Operation Storm was not the honourable victory that Croats celebrate each year. It resulted in the departure *en masse* of some 200,000 Serbs from the Krajina (Prosecutor v. Gotovina, Čermak and Markač 2011: §1712); and those who were unable or unwilling to leave their homes – primarily elderly Serbs – suffered gross human rights violations (Subotić 2009: 84). Many were killed, often in revenge attacks (Peskin 2008: 103). While the ICTY Appeals Chamber acquitted Gotovina and his co-defendant, Mladen Markač, in 2012, thus overturning the convictions handed down by the Trial Chamber a year earlier, this does not and should not in any way detract from the crimes committed against Croatian Serbs during Operation Storm.

In military terms, however, Operation Storm was highly successful and had an important impact on the fighting still raging in BiH. The destruction of the RSK in Croatia fundamentally weakened the VRS's three-year hold on Bihać in north-western BiH. This, combined with the NATO bombing of Bosnian Serb positions, allowed the allied ABiH and HVO to make significant military gains for the first time; 'After two years of stalemate or Serb victories, over 100 square miles of Serb territory fell in a week' (Rohde 2012: 339). The inroads made by the Bosnian Muslims and Bosnian Croats, however, became a new source of problems. The ABiH and the HVO were closing in on Banja Luka, the largest city under VRS control, and according to UN estimates they would have captured it within just 72 hours (Rohde 2012: 40). This scenario had to be avoided at all costs; if Banja Luka were to fall, thousands of Bosnian Serbs would flee into Serbia, potentially destabilizing Milošević – and at this stage the US needed Milošević to make peace in BiH.

Up until the summer of 1995, the VRS had controlled approximately 70 per cent of BiH's territory. Now it held approximately 50 per cent, while the ABiH and HVO jointly held the remaining 50 per cent. These changes on the ground were critical to enabling the start of peace negotiations, which took place at a US military base in Dayton, Ohio. Neither Karadžić nor Mladić travelled to Dayton, and indeed both men were indicted by the ICTY during the negotiations. Milošević negotiated on behalf of the Bosnian Serbs. On 21 November 1995, the Dayton Peace Accords (DPA) were signed and the war that had ravaged BiH for three long years finally ended. Over 150,000 people were dead, some 30,000 individuals were missing and thousands more were internally displaced. While the DPA brought peace to BiH, in the sense of Galtung's negative peace (1969: 183), they contributed to a deteriorating situation in Kosovo.

War in Kosovo

Kosovo was an autonomous province of Serbia with extensive powers, but this was to change when Milošević came to power in Serbia. Under his presidency, Kosovo's autonomy was effectively abolished and Kosovo Albanians, the over-whelming majority in Kosovo, were subjected to extreme abuse and discrimination. This led to widespread popular support for Ibrahim Rugova and his League for a Democratic Kosovo. Rugova's strategy of peaceful resistance, however, was gradually discredited, not least as a result of the DPA which, contrary to Kosovo Albanian expectations, made no mention of Kosovo or a possible solution. As Ker-Lindsay writes, 'Although some in the US Administration wished to raise the issue, the need to keep Milošević – who insisted that Kosovo was an internal matter for Serbia – engaged in the overall process meant that it was kept off the agenda' (2012: 11). Hence, after Dayton, Kosovo Albanians now sought a more direct way to fight against the Milošević regime, and the KLA, which began to form in 1994, was waiting in the wings to take the struggle to the next level.

Initially, there was little international sympathy for the KLA; and indeed up until 1998, it was widely regarded as a terrorist group (see, for example, UN 1998a). After a series of major Serb offensives throughout 1998, however, perceptions began to change and by early 1999, much of the international community – and in particular the US – had strongly sided with the KLA. Following the failure of the Rambouillet peace talks, NATO forces – without the authorization of the UN Security Council – bombed Serbia and Kosovo for 78 days, until Milošević finally agreed to a peace deal. At that point, Kosovo became an international protectorate. Nevertheless, its final status remained uncertain, and Kosovo Albanians became increasingly frustrated with the lack of progress on the issue. The situation reached boiling point in March 2004; for three days, widespread rioting occurred throughout Kosovo, Serb homes and monasteries were attacked and over 4,000 people (primarily Serbs and Roma) were expelled from their homes. Eight Serbs and 11 Kosovo Albanians were killed (Ker-Lindsay 2010: 20). These riots caught the international community off guard and helped to put the issue of Kosovo firmly back onto the international agenda. Four years later, on 17 February 2008 – and with strong backing from the US – Kosovo declared independence.

Since Kosovo proclaimed its independence, which Serbia has never recognized, Kosovo Serbs and other minorities have frequently faced serious discrimination and human rights abuses. According to the OSCE, 'Safety and security remain key matters of concern for members of the non-majority communities…' (2011c). Serbs living south of the River Ibër/Ibar, surrounded by Kosovo

Albanians, have always been the most vulnerable and have therefore had to accept Kosovo identity cards, driving licenses, number plates and so on, despite the fact that they do not recognize Kosovo's independence. It is a different story in the north of Kosovo, however, where Serbs constitute the majority and are thus in a much stronger position. Separated from the rest of Kosovo by the Ibër/Ibar, the northern municipalities of Leposavić/q, Mitrovica/ë, Zubin Potok and Zvečan/Zveçan are a Serbia in miniature. Here the Serbian flag flies, street signs are written in Cyrillic, the Serbian language and currency are used and only those Serbs who need to travel south of the Ibër/Ibar have obtained Kosovo documents.

This seemingly intractable northern problem has long been a major thorn in the side of the Kosovo government. On 19 April 2013, however, after intensive European Union (EU)-facilitated dialogue, the Prime Ministers of Kosovo and Serbia – Hashim Thaçi and Ivica Dačić respectively – reached an historic agreement (EU 2013, UN 2013). The four aforementioned northern municipalities will be allowed to form an association, which will have sole responsibility for economic development, health, education and urban planning. On the critical issues of security and law enforcement, the Kosovo Police Service will be deployed in the north (where until now only Serb institutions have operated), but in a way that reflects the ethnic composition of the northern municipalities, and the regional police commander in the north will be a Kosovo Serb. In addition, a division of Kosovo's Appellate Court will permanently sit in north Mitrovica/ë and each of its panels will have a Kosovo Serb majority. Finally, as part of the agreement reached, which does not require Serbia to recognize Kosovo's independence, each side has undertaken not to obstruct the other's journey towards eventual EU membership. The April agreement is an important step forward after so many years of uncertainty and stalemate. However, as the election violence in November 2013 powerfully highlighted (Bilefsky 2013; Verbica 2013), there is still a very long and difficult road ahead, and the final status of the north remains uncertain.

Throughout the wars in the former Yugoslavia, the international community was often ineffective, divided and hesitant, unsure of how to deal with the spiralling situation. At the height of the war in BiH, however, the scale of the atrocities taking place no longer permitted inaction and prevarication. The international community needed to react, and it did so in the form of a judicial response – the creation of the ICTY.

The establishment of the ICTY

After the end of WWII, the Allies were divided on how to deal with Nazi war criminals. The British government was in favour of simply shooting them (Scharf 1997: 5), and Stalin similarly supported the idea of summary executions (Bass 2000: 147). The course of history would have been very different if the British and Soviet positions had prevailed. In Washington, however, although both President Roosevelt and his Treasury Secretary, Henry Morgenthau Jr., shared the view that Nazi war criminals should be shot, the Secretary of War, Henry Stimson, argued the case for criminal trials; and after Roosevelt's death, 'His successor, Harry Truman, a former small-town judge, was adamant that a trial was both necessary and feasible' (Overy 2003: 5). So it was that the International Military Tribunal for Nuremberg was created on 8 August 1945, under the London Agreement. Between November 1945 and October 1946, 22 leading Nazis stood trial at Nuremberg, among them Hermann Göring, Rudolf Hess and Joachim von Ribbentrop. Nineteen of the defendants were found guilty, of whom 12 were sentenced to death. The remaining seven defendants received prison terms of between ten years and life. Three defendants were acquitted. For all their flaws (see, for example, Overy 2003: 7; Owen 2006: 7), the trials were an innovative, and ultimately successful, experiment in international criminal justice whose legacy would leave a deep and indelible mark (Robertson QC 2012: 309). Nevertheless, it would be several decades before any serious attempt was made to build upon this legacy.

It was the Belgrade journalist Mirko Klarin who first called for the creation of a tribunal to deal with unfolding events in the Balkans. In an article entitled '*Nirnberg sada*!' (Nuremberg Now), published in the Serbian newspaper *Borba* on 16 May 1991, Klarin, who is now the editor-in-chief of the South East News Service Europe (SENSE), argued that it was necessary to establish a tribunal sooner rather than later (Klarin 2001: 97). Klarin's appeals, however, went unheeded; at this time, there was little enthusiasm in Washington for dealing with the former Yugoslavia. According to Zimmermann, 'Nobody wanted to touch it. With the American presidential election just a year away, it was seen as a loser' (1995: 15). The fighting in the former Yugoslavia nevertheless triggered a series of UN Security Council Resolutions. Although these were initially limited to reminding the parties of their duty to comply with international humanitarian law (see, for example, UN 1992a), it quickly became clear that the escalating bloodshed in BiH required more than verbal warnings and condemnation.

On 6 August 1992, a report by Penny Marshall, a British news correspondent, on the Omarska camp in Prijedor municipality was broadcast; 'Around the world, people turned on their television sets and recoiled at seeing images they thought relegated to the past – skeletal men, ribs protruding, eyes blank and empty with terror' (Neuffer 2003: 47). It is often argued that the screening of such images was a major catalyst for the creation of the ICTY (see Schrag 1995: 193). Certainly, during the London Conference in late August 1992, Germany's then Foreign Minister, Klaus Kinkel, insisted on the creation of an international court to prosecute those responsible for war crimes in the former Yugoslavia (Neuffer 2003: 47–48). It is not the case, however, that the discovery of camps in Prijedor municipality triggered immediate action on the part of the international community.[7] According to Scharf, 'Even after receiving reports of Serb-run death

---

7 Despite Kinkel's calls, for example, no decisive action was taken at the London Conference. Instead, diplomats relied on the promises of Milošević and the Bosnian Serb leader, Radovan Karadžić to, *inter alia*, close the camps and halt the siege of cities such as Sarajevo.

camps in Bosnia, Washington was hesitant to act' (1997: 31). Moreover, it would seem that the US was already cognizant of the camps' existence when the news story broke. After Marshall's report was aired, '...State Department spokesman Richard Boucher told reporters that administration officials had been aware that "Serbian forces are maintaining what they call detention centres", and also knew about the "abuses and tortures taking place"' (LeBor 2002: 179).

Nevertheless, in response to the broadcast of footage from inside the Omarska camp, William Scharf – as the Attorney-Adviser for UN Affairs at the US State Department – drafted Security Council Resolution 771 (13 August 1992). In addition to demanding that all parties to the conflict in BiH 'immediately cease and desist from all breaches of international humanitarian law...', Resolution 771 also called upon states and international humanitarian organizations 'to collate substantiated information in their possession or submitted to them' relating to violations of international humanitarian law being committed in the former Yugoslavia, and 'to make this information available to the Council' (UN 1992b). The original version of the Resolution, however, went a step further. Scharf explains that while he was drafting it, 'I was aware of a proposal that had been recently circulated within the Office of the Legal Adviser to establish an international commission to investigate Iraqi war crimes committed during the Persian Gulf War. Although that proposal was never pursued, I thought such language might be appropriate for Resolution 771' (1997: 39). He believed that although the Bush administration was not in favour of creating an international court, it might support the establishment of an international commission to investigate the crimes being committed in the former Yugoslavia. This was not the case. When the draft resolution was circulated in the Department of State, 'the consensus was to defer the proposal for the time being in favor of the formulation calling on the Secretary General to recommend additional measures' (Scharf 1997: 40).

When Milošević and Karadžić reneged on the promises they made at the London Conference, however, the UN Security Council took the decision to create an international commission. Resolution 780 (6 October 1992) requested the UN Secretary-General,

> ...to establish, as a matter of urgency, an impartial Commission of Experts to examine and analyse the information submitted pursuant to resolution 771 (1992) and the present resolution...with a view to providing the Secretary-General with its conclusions on the evidence of grave breaches of the Geneva Conventions and other violations of international humanitarian law committed on the territory of the former Yugoslavia.
>
> (UN 1992c)

Although Resolution 780 was unanimously adopted, the creation of a five-member Commission of Experts – headed by Professor Frits Kalshoven from the Netherlands – generated disagreement within the Security Council. In particular, Britain and France were concerned that the Commission's work might jeopardize ongoing attempts to end the war and secure a peace agreement (Bass 2000: 211); and the British government 'made no secret of its preference that the commission be limited to passively analyzing and collating information that it received' (Scharf and Schabas 2002: 46). The fact that the Commission did not enjoy the full support of all Security Council members resulted in the head of the Commission resigning in protest in September 1993. It also meant that the Commission was always severely under-funded, forcing Kalshoven's successor, Professor M. Cherif Bassiouni, to seek donations from the Soros and MacArthur Foundations.

While Security Council Resolution 780 did not explicitly refer to a possible international tribunal for the former Yugoslavia, 'the language deliberately left the door open for an international judicial response' (Scharf 1997: 42). Moreover, by this stage the idea of establishing a tribunal was gathering momentum. In December 1992, for example, in his 'Naming of Names' speech in Geneva, the US Secretary of State, Lawrence Eagleburger, announced that the US government had identified ten suspected war criminals – among them Milošević, Karadžić, Mladić and Željko Ražnatović (Arkan), a Serbian paramilitary leader – whom it believed should stand trial. The speech, however, received a mixed reception. At the time, Cyrus Vance and David Owen were attempting to negotiate a peace agreement in BiH, and their peace plan 'was dependent upon the cooperation of the ten people Eagleburger had just labelled as war criminals...' (Scharf 1997: 44).

Notwithstanding British and French concerns regarding a possible tension between justice and peace, the Security Council went on to adopt Resolution 808 (22 February 1993). After noting the interim report of the Commission of Experts, and the latter's observation that an *ad hoc* (temporary) international tribunal 'would be consistent with the direction of its work', Resolution 808 expressed the Security Council's determination to put an end to the war crimes being committed in the former Yugoslavia and 'to take effective measures to bring to justice the persons who are responsible for them' (UN 1993a). Further articulating the Security Council's conviction that an international tribunal 'would contribute to the restoration and maintenance of peace', Resolution 808 decided that, 'an international tribunal shall be established for the prosecution of persons responsible for serious violations of international humanitarian law committed in the territory of the former Yugoslavia since 1991' (UN 1993a). Three months later, on 25 May 1993, the Security Council unanimously adopted Resolution 827 and established the ICTY (UN 1993b).

According to Klarin, 'Opinions were divided on whether this move by the Security Council was an exercise in futility or should be more accurately described as an exercise in hypocrisy' (2004: 547). As an exercise in hypocrisy, some commentators have claimed that the ICTY was created simply in a bid to avert calls for military intervention in the former Yugoslavia (see, for example, Bass 2000: 207; Neuffer 2003: 65). However, this is an overly simplistic argument (Scheffer 2004: 354); the privileging of military action not only denies the significance of judicial responses, but also assumes that military intervention is always the best option. If the creation of the ICTY was not a simple exercise in hypocrisy, it was certainly not an exercise in futility. Nevertheless, when the Tribunal was first established, it was far from clear whether it would become a fully functioning court of law because at that time it faced enormous challenges. Firstly, the ICTY did not enjoy universal support, notwithstanding the unanimous adoption of Resolution 827. Justice Richard Goldstone, for example, recalls that during the week that he was elected as the ICTY's first Prosecutor, he met the former British Prime Minister, Edward Heath, at a party in Cape Town. The latter asked him why he had accepted 'such a ridiculous job'. When Goldstone explained his reasons, 'Heath replied to the effect that if people wished to murder one another, as long as they did not do so in his country, it was not his concern and should not be the concern of the British government' (Goldstone 2000: 74). While such opinions deeply shocked Goldstone at the time, he soon realized that Heath 'was candidly stating what many leading politicians in major Western nations were saying privately...' (Goldstone 2000: 74).

Secondly, it took the ICTY over a year to select a Prosecutor. Various names were put forward and one in particular stood out – Luis Moreno Ocampo (who later became the first Prosecutor of the ICC). The Argentine government, however, declined to support Ocampo's nomination, as a result of which the process of finding a Prosecutor became long and protracted – and seriously hindered the Tribunal during the first year of its existence. The former US Ambassador at Large for War Crimes Issues, David Scheffer, has insisted that, '...with Argentine support, we could have prevailed in August 1993 to elect Mr Ocampo as Prosecutor and launch the ICTY's investigative and prosecutorial work quickly' (2004: 359). The Clinton administration put forward Professor M. Cherif Bassiouni, a legal scholar, and Charles Ruff, a lawyer, as possible alternative candidates, but both nominations met with opposition in the Security Council (Scheffer 2004: 360). Britain was particularly opposed to Bassiouni, a Muslim, fearing that he would quickly issue indictments against Serb leaders and thereby threaten the Vance-Owen negotiations (Scharf 1997: 76). It was thus agreed that the Prosecutor could only be elected by consensus, which in turn led to further delays. Finally, on 7 July 1994, following a suggestion by the then ICTY President, Antonio Cassese, the UN Secretary-General proposed Justice Richard Goldstone of South Africa as ICTY Prosecutor. However, as Goldstone was needed in South Africa's Constitutional Court, it was agreed (with input from President Nelson Mandela) that he would only serve half a term (i.e. two years) as Prosecutor.

Thirdly, there were serious funding issues hampering the Tribunal. According to Goldstone, 'I had assumed that a United Nations tribunal, which was a sub-organ of the Security Council itself and established by the unanimous vote of its members, would be adequately funded and well supported by the international body. That, unfortunately, turned out to be a naïve assumption' (2000: 77). President Cassese, for example, reportedly rejected the offer of an official car and instead travelled around by bicycle, in order to save the Tribunal money (Stephen 2004: 98); and the start of the ICTY's first trial, of Duško Tadić, had to be postponed for six months 'for want of $78,000 for expenses for defense counsel and investigators' (Scharf 1997: 83).

Despite all of these difficulties, the ICTY has established itself as a credible and, in many respects, a successful international tribunal. With jurisdiction to prosecute genocide, crimes against humanity, grave breaches of the Geneva Conventions and violations of the laws or customs of war, it has indicted 161 individuals, prosecuted many of the major protagonists in Yugoslavia's wars of secession and significantly contributed to the development of international criminal law through its jurisprudence. Setting a positive precedent, moreover, its work has paved the way for the creation of other international courts – including those for Rwanda, Sierra Leone and Lebanon – and ultimately the ICC. Notwithstanding the Tribunal's successes, however, the purpose of this research is to explore – and to fundamentally problematize – the argument that the ICTY has contributed/is contributing to reconciliation in the former Yugoslavia.

The ICTY, peace and reconciliation

Security Council Resolution 827 established the threefold mandate of the ICTY, namely: to bring to justice persons responsible for war crimes, to deter the commission of further crimes and to 'contribute to the restoration and maintenance of peace' (UN 1993b). Justice and deterrence are standard core objectives of any criminal justice system. The idea that the administration of justice can facilitate peace, in contrast, is far more novel. Indeed, justice and peace have often been regarded as dichotomous goals which cannot be simultaneously pursued (Boraine 2006: 27; Sarkin 2001: 144; Tutu 1999: 27). Today, the debate has shifted somewhat and the simplicity of the 'peace versus justice' dilemma is increasingly recognized. As Sriram underscores, 'In reality the choice is seldom simply "justice" or "peace" but rather a complex mixture of both' (2009: 1). When the ICTY was established in 1993, however, the inclusion of peace as part of its mandate was a significant innovation (Lescure and Trintignac 1996: 4). A year later, on 8 November 1994, the Security Council adopted Resolution 955 and thereby established the ICTR, with a mandate, *inter alia*, 'to contribute to the process of national reconciliation and to the restoration and maintenance of peace' (UN 1994). Two decades on, important questions persist as to whether peace and reconciliation are appropriate objectives for criminal tribunals whose primary function is judicial. To understand why Security Council Resolutions 827 and 955 refer to peace (and, in the case of Resolution 955, reconciliation), it is essential to consider the legal basis on which they were adopted.

The Security Council judged that the situation in the former Yugoslavia and Rwanda respectively posed a threat to international peace and security. In these circumstances, the traditional way of establishing an international tribunal, by treaty, was discounted; it would have taken too long. Instead, recourse was made to Chapter VII of the UN Charter, which authorizes the Security Council to take action with respect to, *inter alia*, threats to the peace. The fact, therefore, that the ICTY and ICTR were created in response to such threats logically meant that their mandates needed to include a peace component (Robertson QC 2012: 452). According to a former ICTY deputy Prosecutor, 'To expect any court to do anything other than try individual cases is to ask a lot. But our mandate is based on Chapter VII, and the UN Security Council saw that it could not act completely legally under Chapter VII unless there was some connection to the restoration of peace'.[8]

Although peace and reconciliation are closely inter-linked, the fact that the ICTR has a mandate 'to contribute to the process of national reconciliation *and* to the restoration and maintenance of peace' suggests that the Security Council at the time made a clear distinction between peace and reconciliation; and the ICTY's mandate only refers to the former. One possible explanation is that when the ICTY was created in 1993, war was still raging in BiH. Hence, the main priority was the restoration of peace. In contrast, the ICTR was created in a post-conflict situation where national reconciliation could at least be contemplated. Although reconciliation is not an official prong of the ICTY's mandate, this research is an attempt to empirically explore and test a posited linkage between the ICTY and reconciliation which the Security Council and members of the Tribunal have *themselves* established.

Resolution 827 expressed the Security Council's determination to end the war crimes occurring in the former Yugoslavia and to bring the perpetrators to justice, as well as its conviction that, 'in the particular circumstances of the former Yugoslavia, the establishment as an *ad hoc* measure by the Council of an international tribunal and the prosecution of persons responsible for serious violations of international humanitarian law...would contribute to the restoration and maintenance of peace' (UN 1993b). Five years later, on 13 May 1998, the Security Council adopted Resolution 1166, which established a third Trial Chamber of the ICTY and reiterated the conviction that, 'the prosecution of persons responsible for serious violations of international humanitarian law...contributes to the restoration and maintenance of peace in the former Yugoslavia' (UN 1998b). The subtle change in wording from 'would contribute' to 'contributes', moreover, suggested renewed conviction in this regard. Again, nowhere was the word reconciliation used.

Resolution 1329 (30 November 2000) conveyed the idea, like Resolution 955 previously, that peace and reconciliation are two separate entities. Establishing a pool of more specialized *ad litem* judges for the ICTY and enlarging the membership of the Appeals Chamber which both the ICTY and ICTR share, it expressed the Security Council's continuing conviction that the prosecution of persons responsible for serious violations of international humanitarian law 'contributes to the restoration and maintenance of peace in the former Yugoslavia' and also 'contributes to the process of national reconciliation and to the restoration and maintenance of peace in Rwanda and the region' (UN 2000). In contrast, Resolution 1503 (28 August 2003) did not mention reconciliation at all, even vis-à-vis the ICTR. Instead, it simply commended 'the important work' of both the ICTY and ICTR 'in contributing to lasting peace and security in the former Yugoslavia and

---

8 Author interview, via telephone, 24 January 2008.

Rwanda and the progress made since their inception' (UN 2003). Resolution 1503 adopted the Tribunals' completion strategies, according to which they would endeavour to complete all investigations by 2004, all first instance trials by the end of 2008 and all work by 2010. This focus on the completion of the Tribunals' work may help to explain the absence of any reference to reconciliation, a long-term process. Seven months later, the Security Council adopted Resolution 1534 (26 March 2004), which called on the ICTY and ICTR 'to take all possible measures' to adhere to the completion schedule set out in Resolution 1503 (UN 2004). What is particularly interesting about Resolution 1534 is that it associated not just the ICTR but also the ICTY with reconciliation, commending 'the important work of both Tribunals in contributing to lasting peace and security and national reconciliation and the progress made since their inception...' (UN 2004).[9]

The idea that the ICTY can contribute, and indeed is contributing, to reconciliation in the former Yugoslavia, however, can primarily be traced to certain prominent figures (past and present) within the institution itself. In a speech to the UN General Assembly on 20 November 2000, for example, the Tribunal's then President emphasized that, 'As an *ad hoc* institution, the Tribunal accomplishes the goal assigned to it by Security Council resolution 827, that is, to restoring a peace of reconciliation in the Balkans by trying those guilty of crimes' (Jorda 2000). The rather odd phrase 'a peace of reconciliation' appears to suggest that there can be no genuine peace without reconciliation, the latter thus an implicit part of the Tribunal's mandate of contributing to the restoration and maintenance of peace. Despite this, Judge Jorda made no further references to reconciliation, and later in the speech he insisted that, 'Only justice can guarantee long-lasting peace' (2000).

In an address to the UN Security Council on 10 October 2003, the then Prosecutor of the ICTY, Carla Del Ponte, also seemed to imply that reconciliation is an official part of the Tribunal's mandate. 'By completing these investigations', she declared, 'the ICTY will have proven that it worked impartially towards achieving justice, peace and reconciliation in the former Yugoslavia' (Del Ponte 2003). During an address to the NATO Assembly in Belgrade four years later, she made this point more explicitly and claimed that, 'The Tribunal was established as a measure to restore and maintain peace and promote reconciliation in the former Yugoslavia' (Del Ponte 2007). Moreover, echoing Jorda, and similarly highlighting a crucial interplay between justice, peace and reconciliation, Del Ponte underlined that, 'True peace will only be maintained if the need for justice

---

9 Subsequent Security Council Resolutions relating to the ICTY have focused exclusively on, *inter alia*, the Tribunal's completion strategy, the extension of judges' terms and the Mechanism for International Criminal Tribunals, created by the Security Council in 2010. Resolution 1966 (22 December 2010), however, recalled that the ICTY and ICTR 'were established in the particular circumstances of the former Yugoslavia and Rwanda respectively as *ad hoc* measures contributing to the restoration and maintenance of peace' (UN 2010).

is satisfied, if facts about the war are undisputed and if reconciliation is achieved' (2007). While strongly associating the Tribunal's work with reconciliation, she nevertheless cautioned that, '…it is not and should not be perceived as the sole or principal factor of reconciliation' (Del Ponte 2007).

More than any other member of the Tribunal, it is the ICTY's former and current President, Judge Theodor Meron, who has most frequently and directly linked the ICTY's work to reconciliation. In a 2004 address, for example, he emphasized the hopes of the Tribunal's creators. The Security Council, he claimed, hoped that in addition to delivering justice, the ICTY would establish an impartial record of the crimes committed in the former Yugoslavia and restore a sense of dignity to victims – and that in so doing, '…it would contribute to reconciliation and reconstruction in the republics of the former Yugoslavia' (Meron 2004b). At the end of his address, Meron added that he was proud to say that, '…the Tribunal, with the General Assembly's support, is tirelessly striving to fulfill these hopes' (2004b). In subsequent speeches and writings, moreover, he has continued to underscore the theme of reconciliation and to highlight a strong linkage between justice and reconciliation. In a 2004 article, he wrote that, 'The trials [at the ICTY] have sent a powerful message that only through justice can all the peoples of the former Yugoslavia achieve reconciliation and create thriving societies' (2004a: 520). This seems to imply that reconciliation is a side-effect of the Tribunal's commitment to dispensing justice; but in a 2005 address, Meron suggested that the ICTY is actively seeking to promote reconciliation. In his words, 'We have known from the beginning that successfully prosecuting war crimes in Bosnia and Herzegovina is an essential component to showing that justice is being served, promoting reconciliation among Bosnia and Herzegovina's communities and bringing closure to the families of the victims of the war' (Meron 2005). More recently, in an address to the UN General Assembly in October 2012, the ICTY President delivered his most unequivocal argument apropos of reconciliation, maintaining that the ICTY's achievements have 'contributed to bringing peace and reconciliation to the countries of the former Yugoslavia' (Meron 2012).

During the author's fieldwork at the ICTY in 2008, however, interviewees expressed extremely diverse opinions on this issue. Fundamentally, there was a clear absence of consensus on whether reconciliation is one of the Tribunal's actual objectives or merely a possible side-effect of its work. An interviewee working in the Transition Unit, for example, maintained that reconciliation is absolutely one of the ICTY's goals, but also emphasized that it is a long process which requires more than criminal trials alone.[10] For his part, a member of the Trial Division described reconciliation as the 'third prong' of the Tribunal's mandate, while also stressing the difficulties of achieving reconciliation; 'If all the sides say

10 Author interview, The Hague, 12 February 2008.

it wasn't them, then how can you have reconciliation?'[11] A member of the Registry, who believed that reconciliation is in fact an element of the Tribunal's official mandate, expressed the view that, 'Our work, by definition, aids reconciliation'. Underscoring the importance of bringing senior perpetrators to justice, he insisted that, 'Justice is an absolutely necessary part of reconciliation'.[12] A fellow member of the Registry, in contrast, sought to strongly disassociate the Tribunal from reconciliation. Keen to begin the interview 'with a few basic structural observations', he vigorously argued that, 'At no point in any of the key documents, Security Council Resolutions and such like in which we have our mandate codified is the word "reconciliation" used…'.[13] A spokesperson for Registry and Chambers similarly sought to distance the Tribunal from the idea of reconciliation and stressed that the latter is a deeply individual process. In her view, therefore, 'All that any war crimes court can do is to contribute to the creation of the atmosphere and the facts for those individuals to decide to forgive and to move on, to reconcile'.[14] Finally, a member of the OTP opined that although the ICTY has the potential to contribute to reconciliation, societies in the former Yugoslavia must ultimately drive the process.[15]

What has strongly emerged from the foregoing analysis is that considerable ambiguity and inconsistency surround the issue of reconciliation in the context of the ICTY's work. The author's own position is that while reconciliation is not an official part of the Tribunal's mandate, Security Council Resolution 827 refers to 'the restoration and maintenance of peace'; and the maintenance of peace arguably requires a 'thicker' form of peace than simply negative peace – characterized by an absence of personal violence. A sustainable form of peace, in short, requires at least some degree of reconciliation. This, together with the fact that the Tribunal's work has been regularly and explicitly associated with reconciliation, means that it is both important, and entirely appropriate, to examine whether the ICTY has indeed contributed to inter-ethnic reconciliation in the former Yugoslavia. While the notion that a court can aid reconciliation has attracted considerable scepticism (see, for example, Hayden 2011: 316; Weinstein 2011: 2; Weinstein et al. 2010: 47) – scepticism which this author shares – it is also the case that very few scholars have sought to systematically assess the Tribunal's impact on reconciliation. Certainly, no one has created clear methodological tools for doing so. The following conceptual chapter does precisely this.

11 Author interview, The Hague, 11 February 2008.
12 Author interview, The Hague, 15 February 2008.
13 Author interview, The Hague, 7 February 2008.
14 Author interview, The Hague, 13 February 2008.
15 Author interview, The Hague, 8 February 2008.

Chapter 2

Reconciliation, the ICTY and the issue of impact

Critical Challenges and Foundations

In everyday language, the term 'reconciliation' is often used as though its meaning were self-explanatory. When we begin to grapple with definitional issues, however, it immediately becomes apparent that reconciliation is by no means a straightforward concept. Variously referred to as 'an ambiguous term' (Stover 2007: 117), 'an abstract and ambiguous term' (Chapman 2009: 144), 'an imprecise term' (Weinstein 2011: 6) and 'a notoriously fuzzy and contested notion' (De Grieff 2007: 127), there is little academic consensus on how to define reconciliation. Indeed, one author maintains that, 'The amount of writing on what constitutes reconciliation reinforces the view that we are searching for a concept that defies clarity' (Weinstein 2011: 7). While this is not an opinion that this research endorses, it cannot be denied that the challenges inherent in disambiguating the notion of reconciliation are significant. Three in particular can be highlighted.

Firstly, reconciliation is both an outcome and a process, 'the *place* we are trying to reach and a *journey* we take to get there' (Lederach 1999: 24). Its progressive character, in turn, means that reconciliation is continually evolving and changing shape, and this innate fluidity makes it difficult to define with precision; 'its interpretation is growing and changing' (Quinn 2009: 12). Even when we focus on reconciliation as an outcome, this by no means eliminates definitional difficulties since we may disagree on what an end state of reconciliation looks like. As one author fittingly asks:

> Is it peace, the end of violence; is it contented individuals and families; is it communities where it is safe to walk the streets, to shop, to go to the mosque or church or synagogue, where women do not fear rape and where men and women feel no pressure to take up arms; is it economic opportunity, education for the children and dignity in old age?
>
> (Weinstein 2011: 3)

Secondly, and linked to the previous point, reconciliation is a highly elastic concept which can easily accommodate a variety of related concepts – such as peace, coexistence and forgiveness. This, together with the fact that reconciliation is not part of any specialized lexicon, means that it signifies different things to different people. 'The problem with reconciliation', as Gibson argues, 'is not that it is devoid of content; the problem is that reconciliation is such an intuitively accessible concept that everyone is able to imbue it with her or his own distinct understanding' (2004a: 12).

Thirdly, the need for reconciliation arises from the particular events – armed conflicts, war crimes, ethnic cleansing – that have occurred within an individual society. Hence, the meaning of reconciliation may vary from one context to another (Mukherjee 2011: 333). The degree of atrocities committed, the level of popular participation in those atrocities and the duration of the conflict are factors, among others, that help to create contextual definitional variation. The result, thus, is that, 'Competing understandings of reconciliation are apparent in most societies coming out of conflict' (Hamber and Kelly 2005: 13).

If reconciliation raises acute definitional challenges, finding a way to quantify and measure it is yet more difficult. If we cannot agree on what reconciliation actually means, how do we know when it exists? According to Meierhenrich, '... operationalization is the linchpin that connects categories and cases – or ideas and facts – and constitutes a methodological task second only to that of conceptualization' (2008: 224). This chapter specifically addresses that methodological task. In order to assess whether the ICTY has contributed to inter-ethnic reconciliation in BiH, Croatia and Kosovo, it is first necessary to define reconciliation, to operationalize the concept and finally to develop a model for assessing the Tribunal's impact on inter-ethnic relations.

Defining an essentially contested concept

At the most basic level, 'Reconciliation is first and last about people and their relationships' (Lederach 2001: 842). Where authors disagree is on the details and specifics of those relationships – on what it practically means to say that people have reconciled with each other. Most prominently, there is a clear distinction within academic literature between 'thin' and 'thick' definitions of reconciliation.

Reconciliation 'thinly' defined

Authors who embrace a 'thin', minimalist definition typically understand reconciliation as a process wherein relationships are improved to the extent that is necessary for society to function normally (without conflict). Accordingly, reconciliation has been variously described as 'mutually conciliatory accommodation between former antagonists' (Long and Brecke 2003: 1), as 'a capacity to restore and create relationships in an ongoing way...' (Gready 2011: 196) and as acceptance of others (Morton 2004: 125). 'Thin' reconciliation, in short, is little more than coexistence, 'wherein a certain level of day-to-day trust is established by people living in close proximity but the level of profound empathy and dialogue associated with "thick reconciliation" is foreclosed by a determined silence over

war-time injustices and suffering' (Helms 2010: 18). The advantage of thin definitions is that they encourage a view of reconciliation that does not expect too
much of post-conflict societies. People living in these societies, moreover, are less
likely to oppose reconciliation if they feel no sense of pressure 'to forgive for the
sake of peace' (Bloomfield 2006: 28).

The extent to which these thin definitions can aid the task of developing a
measurable concept of reconciliation, however, is arguably limited for three main
reasons. Firstly, such definitions often tell us very little about what reconciliation
actually looks like, particularly when they operate at high levels of abstraction. If,
for example, reconciliation is 'an agreement among antagonistic subjects to
depart from violence in a shared present' (Borneman 2002: 300), 'the preparedness of people to anticipate a shared future' (Rigby 2001: 12) or 'a process
through which a society moves from a divided past to a shared present' (Bloomfield
2003: 12), how do we know when it exists and where is the end point?

Secondly, thin definitions encourage conceptual blurring by equating reconciliation with the related concepts of, *inter alia*, coexistence and co-operation.
While coexistence and co-operation can certainly be viewed as indicators of reconciliation, the latter loses its specificity if it is merely seen as a derivative of these
terms. This, in turn, compounds the challenges inherent in quantifying reconciliation; measuring coexistence and co-operation should not become a substitute
for measuring reconciliation, but we will always struggle to find the tools to
measure reconciliation if we define it in ways that conflate it with other similar
concepts.

Thirdly, if we embrace a highly functional view of reconciliation as something
that needs to exist in order for people to go about their daily lives, reconciliation
thus becomes highly contiguous with negative peace (Galtung 1969). An absence
of physical violence within a society, however, may tell us little about inter-personal and community relationships within that society; and 'It is the interpersonal
ruins, rather than the ruined buildings and institutions, that pose the greatest
challenge for rebuilding society' (Halpern and Weinstein 2004: 304). Hence,
although reconciliation cannot endure in the absence of negative peace, the latter
can never be a sufficient basis for measuring reconciliation. A lack of physical
violence, in short, does not necessarily mean that reconciliation exists on an emotional and attitudinal level, and it is these critical affective dimensions that distinguish mere functional reconciliation – which can be found among primates and
other animals (Cords 1993; Silk 2002; Wahaj, Guse and Holekamp 2001) – from
much 'thicker' forms. It is the latter, moreover, that provide a critical starting
point for developing a measurable concept of reconciliation.

Reconciliation 'thickly' defined

Reconciliation, to reiterate, is about relationships (Gready 2011: 196; Villa-
Vicencio 2009a: 5). When 'thickly' defined, however, it is not simply about
improving those relationships at a functional level, but about re-building them at

a much deeper level. Weinstein and Stover, for example, 'loosely' use the term reconciliation to signify 'people re-forming prior connections, both instrumental and affective, across ethnic, racial, or religious lines' (2004: 4); Kriesberg defines reconciliation as 'a relatively amicable relationship typically established after a rupture in relations involving one sided or mutual infliction of extreme injury' (1998: 351); and Hamber and Kelly understand reconciliation as 'the process of addressing conflictual and fractured relationships' (2009: 291). In a similar vein, Trimikliniotis emphasizes that societal reconciliation is 'the Greek *symphiliosis* (i.e. the process of reaching *philia*, friendship)', which requires a 'transcendence' of social divides (2012: 255); for Amstutz, 'Fundamentally, reconciliation involves the rebuilding of understanding and harmonious relationships' (2005: 97); and Villa-Vicencio explains that while reconciliation 'often begins with little more than a cautious openness towards others', a deeper relationship may develop as trust and confidence grow (2009a: 5).

There is a widespread consensus, moreover, that this re-building of relationships cannot occur in the absence of 'a changed psychological orientation toward the other' (Staub et al. 2005: 301; see also Jeong 2005: 155; Kubai 2007: 64). In terms of what exactly this entails, three key (and inter-linked) sub-processes can be identified. The first of these is re-humanization. When societies begin to fragment and fracture, 'us' and 'them' divides quickly emerge; and as the 'negative other' is progressively stigmatized and demonized (Feierstein 2012: 23), this can ultimately culminate in the de-humanization of the entire 'out group'. At this point, the slide into violence and bloodshed is all but inevitable as 'the normal human revulsion against murder' is overcome (Baum 2008: 33). In societies recovering from conflict, therefore, re-humanization is a necessary prerequisite for any re-building of relationships (Halpern and Weinstein 2004: 305; Jeong 2005: 156; Lederach 1999: 24; Staub 2000: 376). One possible way in which to facilitate re-humanization – and this brings us to the second aforementioned sub-process – is through the medium of empathy. When former enemies listen to each other, share their experiences and recognize that 'victims and offenders share a common identity, as survivors and human beings' (Huyse 2003: 21), this creates the basis for an 'empathic connection' to occur (Halpern and Weinstein 2004: 306). This connection cannot endure and deepen, however, in the absence of the third crucial sub-process, namely trust. As the 'glue that holds relationships together' (Lewicki and Wiethoff 2000: 86), trust is a critical component of reconciliation. Its existence, moreover, creates an enabling environment for reconciliation to develop (Nadler and Leviatan 2006: 461).

From all of the above, an important strength of thick definitions can be discerned. By focusing heavily on the psychological processes that are necessary in order for former enemies to fundamentally change how they view each other, and thus to begin to re-build relations, such definitions implicitly suggest potential ways of measuring reconciliation. To what extent do perceptions of 'otherness' persist; are people open to hearing the stories of their former enemies; is there trust between them and to what degree? These are some of the questions that might be asked in order to ascertain whether reconciliation exists. Thick definitions, however, are by no means unproblematic. One issue is that in contrast to thin definitions of reconciliation, it might be argued that thick definitions demand too much of people. While it may be very difficult, at least initially, for the members of formerly rival groups to peacefully coexist and co-operate, asking them to empathize with each other, to trust one another, and so on, is another matter entirely. De Grieff, for example, maintains that if we reduce reconciliation to a psychological state which requires 'attributes that are, according to most views of human beings, absolutely extraordinary' (2007: 121), it will never be easily accepted. If, moreover, reconciliation is defined in an unrealistic way that has no resonance among communities on the ground, it thus becomes almost impossible to measure since evidence of its existence will likely remain lacking. A second issue is that although thick definitions provide a number of possible ways of gauging reconciliation, it is extremely difficult to measure psychological processes because we cannot know with complete certainty what other people think and feel. In order to portray themselves in a positive light, for example, individuals may not reveal their true feelings, and indeed may not fully recognize their views and prejudices for what they actually are. A classic example of this is the person who claims: 'I'm not a racist but...'.

The above problems, however, can be addressed in two main ways. Firstly, many authors approach reconciliation as a multi-layered concept consisting of several inter-related elements or stages. Hamber and Kelly, for example, argue that reconciliation consists of, and is the process of addressing, five inter-woven strands, namely: developing a shared vision of an independent and fair society; acknowledging and dealing with the past; building positive relationships; significant cultural and attitudinal change; and substantial social, economic and political change (2009: 282). Kelman similarly pinpoints five conditions that are necessary for reconciliation. These are: mutual acknowledgement of the other's nationhood and humanity; development of a common moral basis for peace;[1] confrontation with history; acknowledgement of responsibility; and establishment of patterns and institutional mechanisms of co-operation (Kelman 2008: 27–29). Huyse, for his part, identifies three key stages of reconciliation. As a first stage, non-violent coexistence must replace fear, which 'requires first of all that victims and perpetrators be freed from the paralyzing isolation and all-consuming self-pity in which they often live...' (2003: 20). Once coexistence (thin reconciliation) exists, the reconciliation process can move into its more difficult stages of confidence/trust-building and empathy creation (Huyse 2003: 21). Such composite definitions (see also Auerbach 2005: 474; Gibson 2004a: 117; Kriesberg 2007: 251–252; Lederach 1997: 29), which often encapsulate the idea that

---

1 Here, Kelman makes the excellent point that, 'To create the conditions for reconciliation, it is necessary to move beyond a peace anchored entirely in pragmatic considerations – essential as these are – to a peace based on moral considerations' (2008: 28).

reconciliation progresses along a continuum, demonstrate that thick conceptions of reconciliation do not need to be unrealistic or overly demanding. When reconciliation is theorized as consisting of different strands and dimensions, this helps to ensure that the demands which reconciliation inevitably creates are more evenly spread as the process develops and unfolds.

Secondly, and linked to the above, we can address at least some of the difficulties of measuring psychological processes, such as trust and empathy, by holistically defining reconciliation as consisting of both affective/attitudinal and behavioural elements. Kelman, for example, argues that, 'Changes in the ways in which former enemy populations think about each other, feel about each other and act toward one another, as they learn to live together, are the essence of what is generally meant by reconciliation' (2008: 16). These dimensions of reconciliation necessarily complement and reinforce each other. People cannot truly behave in a reconciliatory way if they continue to harbour negative beliefs and feelings about 'the other'. As Pillay underlines, 'Ending the fighting between warring parties may create only a short-term peace if the animosities, mistrust and bitterness that are produced during conflict are not addressed but instead are allowed to linger into the future, often overshadowing the everyday practices of social and political life after the conflict' (2009: 353). By the same token, however, even if progress is made along the affective/attitudinal axis, this must be translated into practical behaviour. Observing how people act towards, and interact with, each other, moreover, can provide important insights into whether they do in fact hold the attitudes and views that they claim to.

While multi-stranded, compound definitions can help to reduce some of the difficulties associated with conceptualizing reconciliation in thick terms, they too have their own weaknesses. Two in particular merit attention. The first is that composite definitions can potentially encourage a template approach to reconciliation that is insufficiently responsive to the circumstances and nuances of individual post-conflict societies. As the need for reconciliation arises out of particular events that have occurred within these societies, the precise form that reconciliation takes, and the specific challenges that it poses, can be expected to vary from one context to another. When reconciliation is presented as a specific set of elements and stages, however, this can engender an overly prescriptive view of what it *should* look like.

Turning to the second weakness associated with composite definitions, it is of course the case that, 'The more abstract our concepts, the less clear will be the observable consequences and the less amenable the theory will be to falsification' (King, Keohane and Verba 1994: 110). Conversely, rendering operational and quantifiable a highly dense and multi-faceted concept presents its own challenges. Indeed, overly-complex definitions can deter us from even attempting to broach difficult measurement issues. This research, therefore – which to reiterate is specifically concerned with reconciliation at the inter-personal and community level – adopts a somewhat loose, albeit thick, definition of reconciliation as the *repair and restoration of relationships and the re-building of trust*. This definition makes clear that reconciliation is far more than simply coexistence.[2] It also emphasizes the dual nature of reconciliation as both psychological (affective, attitudinal) and behavioural. Defining reconciliation in this way, however, can only take us so far. Multiple definitions of the term already exist. The key question is how do we *measure* reconciliation?

From definitional to operational issues

Reconciliation, according to one commentator, 'is like the old saw about pornography – we know it when we see it' (Weinstein 2011: 3). What is critically needed is a scientific way of assessing reconciliation,[3] yet few authors have embraced this challenge. The result is that beyond definitional issues, the practical question of how to measure reconciliation remains largely unanswered. This, in turn, has created significant gaps within an otherwise rich literature. Lederach, for example, one of the leading scholars on reconciliation, conceptualizes reconciliation as truth, mercy, justice and peace (1997: 29). Unless we devise a method for gauging and quantifying these four components, however, we cannot know whether reconciliation thus defined actually exists and/or is feasible. Understanding reconciliation as the repair and restoration of relationships and the re-building of trust raises similar issues. How do we assess whether and to what extent these processes have occurred or are occurring? Ultimately, '...we need to develop empirical tools for...measuring reconciliation and how it unfolds at the individual, community and societal level' (Stover and Weinstein 2004b: 340). Some attempts, albeit small in number, have been made to identify and explore possible ways of quantifying reconciliation, and it is important to briefly review a selection of these.

Approaches to measuring reconciliation

Starting with the work of Long and Brecke, these authors draw a key distinction between reconciliation – defined as 'mutually conciliatory accommodation between former antagonists' (2003: 1) – and what they term 'reconciliation events'. Rather than seeking to measure reconciliation per se, the authors use reconciliation events 'to identify potential reconciliations...' (Long and Brecke 2003: 7). The advantage of doing so, as they point out, is that reconciliation events are more concrete and hence more clearly recognizable; 'Reconciliation events can be identified in the historical record, whereas reconciliation...ultimately occurs within the minds of many, perhaps most individuals in a society and is difficult to measure' (Long and Brecke 2003: 7). The problem is that the authors define

2 Trust is a key factor that critically distinguishes reconciliation from mere coexistence (Ogata 2003: xiii).
3 Gibson, for example, underlines that reconciliation is a concept 'that can be (and should be) measured and assessed using rigorous and systematic social science methods' (2004a: 3).

such events in an overly-narrow way, thereby limiting their use. According to them, reconciliation events consist of the following components:

> direct or physical contact or proximity between opponents, usually senior representatives of respective factions; a public ceremony accompanied by substantial publicity or media attention that relays the event to the wider society; and ritualistic or symbolic behavior that indicates the parties consider the dispute resolved and that more amicable relations are expected to follow.
> (Long and Brecke 2003: 6)

Thus defined, reconciliation events are clearly pertinent to issues of national reconciliation. However, in order to act as measurable indicators of reconciliation at the grassroots level, which is precisely the focus of this research, they would need to be defined more broadly. Former enemies jointly taking part in commemorations to honour and remember the dead, or working together to improve the life of their community (for example, by setting up a youth club, protesting against development plans that would harm the local eco-system or cleaning up a vandalized church), could be viewed as reconciliation events at an inter-personal and community level. Indeed, ultimately, Long and Brecke do allow for a wider application of the term reconciliation events, notably by identifying the core factors and processes that create a favourable context for such events to be successful. In their words, '... reconciliation events restore lasting order when they are part of a forgiveness process characterized by truth telling, redefinition of the identity of the former belligerents, partial justice, and a call for a new relationship' (Long and Brecke 2003: 3). These elements are relevant to reconciliation at any level. They also enrich the concept of reconciliation events, by highlighting the significance of psychological processes. Dealing with these processes as a corollary or dimension of reconciliation events, moreover, potentially lessens the difficulties of measuring them.

Despite the obvious value of Long and Brecke's work, this research does not utilize the concept of reconciliation events for three reasons. The first is that this is a comparative study focused on BiH, Croatia and Kosovo. Since each of these post-conflict societies faces its own particular problems and challenges, which in turn means that they are in many ways at different stages of the reconciliation process, this creates important contextual variation which potentially challenges the concept of reconciliation events. An event which could be deemed reconciliatory in Croatia, for example, may not have the same meaning and import in Kosovo. The second reason is that this research is concerned with inter-personal and community reconciliation, and the notion of reconciliation events arguably has greater application vis-à-vis national reconciliation. This is because events that attract attention and are deemed significant are more likely to occur at the macro level – and to involve political leaders – than at the grassroots level where reconciliation is less about one-off memorable events and more about small steps, gradual changes and everyday life. The third reason is that the concept of reconciliation events can only take us so far. If we focus on reconciliation events rather than on reconciliation itself, this means that we are not measuring reconciliation per se; and given that the latter is heavily contested, how do we know that reconciliation events are reliable indicators of reconciliation? The concept of reconciliation events, moreover, leaves unanswered the issue of how to measure the processes, such as truth telling and partial justice, which, according to Long and Brecke, critically impact on the ultimate success of such events.

If the concept of reconciliation events works best at the level of national reconciliation, Biro et al. underscore that, '...the elements of reconciliation occur at multiple levels...' (2004: 198). Rather than specifically discussing how we might measure reconciliation at these different levels, however, the authors focus on developing a multi-variate prediction of readiness for reconciliation, with the purpose of identifying which factors contribute to or prevent reconciliation. Underlining the complexity of reconciliation, they define the term operationally using three key variables, namely: 'Readiness to accept the presence of members of the "opposing" nationalities in eight different situations (stores, parks, sporting events, sport teams, concerts, parties, schools/offices and non-governmental organizations)'; 'Readiness to be reconciled with the conflicted nationalities'; and 'Readiness to accept interstate cooperation' (Biro et al. 2004: 197). These three variables, in turn, are combined to create a composite 'Readiness for Reconciliation' variable, which is tested as part of a survey of 1,624 people in BiH (Mostar and Prijedor) and Croatia (Vukovar) in 2000–2001. While the research is innovative and has potential practical significance, it provides important insights into how reconciliation can be facilitated or impeded, rather than a way of assessing whether reconciliation exists. A readiness to reconcile could be used as one possible measure of reconciliation, but it would be a necessarily limited indicator. Reconciliation, to reiterate, has a critical behavioural component, and the fact that a person expresses a readiness to accept members of another group in a variety of situations does not necessarily mean that this readiness will be translated into practice.

Moving from the former Yugoslavia to South Africa, Gibson has sought to ascertain whether the truth established by the country's TRC contributed to inter-racial reconciliation. As a starting point, he deconstructs the concept of reconciliation in order to identify what he regards as an 'elemental component', namely mutual respect. Maintaining that 'a fundamental ingredient in mutual respect is the willingness to judge people as individuals rather than brand them with group stereotypes...' (Gibson 2004a: 118), Gibson approaches the challenge of measuring reconciliation by exploring how the members of the country's different racial groups view and feel about each other. In order to do this, he has developed nine different statements[4] as a way of gauging popular attitudes; and

4 The statements were: 'I find it difficult to understand the customs and ways of [the opposite racial group]; it is hard to imagine being friends with [the opposite racial group]; more than most groups, [the opposite racial group] are likely to engage in crime; [the opposite racial group] are

during a survey conducted in 2000–2001, which involved 3,727 face-to-face interviews, participants were asked to agree or disagree with each of these statements. Using the responses to these nine statements to develop a 'Reconciliation Index' – which he explains 'is simply the number of "reconciled responses" minus the number of "nonreconciled" answers' (Gibson 2004b: 206) – he finds that white South Africans hold more positive views of black South Africans than vice versa (Gibson 2004b: 207).

Gibson's work is methodologically rigorous and it provides an interesting way of measuring reconciliation. It does, however, privilege breadth over depth. Simply asking people whether they agree or disagree with a set of statements cannot tell us anything about their reasons for agreeing or disagreeing, and this is an important limitation of Gibson's work. In short, it cannot yield the highly nuanced answers that any assessment of reconciliation demands. Meierhenrich, moreover, identifies a further limitation. Gibson is only measuring attitudes, yet these do not constitute the totality of reconciliation; the critical behavioural dimension is neglected in his analysis. According to Meierhenrich, therefore, 'By adopting a unilateral conception of interracial reconciliation that deems unnecessary *action* regarding another group and is centered solely on *attitudes* toward another group, Gibson set a low bar for interracial reconciliation' (2008: 218). This is because it is often easier for people to change 'their attitudes toward adversaries than their actions' (Meierhenrich 2008: 218).

Like Gibson, the Institute for Justice and Reconciliation (IJR), based in Cape Town, has also devised a way of measuring reconciliation in South Africa, in the form of its Reconciliation Barometer surveys.[5] These longitudinal surveys, which have been conducted on an annual basis since 2003, are structured around the construct of the Reconciliation Barometer. This consists of six variables – namely human security, political culture, cross-cutting political relationships, dialogue, historical confrontation and race relations – which in turn form the basis of six hypotheses. According to the IJR's approach, however, 'the intangible and highly ambiguous concept of reconciliation needs to be unpacked in relation to a number of critical indicators or benchmarks' (Lombard 2003: 3). Hence, for each of the six hypotheses, there are between one and four indicators. For the human security variable, for example, the hypothesis is: 'If citizens do not feel threatened, they are more likely to be reconciled with each other and the larger system'; and the respective indicators are physical security, economic security and cultural security (Lefko-Everett 2012: 12). While the IJR acknowledges '[t]he

untrustworthy; [the opposite racial group] are selfish, and only look after the interests of their group; I feel uncomfortable when I am around a group of [the opposite racial group]; I don't believe what [the opposite racial group] say to me; South Africa would be a better place if there were no [the opposite racial group] in the country; and I could never imagine being part of a political party made up mainly of [the opposite racial group]' (Gibson 2004b: 205).

5 See http://www.ijr.org.za/political-analysis-SARB.php

obvious dangers of excessive reductionism in translating such a complex process [as reconciliation] in relation to a handful of critical indicators...' (Lombard 2003: 7), it is the identification of measurable indicators of reconciliation (although we may not agree on how to actually measure these indicators) that makes the Reconciliation Barometer a useful methodological tool. It is, therefore, a tool which this research utilizes and adapts, by using it as the basis for developing a Reconciliation Matrix – a term which conveys the essence of reconciliation as a composite concept of inter-connected strands and fibres.

Constructing a reconciliation matrix

The Reconciliation Matrix used in this research consists of a set of four variables, which can be viewed as broad indicators of reconciliation, and a set of more specific indicators or markers for identifying, exploring and measuring each of these variables (see Table 2.1). These variables and indicators reflect both the attitudinal/affective and behavioural dimensions of reconciliation.

It is not the case that reconciliation can only be said to exist if all of the four variables are found to be present, as measured using the associated indicators. Reconciliation is a process and different combinations of different variables, and different gradations of those variables, are merely indicative of varying levels of progress along the reconciliation continuum. It is, however, necessary to elaborate upon each of the variables and indicators that constitute the Reconciliation Matrix, beginning with human security and its markers.

There is a close nexus between reconciliation and security; if people do not feel safe and secure in their homes and communities, they will not be able to reach out to their former enemies or to begin the process of re-building trust. Highlighting this point, Atashi observes that, 'The necessary element for the

Table 2.1 Reconciliation Matrix

Variables	Indicators
Human Security	Physical security Prevalence of inter-ethnic incidents Economic security
Deep Contact	Frequency Type (formal/informal; required/chosen) Social setting (public/private)
Trust	Levels of social distance Perceptions of the 'other' Trust-inducing/trust-impeding behaviour
Mutual Acceptance	Respect Empathy Positive gestures and signals

transformation from victimhood and suffering to healing is the perception of security and safety' (2009: 56). In order to assess levels of human security, three particular indicators can be used. The first is physical security, which is both a subjective and objective concept. Do people feel safe going about their daily business; do they fear any members of the community; have they ever been a victim of physical violence? The second indicator is the frequency of inter-ethnic incidents, involving not only attacks on individuals but also damage to properties, land and livelihoods. The prevalence of such incidents can shed important light on levels of physical security. The third indicator is economic security. If people have jobs, if they are able to make ends meet, if they are not preoccupied with basic existential issues, they will be less inclined to view themselves as fundamentally disadvantaged, and hence potentially less likely to resent and blame members of the other ethnic group. In short, 'Economic problems intensify the relative deprivation that less privileged groups may experience in normal times' (Staub 2011: 116).

Turning now to the second variable, deep contact, this research endorses the so-called contact hypothesis: the idea that contact helps to reduce the stereotypes and prejudices that people hold about each other (Allport 1954; Amir 1969; Cook 1985; Pettigrew 1998; Staub 1989, 2011). Although this hypothesis has been heavily criticized over the years (see, for example, Babbitt 2003; Nesdale and Todd 2000; Ray 1983), it is difficult to envisage how reconciliation can make significant inroads in a context where only very limited contact is occurring. To cite Jansen, 'Any concrete form of reconciliation, however we understand it, requires encounters on the ground between actual persons' (2013: 235). Contact constitutes a critical foundation for the repair and restoration of relationships and the re-building of trust, but it is not the case that simply any contact will suffice. As Donnelly and Hughes point out,

> The classic version of the hypothesis posited by [Gordon] Allport has always emphasized that contact must have "acquaintance potential", meaning that relationships must move beyond mere "sightseeing" and have the capacity to develop into meaningful friendships where participants have the opportunity to take the perspective of the "out group" in general.
>
> (2009: 150)

Staub has expanded upon this by using the term 'deep contact' (2011: 290). Contrasting this with superficial contact,[6] he maintains that, 'Deeper contact, more significant engagement, in which ideally people work together for shared

---

6 According to Staub, 'A statistical summary of over 500 studies on the effects of contact shows that contact reduces prejudice. It creates a more positive attitude toward members of another group. But superficial contact, people belonging to different groups living in the same neighborhood, seeing but not engaging with each other, will have limited effects' (2011: 330).

goals, is more effective in overcoming prejudice and humanizing the other' (Staub 2011: 330). This raises the important question of how to distinguish between these two types of contact, and to this end this research uses three indicators. The first is the frequency of the contact; does it occur on a regular and periodic basis or is it irregular and sporadic? The second is the type of contact; is it purely formal (for example, an exchange between a buyer and seller) or is it more informal and relaxed; and is it contact that occurs out of necessity (for example, in a hospital) or through choice? The final indicator is social setting; does the contact happen only in public (such as in cafes and restaurants) or also in the more private setting of people's homes?

The third key variable is trust, a core element of reconciliation. In the words of Archbishop Desmond Tutu, reconciliation is a 'gradual growing into a common space that allows us to trust one another enough to work together, eventually to be friends and neighbors and, yes, even to forgive and love one another' (2009: x). Reconciliation cannot occur, therefore, in the absence of fundamental attitudinal change, and hence two significant indicators of trust are social distance (what types of relationships do people accept and reject?) and perceptions of the 'other' (to what extent do individuals continue to think in terms of 'us' and 'them',[7] do they generalize about members of another ethnic group, do they regard the members of that group as collectively guilty?). Trust, however, also has an important behavioural dimension; the particular ways in which people act may either encourage or inhibit the process of re-building trust. Hence, a third indicator that this research uses for measuring trust is trust-inducing/trust-impeding behaviour. An example of the former might include an apology. As Barkan remarks, 'An apology does not mean the dispute is resolved but it is, in most cases, a first step' (2003: 98). An example of trust-impeding behaviour, on the other hand, would be the deliberate withholding of information about the whereabouts of missing persons.

Mutual acceptance is the fourth and final variable. We cannot reconcile with those whom we do not accept; acceptance of others, and acceptance of difference, is a foundational prerequisite (Gibson 2004c: 133). One important indicator of mutual acceptance is mutual respect, which can be observed in the way that people speak about each other, their willingness to listen to each other's views and their acceptance of each other's right to live in the community or area. The second indicator is empathy (Halpern and Weinstein 2004: 306). For Staub, 'Seeing as similar to ourselves people who have been historically devalued or with whom our group is in conflict is an important condition for empathy' (2011: 327). In particular, empathy is about being receptive to others' stories of pain and suffering, and ultimately recognizing inter-group shared experiences. When

---

7 Bar-On opines that as part of the process of reconciliation, 'A "hard" and simplistic identity construction that has been developed to support the conflict has to be replaced by a "softer", more complex and less monolithic construction' (2007: 74–75).

individuals are ready to acknowledge that there was suffering on both/all sides and that women losing husbands and sons, children losing fathers, people being forced to leave their homes were common *cross-ethnic* experiences, this is an important expression of mutual acceptance. The third indicator is positive gestures and signals, namely acts which convey to members of a particular group the message that they are welcome and fully accepted. Such gestures and signals might include offering assistance (for example, in regard to re-building a house or cultivating a plot of land) and showing respect for the other group's religious and cultural heritage.

The above variables and their respective indicators constitute a tool, a Reconciliation Matrix, for assessing whether and to what extent reconciliation exists at an inter-personal and community level. This research, however, is not simply interested in the question of how to measure reconciliation. Its far more ambitious objective is to evaluate the ICTY's impact on inter-ethnic reconciliation, which necessarily raises difficult issues of causation. Establishing causality, according to Gibson, '...is one of the most demanding tasks facing empirical social scientists, and one can virtually never do better than drawing probabilistic conclusions about causation' (2004a: 29). This research seeks to do more than simply offer such conclusions, and the final part of this chapter develops a model specifically for measuring the ICTY's contribution – if any – to reconciliation.

The ICTY's impact on inter-ethnic reconciliation: A three-pronged model

As discussed in the previous chapter, the idea that criminal trials can contribute to peace and reconciliation has become an oft-cited claim within the TJ literature. However, the relationship between international courts and reconciliation, to reiterate, remains empirically under-explored. Although the putative merits of these courts are confidently asserted, '...we still know surprisingly little about their tangible domestic effects' (Stromseth 2009: 88). Existing TJ literature nevertheless provides a useful starting point for measuring the ICTY's impact on reconciliation.

Among the various ways in which criminal trials reputedly facilitate reconciliation, two in particular are frequently emphasized. The first of these can be termed the 'justice route'. Justice is often viewed as essential for peace and reconciliation (Bassiouni 2003: 204; Bloomfield 2003: 14; Oette 2010: 353; Staub 2011: 459), and an extension of this is the argument that the ICTY can aid reconciliation by delivering justice to the people of the former Yugoslavia (see, for example, Cassese 1998: 6; Moghalu 2004: 216; Scharf and Williams 2003: 190). Chapter 1 demonstrated that prominent figures within the Tribunal have similarly emphasized this justice-reconciliation relationship, and it is important to underline this point. In a speech delivered in 2005 to mark the opening of BiH's War Crimes Chamber, for example, the ICTY's President declared that, '[The] creation of the

War Crimes Chamber is further evidence of the international community's commitment to ensuring justice in Bosnia and Herzegovina, and reflects the understanding that justice and accountability are necessary components of post-war reconciliation and reconstruction' (Meron 2005). More recently, the ICTY's Registrar referred to justice as the '*condicio sine qua non* to national reconciliation and peace' (Hocking 2012).

In order to measure the ICTY's impact on reconciliation, this research thus begins by empirically exploring the idea that the Tribunal has positively aided reconciliation via the dispensation of justice. Justice therefore provides a useful criterion for measuring the ICTY's contribution to reconciliation. It is essential to acknowledge that, 'Justice is not easily observed or measured, its attached meaning and symbols cannot escape cultural particularity and it will always be the controversial subject of ideological and political contestation, rather than causal certitudes' (Dancy 2010: 355). However, the quintessential point about justice is that it must not only be done but must also be *seen* to be done, and this in turn highlights the critical importance of perceptions. How local people perceive the ICTY can thus be viewed as a key indicator of justice. In short, do local people in the former Yugoslavia associate the ICTY and its work with justice? Whether or not they do so may be strongly influenced by how much they actually know about the Tribunal, particularly in view of the fact that the latter is not located within the former Yugoslavia. Hence, the extent to which people are well-informed about the ICTY's trials can be used as a second important indicator. Yet, even if local people comprehend the justice process, this does not necessarily mean that 'justice' – as *they* understand the term – is being delivered. The ICTY defines justice, as we might expect, in a narrow, legalistic way: 'By holding individuals responsible for crimes committed in the former Yugoslavia, the Tribunal is bringing justice to victims' (ICTY n.d.). Justice, however, is a fluid and elastic term that may mean different things to different people (Volf 2000: 870). Accordingly, '...we need to be very careful about how we define the term "justice". For many survivors, justice may not mean trials but a much more personal sense of what they need in order to move on with their lives' (Biro et al. 2004: 201). How local people personally understand the concept thereby constitutes a third marker.

Closely inter-woven with the aforementioned 'justice route' is what might be called the 'truth route' – the idea that tribunals assist reconciliation by documenting the facts, establishing an incontrovertible historical record which cannot be challenged and tackling denial (see, for example, Akhavan 1998: 741; Scharf and Williams 2003: 195; Wilson 2005: 909). The ICTY itself has underscored the relationship between its trials, truth and reconciliation. According to its website, for example, 'The Tribunal's judgements have contributed to creating a historical record, combatting denial and preventing attempts at revisionism' (ICTY n.d.). During her time as the ICTY Prosecutor, Carla Del Ponte similarly maintained that, 'The Tribunal's primary contribution to peace and security, to regional stability and reconciliation is in establishing the facts and individual criminal responsibility' (2007). More recently, on the occasion of the Tribunal's twentieth anniversary, the current Prosecutor declared that, 'Over the past 20 years our cases have not only ensured individual accountability for crimes but they have also set down a record of events that will be an important barrier to revisionism in the years to come' (Brammertz 2013a).

Truth, therefore, is a second important element in measuring the ICTY's impact on reconciliation, and three indicators can be used in conjunction with it. The first is truth acceptance. It is not sufficient simply for a court such as the ICTY to establish the truth, because '...the truth will not necessarily be believed...' (Ignatieff 1998: 186). What is essential is that local people endorse and internalize that truth. Levels of truth acceptance (which of course are intertwined with people's knowledge of a court's findings) thus constitute an important indicator of truth. The second indicator is acknowledgement, and more specifically what Govier terms 'aversive acknowledgement'; that is to say 'the admission that one bears or shares responsibility for wrongs against others, has harmed them, and accepts one's responsibility in that context' (Govier 2009: 38). Aversive acknowledgement is, in turn, a critical prerequisite for the re-building of trust, which cannot progress in the absence of honesty and openness. During his research with 87 witnesses who had testified at the ICTY, for example, Stover found that, '...the witnesses said that the *inability* and *unwillingness* of their neighbors from other national groups to accept and acknowledge that they had stood by as other members of their group had committed war crimes in their name was one of the biggest hindrances to reconciliation' (2007: 123–124). The third and final indicator, which is inextricably linked to truth acceptance and aversive acknowledgement, is denial. Regardless of the establishment of official truths, are there individuals who continue to deny particular events and war crimes? When people engage in denial, and thus deny the suffering of others, there is no basis for reconciliation.

In order to assess the ICTY's impact on inter-ethnic reconciliation, justice and truth thus represent two critical measurement criteria. That both TJ scholars and the ICTY itself have emphasized the Tribunal's potential contribution to reconciliation specifically via the dispensing of justice and the establishment of truth means that justice and truth provide a framework for measuring the ICTY's *direct* impact on reconciliation. A finding that the Tribunal has not aided reconciliation either through the medium of justice or the medium of truth, however, does not necessarily mean that the institution has had no positive impact on reconciliation. It might have done so in other, more indirect ways, and hence it is essential to examine everyday inter-ethnic relations, the third prong of the measurement model. The Reconciliation Matrix constitutes a tool for evaluating these relations. Specifically, based on the four key variables of human security, deep contact, trust and mutual acceptance, to what extent is there evidence of inter-personal and community reconciliation in BiH, Croatia and Kosovo?

If, using the indicators that relate to each of the above variables, some level of reconciliation is found to exist (outcome monitoring), the next task is to establish whether and to what extent the ICTY has contributed to this positive outcome (outcome evaluation).[8] If, for example, people feel physically secure, can this be traced back to the ICTY's work and the prosecution of major war criminals? If there are few allegations of collective guilt, to what extent can this be attributed to the Tribunal's efforts to individualize guilt? Conversely, if there is little evidence of reconciliation, based on the aforementioned variables and indicators, it is necessary both to identify some of the factors that are impeding reconciliation and to examine whether the ICTY itself is part of the problem in this regard. If, for example, there are high levels of social distance and low levels of deep contact, could this be – at least in part – because the Tribunal's work is helping to keep wartime memories alive?

To summarize, this research uses a three-pronged model to measure the ICTY's impact on inter-ethnic reconciliation in BiH, Croatia and Kosovo. The three prongs consist of justice, truth and the nature of inter-ethnic relations on the ground. Justice and truth, and their respective indicators, provide a gauge for measuring the ICTY's direct impact on reconciliation. Conversely, the complementary focus on inter-ethnic relations, conceptualized in the form of a Reconciliation Matrix, allows for an exploration of whether reconciliation exists and, by extension, whether the ICTY has thus contributed to reconciliation in more indirect ways. The basic and expanded measurement models which this research uses are presented in Figure 2.1 and Table 2.2 respectively.

There is no obvious, correct or problem-free way of assessing the ICTY's effects on reconciliation, and this research does not claim to have developed the perfect model. Nevertheless, what it has created is a novel, comprehensive and workable model that can help to answer the critical question of whether and to what extent the ICTY had aided inter-ethnic reconciliation in the former Yugoslavia.

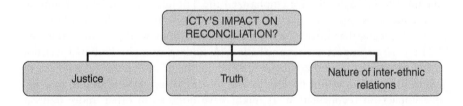

Figure 2.1 Basic measurement model.

8 The terms outcome monitoring and outcome evaluation are borrowed from Pham and Vinck (2007: 237).

Table 2.2 Expanded measurement model

PRONGS 1 AND 2 (DIRECT)		PRONG 3 (INDIRECT)	
1. Justice	*2. Truth*	*3. Ethnic relations*	
Indicators	*Indicators*	*Reconciliation Matrix*	*Indicators*
Perceptions of ICTY trials	Truth acceptance	Human security	Physical security Economic security Prevalence of inter-ethnic incidents
Knowledge of the ICTY's work	Aversive acknowledgement	Deep contact	Frequency Type (formal/informal; required/chosen) Social setting (public/private)
Understanding of justice	Levels of denial	Trust	Levels of social distance Perceptions of the 'other' Trust-inducing and trust-impeding behaviour
		Mutual acceptance	Respect Empathy Positive gestures and signals

Chapter 3

Part One of a Tripartite Case Study of Bosnia-Hercegovina

Justice

It is not possible to assess the ICTY's impact on reconciliation in BiH in a single chapter, due to the volume of material to be covered. Hence, with respect to the three measurement criteria outlined in the previous chapter, this chapter focuses exclusively on the first of these – justice. It argues that if a court is to potentially aid reconciliation through the medium of justice, it is not enough that justice is done in a legal sense (Menkel-Meadow 2002: 1774). Communities on the ground, and in particular victims, must themselves feel that some level of justice has been done (Stover 2007: 141). It is therefore imperative to examine how local communities view and evaluate the ICTY's work.

When we look at how the ICTY is perceived in BiH, two key points stand out. The first is that, '...delivering justice has proved easier in theory than in practice' (Stover 2007: 35). Part of the explanation is that because justice and ethnicity are deeply intertwined in BiH, it is almost impossible to achieve a cross-ethnic consensus that justice has been done. Quintessentially, 'The notion of what justice means is shaped by one's allegiance to an ethnic group and each ethnic group has a starkly different interpretation' (Simić 2011: 140). This, in turn, has important implications for the claim that the ICTY is contributing to reconciliation. Unless its work is able to satisfy all sides, the justice-reconciliation nexus becomes extremely tenuous (Barria and Roper 2005: 363). The second point is that widespread dissatisfaction and disappointment with the ICTY exist among Bosnian Muslims (Bosniaks),[1] Bosnian Serbs and Bosnian Croats alike. Indeed, while undertaking fieldwork in the country between 2008 and 2013, it was a somewhat rare occurrence to encounter individuals who spoke in positive terms about the Tribunal. As Hayden argues in his typically forthright manner, 'Gaining agreement on almost any political topic in the formerly Yugoslav republics is difficult, but the ICTY has nearly achieved it: majorities of almost all of the major national groups dislike the Tribunal' (2011: 317). Reflecting on the *Assessing the Legacy of the ICTY* conference that took place in The Hague in February 2010, the

---

1 The terms 'Bosnian Muslims' and 'Bosniaks' will be used interchangeably throughout.

Tribunal's then President, Judge Patrick Robinson, himself acknowledged that, 'From the contributions made by victim groups, it is clear to me that there is a perception amongst victim communities that the Tribunal has failed to deliver all that was expected' (2011: 268). While negative popular perceptions are not entirely the fault of the Tribunal (Ivanišević 2011a: 131; Klarin 2011: 112), an unpopular institution will necessarily struggle to deliver justice that is perceived as such by local communities.

Bosniak viewpoints, multiple grievances and demands for greater justice

In general, Bosnian Muslims are extremely glad that the ICTY exists. They readily concede that without it, very few war criminals would have ever stood trial. Notwithstanding widespread support for the Tribunal as a concept, however, there is deep-felt dissatisfaction with the quantity and quality of the 'justice' it delivers. Specifically, Bosniak interviewees consistently expressed three main grievances with the ICTY: it has not prosecuted enough people, its sentences are too lenient and it unjustly rewards defendants who plead guilty to the charges against them.

Not enough war criminals have been prosecuted

While acknowledging that the ICTY could have indicted more than 161 individuals, a former senior trial attorney has underlined that, 'The Tribunal was never designed to prosecute every criminal who committed a crime during the wars in the former Yugoslavia. Its mandate has been to prosecute the persons who are most responsible for these crimes and defer to the domestic courts to prosecute people for the remaining crimes' (Harmon 2005: 67). Among Bosniak interviewees, however, who in many cases had little confidence in local courts and were often unfamiliar with the specificities of the Tribunal's mandate, a major grievance with the ICTY was precisely that it has not, in their eyes, indicted enough suspected war criminals. To cite Edin Ramulić from the Prijedor-based victims' group *Izvor*, 'When the ICTY determined that it would ultimately handle fewer than 200 cases in total, it was a surprise to most groups and created disappointment in the victim and survivor communities' (2011: 103).

There is no doubt that some victims initially had extremely high expectations of the ICTY (a fact that several interviewees themselves conceded), and hence a certain level of disappointment was always inevitable. Moreover, some interviewees continued to insist that there can be no justice until *all* war criminals are prosecuted. Yet, even among those who recognized that such maximalist demands are unrealistic, there was a widespread sense that the ICTY could and should have indicted and prosecuted more people. Throughout the country, interviewees frequently maintained that there are war criminals living freely in their communities, and even working in local institutions. Indeed, the deputy commander of the local police in Srebrenica acknowledged that there are suspected war criminals still working in the force, although he stressed that these individuals would be dealt with.[2] Hence, contrary to the former ICC Prosecutor's assertion that the success of courts cannot be measured by the number of trials (Moreno-Ocampo 2003), it is clear that the number of trials *is* an important evaluative yardstick as far as local communities and victims are concerned.

It was often the case that interviewees did not know exactly how many people the ICTY has indicted, despite vigorously asserting that the number was insufficient. Those who were more informed, however – in particular those who led or worked for victims' associations – expressed additional concerns. Some objected not only to the relatively small number of ICTY indictments, but also to the fact that not all of the 161 persons indicted have actually been prosecuted. The ICTY President has declared that, 'Among other achievements, the Tribunal has: accounted for all 161 individuals it indicted, including high-level military and political leaders...' (Meron 2013b). While this is true, 20 indictments have been withdrawn, due to practical reasons pertaining to time and resources. As 14 of these 20 indictments related to crimes committed in Prijedor municipality, their withdrawal[3] was a matter of concern for interviewees in this area. One interviewee, who lost several members of his family during the war in BiH, was particularly insistent that the Tribunal's statistics are not a true reflection of reality as they suggest that the ICTY has done more than it has.[4]

If a common belief exists that the ICTY has not indicted or prosecuted enough people, some interviewees also expressed the view that it is not necessarily dealing with the right people. Although the Tribunal was officially established to deal with the so-called 'big fish' – those in positions of power and authority who, *inter alia*, planned, organized and ordered the commission of war crimes – when it first began its work it focused on lower-ranking perpetrators. The first person to be indicted, for example, on 4 November 1994, was not Milošević or Karadžić but Dragan Nikolić, the former commander of the Sušica detention camp in the municipality of Vlasenica in eastern BiH. The Tribunal's first Prosecutor, Justice Richard Goldstone, has acknowledged that Nikolić 'was hardly an appropriate defendant for the first indictment issued by the first ever international war crimes tribunal' (2000: 106). The fact is that at a time when the Tribunal did not even have a budget, its early indictments reflected important practical considerations.

2 Author interview, Srebrenica, 25 June 2008.
3 On 8 May 1998, the ICTY's then Prosecutor, Louise Arbour, issued a statement explaining her decision to withdraw all charges against 14 accused in connection with the Omarska and Keraterm camps. Welcoming the fact that a growing number of indictees had been arrested or had voluntarily surrendered to the Tribunal, she explained that this had necessitated a review of existing indictments. She also emphasized that her decision to withdraw the charges was 'not based on any lack of evidence in respect of these accused' (Arbour 1998).
4 Author interview, Prijedor, 1 April 2013.

As Goldstone recalls, 'The initial indictments were issued under tremendous pressure to obtain crucial funding from the United Nations' (2002: 281). The pursuit of smaller fry, however, allowed the Tribunal to build up an evidence base against high-level perpetrators, who are now the primary focus of its work. To cite a member of the ICTY's Trial Division, 'In a way, the early cases were test-beds. They were serious cases in their own right that merited prosecution, but they were also stepping stones in the development towards later cases'.[5]

There is, of course, an obvious rationale for a temporary court with finite resources to concentrate its efforts on those in positions of power. Nevertheless, victims themselves may not appreciate this (Arriaza and Roht-Arriaza 2008: 159). As Mirsad Tokača from the Research and Documentation Centre (RDC) in Sarajevo underscores, 'Every victim believes that her case is the most serious. For her there are no less important perpetrators' (2005: 7).[6] The distinction between different categories of perpetrators can thus appear artificial. A camp survivor who lost ten members of his family, for example, explained that those who physically killed his loved-ones are more culpable, in his eyes, than men such as Karadžić, and hence he needs to see these direct perpetrators face justice.[7] Accordingly, interviewees often complained that the Tribunal's focus on the top echelon of perpetrators is too restrictive and should be broadened (they thus neglected the role of local courts, whose *raison d'être* is the prosecution of lower-ranking perpetrators). A widow in Bratunac, for instance, opined that while the ICTY must prosecute the so-called big fish, more of the smaller fish should have also been prosecuted, a view which certain commentators share (see, for example, Askin 2003: 906). Highlighting the examples of Miroslav Deronjić and the afore-mentioned Dragan Nikolić, both of whom admitted their guilt,[8] she claimed that lower-level perpetrators are more likely than political and military elites to tell the truth as they have less to lose in terms of their image, reputation and status.[9] Although interviewees complained that the ICTY has not dealt with enough of the actual perpetrators and has focused too much on the masterminds behind the crimes committed, it is interesting to note that in the early years, the Tribunal was conversely criticized for failing to pursue the top leadership. It would thus seem

5   Author interview, The Hague, 11 February 2008.
6   Author's translation from Bosnian.
7   Author interview, Prijedor, 1 April 2013 (see also Stover 2007: 111).
8   Deronjić was the president of the Bratunac Crisis Staff. Indicted for crimes against humanity in Glogova, a village near Bratunac, he initially pleaded not guilty, but a year later, in 2003, he pleaded guilty. On 30 March 2004, he was sentenced to ten years' imprisonment (Prosecutor v. Deronjić 2004). He died on 19 May 2007 while serving his sentence. Dragan Nikolić, the commander of the Sušica camp, similarly pleaded not guilty to all charges, but subsequently changed his plea. On 18 December 2003, he was sentenced to 23 years' imprisonment for crimes against humanity, reduced to 20 years on appeal (Prosecutor v. Nikolić 2003a, 2005).
9   Author interview, Bratunac, 28 March 2013.

that regardless of whom it indicts and prosecutes, the ICTY is always in a no-win situation.

Finally, it should be noted that some interviewees regarded as unjust the fact that the ICTY is only prosecuting individuals from the former Yugoslavia. Reflecting a prevalent viewpoint that Western powers inexcusably failed the Bosnian Muslims, an ex-combatant in Sarajevo passionately argued that the Tribunal should have also prosecuted, *inter alia*, members of the EU and US officials for failing to stop the war;[10] while interviewees in, or connected with, Srebrenica widely expounded the belief that the UN and the Dutch government should face prosecution for allowing genocide to occur.[11] While, on one hand, such views demonstrate that people are not necessarily well-informed about the Tribunal and its mandate, on the other hand they powerfully highlight that, '... the importance of the ICTY is diminished by the widespread belief that this tribunal does not judge those who are truly and primarily responsible for the war, like the French, the American or the Dutch governments' (Delpla 2007: 226). This, together with the various grievances that interviewees expressed pertaining to the number and content of ICTY indictments, has given rise to a perceived 'justice gap' (Stromseth 2009: 90), rather than a sense of justice done.

The ICTY does not sufficiently punish war criminals

Without exception, interviewees expressed deep dissatisfaction with the Tribunal's sentencing practices. As Orentlicher remarks, 'ICTY sentences have on the whole been cause for profound disappointment and at times anger among victims and others in Bosnia' (2010: 14). At the core of such disappointment is the common belief that ICTY sentences are too lenient and do not constitute sufficient punishment. Certainly, in view of the gravity of the crimes which the Tribunal is prosecuting, some of its sentences have unquestionably been very low. Defendants have been sentenced, for example, to prison terms of as little as two years (Amir Kubura), three years (Rasim Delić, Dragan Kolundžija,), three-and-a-half years (Enver Hadžihasanović) and five years (Damir Došen, Dražen Erdemović, Milan Gvero, Dragoljub Prcać, Milan Simić). Of course, these light sentences – which

---

10 Author interview, Sarajevo, 5 July 2008.
11 The Mothers of Srebrenica brought a legal case against the Dutch government and the UN. The Dutch Supreme Court ultimately ruled that, '...the UN cannot be summoned before any national court' (SENSE 2012a). The Mothers' claim against the Dutch government, in contrast, has been more successful. In September 2013, the Supreme Court found that the Netherlands was responsible for the deaths of three particular victims of the Srebrenica genocide, including the father and brother of the former UN translator Hasan Nuhanović, the author of a powerful and compelling book about the genocide (Nuhanović 2007). The Supreme Court thus upheld an earlier decision of the Dutch Appeals Court; in 2011, the latter ruled that the Dutch peacekeeping force in Srebrenica fundamentally erred in handing over Rizo Mustafić, Ibro Nuhanović and Muhamed Nuhanović to the VRS (BBC 2013d).

have led to speculation that the ICTY may have implicitly prioritized 'defendant-relative proportionality over offence-gravity proportionality...' (Ohlin 2011: 328) – do not represent the entire picture. The length of ICTY sentences does in fact vary enormously, and its highest sentences include 40 years (Goran Jelišić, Milomir Stakić), 35 years (Radislav Krstić, Milan Martić), 30 years (Radoslav Brđanin) and 29 years (Dragomir Milošević). In addition, five defendants have been sentenced to life imprisonment (Ljubiša Beara, Stanislav Galić, Milan Lukić, Vujadin Popović and Zdravko Tolimir) (for an overview of all sentences, see ICTY 2013a).

When interviewees complained that ICTY sentences are low, they often spoke in general terms instead of giving concrete examples. Moreover, when they did cite particular cases, they always focused on the lowest sentences. During field-work in 2013, for example, it was striking how nobody referred to the recent genocide verdicts and life sentences against Vujadin Popović and Ljubiša Beara (Prosecutor v. Popović et al. 2010) and Zdravko Tolimir (Prosecutor v. Tolimir 2012). In addition, almost without exception, interviewees concentrated entirely on cases relating to their own particular area. Those in Prijedor, for example, repeatedly pointed out that almost every war criminal convicted of crimes in the municipality is now free. Insisting, therefore, that crime pays, a camp survivor asserted that victims can expect little from the Tribunal.[12] In nearby Kozarac, an interviewee whose son was killed at Korićanske Stijene on Vlašić Mountain, in central BiH, spoke solely about the sentence imposed on Darko Mrđa, a member of a special Bosnian Serb police unit (the 'intervention squad') in Prijedor during the war. The only person prosecuted at the ICTY in connection with the massacre of more than 200 unarmed men at Korićanske Stijene in August 1992, Mrđa – who ultimately pleaded guilty to crimes against humanity and violations of the laws or customs of war – was sentenced to 17 years' imprisonment on 31 March 2004 (Prosecutor v. Mrđa 2004). Repeatedly asking how she can be satisfied with this sentence, the interviewee – who has not been able to bury her son as his remains have never been found – was adamant that 17 years is not an adequate punishment for someone who played a part in ending so many lives.[13]

In a similar vein, Bosniak interviewees in the central Bosnian village of Ahmići had formed their views of ICTY sentences almost exclusively on the basis of a very specific set of sentences pertaining to crimes committed in the Lašva Valley – in particular the massacre in Ahmići on 16 April 1993. Interviewees referred with particular frequency to the case of Tihomir Blaškić. On 3 March 2000, the ICTY sentenced Blaškić, the former commander of the HVO in central BiH, to 45 years' imprisonment for crimes against humanity, grave breaches of the Geneva Conventions and violations of the laws or customs of war (Prosecutor v. Blaškić

12 Author interview, Prijedor, 2 April 2013.
13 Author interview, Kozarac, 29 July 2008.

2000). On 29 July 2004, however, the Appeals Chamber found that the Trial Chamber had committed a number of serious legal errors. Accordingly, it reversed the majority of the Trial Chamber's convictions and sentenced Blaškić *de novo* to nine years' imprisonment (Prosecutor v. Blaškić 2004).[14] Just four days later, he was granted early release. Commenting on the immediate aftermath of the verdict, Stover observes that, 'Within hours of the ruling, Bosnian Radio broadcast angry reactions from relatives of people murdered in Ahmići. One man who lost his parents said the decision made no sense and was a political game and a mockery of justice' (2007: 66). Today, the appeal verdict continues to generate strong emotions. Interviewees in Ahmići struggled to make sense of such a dramatic reduction in Blaškić's sentence[15] and felt deeply let down by the Tribunal.

Regardless of whether any prison sentence can truly satisfy those who have lost loved-ones in horrific circumstances (Hodžić 2011:118), sentences must at least meet the threshold of fairness – and hence they need to be 'clear, predictable, and proportionate, or, in other words, consistent' (Holá, Smeulers and Bijleveld 2009: 80). In BiH, the fundamental problem is that ICTY sentences are not seen as fair because they make little sense to affected communities (King and Meernik 2011: 21), and this problematizes the Tribunal's claim that it is delivering justice to victims. Justice means little to victims in abstract terms. They are seeking justice that is tangible and concrete, and punishment epitomizes these properties. Consequently, victims attach enormous importance to the length of sentences. Based on his research in Prijedor, for example, Hodžić argues that, 'In terms of impact on the perceptions of justice delivered, the length of sentence takes precedence over all the other aspects of the trial, including the facts established ("the truth"), the opportunity to testify, the material compensation and other forms of redress' (2010: 133).

---

14 A key issue in Blaškić's appeal was the standard of *mens rea* required for ordering acts under Article 7(1) of the Tribunal's Statute. According to the Trial Chamber, it was sufficient that the person ordering an act knew that there was a risk of crimes being committed and accepted such a risk (Prosecutor v. Blaškić 2000: §474). The Appeals Chamber, in contrast, fundamentally disagreed, and found that simple knowledge of risk is insufficient (Prosecutor v. Blaškić 2004: §41). Instead, it adjudged that in order to be liable under Article 7(1),'...a person who orders an act or omission' must be aware of 'the substantial likelihood that a crime will be committed in the execution of that order' (Prosecutor v. Blaškić 2004: §42). Another important issue in Blaškić's appeal was whether he had ordered an offensive attack on Ahmići and neighbouring villages. The Trial Chamber found that Defence Exhibit D269 – an order that Blaškić had issued on 16 April 1993 at 1.30am – was very clearly an order to attack (Prosecutor v. Blaškić 2000: §437). Based on additional evidence admitted during the appeals process, however, the Appeals Chamber took a different view and concluded that there was a military justification for order D269 (Prosecutor v. Blaškić 2004: §333).

15 Commenting on the Blaškić appeal judgement, the Tribunal's former Prosecutor, Carla Del Ponte, recalls that, 'In our offices, shock and gloom fell over the Blaškić trial team. This Appeals Chamber decision was scandalous. The appeals process had effectively turned into a second trial, but one in which the judges assessed the credibility and reliability of the evidence without ever having seen or heard the witnesses who appeared at trial' (2008: 260).

The fact, therefore, that defendants who are found guilty will typically only serve two-thirds of their sentence has further compounded popular dissatisfaction and resentment on the issue of ICTY sentences. In 2001, for example, Mlađo Radić, a shift leader at the Omarksa camp, was sentenced to 20 years' imprisonment (Prosecutor v. Kvočka et al. 2001), but was granted early release with effect from 31 December 2012. In a decision issued on 13 February 2012, the ICTY President reiterated that, 'the Tribunal's practice of considering applicants eligible for early release once they reach two-thirds of their sentence is not an entitlement to early release at that time...' (Meron 2013a: §30). Despite the fact that Radić had at that stage completed two-thirds of his sentence, the President reached the conclusion that he should not be granted early release until the end of the year. This decision, however, provoked anger in Prijedor. Describing Radić as a monster who raped most of the women in the Omarska camp, a member of a local victims' group opined that by sentencing those it convicts to lenient sentences and subsequently granting them early release, the ICTY thus allows war criminals to carry on with their lives while their victims continue to suffer.[16]

The abhorrent use of plea agreements

What has further fuelled a widespread sense of injustice among Bosnian Muslims is the controversial use of plea agreements; to date, 20 defendants have pleaded guilty at various stages of the proceedings. From the Tribunal's point of view, plea agreements – defined as 'bargaining through which a defendant agrees to plead guilty in exchange for sentencing or charging reductions' (Combs 2002: 10) – are very useful. By entering a guilty plea, a defendant waives certain procedural rights, including the right to plead not guilty, the right to require the Prosecution to prove the charges made against him at a fair and public trial and the right to put forward a defence to those charges at trial. Admissions of guilt, in other words, save the Tribunal valuable time and resources, and this is extremely important in the context of its completion strategy (UN 2003).

Guilty pleas can also result in the disclosure of vital information that might have otherwise remained hidden. Harmon, a former senior trial attorney, uses the example of Dražen Erdemović, a soldier in the 10th Sabotage Detachment of the VRS who pleaded guilty to participating in the killing of hundreds of men from Srebrenica in Zvornik municipality in eastern BiH (2005: 60–61). Erdemović's guilty plea brought to light valuable information – which local Serbs were unwilling to reveal – about his crimes. What is unusual about Erdemović's first guilty plea in May 1996 is that it was not the result of a plea agreement. Initially pleading guilty to murder as a crime against humanity, he confessed to his involvement in the Pilica massacre 'at a time when no authority was seeking to prosecute him

16 Author interview, Prijedor, 1 April 2013.

in connection therewith, knowing that he would most probably face prosecution as a result' (Prosecutor v. Erdemović 1998: §21). In other words, Erdemović's first guilty plea was not induced through any bargaining process.[17] Typically, however, defendants will not plead guilty unless they receive something in return, and it is precisely this granting of concessions that renders plea agreements so unpopular among victims.

Only interviewees in Bratunac acknowledged that plea agreements can be useful, citing the case of Miroslav Deronjić, the wartime president of the Bratunac Crisis Staff. On 8 May 1992, Deronjić ordered an attack on the nearby village of Glogova which resulted in the deaths of 65 unarmed Bosniaks. After pleading guilty to crimes against humanity, Deronjić was sentenced to ten years' imprisonment in March 2004 (Prosecutor v. Deronjić 2004). While interviewees in Bratunac maintained that he should have been more severely punished, they noted with approval that Deronjić had revealed important information and provided significant assistance to the OTP (see Prosecutor v. Deronjić 2004: §245). They thus believed that he was genuinely repentant. Deronjić also delivered a powerful statement to the Tribunal, in which he declared:

> Your Honours, I bow to the spirit of innocent victims in Glogova. Everything that I did in this Tribunal, for whatever it's worth, I dedicate to them in the hope that it will at least somewhat alleviate the pain of their dear ones. I am familiar with that pain because I also carry that pain. I regret the expulsion that I committed, and I express my remorse about all the victims of war, no matter in which graveyards they lie. I apologize to all of those whom – to whom I caused sorrow and whom I let down.
> (Prosecutor v. Deronjić 2004: §263)

More commonly, however, interviewees were extremely sceptical regarding expressions of remorse,[18] insisting that defendants only apologize in order to

---

17 Erdemović was initially sentenced to ten years' imprisonment (Prosecutor v. Erdemović 1996). He subsequently appealed, asking to be excused from serving his sentence on the grounds that he committed crimes under duress. While the Appeals Chamber rejected this claim, it found that Erdemović's guilty plea was not informed (Prosecutor v. Erdemović 1997: §20), and accordingly remitted the case to a new Trial Chamber. In his second trial, Erdemović pleaded guilty to murder as a violation of the laws or customs of war. As part of a plea agreement, the Prosecutor withdrew the alternative count of murder as a crime against humanity. In its second sentencing judgement, the Trial Chamber sentenced Erdemović to five years' imprisonment (Prosecutor v. Erdemović 1998).

18 Apologies are more likely to be taken seriously when they are not part of a plea agreement. In January 2013, for example, the former VJ general Dragoljub Ojdanić, sentenced by the ICTY in 2009 to 15 years' imprisonment for crimes committed in Kosovo (Prosecutor v. Šainović et al. 2009), apologized to his victims in a written letter sent to the Tribunal. While Kosovo Albanian reactions to the apology were inevitably mixed, some victims appreciated the gesture. According to the head of one victims' association, 'For me and my colleagues,

secure a reduced sentence (see also Hodžić 2010: 129).[19] Accordingly, they demanded more of defendants. Specifically, while the ICTY claims that, 'admissions of guilt from a number of accused have...greatly contributed to the establishment of facts' (ICTY n.d.), several interviewees underlined that those who plead guilty should be required to disclose *more* of the facts, particularly regarding the whereabouts of mass graves and missing persons (discussed more in Chapter 5). A camp survivor in Prijedor, for example, demanded to know how the remaining mass graves in BiH remain undiscovered, despite the fact that a number of defendants have pleaded guilty. The guilty need to tell the truth and to show humility, not crocodile tears, he underscored.[20] Those interviewees who heavily focused on the issue of guilty pleas further asserted that if the Tribunal is going to enter into plea agreements with defendants, it should first consult with victims' groups, an argument which Henham and Drumbl have similarly advanced (2005: 58–59). Practicalities aside, including victims in the process would be a way of giving them back their voice – which guilty pleas typically take away by depriving victims of having their day in court. An interviewee in Prijedor, for example, had been called to testify against the aforementioned Darko Mrđa, but ultimately he never had this opportunity as the accused pleaded guilty.[21]

Recent acquittal verdicts

During the author's final two research trips to BiH in 2013, Bosniak interviewees had an additional grievance with the ICTY, pertaining to a string of recent acquittal verdicts. On 16 November 2012, for example, the Appeals Chamber acquitted the Croatian generals Ante Gotovina and Mladen Markač (Prosecutor v. Gotovina and Markač 2012a), both of whom were convicted the previous year of crimes against humanity and violations of the laws or customs of war and sentenced to prison terms of 24 years and 18 years respectively (Prosecutor v. Gotovina, Čermak and Markač 2011a). This acquittal verdict, which will be discussed in more detail in Chapter 6, elicited strong views from some Bosniak interviewees, and particularly from interviewees in Prijedor, perhaps due to the latter's proximity to the Croatian border. One interviewee, for example, maintained

Ojdanić's confession is a sign of respect and a relief' (cited in Kabashaj and Jovanović 2013). On 10 July 2013, Ojdanić was granted early release.

19 Combs shares this view (2002: 149). The case of Biljana Plavšić, a former President of RS, is particularly illustrative. In 2002, Plavšić pleaded guilty to persecutions on religious, racial and political grounds, in return for which the genocide charge against her was dropped. A year later, on 27 February 2003, she was sentenced to 11 years' imprisonment (Prosecutor v. Plavšić 2003). While she appeared to express genuine remorse for her conduct during the war, in an interview with a Swedish newspaper in January 2009, she revealed that she pleaded guilty simply in an effort to have all remaining charges against her dropped (Drakulić 2009). Just eight months later, Plavšić was granted early release and greeted with a hero's welcome in RS.

20 Author interview, Prijedor, 1 April 2013.

21 Author interview, Prijedor, 2 April 2013.

that the verdict was a huge injustice and expressed his support and sympathy for the Serb victims of Operation Storm.[22] Another interviewee opined that while Serbs have always argued that the ICTY is a political court, they now have good reason to make such claims.[23]

It was, however, the Appeals Chamber's acquittal of Momčilo Perišić, the former Chief of the VJ General Staff, which had piqued a particularly acute sense of injustice among interviewees. Charged with aiding and abetting crimes committed in Sarajevo and Srebrenica by providing military logistical and personnel assistance to the VRS, Perišić was found guilty in 2011 of crimes against humanity and violations of the laws or customs of war and sentenced to 27 years' imprisonment (Prosecutor v. Perišić 2011). His appeal centred on whether specific direction is a requisite element of the *actus reus* of aiding and abetting. Quintessentially, the issue was whether acts that constitute aiding and abetting must be *specifically directed* at assisting the crimes of the principal perpetrators. Relying on the judgement of the Appeals Chamber in the case of Mrkšić and Šljivančanin, discussed in Chapter 6, the Trial Chamber found that specific direction was not a requirement (Prosecutor v. Perišić 2011: §126).

The Appeals Chamber, in contrast, disagreed. While Judge Liu Daqun dissented (Prosecutor v. Perišić 2013b: §3), the Majority was 'not persuaded that the Mrkšić and Šljivančanin Appeal Judgement reflected an intention to depart from the settled precedent established by the *Tadić* Appeal Judgement' (Prosecutor v. Perišić 2013a: §32).[24] Finding, moreover, that, '...Perišić's assistance to the VRS was remote from the relevant crimes of the principal perpetrators' (Prosecutor v. Perišić 2013a: §42), in part because he was not physically present when the crimes in question were planned or committed, the Appeals Chamber deemed that, 'explicit consideration of specific direction' was therefore necessary (Prosecutor v. Perišić 2013a: §39).[25] Recalling that 'the VRS undertook, *inter alia*, lawful combat activities and was not a purely criminal organisation' (Prosecutor v. Perišić 2013a: §69), the Appeals Chamber ultimately concluded that Perišić's assistance to the VRS was not specifically directed at facilitating the commission of VRS crimes in Sarajevo and Srebrenica.[26] Rather, '...a reasonable interpretation of the record is that VJ aid facilitated by Perišić was

---

22 Author interview, Prijedor, 31 March 2013.
23 Author interview, Prijedor, 2 April 2013.
24 According to the Appeals Chamber in the Duško Tadić case, 'The aider and abettor carries out acts specifically directed to assist, encourage or lend moral support to the perpetration of a certain specific crime (murder, extermination, rape, torture, wanton destruction of civilian property, etc.), and this support has a substantial effect upon the perpetration of the crime' (Prosecutor v. Tadić 1999: §229).
25 Judge Liu again dissented.
26 In his partially dissenting opinion, however, Judge Liu opined that, '...even assuming specific direction were a required element of aiding and abetting liability, I am not convinced that an acquittal would be justified given the magnitude, critical importance, and continued nature of the assistance Perišić provided to the VRS' (Prosecutor v. Perišić 2013b: §9).

directed towards the VRS's general war effort rather than VRS crimes' (Prosecutor v. Perišić 2013a: §71).

Among Bosniak interviewees, the acquittal of Perišić was deeply shocking and controversial for two main reasons. Firstly, because interviewees repeatedly maintained that Serbia was the mastermind behind everything that happened in BiH (leading many to insist that the Serbian state should itself be prosecuted), they wanted high-ranking political and military figures – those who constituted Serbia's 'criminal structures' – to face justice (while also calling for more of the 'smaller fish' to be prosecuted). As Perišić was the top figure within the VJ, his conviction in 2011 was immensely significant to Bosniaks. Interviewees were therefore unwilling to accept his acquittal.

Secondly, and more broadly, interviewees demanded to know what sort of justice they can expect from the ICTY when the latter convicts defendants like Perišić and subsequently finds them not guilty. There is no doubt that the recent acquittal verdicts have (further) undermined the Tribunal's credibility among Bosniaks and left many people confused and struggling to make sense of these decisions. Robertson QC, pointing out that the Nuremberg Tribunal did not have an appeals procedure, maintains that, 'The Hague Tribunal reflects another development in human rights law by providing a right of appeal against errors of law and fact...' (2012: 467). Due to the challenges of translating highly complex legal judgements into simple layman's terms, however, combined with the inadequacy of the Tribunal's outreach work (discussed below) and the often biased local media coverage of the ICTY's work (Nettelfield 2010: 159), high-profile acquittal verdicts necessarily generate significant controversy – and thus negatively impact on how the Tribunal is popularly perceived.

More recently, a Trial Chamber of the ICTY acquitted Jovica Stanišić, the former head of the State Security Service of the Ministry of Internal Affairs (MUP) of Serbia, and Franko Simatović, Stanišić's right-hand man. According to the indictment against them, both men – who were charged with crimes against humanity and violations of the laws or customs of war – were participants in a JCE aimed at forcibly and permanently removing the majority of non-Serbs from large areas of BiH and Croatia. Other members of this JCE allegedly included Slobodan Milošević, Radovan Karadžić, Biljana Plavšić and Arkan. Five years after the trial commenced, the Trial Chamber delivered its long-awaited verdict. It found that the defendants had established a special unit of the State Security Service, known as the Special Purpose Unit or 'Red Berets', and that, '...from at least September 1991, the Accused were in command of the Unit and controlled its deployment and training activities...' (Prosecutor v. Stanišić and Simatović 2013b: §1489). The Trial Chamber also found that the Unit committed the crime of deportation (a crime against humanity) in numerous locations in BiH and Croatia, as well as the crimes of murder, deportation and forcible transfer in the municipality of Bosanski Šamac (Prosecutor v. Stanišić and Simatović 2013a: section 3.4) and the crimes of deportation and forcible transfer in Doboj municipality in 1992 (Prosecutor v. Stanišić and Simatović 2013a: section 3.5).

Despite this, two of the three judges (Judge Picard dissenting) decided that they could not conclude from the actions of the defendants that the latter intended to further the common purpose of the JCE. While finding that both Stanišić and Simatović had provided assistance to the Bosanski Šamac and Doboj operations, the Majority adjudged that it was reasonable to conclude that this assistance was aimed at establishing and maintaining Serb control over the aforementioned areas, rather than specifically directed towards the commission of murder, deportation, forcible transfer or persecution (Prosecutor v. Stanišić and Simatović 2013b: §2360).[27] Accordingly, the Trial Chamber acquitted the defendants of aiding and abetting the commission of these crimes. The fact, moreover, that the defendants were shown to have links to other groups which committed crimes, including the Serbian Volunteer Guard and the Scorpions, was found to be insufficient for the purpose of establishing that they played a specific role in assisting these groups to perpetrate crimes (Prosecutor v. Stanišić and Simatović 2013b: §2361).

Again, this is a verdict that has created disbelief and anger. Fadila Memišević, the president of the Society of Endangered Peoples in BiH, has argued that, 'According to this ruling, Serbia never participated in the war. This is sham justice. In 20 or 30 years' time, we'll have another war here because we failed to deal with our past, we just brushed it under the carpet' (cited in Karabegović and Zorić 2013); and a victim who travelled to The Hague to hear the verdict explained that, 'We expected a guilty verdict, knowing the evidence. We know Stanišić and Simatović are directly involved in crimes. The only thing left is to hope for changes in the appeals process' (cited in Džidić 2013d). It is not only Bosniaks who have criticized the Trial Chamber's judgement, however. Sonja Biserko and Nataša Kandić, leading human rights activists in Serbia, have expressed their surprise and shock at the verdict (Karabegović and Zorić 2013); and according to Savo Štrbac from the Veritas Documentation Centre in Belgrade, 'It is really difficult to assess what is going on with the Hague Tribunal...But since last November [2012], when the Croatian generals Gotovina and Markač were acquitted, the decisions issued either by the trial or appellate panel are surprising and unexpected and causing a lot of conflicting views and opinions' (cited in Mitić 2013).

27 Judge Michèle Picard, who issued a strong dissenting opinion, disagreed. Maintaining that it was necessary to look at the entire picture, and criticizing her fellow judges for reviewing the evidence 'in an isolated fashion' (Prosecutor v. Stanišić and Simatović 2013c: §2367), she opined that, '...the sole reasonable interpretation of the vast amount of evidence that the Tribunal has received is that the Accused shared with other members of the JCE the intent to establish their control over the regions pertinent to the Indictment by deporting the non-Serb population by criminal means' (Prosecutor v. Stanišić and Simatović 2013c: §2365). While acknowledging that there was no direct evidence of the defendants' intention to achieve the common purpose of the JCE, Judge Picard opined that, 'one can infer it from the circumstantial evidence available' (Prosecutor v. Stanišić and Simatović 2013c: §2370).

Even Serge Brammertz, the ICTY Prosecutor, has disclosed that he was not expecting Stanišić and Simatović to be acquitted (Hina 2013). He has further asserted that following this verdict and the acquittal of Perišić, the ICTY has introduced a new element – the 'specific direction' requirement – that will make it more difficult to convict war commanders (Hina 2013). Judge Picard expressed similar concerns in her dissenting opinion in Stanišić and Simatović. In a powerful concluding statement, she remarked that if the Trial Chamber was unable to find that the defendants had aided and abetted war crimes, '...I would say we have come to a dark place in international law indeed. It is a place, in the words spoken by the Honourable Judge Robert H. Jackson in 1949, where "law has terrors only for little men and takes note only of little wrongs"' (Prosecutor v. Stanišić and Simatović 2013c: §2406; but see Prosecutor v. Perišić 2013a: §72).

To reiterate, these highly contentious acquittal verdicts have undoubtedly tarnished (or further tarnished) the image of the ICTY (Ivanišević 2013). While Serbs have long insisted that the Tribunal's work is politically-motivated, the recent acquittals have left others similarly questioning whether political considerations influence developments in The Hague; and as Arzt underscores, '...if international criminal courts are to achieve their aims...perception of their legitimacy by the local population is a crucial factor' (2006: 227). In view of the above developments, the shocking allegations made by one of the Tribunal's *ad litem* judges could not have come at a worse time. In a leaked letter that was published by a Danish news website in June 2013, Judge Frederik Harhoff claimed that US judge Theodor Meron, the ICTY President and the presiding judge of the Appeals Chamber, exerted 'tenacious' pressure on his fellow judges to acquit Gotovina, Markač and Perišić, as well as Stanišić and Simatović (Harhoff 2013). The letter, which Judge Harhoff had circulated to 56 people, further suggested that Meron himself may have been under strong pressure to secure these acquittal verdicts from US or Israeli officials, whose own military leaders can now, as a result of the acquittal verdicts, 'breathe a sigh of relief' (Harhoff 2013).[28] Regardless of whether and to what extent such allegations are true, or partly true,

---

28 As a result of his letter, Judge Harhoff was subsequently disqualified from the trial of Vojislav Šešelj, the leader of the Serbian Radical Party (SRS). According to Šešelj's defence team, the letter raised serious questions regarding Judge Harhoff's impartiality, particularly in view of the latter's claim that, 'Right up until autumn 2012, it has been more or less set practice at the court [ICTY] that military commanders were held responsible for war crimes that their subordinates committed during the war in the former Yugoslavia from 1992–95...' (Harhoff 2013). The Trial Chamber agreed (Judge Liu dissenting) with Šešelj's defence counsel, and found that: 'By referring to a "set practice" of convicting accused persons without reference to an evaluation of the evidence in each individual case...there are grounds for concluding that a reasonable observer, properly informed, would reasonably apprehend bias on the part of Judge Harhoff in favour of conviction' (Prosecutor v. Šešelj 2013: §13). In view of this 'unacceptable appearance of bias' (Prosecutor v. Šešelj 2013: §14), Šešelj's application to have Judge Harhoff disqualified from his trial was upheld.

they are extremely damaging and will strengthen the hand of the Tribunal's detractors both in BiH and elsewhere in the former Yugoslavia. Indeed, in response to both the acquittal verdicts and the allegations made by Judge Harhoff, 15 victims' associations in BiH wrote a letter to Judge Meron demanding his resignation (SENSE 2013b).

Developments regarding Karadžić and Mladić

While interviewees thus had additional grievances in 2013 which they did not have in 2008 and 2009, it was nevertheless anticipated that some of them might have a more positive view of the ICTY now that Karadžić and Mladić are on trial. This expectation was based on the fact that during the author's earlier fieldwork, interviewees – particularly those in Srebrenica – had frequently criticized the ICTY for failing to arraign Karadžić and Mladić (crucially overlooking the reality that the Tribunal has no powers of arrest) and repeatedly argued there would never be justice for victims as long as these two men remained free.[29] During her own research in BiH, Orentlicher similarly found that, '…on one point, our Bosniak interlocutors almost universally expressed crystalline clarity: Justice will not be served if the ICTY fails to gain custody over Ratko Mladić, who is widely seen to be even more culpable than Karadžić' (2010: 17). When the author returned to BiH in 2013, however, reactions to the fact that both Karadžić and Mladić are now on trial at the ICTY were generally muted, including among the six men and women who were first interviewed in 2008. As Delpla remarks, 'Most Bosniacs denounce the impunity of suspected war criminals but, once these criminals are arrested, their trials attract less attention' (2007: 224). What this partly demonstrates is that while justice is a contested concept, particularly along ethnic lines, people's very perceptions and views of what constitutes justice are fluid and changeable. This adds to the difficulties that any court faces in delivering 'justice' that satisfies local communities.

Only a handful of interviewees professed to feelings of happiness when Karadžić and Mladić were arrested. An interviewee who had spent time in the Trnopolje camp in Prijedor municipality, for example, explained that Karadžić's arrest was particularly important to her. He is worse than Mladić, she claimed, because he is a psychiatrist and he misused his knowledge and expertise to harm and destroy people's mental health;[30] and a camp survivor in Prijedor, who had recently testified as a prosecution witness in Karadžić's trial, described feeling a sense of satisfaction at seeing the former Bosnian Serb leader in the dock.[31] More commonly, however, interviewees simply expressed indifference. A camp survivor and war

29 Karadžić was arrested in Belgrade on 18 July 2008, during the author's first fieldtrip to BiH. Mladić was arrested three years later, on 26 May 2011, in the Serbian village of Lazarevo.

30 Author interview, Kozarac, 31 March 2013.

31 Author interview, Prijedor, 30 March 2013.

invalid in Sarajevo, for example, explained that for him, what is most important is that the bodies of the missing are exhumed and buried with dignity. Only when this happens, he underlined, will he be happy that Mladić is in The Hague.[32] For her part, a widow in Prijedor simply expressed disbelief that the two men were able to evade justice for so long.[33] Contrary to expectations, the author encountered similar views and reactions in eastern Bosnia. An interviewee in Potočari emphasized that although Mladić is now where he should be, she does not feel any satisfaction. How can she, she asked, when she lost her 19-year-old son during the genocide and has still not been able to bury him?[34] Underlining that there is no bigger injustice than waiting for justice, an interviewee who lost her entire family during the genocide similarly disclosed that she feels no strong emotions regarding the trials of Karadžić and Mladić; without her children, her heart is empty.[35]

While the ongoing proceedings against Karadžić and Mladić generally failed to evince strong emotions among interviewees, there was an important exception. Specifically, Karadžić's trial had generated considerable resentment among victims in Bratunac, who were angry that a number of local Serbs – including the town's mayor and a school director – had testified as witnesses for the Defence. Demanding to know why 'war criminals' are being allowed to defend Karadžić, interviewees communicated a deep sense of injustice. Compounding their frustration was the fact that in contrast to victims from Srebrenica, victims from Bratunac have not been given a voice at the ICTY. Interviewees thus felt forgotten, their suffering overshadowed by nearby Srebrenica, and they accused the Tribunal of giving a greater voice to war criminals than to victims. Asking what she can therefore expect from the ICTY, an interviewee whose brother remains missing emphatically answered her own question: nothing at all.[36]

What is clear, to sum up, is that Bosnian Muslims have a number of serious grievances with the Tribunal, and these have increased since the author first conducted fieldwork in BiH in 2008. While interviewees generally appreciated the fact that the Tribunal exists and viewed its work as important, there was also a widespread feeling that it has not done enough and has not lived up to expectations. There are too many aspects of the ICTY's work which do not make sense, and few interviewees endorsed the Tribunal's claim that it is delivering justice to victims. In the aftermath of heinous war crimes, courts will always struggle to satisfy victims. What further adds to the complexity of the challenge is that 'victims' are not a homogenous group with uniform ideas about justice and 'they may not think in the same way about the meaning of justice...' (Weinstein et al. 2010: 47). Some interviewees, for example, demanded that all war criminals must be

---

32 Author interview, Sarajevo, 22 March 2013.
33 Author interview, Prijedor, 2 April 2013.
34 Author interview, Potočari, 24 March 2013.
35 Author interview, Potočari, 26 March 2013.
36 Author interview, Bratunac, 28 March 2013.

tried, while those who had lost loved-ones particularly underlined the importance of locating the missing; and torture survivors – due to their lack of status (discussed in Chapter 5) – underscored the importance of reparations. Some opined that justice is impossible after genocide and war crimes, and some elderly interviewees believed that Allah will ultimately deliver justice. Hence, the meaning of justice varies not only inter-ethnically but also intra-ethnically, thereby highlighting the reality that ICTY 'justice' will always be vigorously disputed and contested.

Bosnian Serb viewpoints and claims that the ICTY negates Serb victimhood

Klarin remarks that, 'Statistically speaking, the Tribunal's popularity in the former Yugoslavia is inversely proportionate to the number of accused that come from the countries, entities and, particularly ethnic communities concerned' (2009: 553). Hence, in BiH, the ICTY's primary and most vocal detractors are Bosnian Serbs. While Bosniak interviewees expressed multiple grievances, Bosnian Serbs had fewer but more fundamental issues with the Tribunal. Quintessentially, the fact that the Tribunal has prosecuted more Serbs than any other group has created and entrenched the pervasive perception of the ICTY as a deeply political and biased institution. The results of Kostić's research are thus unsurprising; only 4.0 per cent of Bosnian Serbs agreed with the statement that trials at the ICTY are fair, while 67.6 per cent totally disagreed (in contrast to 33.7 per cent of Bosnian Croats and 24.0 per cent of Bosniaks) (2012: 659). Further fuelling a profound sense of injustice is the widespread belief that the Tribunal is deliberately ignoring Serb victims.

An absence of justice for Serb victims

No tribunal can prosecute every potential war criminal, and hence 'selectivity of prosecution will remain an issue with which communities must grapple' (Fletcher and Weinstein 2002: 579). Bosnian Serb interviewees, however, rebuked the ICTY for adopting, in their view, a purposefully selective approach which ignores crimes committed against members of their ethnic group. Resolutely asserting that all sides must be treated equally, interviewees repeatedly cited the case of Naser Orić as the ultimate proof of the ICTY's selectivity and lack of commitment to justice. Interviewees in Srebrenica were particularly embittered by the outcome of Orić's trial. During the war in BiH, Orić was the senior commander of ABiH forces in eastern BiH, including in the municipality of Srebrenica. Indicted for violations of the laws or customs of war, his trial began on 6 October 2004. On 30 June 2006, Orić was acquitted of wanton destruction of cities, towns or villages not justified by military necessity (Prosecutor v. Orić 2006: §716). Finding insufficient evidence to support the Prosecution's claim that Orić had exercised effective control over the various groups who participated in attacks on Serb villages in Srebrenica, the Trial

Chamber concluded that, 'The picture that emerges from the evidence is not one of an organised army with a fully functioning command structure, but one of pockets of desperate men willing to fight, mainly to defend themselves, that grouped together around trusted leaders...' (Prosecutor v. Orić 2006: §707). On the additional charge of murder and cruel treatment, however, Orić was convicted (on the basis of superior criminal responsibility); the Trial Chamber opined that he had failed to take reasonable and necessary measures to prevent crimes committed by the Military Police (over whom he was deemed to have had effective control from 22 November 1992 onwards) against Serbs in Srebrenica between December 1992 and March 1993. Orić was sentenced to two years' imprisonment, but as he had been in detention since 10 April 2003, the Trial Chamber ordered his immediate release.

Orić appealed and on 3 July 2008, the Appeals Chamber reversed the Trial Chamber's judgement and acquitted Orić of murder and cruel treatment. It was a unanimous verdict, although Judge Liu and Judge Schomberg issued partially dissenting opinions. Noting that, 'Where an accused is charged with command responsibility pursuant to Article 7(3) of the [ICTY] Statute, as in the present case, the Prosecution must prove, *inter alia*, that his subordinate(s) bore criminal responsibility and that he knew or had reason to know of his/their criminal conduct', the Appeals Chamber found that the Trial Chamber had not adequately addressed either of these critical issues (Prosecutor v. Orić 2008: §189). This meant that the appellate judges were unable to decipher the basis on which the Trial Chamber held Orić's subordinate criminally responsible, leading them to the conclusion that, 'the Trial Chamber erred in failing to resolve the issue of whether Orić's subordinate incurred criminal responsibility' (Prosecutor v. Orić 2008: §47). The Trial Chamber identified Atif Krdžić, the commander of the Military Police, as Orić's subordinate, and deemed him 'ultimately responsible for murder and cruel treatment' (Prosecutor v. Orić 2006: §496, 533). According to the Appeals Chamber, however, it did so without specifying the basis of Krdžić's criminal responsibility (Prosecutor v. Orić 2008: §38). On the second issue of whether Orić knew or had reason to know of his subordinate's alleged criminal conduct, the Appeals Chamber assessed that the Trial Chamber committed an error of law by failing to establish 'whether Orić knew or had reason to know that his subordinate was about to or had committed crimes' (Prosecutor v. Orić 2008: §61). The Appeals Chamber thus concluded that Orić's conviction for violations of the laws or customs of war must be overturned.

Interviewees attached enormous significance to this particular trial. Not only have very few prosecutions at the ICTY focused on crimes against Serbs, but 'Orić was the first and only indictee for crimes against the Serb population in Srebrenica' (Simić 2011: 1392). Insisting that the outside world does not know the full truth about Srebrenica, interviewees always maintained that approximately 3,500 Serbs were killed in this area during the war. Hence, particularly for Serbs in Srebrenica, Orić's trial was an opportunity to finally see justice done. Inevitably, therefore, his acquittal created a profound sense of outrage and anger.

If the initial two-year sentence handed down by the Trial Chamber was deemed laughable and a mockery of justice, the ultimate acquittal verdict was interpreted as a negation and dismissal of Serb suffering in Srebrenica. To thus construe the appeal judgement, however, is fundamentally erroneous. A key paragraph in the judgement underlines that,

> Like the Trial Chamber, the Appeals Chamber has no doubt that grave crimes were committed against Serb detainees at the Srebrenica Police Station and the Building [the Srebrenica Municipal Building] between September 1992 and March 1993. The Defence did not challenge that crimes were committed against Serb detainees. However, proof that crimes have occurred is not sufficient to sustain a conviction of an individual.
>
> (Prosecutor v. Orić 2008: §189)

In other words, far from finding that the alleged crimes against Serbs did not occur, the Appeals Chamber simply reached the conclusion that Orić could not be held responsible for those crimes under the principle of command responsibility. Unfortunately, this crucial point was not conveyed to the general public. Moreover, it is not an exaggeration to argue that it was the verdict against Orić which most decisively turned Bosnian Serb public opinion against the ICTY. Expressing a common viewpoint, an ex-combatant and camp survivor in Bratunac maintained that Orić's trial extinguished all hope among Serbs that they would ever receive any justice from the Tribunal.[37]

Just as Bosnian Serb interviewees in Srebrenica stressed that there can be no impunity for crimes committed against Serbs in this area in 1992 and 1993, those in nearby Bratunac were similarly emphatic that the ICTY can never deliver justice as long as crimes such as Bjelovac remain unpunished. On 14 December 1992, the ABiH attacked the mainly Serb village of Bjelovac; Serb houses were set alight and lives were lost. The exact number of deaths, however, remains unclear. While an interviewee whose husband was killed in the attack claimed that 68 people died,[38] a booklet given to the author by a Bosnian Serb interviewee in Srebrenica lists the names of 25 victims (Ivanišević 2011b: 39) and the website of the Serbian radio and television station B92 refers to 109 victims (B92 2008). In delivering its judgement against Orić, who was involved in planning the attack on Bjelovac, the Trial Chamber found that, '...property was destroyed on a large scale in Bjelovac and Sikirić [an adjoining hamlet] between 14 to 19 December 1992' (Prosecutor v. Orić 2006: §656). It further found that, 'Undoubtedly, there is evidence that Bosnian Muslims burned down houses both in Bjelovac and Sikirić' (Prosecutor v. Orić 2006: §657). It also noted, however, that it was not in a position to establish exactly how many houses the ABiH had destroyed, on account of the fact that,

---

37 Author interview, Bratunac, 25 March 2013.
38 Author interview, Bratunac, 26 March 2013.

In Bjelovac and its surroundings, there was ongoing fighting between Bosnian Muslims and Bosnian Serbs from 14 to 19 December 1992. This fighting involved the conflicting parties alternately controlling and defending Bjelovac and Sikirić, resulting in exposing property to destruction. The damage caused to houses in Bjelovac and Sikirić likely resulted from all these circumstances.

(Prosecutor v. Orić 2006: §657)

Bosnian Serb interviewees in Bratunac offered a very different and more black and white version of events. They did not mention that, 'there was a Serb and Bosnian Serb military presence in the area'; or that the school in Bjelovac 'was used as a kitchen to feed passing Bosnian Serb fighters' (Prosecutor v. Orić 2006: §651). For them, Bjelovac was a fundamental war crime which the ICTY has inexplicably and unjustifiably ignored. Emphasizing that her own pain is no less than the pain of any other woman who has lost her husband, an interviewee whose spouse was killed in the attack accused the ICTY of privileging Bosnian Muslim victims and according them a status which is denied to Serb victims.[39]

One interviewee in Bratunac had recently testified as a defence witness in Karadžić's trial at the ICTY. She explained that she agreed to testify in the belief – and hope – that this would be an important opportunity to speak about the suffering of Bosnian Serbs during the war. Prior to travelling to The Hague, she had prepared a nine-page statement, but upon her arrival at the Tribunal she was informed that large chunks of it (notably those parts describing her time in the Silos camp near Sarajevo) were irrelevant – and thus inadmissible. During the interview, she produced a copy of her statement for the author to see; pages three through to six had been blacked out in their entirety. This interviewee had spent 1,339 days in the Silos camp (discussed in the next chapter), before finally being released on 20 January 1996, and claimed that her time at the ICTY was worse than her time in the camp. The Tribunal had made her feel less important and of less worth than Bosnian Muslim victims, she explained.[40] Her experience in The Hague had inevitably become common knowledge among Serbs in Bratunac, and for them it was yet further confirmation that the Tribunal has no interest in hearing about crimes against Serbs.

---

39 Author interview, Bratunac, 26 March 2013. Bosnian Serb interviewees in both Bratunac and Srebrenica also expressed a deep sense of injustice that nobody has been held responsible for the ABiH attack on the Serb village of Kravica on 7 January 1993. In its judgement against Naser Orić, the Trial Chamber found that, 'By 8 January 1993, an indeterminate number of houses in Kravica were burned...Witnesses arriving in the Kravica area by mid-March 1993 found most of the houses and out-buildings burned down' (Prosecutor v. Orić 2006: §669). As in the case of Bjelovac, however, it also concluded that, 'Regarding Kravica, while there is evidence that large scale destruction occurred on 7 and 9 January 1993, the Trial Chamber is not satisfied that it can be attributed solely to Bosnian Muslims' (Prosecutor v. Orić 2006: §671).

40 Author interview, Bratunac, 27 March 2013.

The ICTY is a political court

Courts, to reiterate, are forced to be selective. They would 'gain greater credibility', however, by providing 'greater clarity and transparency in justifying selectivity' (Stahn 2011: 15). In short, if local communities do not understand, or sufficiently understand, how a court decides which cases to prosecute, they will necessarily arrive at their own conclusions. For Serbs, the Tribunal's selectivity and, in their eyes, lack of concern for Serb victims fundamentally attest to its inherently political nature. Again and again, interviewees expressed their conviction that the ICTY was created with the sole or primary purpose of prosecuting Serbs and establishing Serb guilt.[41] Even the recent acquittal of Momčilo Perišić, in February 2013, was widely interpreted as further incontrovertible proof that politics, rather than justice, is driving the Tribunal's work. Voicing a common opinion among Bosnian Serb interviewees, an ex-combatant in Srebrenica insisted that Perišić was only acquitted as a trade-off for the earlier acquittals of Gotovina and Markač.[42] This interviewee further explained that ex-combatants in RS have organized a petition against the ICTY to demand that its trials are fair and untainted by political considerations. Providing the author with three small leaflets that contained information about the petition and expressed Serb grievances with the Tribunal, he drew attention to a particular sentence: 'The most powerful method for the destruction of the truth about the last civil war on the territory of BiH is the Hague Tribunal...'.[43]

This petition also targets the work of the State Court of BiH, and specifically the work of its War Crimes Chamber which commenced work in 2005. During fieldwork in BiH in 2008 and 2009, interviewees from all three main ethnic groups almost never mentioned the State Court. In 2013, in contrast, Bosnian Serb interviewees in particular made frequent reference to it and typically described it as a Muslim court. It was clear that they disliked the State Court just as much as they abhorred the ICTY, regarding both institutions as strongly anti-Serb. There is no doubt that the ICTY's geographical remoteness from the former Yugoslavia has contributed to its image problem, particularly among Serbs. To cite Hagan and Kutnjak Ivković, 'Fundamentally, to be seen as legitimate, legal justice must ultimately also be seen as local justice...' (2006: 146). Bosnian Serb hostility towards the State Court of BiH, however, strongly suggests that even if the ICTY had been located within the former Yugoslavia, it would still have struggled to gain legitimacy among local (and notably Serb) communities.

41 Such views do not only exist among Serbs in BiH. According to a 2011 survey by Ipsos Strategic Marketing in Belgrade, for example, 73 per cent of respondents believed that the ethnicity of defendants influences how they are dealt with at the Tribunal (Ipsos Strategic Marketing 2011: 22).

42 Author interview, Srebrenica, 27 March 2013.

43 Author's translation from Serbian.

Bosnian Croat viewpoints and the mirroring of Serb grievances

Bosnian Croat interviewees rarely had anything positive to say about the ICTY, and indeed they expressed many of the same grievances as Bosnian Serb interviewees. Frequently deriding the Tribunal as a political court, they repeatedly accused it of unjustly targeting Croats (both in BiH and Croatia) and overlooking Croat victims.

A court that pursues Croatian 'heroes'

Just as the trial and ultimate acquittal of Naser Orić had a hugely negative and damaging effect on Serb perceptions of the ICTY, certain trials have been similarly decisive in turning (or further turning) Bosnian Croat public opinion against the Tribunal. One particularly notable trial in this regard is that of Tihomir Blaškić, the aforementioned wartime commander of HVO forces in central BiH. Interviewees viewed the trial and conviction of Blaškić as a gross injustice, despite the fact that his original 45-year sentence was reduced to just nine years on appeal – and despite the additional fact that he was granted early release just four days after the Appeals Chamber delivered its judgement. As they saw it, Blaškić had courageously defended his people. Interviewees had similarly strong views about Gotovina. During the author's fieldwork in 2008, three years before the Trial Chamber convicted Gotovina and his co-defendant, Markač, Bosnian Croats were extremely vocal in proclaiming Gotovina's innocence. They were also deeply resentful that this 'Croatian hero' who liberated Croatia from Serb aggression was in The Hague and widely viewed his trial as overwhelming proof that the Tribunal is a political institution. Gotovina had been both convicted and subsequently acquitted by the ICTY before the author returned to BiH in 2013. The appeal verdict, however, had not softened attitudes towards the ICTY; the sense that justice had finally been done was seemingly overshadowed by a deep and parallel sense of injustice provoked by the very prosecution of Gotovina and the Trial Chamber's finding of guilt.

A court that ignores Croat victims

Bosnian Croat interviewees continually accused the ICTY of ignoring crimes committed against members of their ethnic group. This argument was most frequently voiced by Croats in central BiH, who claimed that the ICTY's trials relating to the Lašva Valley had detracted attention from Bosnian Croat suffering. Interviewees in Ahmići, for example, as well as in nearby Vitez, were bitterly aggrieved that while the ICTY has prosecuted several Bosnian Croats in connection with crimes committed in the village in 1993, it has not prosecuted anybody for crimes against Bosnian Croats in nearby villages such as Dušina[44] and Križančevo Selo.[45] One interviewee – who had himself stood trial at the ICTY – argued that while Croats were the biggest victims of the Bosnian war, they have received the least justice.[46] Hence, like Serb interviewees, Croat interviewees accused the Tribunal of discriminating between victims on ethnic grounds. With regard to Dušina, it should be noted that the State Court of BiH has charged Vehid Subotić, who fought in the Seventh Muslim Brigade of the ABiH, with murders (violations of the Geneva Conventions) committed in the village on 26 January 1993. According to the indictment, which was issued on 7 June 2013, Subotić and other members of the 2nd Battalion of the 7th Muslim Brigade stormed the village of Dušina and ordered the capture of approximately 40 civilians and some disarmed members of the HVO. Subotić personally singled out several civilians, three of whom were killed. A further four civilians from a different group were also killed (State Court of BiH 2013). This indictment was issued shortly after the conclusion of the author's fieldwork in BiH in March–April 2013.

Interestingly, Croat interviewees – and particularly those in central BiH – never referred to the trial of Enver Hadžihasović, a senior officer in the ABiH, and Amir Kubura, the Chief of Staff of the 7th Muslim Mountain Brigade of the ABiH 3rd Corps. This was the first ICTY trial to deal with the presence of Mujahedin in central BiH. The Tribunal indicted Hadžihasović and Kubura for violations of the laws or customs of war in central BiH, including in the municipalities of Kakanj, Travnik and Zenica; and on 15 March 2006, the Trial Chamber found the men guilty of failing to take necessary or reasonable measures to prevent or punish crimes committed by forces under their command in 1993 and early 1994 (Prosecutor v. Hadžihasović and Kubura 2006). In April 2008, the Appeals Chamber ultimately sentenced Hadžihasović and Kubura to prison terms of three-and-a-half years and two years respectively (Prosecutor v. Hadžihasović and Kubura 2008) – although both men were granted early release. Undoubtedly, such low sentences would not have satisfied Bosnian Croat interviewees or delivered any meaningful sense of justice. This may explain why nobody referred to them. However, the more likely explanation is that interviewees were either not familiar with this particular case or considered it irrelevant in view of the fact that it did not focus on crimes in their specific area.

44 In its judgement against Josipović et al., the Trial Chamber noted that, 'On 25 January 1993, Muslim forces massacred some fourteen captured Croat soldiers and several civilians in Dušina' (Prosecutor v. Josipović et al. 2000: §61).

45 According to Shrader, '...between 60 and a hundred HVO soldiers and Croat civilians were killed in the village [Križančevo Selo] in December 1993' (2003: 153).

46 Author interview, Ahmići, 12 July 2008.

Justice neither seen nor understood

While people on all sides hold strong views about the ICTY, they are seldom well-informed about its work. An interviewee in Potočari, for example, erroneously claimed that only Radislav Krstić has been convicted of genocide.[47] In fact, Krstić was ultimately convicted of aiding and abetting genocide (Prosecutor v. Krstić 2004), but more recently three defendants – Ljubiša Beara, Vujadin Popović and Zdravko Tolimir – have been convicted of genocide (Prosecutor v. Popović et al. 2010; Prosecutor v. Tolimir 2012). Several interviewees confused the ICTY with the International Court of Justice, also based in The Hague, demanding to know how the former was able to reach the implausible conclusion that Serbia was not responsible for genocide in Srebrenica; and some wanted to know why the Tribunal is only dealing with the former Yugoslavia and Rwanda. The majority of interviewees also revealed that they do not follow the ICTY's work, frequently complaining that its trials take too long. As Saxon underlines, due to the complexity of the trials, '…it is very difficult to maintain the public's interest in a particular proceeding…' (2005: 563).

Some commentators downplay the extent to which the ICTY could and should have undertaken greater outreach work. Nice, for example, contends that the ICTY can take little or no credit for 'failing adequately to educate or inform the population about what the Tribunal does' (2006: 51); and Kerr argues that, 'Combating a propaganda machine intent on distributing malicious rumours and fostering negative perceptions of the ICTY may have been more than any tribunal outreach programme could be expected to achieve' (2007: 379). This research, in contrast, adopts a fundamentally different view, while acknowledging that it is not solely the job of a court to inform local communities about its work. The media, politicians and intellectuals have all contributed to undermining the ICTY's credibility (Hodžić 2011: 115–116), but this does not mean that the Tribunal 'could not have done more to improve its image and get its message across to the region' (Klarin 2011: 111; see also Arbour 2004: 401–402; Orentlicher 2008: 27; Stover 2007: 37). Why has the ICTY mainly indicted Serbs? Why has it only indicted a relatively small number of perpetrators? How did the Tribunal decide who to prosecute? Why has it not prosecuted particular crimes? How can it convict a defendant and subsequently acquit him? Why is the Tribunal only focusing on the former Yugoslavia? These are the sorts of questions that outreach work needed to address. The fact that many people remain ill-informed about the Tribunal, two decades after it was created, is a serious problem, not least because 'a lack of information breeds misinformation, misinformation breeds mistrust' (Wu 2013: 77).

Outreach work is especially important in the aftermath of highly controversial judgements. In the wake of Perišić's acquittal, for example, an outreach event

---

47 Author interview, Potočari, 26 March 2013.

explaining the verdict would have been extremely valuable. Unfortunately, on this and so many other occasions, the ICTY missed a critical opportunity to engage with local communities. Between May 2004 and June 2005, the Tribunal's outreach office organized a series of five conferences in Brčko, Foča, Konjic, Prijedor and Srebrenica (Clark 2009: 102–103; Nettelfield 2010: 155). The aim was to provide local people with key information – in layman's terms – about the Tribunal's work in these areas, from the investigations stage to the judgements themselves. In addition to the outreach team, others including ICTY senior investigators and trial attorneys also addressed the audiences. A strong focus on the grassroots level is crucial to the overall success of any outreach programme, and hence it is deeply regrettable that the Tribunal never built upon or repeated this 'Bridging the Gap' series. While emphasizing the importance of outreach work, the Tribunal's former President, Judge Patrick Robinson, has also underlined that, 'Members of the affected communities are entitled to have their opinions about the work of the Tribunal and to express them' (2011: 267). This is true, but it is at least part of the Tribunal's responsibility to ensure that people are able to express *informed* opinions.

To conclude, as interviewees on all sides overwhelmingly criticized various aspects of the Tribunal's work and identified numerous injustices, this chapter has not been able to fully assess whether 'justice' can in fact contribute to reconciliation. Based on the prevalence of negative perceptions of the ICTY, however, and the multiple grievances that interviewees expressed, it has fundamentally problematized and challenged the argument that the ICTY is contributing to inter-ethnic reconciliation in BiH by delivering justice. The next chapter continues this analysis by focusing on the second prong of the measurement model developed in Chapter 2.

Chapter 4

Bosnia-Hercegovina Part Two
Truth

Denial is an obvious and significant impediment to reconciliation. In particular, 'it hinders healing by survivors, for whom the truth and acknowledgement of their suffering is of great importance' (Staub 2011: 178). Hence, one of the oft-cited ways in which criminal trials can purportedly contribute to reconciliation is by establishing the facts, documenting the truth and thus eliminating – or at least marginalizing – the scourge of denial and revisionism. According to Tieger and Shin, for example, '...there is little doubt that a reliable historical record generated in the course of criminal litigation can play a meaningful role in combating revisionism and creating a climate of consensus upon which reconciliation can be built' (2005: 670). The Tribunal itself has similarly voiced such claims, maintaining that, 'The detail in which the ICTY's judgements describe the crimes and the involvement of those convicted makes it impossible for anyone to dispute the reality of the horrors that took place in and around Bratunac, Brčko, Čelebići, Dubrovnik, Foča, Prijedor, Sarajevo, Srebrenica and Zvornik, to name but a few' (ICTY n.d.).

The reality, however, is more complex (Del Ponte 2005). Courts like the ICTY can create a detailed record of events, an enduring archival legacy of documents, witness statements, trial transcripts, decisions and judgements for future generations to study and consult. The problem is that the truths established in a courtroom may fail to resonate among local communities, particularly in deeply-divided societies where 'truth' is unavoidably a fundamentally contested concept (Mukherjee 2011: 335). In BiH, for example, each side has its own version of truth, according to which it was simply defending itself during the war. A survey undertaken by Kostić in 2010 highlights this point. When asked whom they regarded as the main defenders of the Bosnian war, 91.2 per cent of Bosniaks predictably identified the ABiH, 92.1 per cent of Bosnian Croats named the HVO and 88 per cent of Bosnian Serbs answered the VRS (2012: 656). The reality of these multiple truths and competing ethnic narratives exposes the naïve simplicity of extolling the Tribunal as a truth-telling body. Inter-ethnic disagreement on almost every aspect of the war necessarily 'makes the task of the ICTY impossible, since whatever it does will be rejected by most members of at least one group' (Hayden 2011: 319).

Not only have too many of the ICTY's truths failed to penetrate, but they have also contributed to a critical hardening of BiH's opposing ethnic narratives. Cherry observes that, 'In some circumstances, communities may cling to "truths" about events that happened, even if the transitional justice process exposes those "truths" as myths' (2009: 253), and this is precisely what is happening in BiH. When one of their ethnic kin is convicted at the ICTY, communities in BiH commonly react by reasserting their own collective version of events. The latter thus becomes a form of resistance to any judicial findings that challenge and problematize the group's meta narrative and victim identity. Each side emphasizes its own suffering, and this 'arms race' of victimhood (Helms 2012: 198) is a critical obstacle to reconciliation and positive inter-group relations (Bilali and Vollhardt 2013: 145). More importantly, the fact that the Tribunal's work has fuelled and strengthened competing claims of victimhood 'challenges the theory that criminal trials promote social healing by documenting and acknowledging the atrocities of the past' (Fletcher and Weinstein 2002: 603).

Although the Tribunal maintains that its work is individualizing guilt, its judgements necessarily have wider implications in a context where they encounter and frequently contradict a group's own version of events. To claim that the ICTY's work is combatting denial is thus to overlook the critical fact that, 'what a community chooses to deny about its past is largely defined by its group identity' (Stover 2007: 143). Hence, far from minimizing denial, in some cases the Tribunal's work has had precisely the opposite effect. As Saxon remarks, 'The majority populations of all three communities are still in deep denial about their past and the conduct of their forces during the armed conflict' (2005: 562). Some of the most interesting and persistent examples of denial can be found among Bosnian Serbs.

Bosnian Serb truths versus ICTY truths

Two key points strongly emerged from interviews with Bosnian Serbs between 2008 and 2013. The first is that interviewees did not associate the ICTY with truth, based on the widespread belief – discussed in the previous chapter – that only Serbs are being prosecuted. An interviewee in the village of Kravica, for example, stressed that not a single Bosnian Muslim has been held responsible for crimes against Serbs in the municipalities of Bratunac and Srebrenica;[1] and emphasizing the acquittals of Orić, Gotovina, Markač and 'shqiptars'[2] from Kosovo, an ex-combatant in Bratunac vigorously rejected any suggestion that the Tribunal's work is establishing the truth about the war.[3] A poll conducted by Prism Research in Sarajevo, in 2010, further highlights Bosnian

---

1 Author interview, Kravica, 1 July 2008.
2 'Shqiptars' is a derogatory term that Serbs often use to refer to Kosovo Albanians.
3 Author interview, Bratunac, 25 March 2013.

Serb scepticism vis-à-vis the Tribunal. While overall 58.2 per cent of respondents agreed that the documentation of international courts represents the best basis for discussing what happened during the war in BiH, only 26.5 per cent of Bosnian Serbs endorsed the statement – in contrast to 59.4 per cent of Bosnian Croats and 83.4 per cent of Bosnian Muslims (Pajić and Popović 2011: 23). The second point is that Bosnian Serb hostility towards the ICTY has inevitably generated deep resistance to its judgements. If, as Ford argues, 'The dominant narrative of ethnic Serbians immediately after the conflict in the Balkans is best described as "we were not responsible"' (2012: 427), what strongly emerged during the author's fieldwork in BiH is that this narrative substantially continues to persist today. It is sustained through repeated denial of Serb crimes and a parallel emphasis on crimes committed *against* Serbs. Its existence and functionality are most striking with respect to Srebrenica, an example which casts serious doubt on the claim that the ICTY has 'set down a record of events that will be an important barrier to revisionism in the years to come' (Brammertz 2013a).

Interpreting Srebrenica

On 2 August 2001, the ICTY delivered its verdict against Radislav Krstić, the deputy commander and, later, commander of the Drina Corps of the VRS. The Tribunal convicted him of genocide and sentenced him to 46 years' imprisonment (Prosecutor v. Krstić 2001). Although the Appeals Chamber subsequently found that Krstić lacked the requisite genocidal intent (Prosecutor v. Krstić 2004: §134), and thereby convicted him of the lesser charge of aiding and abetting genocide (his sentence was accordingly reduced to 35 years), this does not detract from the particular significance of the case. Notably, this was the first trial in which the ICTY determined that genocide was committed in Srebrenica in 1995. Notwithstanding the critical importance of the Krstić trial, it has not had the impact that some commentators anticipated at the time. Drumbl, for example, confidently asserted that, '...the Krstić decision will have repercussions among victims, bystanders, and perpetrators in the former Yugoslavia, and accordingly may play some role in the essentially political process of peace and reconciliation in the wake of the endemic violence that has occurred there' (2004: 436). During the author's fieldwork in BiH, however, Bosnian Serb interviewees never referred to the Krstić verdicts; and whilst acknowledging that killings took place in Srebrenica, they always forcefully denied that genocide had taken place. Indeed, from the first interviewees in 2008 to the final interviewees in 2013, respondents continued to voice the same set of arguments to challenge the ICTY's account of what occurred in Srebrenica.

Interviewees essentially engaged in two types of denial – namely denial regarding the victims and denial vis-à-vis the perpetrators. The first type was the most prevalent and manifested itself in a number of inter-related assertions. One of the most frequent was that events in Srebrenica in July 1995 cannot be defined as

Figure 4.1 Srebrenica.

genocide on the grounds that only men were killed. According to an ex-combatant in Srebrenica, for example, genocide signifies the systematic destruction of an entire people[4] and this was never the aim in Srebrenica. If it had been, he maintained, Serbs would not have transported women and children away to Kladanj and Tuzla – areas that were under the control of the ABiH.[5] Building upon such arguments, interviewees always alleged that those killed in Srebrenica were overwhelmingly soldiers rather than civilians, a statement fundamentally at odds with the Tribunal's findings. In delivering its verdict in the trial of Popović et al., for example, the Trial Chamber noted that, 'The mood during the night between 12 and 13 July was fearful. Bosnian Serb Forces moved through the crowd and repeatedly took men away, regardless of their age, after which shouting, moaning, screaming and bursts of fire would be heard' (Prosecutor v. Popović et al. 2010: §313). Indeed, several Bosniak interviewees had lost sons under the age of

---

4   This interviewee had a clearer understanding of genocide than most; in general, interviewees used the term extremely loosely to simply mean unlawful killing. What fundamentally distinguishes the act of genocide, as defined in the 1948 Convention on the Prevention and Punishment of the Crime of Genocide, is that it must be: 'committed with intent to destroy, in whole or in part, a national, ethnical, racial or religious group, as such' (UN 1948).

5   Author interview, Srebrenica, 25 June 2008.

18, including an elderly woman in Potočari whose son was just 15 years old when he was killed. When the author pointed this out to a Serb ex-combatant in Srebrenica, he explained that he was sorry for every victim but emphasized that Serb children were also killed.[6] When similarly pressed, another interviewee presented the author with a small book entitled *Serbian Ruins of Srebrenica*, which as the name suggests focuses entirely on Serb victims (Ivanišević 2011b). Indeed, this was a common trait among interviewees on all sides: whenever they were specifically asked about crimes committed by members of their own ethnic group, they typically avoided answering the question and instead drew attention to crimes against their group.

If Bosnian Serb interviewees repeatedly argued that the vast majority of those killed in Srebrenica were combatants, some – and in particular those interviewed in 2013 – additionally asserted that many of the dead who are buried in the Potočari Memorial Centre near Srebrenica were in fact killed in 1992 and 1993 during attacks on Serb villages in the area. A widow in Bratunac thus described the Potočari Memorial Centre as a huge manipulation, a burial ground in which primarily Muslim war criminals are interred.[7] It is important to note that Mirsad Tokača, the director of the RDC in Sarajevo, has disclosed that there are approximately 70 persons buried in the Potočari Memorial Centre who were not in fact killed during the genocide in Srebrenica in July 1995. The director of the Centre has himself confirmed this and emphasized that there was never any secrecy regarding these burials (Balkan Insight 2010a). Moreover, these burials occurred on a modest scale and were not the deliberate ruse that Serb interviewees often claimed.

In addition to disputing the status of those who died in July 1995, interviewees also challenged the numbers, always maintaining that far fewer people were killed than the Bosniaks claim. In the trial of Popović et al., the Trial Chamber found that, 'at least 5,336 identified individuals were killed in the executions following the fall of Srebrenica'. However, it also went on to remark that, '...noting that the evidence before it is not all encompassing, the Trial Chamber is satisfied that the number of identified individuals will rise. The Trial Chamber therefore considers that the number of individuals killed in the executions following the fall of Srebrenica could well be as high as 7,826' (Prosecutor v. Popović et al. 2010: §664).[8] Interviewees, however, accused Bosniaks – and in particular the Mothers of Srebrenica – of deliberately manipulating the figures and constantly increasing them. During the author's fieldwork in BiH in 2013, for example, Bosniak interviewees in Potočari often cited the figure of 10,000 victims. The difficulty of

---

6 Author interview, Srebrenica, 28 March 2013.
7 Author interview, Bratunac, 26 March 2013.
8 The figure of 8,372 is etched into a commemorative edifice at the Potočari Memorial Centre. Written, however, as '8372...', the number precedes the important words: '*Ukupan broj žrtava koji nije konačan*' (Total number of victims which is not final).

Figure 4.2 Bosniak graves at the Potočari Memorial Centre.

arriving at a final, definitive number primarily stems from the fact that some of the dead remain missing nearly 20 years after the genocide occurred, buried in mass graves that have yet to be located and exhumed.[9] Critically overlooking this, however, Bosnian Serb interviewees had their own, far more cynical explanation. Some even claimed that there are two white memorial pillars for every one victim buried in the Potočari Memorial Centre, as a deliberate ruse to make the number of victims appear substantially larger than it actually is.

In addition to victim-based denial, interviewees also engaged in perpetrator-focused denial. Specifically, notwithstanding the ICTY's verdicts against, *inter alia*, Dragan Obrenović, Momir Nikolić, Vujadin Popović, Ljubiša Beara and Zdravko Tolimir[10] – all of whom held various positions within the VRS and have

---

9 According to the International Commission for Missing Persons (ICMP) in Sarajevo, it has aided BiH 'in accounting for almost 90% of those reported missing from the 1995 fall of Srebrenica' (2012); and during his testimony in the trial of Ratko Mladić, the ICMP's director of forensic sciences claimed that as of June 2013, the remains of 6,767 victims from Srebrenica had been identified (SENSE 2013a).
10 Dragan Obrenović was the Chief of Staff and deputy commander of the 1st Zvornik Infantry Brigade of the Drina Corps of the VRS. Following a guilty plea, he was sentenced in December 2003 to 17 years' imprisonment for crimes against humanity following the

been convicted of war crimes in relation to Srebrenica and Potočari – interviewees emphatically denied that any members of the VRS were involved in criminal acts, insisting that the latter were merely defending their homes and families. According to an interviewee in Bratunac, for example, the VRS undertook a legitimate military operation to liberate Srebrenica,[11] during the course of which crimes and 'incidents' occurred. Yet they were not, he passionately averred, either planned or organized; they were spontaneous acts, committed by individuals in a chaotic situation. He immediately contradicted his clam that nobody was in control, however, by pointing out that transport was provided to take women and children out of Potočari.[12] In a similar vein, an interviewee in Foča – who stressed that Serbs were the principal victims in Srebrenica – asserted that those who committed crimes on the Serb side were psychopaths and lunatics and could be counted on two hands.[13] For his part, an ex-combatant who fought in Srebrenica emphatically argued that no crimes were committed in the name of RS. He instead pointed the finger of blame at paramilitaries and mercenaries, and claimed that they, in turn, were assisted by various secret services.[14] Interviewees thus insisted that Ratko Mladić should not be in The Hague – although some also communicated the hope that his trial would allow the 'real truth' about Srebrenica to emerge. Expressing strong support for the former commander of the VRS, they widely maintained that Mladić was not able to control the situation and that

fall of Srebrenica on 11 July 1995 (Prosecutor v. Obrenović 2003). Momir Nikolić was the assistant commander for security and intelligence of the Bratunac Brigade of the VRS. After pleading guilty to crimes against humanity against Bosnian Muslim victims in Srebrenica and Potočari, as well as Bratunac and Zvornik, he received a 27-year prison sentence in December 2003 (reduced to 20 years on appeal) (Prosecutor v. Nikolić 2003b, 2006). Vujadin Popović was the chief of security of the Drina Corps of the VRS. Ljubiša Beara, one of his six co-defendants, was the chief of security of the VRS Main Staff. In June 2010, both men were sentenced to life imprisonment for genocide, crimes against humanity and violations of the laws or customs of war (Prosecutor v. Popović et al. 2010). Their case is currently on appeal. Zdravko Tolimir, the assistant commander for intelligence and security of the VRS Main Staff, was convicted of genocide and crimes against humanity in December 2012 and sentenced to life imprisonment (Prosecutor v. Tolimir 2012) His case is now on appeal.

11 The ICTY has noted how the ABiH was causing problems for the VRS. According to the Trial Chamber judgement against Naser Orić, 'Between June 1992 and March 1993, Bosnian Muslims raided a number of villages and hamlets inhabited by Bosnian Serbs, or from which Bosnian Muslims had been forcibly expelled. One of the purposes of these actions was to acquire food, weapons, ammunition and military equipment. According to the Bosnian Serbs, these actions resulted in considerable loss to Bosnian Serb life and property' (Prosecutor v. Orić 2006: §104).

12 Author interview, Bratunac, 29 June 2008.

13 Author interview, Foča, 5 June 2008. The ICTY has acknowledged that 'opportunistic' killings occurred, but has emphasized that these were 'the natural and foreseeable consequence of the JCE to Forcibly Remove and the JCE to Murder' (Prosecutor v. Popović et al. 2010: §179).

14 Author interview, Srebrenica, 27 March 2013.

had he been able to do so, crimes would not have occurred. He was, they consistently claimed, a professional soldier who always behaved in the correct way and led his forces from the front.

Finally, interviewees, and particularly those in Srebrenica, often sought to further diminish the responsibility of the perpetrators by enumerating a variety of ways in which Bosnian Muslims had died following the fall of Srebrenica. Some of them committed suicide out of fear, they claimed, while others died in the forests from hunger and illness while trying to reach ABiH-controlled territory. Still others were killed in intra-ethnic feuds and fighting. While some Bosniak men did indeed perish in the forests or take their own lives,[15] the overwhelmingly majority did not die in this way; they were massacred. In addition, some interviewees asserted that Naser Orić and/or the Bosnian Muslim leadership were themselves responsible for everything that happened in Srebrenica; the former on account of abandoning his people after Srebrenica fell to the VRS,[16] and the latter by keeping Bosnian Muslim forces in Srebrenica after the town had been declared a UN 'safe area'. They further blamed the international community and stressed that it could have prevented the fall of Srebrenica and the crimes that occurred had it wanted to.

All of the above strongly attests to the fact that the ICTY's trials and findings with respect to Srebrenica have failed to penetrate a thick wall of denial. Rather than simply criticizing the Tribunal or denouncing Bosnian Serbs, however, it is far more constructive to reflect on and understand the continued persistence of genocide denial; and what is clear is that a number of critical factors are sustaining it. Politicians in RS, for example, still refuse to acknowledge that genocide occurred – including President Milorad Dodik (Arslanagić 2010; Halimović 2010).[17] Such dogmatism among the political elite is inextricably linked to the existence of RS. While Bosniak interviewees frequently maintained that the RS is a product of genocide and must therefore be abolished, Bosnian Serbs strongly defended their entity and underlined that many Serb lives were lost in the process of its creation. In short, the existence of RS corroborates and validates the Bosnian Serb narrative of the war. Hence, if politicians were to accept that genocide occurred in the quest to establish a Serb entity, this would problematize

---

15 On 12 July 1995, for example, the VRS ambushed a column of people trying to escape from Potočari. The ICTY has found that, 'During the night of 12 to 13 July, there was an exchange of fire between the Bosnian Serb Forces and members of the column. In addition, some people in the column committed suicide using hand-grenades' (Prosecutor v. Popović et al. 2010: §381).

16 Rohde notes that, 'Why Naser Orić was not in Srebrenica has become a bitter bone of contention. Naser insists the Bosnian government barred him from returning to the enclave. The Bosnian government insists that they ordered Naser to return, but he refused' (2012: 353).

17 In April 2013, the President of Serbia, Tomislav Nikolić, issued a formal apology and 'asked for forgiveness for Serbia for the crime committed in Srebrenica' (BBC 2013b). He did not, however, use the term genocide.

not only the meta narrative but also the very legitimacy of RS, thereby strengthening the hand of those calling for the latter's dissolution.

During the author's fieldwork in BiH, it emerged that two additional factors are essential for explicating the persistence of Bosnian Serb denial. Firstly, specifically in Srebrenica and Bratunac, interviewees maintained that they themselves were victims and hence could never accept that genocide occurred. It seemed that denial was thus a device for drawing attention to crimes committed against Serbs – crimes which they accused the ICTY of purposefully overlooking. Secondly, there was a common belief among interviewees in general (and not just those in Srebrenica and Bratunac) that if genocide was committed in Srebrenica, this would mean that Serbs are collectively guilty for this crime. An interviewee in Brčko District, for example, underlined that Serbs suffered genocide during WWII and thus proceeded to ask how it is possible that they are now a genocidal people.[18] Similarly emphasizing the theme of Serb victimhood, an internally displaced person (IDP) in Prijedor maintained that victims cannot be guilty of genocide.[19]

In addition to the above, the very use of the term 'genocide' has encouraged the persistence of Bosnian Serb denial vis-à-vis Srebrenica. This is not to suggest that the ICTY erred in finding that genocide occurred in Srebrenica. The point, rather, is that precisely because genocide is such a powerful and emotive term that 'evokes greater condemnation in the pantheon of evil than do crimes against humanity or war crimes' (Drumbl 2004: 440), it arguably invites denial and revisionism. Of course, we will never actually know whether the denial that continues to surround Srebrenica would have been less pervasive and deep-rooted had the ICTY defined the crimes committed there as crimes against humanity rather than genocide. As an aside, however, what is certain is that the use of the word genocide has created problems in other ways. In particular, the term is often misused, as part of a process of 'trading in victimization' (Nettelfield 2010: 201). If, when the war began, 'a pronounced tendency to label attacks against one's own group as genocidal was evident' (Axboe Nielsen 2013: 28), this tendency remains similarly evident to this day; interviewees from all three sides insisted that their own ethnic group was a victim of genocide. While primarily inter-ethnic, moreover, this competition for victim status is not exclusively so. Interviewees in Prijedor and Kozarac, for example, maintained that Serbs committed genocide not only in eastern BiH but also in Prijedor municipality, and particularly in the various Serb-run camps that emerged. They accordingly expressed deep disappointment, and even resentment, that the ICTY has acknowledged only the occurrence, and the victims, of genocide in Srebrenica.[20] One interviewee thus suggested that perhaps

18 Author interview, Brčko District , 7 July 2009.
19 Author interview, Prijedor, 27 July 2008.
20 Milomir Stakić, the president of the Prijedor Muncipality Crisis Staff and the head of the Municipal Council for National Defence in Prijedor, was charged, *inter alia*, with committing

the Tribunal does not need to distinguish between genocide, crimes against humanity and so on, as this is very painful for victims.[21]

Turning to the aforementioned camps, during the war in BiH all sides established camps in which they detained, mistreated and killed members of other ethnic groups. As will be seen, denial regarding the purpose and function of these camps is not confined to Bosnian Serbs. It was Bosnian Serb interviewees' claims regarding the camps in Prijedor, however, which, after Srebrenica, stood out as a particularly striking example of denial and one that further challenges the claim that the truths established by the ICTY are mitigating revisionism.

Camps or collective centres?

Of the many camps set up by Bosnian Serbs, the ICTY has particularly focused on those located in the municipality of Prijedor. The most notorious of these camps was Omarska, situated in a mine complex. According to the ICTY, 'Omarska held more than 3,000 prisoners at one time, primarily men, but also had at least 36 to 38 women from the area, many of whom were prominent in local affairs. Boys as young as 15 were seen in the early days of the camp, as were some elderly people' (Prosecutor v. Stanišić and Župljanin 2013: §597). The prisoners were continually beaten, the women were regularly subjected to rape and sexual violence (Prosecutor v. Kvočka et al. 2001: §98), and some of the most brutal crimes were committed in the so-called 'white house' (Prosecutor v. Tadić 1997: §156). In delivering its judgement against Milomir Stakić, the Trial Chamber noted that, 'As early on as the first evening, the detainees were beaten, with fists, rifle butts and wooden and metal sticks. The guards mostly hit the heart and kidneys, when they had decided to beat someone to death' (Prosecutor v. Stakić 2003: §167). Those who were forced to clean up after these beatings 'reported finding blood, teeth and skin of victims on the floor' (Prosecutor v. Tadić 1997: §166).

The Keraterm camp, inside a former ceramics factory, was located two kilometres outside of Prijedor and commenced operating in May 1992. Approximately 4,000 people were held in the camp, primarily Bosnian Muslim and Bosnian Croat men (Prosecutor v. Stanišić and Župljanin 2013: §582). As in Omarska, the conditions were terrible (Prosecutor v. Kvočka et al. 2001: §113), and the prisoners were regularly beaten and abused (Prosecutor v. Banović 2003: §27).

---

genocide in Prijedor. The Trial Chamber, however, found that notwithstanding the scale of the atrocities in Prijedor, it had 'not been provided with the necessary insight into the state of mind of alleged perpetrators acting on a higher level in the political structure than Dr. Stakić to enable it to draw the inference that those perpetrators had the specific genocidal intent' (Prosecutor v. Stakić 2003: §547). Accordingly, it concluded that Stakić did not possess the requisite genocidal *mens rea* (Prosecutor v. Stakić 2003: §547, 554).

21 Author interview, Prjedor, 1 April 2013. On this point, it is important to note that the Appeals Chamber has reinstated the genocide charge against Radovan Karadžić (Prosecutor v. Karadžić 2013: §38).

One of the worst atrocities committed in the camp occurred in Room Three in late July 1992: 'The dead and wounded, approximately 160 to 200 men, were taken away in a truck. None of those whose bodies were removed that morning were ever seen again' (Prosecutor v. Sikirica, Došen and Kolundžija 2001: §103).

The third camp, in which several thousand people were detained, was located in a school building in the village of Trnopolje, near Kozarac. The ICTY has found that although the abuses committed in Trnopolje were not on the same scale as those inflicted on victims in Omarksa, it too was 'a notoriously brutal camp' (Prosecutor v. Kvočka et al. 2001: §115). For example, 'The soldiers used baseball bats, iron bars, rifle butts and their hands and feet or whatever they had at their disposal to beat the detainees. Individuals who were taken out for questioning would often return bruised or injured' (Prosecutor v. Stakić 2003: §242). Often, however, the latter would not return at all (Prosecutor v. Stanišić and Župljanin 2013: §628). As in the other camps, moreover, acts of rape regularly occurred (Prosecutor v. Stanišić and Župljanin 2013: §29).

The first case at the ICTY which dealt, *inter alia*, with crimes committed in the camps, and specifically Omarksa, was the trial of Duško Tadić, the president of the local board of the Serb Democratic Party in Kozarac. On 14 July 1997, Tadić was convicted of crimes against humanity, violations of the laws or customs of war and grave breaches of the Geneva Conventions and sentenced to 20 years' imprisonment (Prosecutor v. Tadić 1997). His crimes included severely beating a number of prisoners in the Omarska camp and the 'white house'. In the wake of the judgement, however, the presiding judge in the trial, Gabrielle Kirk McDonald, was 'devastated' to learn that Serbs in and around Prijedor continued to deny the crimes committed in this area (XY Films 2004).[22] Since the Tadić verdict, a number of other defendants – including Miroslav Kvočka, Mlađo Radić, Zoran Žigić, Predrag Banović and Milomir Stakic[23] – have been convicted of

22 Kirk McDonald accordingly came to realize that, '…there was a need – a necessity, really – for the Tribunal to do more: to actually communicate with the people of the former Yugoslavia…' (2004: 569). The Tadić trial was thus a critical catalyst for the creation of the Tribunal's outreach programme.

23 Miroslav Kvočka was a policeman who participated in the operation of the Omarska camp. On 2 November 2001, he was sentenced to seven years' imprisonment for crimes against humanity and violations of the laws or customs of war. Mlađo Radić, one of Kvočka's co-defendants, was also a policeman and a shift leader in the camp. On 2 November 2001, he received a sentence of 20 years' imprisonment for crimes against humanity and violations of the laws or customs of war (Prosecutor v. Kvočka et al. 2001). Zoran Žigić, another co-defendant, briefly worked as a guard at the Keraterm camp, and regularly entered the Omarska and Trnopolje camps with the specific purpose of beating, torturing and/or killing prisoners. He was sentenced to 25 years' imprisonment for crimes against humanity and violations of the laws or customs of war (Prosecutor v. Kvočka et al. 2001). Predrag Banović, a guard at the Keraterm camp who pleaded guilty to persecutions, was sentenced to eight years' imprisonment on 28 October 2003 for crimes against humanity (Prosecutor v. Banović 2003). Milomir Stakić (see note 20) was ultimately sentenced, on 22 March

crimes committed in the camps. Nevertheless, denial remains prevalent (Subašić and Ćurak 2014: 145). In accordance with interpretative denial, whereby 'it is not the raw facts (something happened) that are being denied, but they are given a different meaning from what seems obvious to others' (Cohen 2001: 7), interviewees typically maintained that there were no camps in Prijedor municipality. Instead, there were only collective/detention centres in which Bosnian Muslims (and some Bosnian Croats) were temporarily held. Interviewees further maintained, moreover, that these centres kept people safe, by protecting them from rogue elements and angry Serbs seeking revenge.[24]

Hodžić has described how during the summer of 2010, one of his friends, a lawyer, travelled to Omarska to visit the former camp, now owned by the global steel producer *ArcelorMittal*. The friend sought directions to Omarska, but 'Not one of the people he asked acknowledged the existence of the camp, claiming that they had no clue about it' (Hodžić 2011: 116). This author had a similar experience when seeking directions to the Keraterm camp in July 2008 (Clark 2011: 74–75). Every person asked immediately wanted to know the author's reasons for visiting Keraterm and always insisted that there was nothing to see there. Upon reaching Keraterm, which is now a garage and warehouse, it was necessary to respond to similar questions from a security guard. This man did acknowledge that Keraterm was a camp, but he also maintained that it had been the subject of lies and propaganda. He was particularly keen to stress that everyone had suffered in Prijedor – after all it was a civil war[25] – and offered to take the author to Orlovača, a place where Serbs had suffered and died. Orlovača is halfway between Keraterm and Prijedor, and in a small courtyard in the town there is a memorial bearing the photographs and names of six Serbs. These men were not civilians, and all of them had died in combat. The Keraterm security guard, however, appeared to make no distinction between these battle-related deaths and the killings that occurred in the camp.

When pressed on the issue of the camps, interviewees always emphasized crimes committed against Serbs during WWII, notably the cruelty and brutality that occurred in the Jasenovac camp,[26] and/or insisted that it was Bosnian Muslims

2006, to 40 years' imprisonment for crimes against humanity and violations of the laws or customs of war, including the murder of approximately 120 men in the Keraterm camp in August 1992 (Prosecutor v. Stakić 2006).

24 This claim is not entirely false with respect to the Trnopolje camp. Ed Vulliamy, the first print journalist to enter the camps in Prijedor municipality, has described Trnopolje as 'a perverse haven' (1994: 114); '...some people have come voluntarily to Trnopolje, simply to avoid the rampaging militias plundering their streets and villages' (1994: 105).

25 Highlighting the problem of competing truths, Bosnian Serb interviewees in Prijedor consistently maintained that a civil war began in Prijedor in 1992. Bosnian Muslim interviewees, in contrast, unanimously insisted that they were victims of Serb aggression.

26 Established by the Ustaše, Jasenovac was in operation from 1941 until 1945. In addition to large numbers of Serbs, Jews and Roma were also interned in the camp. Heinous crimes

who started the war in Prijedor – an argument that critically overlooks the Serb takeover of the municipality at the end April 1992. Although a small number of interviewees did concede that Keraterm and Omarska were camps, they significantly downplayed the brutality that the victims were exposed to. Often blaming a few 'idiots' for the crimes that occurred, interviewees underlined that war is an ugly thing and stressed that many Serbs were also held in camps during the war, including those in Prijedor municipality.[27] They did not accept, however, that Trnopolje was a camp. For them, the latter was simply a place that Bosnian Muslims passed through before being transported to ABiH-controlled territory. Those interviewees who had spent time in the Trnopolje camp, however, described how detainees were ill-treated and beaten on a daily basis, and one interviewee revealed that he still suffers consequences as a result of his experiences in Trnopolje.[28]

Serb denial regarding the camps also assumes a more corporeal form. In Trnopolje, there is nothing to commemorate and remember the 180 souls who died in the camp. Instead, in the centre of the village, there is large, eagle-shaped monument dedicated to fallen Bosnian Serb combatants. The lack of any memorial is similarly striking in Omarska. Bosniak survivors of the camp have been continually thwarted in their efforts to turn the infamous 'white house' into a memorial centre, and their negotiations with *ArcelorMittal* (formerly *Mittal Steel*) came to an abrupt end when the local Bosnian Serb authorities became aware of them.[29] In 2003, women from the Prijedor-based NGO *Izvor* finally succeeded in establishing a simple memorial to the victims of Keraterm. Although this was the first time in RS that a place of slaughter of non-Serbs was marked,[30] the fact that the memorial is very small and located inside the former Keraterm camp, under a tree, means that it cannot be seen from the main road or by any passers-by. Its inconspicuousness stands in complete contrast to many Serb memorials (see Subašić and Ćurak 2014: 138), including the aforementioned memorial in Trnopolje and the large, imposing cross located close to the municipality building in the centre of Prijedor.

---

occurred at Jasenovac and 'Killing was unimaginably cruel there' (Stewart 2007: 139). However, the exact number of people killed in the camp is disputed, with estimates ranging from 100,000 to 700,000. According to Thompson, 'The true figure will never be known; data is too scanty' (1992: 267).

27 The ICTY has noted apropos of Keraterm that in addition to the mostly Bosnian Muslim and Bosnian Croat men held in the camp, 'There were also a couple of Albanians, and a Bosnian Serb accused of not being a loyal Serb' (Prosecutor v. Stanišić and Župljanin 2013: §582). The Tribunal has similarly remarked vis-à-vis Trnopolje that, 'There were several thousand people detained in the camp, the vast majority of whom were Muslim and Croat, although there were some Serbs' (Prosecutor v. Stanišić and Župljanin 2013: §622); and in Omarska, 'The few Bosnian Serbs detained were reportedly there because they were suspected of having collaborated with the Muslims' (Prosecutor v. Kvočka et al. 2001: §21).

28 Author interview, Prijedor, 1 April 2013.

29 Since then, *ArcelorMittal* has started to deny victims access to the former camp, allegedly for safety reasons (Hodžić 2012).

30 Author interview, Prijedor, 26 July 2008.

Figure 4.3 Serb memorial in Prijedor.

In BiH, denial is a critical source of inter-ethnic mistrust and resentment, and hence a major hindrance to reconciliation. Highlighting this point, the president of the Mothers of Srebrenica and Žepa, Munira Subašić, has underlined that, 'It is deeply saddening to see that myths are still used to deny the atrocities that took place in Bosnia and Herzegovina...This hinders our ability to achieve progress and reconciliation' (2011: 135–136). In a similar vein, Bosnian Muslim interviewees throughout BiH repeatedly stressed that there can be no reconciliation until Bosnian Serbs face and accept the truth. Some interviewees, moreover, maintained that the ICTY could and should have done more to tackle Serb denial. A camp survivor in Prijedor, for example, opined that when defendants have pleaded guilty, the Tribunal should have published their admissions of guilt in the local media, reprinted them in the form of leaflets or broadcast them over the radio.[31] Another interviewee, also in Prijedor, suggested that the Tribunal could have been more effective in combatting Serb denial if it had recruited and utilized the skills of BiH's young people to assist with its outreach work.[32] As discussed with respect to Srebrenica, however, the reasons for the persistence of denial are more fundamental. Not only is denial rational – it is a powerful defence mechanism – but

31 Author interview, Prijedor, 1 April 2013.
32 Author interview, Prijedor, 2 April 2013.

it cannot be effectively tackled by a court which, as seen in the previous chapter, is widely viewed among Bosnian Serbs as biased, political and anti-Serb. As Fletcher and Weinstein underline, tribunals like the ICTY 'must be seen as legitimate by those on whose behalf they operate in order for their work to be accepted within affected societies' (2004: 30).

Bosnian Muslim truths and the lack of space for Serb victims

While expressions of denial and revisionism were most blatant and pronounced among Bosnian Serb interviewees, it is not constructive to focus only on Serb denial or to place the responsibility of dealing with the past solely on Serbs. All sides share this responsibility. The fact that more crimes were perpetrated during the Bosnian war against Bosnian Muslims, for example, does not detract from the reality that members of all three groups committed crimes. Nor does it mean that crimes against Bosnian Serbs and Bosnian Croats can be overlooked or viewed as less important. Bosniaks, however, were often unwilling to discuss or acknowledge crimes against Bosnian Serbs.

When asked about the ABiH's attack on the village of Bjelovac in December 1992, for example, which was covered in the previous chapter, Bosniak interviewees in Bratunac insisted on speaking about what had happened in this area *prior* to the attack. Before discussing Bjelovac, one interviewee underscored, it was necessary to talk about the crimes committed against Bosnian Muslims in Bratunac from April 1992 onwards; and to note that by the time that the ABiH attacked Bjelovac, there were no Bosniaks remaining in Bratunac as all of them had been expelled.[33] Certainly, in April and May 1992, Bratunac was the bloodiest town in BiH. During this period, 603 Bosnian Muslim civilians were killed in Bratunac (Pargan 2012: 5), and more than 800 people were interned in the Vuk Karadžić primary school, which had been turned into a camp. Hence, although interviewees did not deny the attack on Bjelovac, for them it paled into significance when compared to the brutality of the crimes committed in Bratunac. Moreover, while they did not deny that Serbs were killed in Bjelovac, they repeatedly underlined that it was necessary to make a distinction between military and civilian casualties – and always accused Serbs of deliberately conflating the two. Throughout BiH, Bosnian Muslim interviewees fully conceded that Serb soldiers were killed during the war, but they were far less willing to acknowledge civilian deaths. Interviewees in Bratunac, Potočari and Srebrenica particularly resisted the idea that Serb civilians were killed in these areas, and the verdict of the ICTY Appeals Chamber against Naser Orić has not helped in this regard. Orić's ultimate acquittal, in short, has been wrongly interpreted on the ground as confirming

33 Author interview, Bratunac, 28 March 2013.

that there were no crimes committed against Serb civilians. Highlighting this, a Bosniak returnee in Srebrenica referred to the verdict as proof that Bosnian Muslims were simply defending themselves.[34]

When interviewees did accept that crimes were committed on all sides, they always stressed that these crimes could not be compared. For them, the critical difference was that only Serb crimes were highly organized, planned and premeditated. To assert that Serb crimes were uniquely heinous, however, does a grave injustice to Serb victims. In October 1992, for example, the UN established a Commission of Experts to investigate alleged human rights allegations in BiH, including rape; it is widely estimated that approximately 20,000 Bosnian Muslim women (and some men) were raped during the Bosnian war (Bassiouni and McCormick 1996: 6). The Commission – headed by Professor M. Cherif Bassiouni – also examined allegations of crimes and acts of rape against Bosnian Serb women. While acknowledging the seriousness of these crimes, it underlined that, 'there was no similar indication of a policy of sexual violence by the Bosnian and Croatian governments' (Bassiouni and McCormick 1996: 22). Regardless of whether rape is committed as part of a systematic policy or not, it has profound and devastating psychological (and sometimes also physical) consequences. Hence, to create a hierarchy of victims is both dangerous and necessarily inhibits reconciliation. In short, there will never be a cross-ethnic consensus on any version of truth which elevates and privileges the suffering and victimhood of only one ethnic group.

Rapes were most frequently committed in camps; and if Bosnian Serb interviewees engaged in denial regarding the aforementioned camps in Prijedor municipality, Bosnian Muslim interviewees evinced little readiness to speak about camps such as Čelebići near Konjic. The Čelebići camp was established by Bosnian Muslims and Bosnian Croats for the purpose of detaining Bosnian Serbs. During the trial of the camp's commander, Zdravko Mucić, and his three co-defendants, the Trial Chamber found that, '[t]hrough the frequent cruel and violent deeds committed in the prison-camp, aggravated by the random nature of these acts and the threats made by guards, the detainees were thus subjected to immense psychological pressures which may accurately be characterized as "an atmosphere of terror"' (Prosecutor v. Mucić et al. 1998: §1091). The Trial Chamber further described how 'the detainees in crowded conditions of detention were obliged to helplessly observe the horrific injuries and suffering caused by this mistreatment, as well as the bodies of detainees who had died from the abuse to which they were subjected' (Prosecutor v. Mucić et al. 1998: §1086). On 16 November 1998, Mucić was thus convicted of grave breaches of the Geneva Conventions and sentenced to seven years' imprisonment, which was subsequently increased to nine years (Prosecutor v. Mucić, Delić and Landžo 2001). The camp's deputy commander

---

34 Author interview, Srebrenica, 27 June 2008.

and Mucić's co-defendant, Hazim Delić, was also found guilty of grave breaches of the Geneva Conventions and sentenced to 20 years' imprisonment (reduced during a second sentencing judgement to 18 years' imprisonment, to reflect the fact that one count of wilful killing was quashed on appeal); and Esad Landžo, a guard at the camp, was sentenced to 15 years.[35]

When asked about the camp, however, Bosnian Muslim interviewees frequently maintained that they had never heard of it or knew nothing about it. Interviewees in Čelebići and Konjic, moreover, typically claimed that they were not in this area during the war and hence did not have any information about the camp. Although no interviewees engaged in explicit denial vis-à-vis the camp, their professed ignorance – whether genuine or not – clearly indicated that the facts and truths established in The Hague have failed to penetrate (see, however, Nettelfield 2010: 209). When the author highlighted some of the acts of violence which occurred in the camp, two interviewees in Konjic stressed that anyone who commits war crimes must be punished. Yet, they also underlined that Serbs had started the war and that Bosnian Muslims were just defending themselves.[36] Similarly, when the author pointed out that Serb women were raped in Čelebići, an interviewee in the village professed that he had never heard this and proceeded to claim that 50,000 Bosniak women were raped during the war.[37]

Questions about the Silos camp in Tarčin, near Sarajevo, elicited similar responses. Two Bosnian Serb interviewees in Bratunac were interned in the Silos camp during the war, one of them for four years, and described how prisoners were regularly tortured and beaten. Indeed, eight Bosnian Muslims – including Nermin Kalembar, a former guard at the camp, and Mustafa Delilović, the former president of the municipal assembly of Hadžići – are currently on trial at the State Court of BiH in connection with crimes committed in the camp. The indictment, which was confirmed on 12 January 2012, states that between May 1992 and January 1996, the eight defendants 'knowingly and willingly participated in the systemic joint criminal enterprise and by planning, ordering, committing, inciting, aiding and abetting committed the criminal offence of War Crimes against Civilians and the criminal offence of War Crimes against Prisoners of War of Serb ethnicity in the facilities such as Silos in Tarčin...' (State Court of BiH 2012). The trial began on 19 April 2012. When asked about the camp, however, Bosnian Muslim interviewees usually claimed that they had never heard of it and always underlined the brutal crimes that occurred in Serb-run camps. Although the ICTY has not prosecuted anyone in relation to Silos, the important point is that questions about this camp – and about Čelebići – evoked a strong tendency to minimize crimes against Serbs. The propensity to focus only on crimes committed

35 The fourth defendant, Zejnil Delalić – the coordinator of Bosnian Muslim and Bosnian Croat forces in the Konjic area – was acquitted.
36 Author interviews, Konjic, 22 June 2009.
37 Author interview, Čelebići, 21 June 2009.

against one's own ethnic group, moreover, exists on all three sides and highlights the persistence of 'competitive victimhood' (Noor, Brown and Prentice 2008: 484). The latter, in turn, is the driving force of the antagonistic ethnic narratives which critically restrict the impact of the Tribunal's work and the truths that it establishes.

Bosnian Croat truths and resistance to alternative truths

During the war in BiH, one of the worst crimes committed by the HVO was the massacre in Ahmići in April 1993, which the ICTY has described as 'one of the most vicious illustrations of man's inhumanity to man' (Prosecutor v. Josipović et al. 2000: §755). The Tribunal has therefore prosecuted and convicted a number of defendants in relation to both this atrocity and other HVO crimes within the wider Lašva Valley area. These defendants include Tihomir Blaškić, Drago Josipović, Dario Kordić and Miroslav Bralo.[38] Notwithstanding these trials, however, Bosnian Croats in this part of BiH remained in strong denial. An interviewee in Ahmići, for example – who had himself stood trial at the ICTY[39] – maintained that prior to the attack on the village, Bosnian Muslims had continually provoked the HVO[40] and created 'non-stop' problems, such as blocking roads. For him, therefore, the attack on Ahmići was militarily justified; Croats had

---

38 The trial of Tihomir Blaškić, who at the time of the attack on Ahmići was the commander of the HVO in the Central Bosnian Operative Zone, was discussed in the previous chapter. Drago Josipović was a member of HVO forces in the village of Šantići. On 14 January 2000, he was sentenced to 15 years' imprisonment for crimes against humanity. A year later, the Appeals Chamber reduced his sentence to 12 years, and on 30 January 2006 he was granted early release (Prosecutor v. Josipović et al. 2000, 2001). He returned to his home in Ahmići and continues to live in the village today. Dario Kordić was the president of the HDZ of BiH and the vice-president of the HZHB. Convicted of crimes against humanity, violations of the laws or customs of war and grave breaches of the Geneva Conventions, he was sentenced to 25 years' imprisonment on 26 February 2001 (Prosecutor v. Kordić and Čerkez 2001). Miroslav Bralo was a member of the 'Jokers', the anti-terrorist platoon of the 4th Military Police Battalion of the HVO. He pleaded guilty to various war crimes in and around Ahmići and the nearby village of Nadioci, also attacked on 16 April 1993. In December 2005, he was sentenced to 20 years' imprisonment for crimes against humanity, violations of the laws or customs of war and grave breaches of the Geneva Conventions (Prosecutor v. Bralo 2005).

39 The Trial Chamber had convicted the interviewee of crimes against humanity and violations of the laws or customs of war. A year later, however, the Appeals Chamber quashed his conviction.

40 On 15 April 1993, for example, the HVO Zenica Brigade commander, Živko Totić, was ambushed and abducted on his way to work. In the trial of Josipović et al. however, the Trial Chamber underlined that, '...the intentional killing of children...cannot be reconciled with the view [put forward by the Defence] that this [the attack on Ahmići] was an action demanded by strategic or tactical necessities' (2000: §762).

to defend themselves. He further claimed that everyone killed in the attack was armed, which fundamentally contradicts the facts established by the ICTY (Prosecutor v. Josipović et al. 2000: §749).[41] Another interviewee in the village, whose husband had fought in the HVO, maintained that what happened in Ahmići was simply an act of revenge for the Bosniak attack on the Croat village of Dušina, discussed in the previous chapter.[42]

Although some interviewees described the attack on Ahmići as a 'mistake' or a 'disgrace', they always distanced the HVO from the crime, instead blaming paramilitaries or lone individuals. An ex-combatant in the town of Vitez, for example, repeatedly argued that two drunken individuals were responsible for the crimes carried out in Ahmići. What happened on that day in April 1993, he claimed, began as an armed combat between two armies, but then two heavily inebriated men got out of control and committed war crimes.[43] Denial regarding the attack, moreover, was not confined to interviewees in Ahmići and Vitez. A Croat family in the village of Milići, also in central BiH, maintained that the HVO did not do anything wrong in Ahmići and stressed that any war crimes committed there were the work of paramilitaries;[44] and in the town of Prozor in northern Hercegovina, an ex-combatant's only response to being told that the author had previously visited Ahmići was to issue an expletive and a loud grunt of disapproval.[45] Despite the ICTY's judgements with respect to Ahmići and the Lašva Valley, moreover, it was clear that men such as Blaškić and Kordić are very much regarded as heroes – not war criminals. All of these examples strongly support the argument that, 'the ICTY has failed as a pedagogical tool in the same territories where it was intended to promote reconciliation' (Saxon 2005: 566).

Upon hearing that Croatian President Ivo Josipović would visit Ahmići in April 2010, Blaškić apologized for his role in the Bosnian war and declared: 'I was very happy to hear that Josipović will go to Ahmići ...To go there, to the place where the actual crimes were committed, and to pay respect to the innocent victims, is the only way' (Balkan Insight 2010b). While this apology was very significant, unfortunately there is very little respect among Bosnian Croats in Ahmići for the 116 Bosnian Muslims who perished in the village that day in April 1993. In October 2001, for example, local Croats celebrated the acquittals (which crucially were never explained to Bosnian Muslims in the village)[46] of Mirjan, Zoran

41 Author interview, Ahmići, 9 July 2008.
42 Author interview, Ahmići, 12 July 2008.
43 Author interview, Vitez, 9 July 2008.
44 Author interview, Milići, 12 August 2008.
45 Author interview, Prozor, 24 June 2009.
46 The most likely explanation is that the Tribunal's outreach office is insufficiently staffed and under-funded (Clark 2009: 105). Nevertheless, it is deeply regrettable that Ahmići was not included in the Tribunal's 'Bridging the Gap' series referred to in the previous chapter.

and Vlatko Kupreškić and threw a party to welcome the men home.[47] Far from being a quiet affair, 'revelers frequently stepped outside and discharged their firearms into the night air' (Stover 2007: 106). Furthermore, every year on the anniversary of the massacre, while Bosniaks remember their dead in a memorial service held at the mosque, their neighbours gather at the local Catholic church in order to commemorate fallen Croats. Standing tall in the grounds of the church is a large white cross in memory of the '*653 Hrvata*' (653 Croats) killed during the '*316 dana muslimanske opsade Viteza*' (316 days of the Muslim siege of Vitez).

What has undoubtedly facilitated denial is the fact that the details of ICTY judgements are not sufficiently communicated to local communities on the ground, and a recent case highlights this point. On 29 May 2013, the ICTY convicted six high-ranking Bosnian Croats of crimes against humanity, violations of the laws or customs of war and grave breaches of the Geneva Conventions, committed as part of a JCE. According to the Trial Chamber, the aim of this JCE – which lasted from 18 November 1991 until April 1994 and also included the former President of Croatia, Franjo Tuđman, and his Minister of Defence, Gojko Šušak – was 'to remove the Muslim population of Herceg-Bosna' (Prosecutor v. Prlić et al. 2013: 8). Jadranko Prlić, the former President of the HZHB and the Prime Minister of the HRHB, was sentenced to 25 years' imprisonment. Bruno Stojić, the head of the Department of Defence of the HVO, Milivoj Petković, the chief of the HVO Main Staff, and Slobodan Praljak, the senior representative of the Croatian Ministry of Defence to the Herceg-Bosna/ HVO government and armed forces, all received sentences of 20 years. Valentin Ćorić, the Minister of Interior in the HRHB, was sentenced to a prison term of 16 years; and Berislav Pušić, who held a command position within the military police, was sentenced to ten years' imprisonment.

47 On 14 January 2000, the ICTY convicted brothers Mirjan and Zoran Kupreškić and their cousin Vlatko – all of whom were members of the HVO – of crimes against humanity in Ahmići. They were sentenced to prison terms of eight, ten and six years respectively. On 23 October 2001, however, the Appeals Chamber acquitted all three defendants and ordered their immediate release. In the case of Mirjan and Zoran Kupreškić, the Appeals Chamber found that there were a number of defects in the amended indictment against the brothers which had rendered their trial unfair (Prosecutor v. Josipović et al. 2001: §119, 124). It further found, *inter alia*, that the Trial Chamber failed 'to consider material discrepancies' in Witness H's statements (Prosecutor v. Josipović et al. 2001: §162) and 'did not direct itself to Witness SA's statements, which raised the distinct possibility that Witness H's identification of her neighbours' in the attack had been a gradual development in the months following the April 1993 atrocity' (Prosecutor v. Josipović et al. 2001: §223). Regarding Vlatko Kupreškić, the Appeals Chamber found that the evidence against him was weak. His conviction was critically linked to the Trial Chamber's findings that he was a police operations officer. According to the Appeals Chamber, however, all of the evidence 'overwhelmingly' suggested that, 'any [police] duties undertaken by Vlatko Kupreškić ceased in February 1993' (Prosecutor v. Josipović et al. 2001: §274).

An important part of the Trial Chamber's lengthy judgement against Prlić and his co-defendants discusses the camps/detention centres which the HVO established in Hercegovina, including Dretelj, Gabela and the Heliodrom. According to the judgement summary,[48]

> Detainees in all the detention centres were undernourished and the sanitary conditions were appalling. Some did not even have access to toilets and had to relieve themselves in makeshift containers. Most of the time they had no access to medical care adequate enough to treat the illnesses resulting from the unsanitary conditions and the injuries resulting from ill-treatment that they suffered at the hands of the HVO. Some of them suffered consequences for the rest of their lives.
>
> (Prosecutor v. Prlić et al. 2013: 5)

The Trial Chamber further found that, 'detainees at the Heliodrom, the Vojno detention centre and the Ljubiški Prison were forced to carry out dangerous work at the front line, during which some of them were wounded or killed in the exchange of fire between the ABiH and the HVO' (Prosecutor v. Prlić et al. 2013: 6); while 'detainees at the Heliodrom were wounded or killed when they were used as human shields on the front line' (Prosecutor v. Prlić et al. 2013: 6).

During the author's fieldwork in BiH in 2008, Bosnian Croat interviewees in Hercegovina typically responded to questions about these detention centres by claiming that they did not know anything about them. More frequently, they simply shifted the focus to crimes against Croats. Moreover, they always blamed lone individuals for any crimes committed by members of their own ethnic group. When the author returned to Hercegovina in August 2013, Bosnian Croat interviewees continued to express the same arguments and to strongly defend the HVO. The Prlić et al. judgement fundamentally challenges the Croat meta narrative. Of particular significance is the Trial Chamber's finding that the majority of crimes committed by HVO forces against Bosnian Muslims between January 1993 and April 1994 followed 'a clear pattern of conduct' and 'were not the random acts of a few unruly soldiers', but were instead 'the result of a plan drawn up by members of the JCE whose goal was to permanently remove the Muslim population from Herceg-Bosna' (Prosecutor v. Prlić et al. 2013: 7). The lack of political will to disseminate such inconvenient truths, however, combined with the inadequacies of the Tribunal's outreach work, means that people on the ground are given only fragments of very minimal information about the ICTY's verdicts – and hence such truths cannot penetrate the group's own narrative. Interviewees in Grude and Široki Brijeg, for example, knew almost nothing about

---

48 The full judgement, which consists of over 2,000 pages divided into six volumes, is only available in French.

the Prlić et al. judgement, other than the fact that six Bosnian Croats had been convicted. Despite this, they strongly criticized the verdict, regarding it as further evidence of the ICTY's bias and continued failure to deliver justice.

What is more encouraging is the way in which Croatian President Ivo Josipović responded to the judgement. Rather than condemning the verdict, Josipović declined to make any comment on it and instead stressed the importance of focusing on the future. He particularly emphasized the victims, declaring: 'When I listen to such a ruling, the first thing that comes to mind is the victims. My heart goes out to the victims and their families, just like in all other cases of horrible crimes that took place in the region of the former Yugoslavia' (cited in Radio.net 2013). If politicians in BiH were to respond to the ICTY's judgements in a similarly balanced way, this would undoubtedly contribute to the minimization of denial.

To conclude, this chapter does not necessarily problematize the frequently-made linkage between truth and reconciliation; interviewees on all sides underscored that relations could not be repaired and trust could not be rebuilt in the absence of truth. What it complexifies is the concept of truth. In BiH, 'truth' is a quintessentially contested concept and one that continues to provoke deep ethnic divisions. As Simić remarks, 'The truth about the BH war is still being made out of competing historical narratives that cannot be agreed upon' (2011: 1407). Conducting fieldwork in the country can thus be an extremely disorientating experience, with members of each ethnic group insisting that their version of events is the correct and truthful one. In such an environment, claims that the ICTY is contributing to reconciliation by documenting the facts, and thus reducing denial, simply fail to stand up to empirical scrutiny. These claims erroneously and simplistically assume that local communities will accept and internalize the truths established in the Tribunal's courtrooms, and this is not the reality. The ICTY's work has in fact intensified what one NGO leader described as a 'war of interpretation'.[49] Indeed, the Tribunal's Prosecutor, Serge Brammertz, has himself acknowledged that, 'Of course, if you look at the different ethnic groups, if I may say, in the former Yugoslavia, we see even today persons prosecuted and convicted by the tribunal are seen as heroes in their local communities...' (UN News Centre 2011).

A critical question is whether the Tribunal could have done more to tackle the problem of denial and competing truths. Ivanišević argues that, 'In closed societies, such as those in the territory of the former Yugoslavia, prevalence of false beliefs is virtually inevitable. It is for this reason that sympathetic commentators should be less severe than they sometimes are when they critically reflect on the ICTY's contribution to reconciliation in the region' (2011a: 132). Stover, for his part, notes that while many of his interviewees (87 ICTY witnesses) insisted that

---

49 Author interview, Sarajevo, 18 June 2008.

for the purposes of reconciliation, their neighbours must accept their complicity in war crimes, 'These are, of course, matters over which the ICTY has little, if any, influence' (2007: 143). While both authors make important arguments, it is submitted that the Tribunal could have been more proactive in countering revisionism, and this again returns us to the critical issue of outreach. Had the Tribunal done more to engage with local communities, to explain its work to them and to promote its achievements,[50] it might have had more credibility on the ground – and hence been more effective in limiting denial (Leebaw 2008: 108). Unfortunately, too many of its senior officials, to cite a former member of the ICTY's outreach team, 'did not consider the impact its work had on the ground or regard the people on the ground as its primary constituents' (Hodžić 2011: 117).

Just as there is little evidence that the ICTY has contributed to reconciliation in BiH by delivering justice, there is a similar lack of evidence to suggest that it has done so by establishing the truth. Are there, however, signs of reconciliation in BiH that might be attributed to the ICTY in other, more indirect ways? To assess this, the next chapter, which completes this tripartite case study of BiH, focuses on the third measurement criterion outlined in Chapter 2 – everyday inter-ethnic relations.

50 Apropos of the Nuremberg Tribunal, for example, Bass remarks that, 'The Allies went to great lengths to make clear to Germans what the defendants at Nuremberg were accused of by broadcasting on German radio, showing documentaries, and distributing pamphlets' (2000: 303).

Chapter 5

Bosnia-Hercegovina
Part Three

Inter-Ethnic Relations

This chapter employs the Reconciliation Matrix developed in Chapter 2 to explore inter-ethnic relations in BiH. More specifically, it uses human security, deep contact, trust and mutual acceptance as critical referents for gauging whether reconciliation exists in BiH. By way of an introduction, three important preliminary points should be made. Firstly, a small number of Bosniak interviewees objected to the word reconciliation, which can be deeply controversial in post-conflict societies (Staub 2011: 305), and viewed it as inappropriate. For them, it implied reciprocity – requiring apologies and forgiveness from two sides – and was thus meaningless in a situation where, from their perspective, one side was clearly the aggressor. They thus rejected the notion of reconciliation, always underlining that they themselves did nothing wrong during the war, and maintained that they have no one with whom to reconcile. Such examples of resistance highlight the fact that while reconciliation is a key term in the international lexicon of peace-building, it may fail to resonate among local communities – and in particular victims (Enns 2013: 182). The use of such potentially contentious terms thus requires contextual sensitivity.

Secondly, and linked to the previous point, some interviewees were adamant that they can never reconcile. There was a widespread sentiment that the war had fundamentally changed everything and that inter-ethnic relations can never return to how they were prior to 1992. An interviewee who lost all of her family in the genocide in Srebrenica, for example, described her life as an unending punishment and explained that she has no interest in reconciliation.[1] A Serb taxi driver in Srebrenica, for his part, opined that while people can be good neighbours, they cannot fully reconcile.[2] While others judged that reconciliation is possible – and indeed some stressed that it is essential[3] – they

---

1 Author interview, Potočari, 24 June 2008. The interviewee repeated this point during a second interview on 26 March 2013.
2 Author interview, Srebrenica, 27 March 2013.
3 An interviewee whose mother and father were killed in the village of Ahmići in April 1993, for example, argued that no normal person wants another war and hence everybody must work for reconciliation. Author interview, Ahmići, 8 July 2008.

always emphasized that it will take a very long time, spanning at least two generations. Munira Subašić, the president of the Mothers of Srebrenica and Žepa, shares this viewpoint. According to her, 'It is apparent that there is still a strong need for social transformation in Bosnia and Herzegovina. Reconciliation is still an ongoing process that will require a lot of time, effort and patience' (2011: 135).

Thirdly, a minority of interviewees opined that the ICTY's work has had some positive effects apropos of reconciliation. Several Bosniak interviewees in Prijedor, for example, argued that during its early years, the ICTY indirectly aided reconciliation by facilitating the return of Bosnian Muslims to Prijedor municipality and giving them hope.[4] The vast majority of interviewees, however, argued that the Tribunal's work has not helped reconciliation in any way.[5] The reasons put forward by Bosniak interviewees reflected their various grievances with the ICTY discussed in Chapter 3. An interlocutor in Bratunac, for example, maintained that victims need to feel as though somebody is being held to account for their destroyed lives, and stressed that currently this is not happening as too few people have been prosecuted in the ICTY's courtrooms.[6] In the village of Trnopolje, an interviewee whose two sons remain missing angrily asserted that no court which imposes a 17-year sentence for the murder of over 200 people[7] can ever help reconciliation.[8] Many also highlighted the issue of Serb denial as a major impediment to the ICTY's work and impact. Others adjudged that reconciliation does not depend on the ICTY but rather on the country's politicians – whom interviewees widely accused of deliberately creating problems – and constitutional reform; among Bosniak interviewees, there was broad agreement that reconciliation requires a unified BiH and the abolition of RS. Bosnian Serb and Bosnian Croat interviewees were even more adamant that the ICTY cannot facilitate reconciliation, on the grounds that it is an entirely one-sided court that does not treat all victims equally.

While interviewees on all three sides overwhelmingly rejected the notion that the ICTY can contribute, or is contributing, to reconciliation in BiH, and while

---

4   By 2004, approximately 25,000 Bosniaks had returned to Prijedor (Moratti 2004). According to the 1991 census, 49,454 Bosniaks were living in the municipality (UN Commission of Experts 1994).
5   Ramulić claims that in the early years, many victims did expect the ICTY's work to have a positive effect on reconciliation (2011: 105). Based on his research in Prijedor, Hodžić similarly argues that, 'Evidently, at the time when Prijedor-related trials were held at the Tribunal, victims strongly believed that these would have a transformative effect on the relationships between the Serb and non-Serb communities in the municipality, fostering a society based on the principles of justice and reconciliation...' (2010: 120–121). The fact that this anticipated transformation did not occur has compounded popular disappointment with the ICTY.
6   Author interview, Bratunac, 23 March 2013.
7   The interviewee was referring here to the case of Darko Mrđa, discussed in Chapter 3.
8   Author interview, Trnopolje, 30 July 2008.

few were optimistic about the prospects for genuine reconciliation (as opposed to simple coexistence), it is impossible to fully assess the ICTY's impact without exploring and analyzing everyday grassroots inter-ethnic relations. Fundamentally, when these relations are measured against the four key criteria of human security, deep contact, trust and mutual acceptance, can it be argued that reconciliation has been achieved in BiH?

Human security

There have been serious security incidents in BiH since the end of the war in 1995. According to a UNHCR report published in the year 2000, for example, in certain areas – including Kula in Gacko municipality in eastern BiH – 'serious security incidents continued to take place for some time, including one on 30 November 1999, when an NGO vehicle hit a partially armed anti-tank mine where the Mine Action Centre did not have any records of mines; 4 people were injured'. The report further noted that, 'Other incidents that have occurred since September 1999 in Kula include reports of automatic gunfire, grenades launched at homes from a 60mm mortar, as well as the discovery of fresh mines in and around destroyed homes' (UNHCR 2000: 7).

Some mines have been newly laid with the express purpose of impeding the returns process, and indeed returnees have often been a significant focus of incidents involving threats to or attacks on human security. According to data from the UN Mission in BiH, for example, between 1 March 2000 and 18 May 2000 'there were approximately 73 reported, but not necessarily confirmed, security incidents in the RS directed against minority returnees or between minority returnees and Serbs'. These incidents included verbal harassment, shootings and explosions (UNHCR 2000: 7). A year later, in May 2001, NATO forces commenced the process of returning Bosnian Muslims to their pre-war homes in Damdžići, a village in the municipality of Vlasenica in eastern BiH. On 14 May 2001, however, a returnee sustained injuries during an attack; and on 11 July 2001, a teenager (female) was shot and fatally wounded (Immigration and Refugee Board of Canada 2003). Recounting further examples of serious security incidents, an interviewee from the UNHCR in eastern BiH disclosed that in October 2007, a hand grenade was thrown through the window of a Bosniak returnee's home in the village of Zubovići in the municipality of Foča. She further recounted the story of a Bosniak woman who, since returning to her home in Gornji Polje in the municipality of Foča, had been made to feel unwelcome and repeatedly called a 'Turk'.[9] Ethnically-motivated harassment, moreover, has not been solely confined to rural areas. According to an Early Warning Report in 2007, 'In towns, there has been a rise in reported harassment on ethnic grounds,

9 Author interview, Goražde, 13 June 2008.

up from 8.1% to 9.2% since last quarter. There was a fall in rural areas, however, from 6.2% to 5.3%' (Duraković et al. 2007: 56).

Today, inter-ethnic incidents continue to occur and to pose an obstacle to the returns process. For example, 'During the year [2010], observers continued to note a trend of attacks directed against symbols of minority groups,[10] rather than attacks against individuals. This hostility continued to affect returns' (US Department of State 2011: 19). The frequency of security incidents, however, has declined. According to Early Warning research by Prism Research in Sarajevo in November 2010, respondents were asked whether they or anyone in their family had been subjected to ethnically-motivated verbal harassment or physical attack during the last year. An overwhelming majority of respondents (95.8 per cent of Bosniaks, 97.8 per cent of Bosnian Serbs and 89.6 per cent of Bosnian Croats) answered 'no – never' (Duraković et al. 2010: 134).

During the author's fieldwork in BiH between 2008 and 2013, the majority of interviewees similarly claimed that they had not experienced any problems on account of their ethnic identity, and always maintained that their community was peaceful. An interviewee who returned to Potočari in 2003, for example, explained that while she does not spend time with her Serb neighbours, she has 'normal' relations with them – in the sense that she greets them and communicates with them – and has never encountered any hostility or trouble.[11] A small number of interviewees disclosed that when they first returned to their pre-war homes, some incidents did occur. An interviewee who lost both her husband and brother in the war, for example, recounted that when she returned to Potočari, Serb neighbours threw rubbish in her front garden;[12] a camp survivor in Prijedor described how when she returned to her apartment, someone daubed the name of the camp on her front door;[13] and an elderly interviewee recalled that when she and her husband returned to the town of Foča in 2003, some local Serbs verbally abused her spouse by shouting '*balija*' – a derogatory and offensive term used to refer to descendants of the Ottoman Empire.[14] One interviewee, however, had faced very serious, and recent, threats. He alleged that there had been two attempts on his life which were linked – he believed – to the fact that he had testified as a prosecution witness in a war crimes trial at the State Court of BiH in Sarajevo.[15]

---

10 The US Department of State notes, for example, that, 'On April 4 [2010], two persons spray-painted swastikas, crosses and Ustasha insignias on 13 tombstones at a Muslim cemetery in Zepče. The local Muslim community and municipal leaders strongly condemned the act' (2011: 31).
11 Author interview, Potočari, 25 March 2013.
12 Author interview, Potočari, 24 March 2013.
13 Author interview, Prijedor, 30 March 2013.
14 Author interview, Foča, 5 June 2008.
15 Author interview, Bratunac, 23 March 2013.

Aside from this particular individual, no interviewees claimed to feel physically unsafe within their communities. Widows in Srebrenica often expressed the sentiment that the worst had already happened – they had lost their loved-ones and, in some cases, their entire families – and hence they had no reason to feel afraid; they had nothing else to lose. Some, moreover, felt safer in their own homes, surrounded by the photographs and memories of those whose lives were prematurely ended in July 1995. Without exception, however, all interviewees strongly emphasized an absence of economic security. From Međeđa (the largest returnee settlement in Višegrad municipality) to Stolac, and from Brčko to Sarajevo, interviewees highlighted a lack of jobs and dearth of economic opportunities as major social issues (see also Oberschall 2007: 228; Stover 2007: 97). At the end of March 2013, for example, the unemployment rate in BiH stood at 46.1 per cent (Intellinews.com 2013), up from 44 per cent the previous year (Alić 2013). Furthermore, 75 per cent of young people in BiH do not have a job and 50 per cent would leave the country if given the opportunity (BBC 2013b). While the World Bank/Department for Economic Planning has estimated that the percentage of BiH's population living below the poverty line decreased from 18 per cent in 2004 to 14 per cent in 2007, it also found that, 'a significant percentage of the population has expenditure levels that are just slightly above the poverty threshold' (Ministry of Finance and Treasury of BiH and UN Country Team 2010: 9–10). Moreover, the Ministry of Finance and Treasury of BiH and the UN Country Team in BiH have estimated, based on the 2007 Household Budget Survey, that approximately 20 per cent of the population are 'susceptible to economic changes that could lead to a decrease of their income, even by rather small amounts, and move them below the poverty line' (2010: 10).

A significant number of interviewees were internally displaced within BiH, and all of them underscored the economic situation and the shortage of jobs – rather than security concerns – as the primary reason why they had not returned to their pre-war homes. In many of BiH's towns, factories that once employed a sizeable workforce have now been privatized and no longer function (Donnais 2002), and hence there is often little incentive for IDPs (and refugees) to return to their homes, other than for sentimental and emotional reasons. Although Annex 7 of the DPA guarantees the right of return,[16] the Accords critically lack any plan for economic reconstruction (Oberschall 2007: 121). A crucial lesson to be learnt from the Bosnian case, thus, is that, '...greater attention needs to be paid to the economic and social well-being of post-war communities' (Stover and Weinstein 2004: 325). The popular protests that have erupted in Bosnian cities such as Tuzla and Sarajevo in 2014 – in response to poverty and corruption – highlight this point.

If lack of economic security negatively impacts upon the returns process, it also has implications for reconciliation. Firstly, it potentially limits the scope for

16 Annex 7 of the DPA states that, 'All refugees and displaced persons have the right freely to return to their homes of origin' (Office of the High Representative 1995).

contact, a critical prerequisite for reconciliation (Gibson and Claassen 2010; Hewstone et al. 2006, Maoz 2011). If people are not returning to former mixed communities, and if they are without jobs, important opportunities for inter-ethnic contact are thereby lost. Secondly, economic concerns are helping to marginalize the issue of reconciliation. If people do not have economic security, how can they be expected to think or even care about reconciliation? The latter cannot be a priority when people are worrying about where their next meal is coming from. Hence, while the Tribunal was established, *inter alia*, to deliver justice to victims, it is somewhat paradoxical that,

> The ICTY is not...the primary concern of victim associations. The foremost concerns of the representatives and members of these associations are widespread in post-war Bosnia: concerns about the material difficulties of everyday life, the meagreness of pensions and salaries, the dire straits of DPs [displaced persons] expelled from their war-time lodgings,[17] the difficulties of return.
>
> (Delpla 2007: 224)

The unfavourable economic situation can, in turn, help to explain why so few people follow the ICTY's work in detail, and hence why significant knowledge gaps remain. Consistently prioritizing economic concerns, interviewees were overwhelmingly preoccupied with the daily struggle to make ends meet, which is unsurprising given that there is little financial support available to war victims. An interviewee in Srebrenica, for example, who lost her husband and two sons during the war, was receiving a monthly pension of just 300 Bosnian Marks (KM) (approximately £127) and demanded to know how much longer people like her would have to suffer.[18] Another interviewee was living with her family in a collective centre in Tuzla, owing to the fact that her house in the municipality of Vlasenica remains a charred ruin. As a rape victim, she was in receipt of a monthly sum of 500 KM (approximately £212), but this was insufficient to support her family of five.[19]

Torture victims are often particularly vulnerable to economic insecurity. In contrast to other categories of war victims in BiH, torture victims do not have a legal status – and hence they have no rights. In short, 'It is estimated that currently, there are about 200,000 persons who were torture victims and who are still waiting for the state to recognise their rights and enable them a dignified life' (Zečević 2013: 5). The physical and psychological consequences of their mistreatment and abuse can further affect the economic status of torture victims. According to research by Kučukalić et al., for example, which focused on 197

---

17 According to the UNHCR, there are still 113,000 IDPs in BiH (2013).
18 Author interview, Srebrenica, 25 March 2013.
19 Author interview, Tuzla, 29 March 2013.

patients at the Centre for Torture Victims in Sarajevo, 71.0 per cent of these patients maintained that their time in detention (acts of torture typically occurred in camps) had detrimentally affected their economic status, and 64.0 per cent opined that it had unquestionably had a strong negative effect on their work and profession (2003: 34). As Arcel et al. explain,

> Physical symptoms arising from bodily injury, or cognitive difficulties as a result of head trauma, psychological problems such as PTSD [post-traumatic stress disorder] syndrome – i.e. generalised anxiety, re-experiencing of frightening traumatic events, avoidance behaviour, difficulties in concentration and memory, depression, irritability in interpersonal relations – may all reduce the social skills of the survivor and reduce the chances of finding employment.
>
> (2003: 65)

Of course, the symptoms of trauma are not exclusive to victims of torture. The key point, however, is that the latter's trauma will often simply feed and exacerbate the problems caused by their lack of legal status. In other words, 'Due to their poverty, torture victims are multiply deprived, particularly in the segment of employment, and with low incomes, they are doomed to poor living conditions, inadequate health care and obstacles in the lifelong learning process, culture, sport and recreation' (Bijedić et al. 2013: 52).

The absence of any state law pertaining to the status of torture survivors in BiH is a powerful testament to the fact that in its current constitutional configuration – specifically its division into two entities – the Bosnian state simply does not function. Torture victims in BiH are in a very weak position precisely because the two entities, the Federation and RS, have been unable to reach any agreement on an issue that has become heavily politicized. For example, although a draft Law on the Rights of Victims of Torture was circulated in February 2012, 'Unfortunately, the representatives of the government of Republika Srpska, despite being invited, have so far not taken part in any meeting to discuss the draft law' (TRIAL 2012: §60). Bosniak torture victims repeatedly argued that the passage of such a law would not be in the interests of RS, and hence expressed deep scepticism regarding the prospects for progress in this regard.

To sum up, although there is only limited human security in BiH, the fact that economic insecurity is the main problem today, rather than physical insecurity, might be viewed as an indicator of progress in respect of inter-ethnic relations. The very existence of widespread economic insecurity, however, is inimical to reconciliation, and it has arguably contributed to a marginalization of the ICTY. Some interviewees, moreover, maintained that the Tribunal is doing more for its own staff – by providing them with comfortable salaries and benefits – than it is for people in the former Yugoslavia. They also questioned whether the large sums of money that have been ploughed into the ICTY[20] could have been put to better use and invested in economic projects in BiH and elsewhere in the former Yugoslavia, such as the construction of new factories (see also Hayden 2006: 390).

Deep contact

In BiH, deep divisions persist in certain areas. In Gornji Vakuf-Uskoplje in central BiH, an invisible line marks the boundary between the Bosniak and Croat parts of the town. It is, moreover, a line that few people cross; Bosniak interviewees always maintained that they had no need to go to the Croat part of the town (Uskoplje), and Croat interviewees similarly saw no reason to visit the Bosniak part (Gornji Vakuf). Likewise, the city of Mostar, in Hercegovina, remains strongly divided; Bosniaks and Croats have separate hospitals, health centres, post offices, schools and so on. The town of Stolac, also in Hercegovina, is not officially divided, but Bosniaks and Croats have their own cafes and there is little significant interaction between the two communities. Even the Bosnian capital, Sarajevo, is divided; Serbs mainly live in eastern Sarajevo, which is part of RS.

The above examples, however, are the exception rather than the rule. Most parts of BiH are not divided and hence inter-ethnic contact is a regular occurrence.[21] Certainly, many interviewees claimed that they have frequent contact with members of the other ethnic group/s. Nevertheless, this contact could rarely be described as deep or 'thick'. When asked about inter-ethnic relations within their community, it was striking how interviewees initially tended to paint a very rosy picture. Yet, as each interview progressed, a more complex reality often emerged. A Bosniak interviewee in Srebrenica, for example, began by claiming that she has good relations with her Serb neighbours, describing how they came to visit her when she suffered a recent bereavement. Later, however, she emphasized that her relations with Serbs have changed. Other than greeting them in the street, she explained that she has little contact or communication with them and underlined that there are 'partition walls' between people now.[22]

Indeed, numerous interviewees echoed this latter point and commonly argued that there are few inter-ethnic friendships. A camp survivor in Bratunac recounted that while he greets local Serbs and shows them courtesy, he does not have any Serb friends and does not want any.[23] In nearby Srebrenica, an ex-combatant observed that while there are no problems between Serbs and Bosniaks in the

20 According to the ICTY's website, the Tribunal's regular budget in 2012–2013 was $250,814,000 (ICTY 2013b).
21 However, many villages in BiH have traditionally always been mono-ethnic, which necessarily limits the opportunities for contact in rural areas (Gallagher 2003: 77).
22 Author interview, Srebrenica, 25 March 2013.
23 Author interview, Bratunac, 23 March 2013.

town, relations are based simply on necessity; people must live together. Insisting that reconciliation is extremely difficult, he stressed that while he communicates with Bosniaks and politely greets them, he does not have any Bosniak friends and feels most comfortable this way.[24] In Prijedor, a Bosniak interviewee claimed that she does not have any Serb friends because Serbs still refuse to accept the truth and to deal with the facts of what happened in Prijedor during the war. While repeating that the town is peaceful and that there are no incidents or acts of violence, she also remarked that divisions are visible.[25] In Ahmići, a Bosnian Croat interviewee similarly emphasized that there are no inter-ethnic problems in the village, but also added that he has no Bosniak friends. He does not trust his Bosniak neighbours, he revealed, because they have distorted what really happened in Ahmići on 16 April 1993.[26] For his part, a Bosniak interviewee in Ahmići disclosed that when he first returned to the village in 1998, he found it very difficult and could not greet any of his Croat neighbours, some of whom may have participated in the attack. He further pointed out that although the situation has slightly improved, he cannot socialize with his Croat neighbours and has only minimal relations with them.[27]

Even when members of different groups were socializing together, this did not necessarily mean that the contact was deep. During fieldwork in the town of Prozor in Hercegovina, for example, the author visited a Bosniak-owned café and met a Bosnian Croat man sitting with a group of Bosnian Muslim men. When they were all together, the Croat stressed that inter-ethnic relations in Prozor were good and that there were no problems between Croats and Bosniaks. When the Bosnian Muslim men went outside, however, the Croat lowered his voice and claimed that the situation was in fact far more complicated. He did not wish to speak openly in the café but agreed to be interviewed the following day. During this interview, he explained that while there were no overt problems between the two ethnic groups, relations had changed and could never return to how they were before the war. He emphasized a dearth of trust and spoke of barriers existing between people.[28]

Critically fuelling the widespread perception of inter-ethnic distance is the fact that many people do not feel comfortable speaking to members of other ethnic groups about the war; the latter largely remains an 'off limits' topic.[29] As part of a survey by Prism Research in Sarajevo, for example, which was conducted between 25 January and 5 February 2010 and involved 1,600 Bosnian citizens

24 Author interview, Srebrenica, 27 March 2013.
25 Author interview, Prijedor, 2 April 2013.
26 Author interview, Ahmići, 12 July 2008.
27 Author interview, Ahmići, 8 July 2008.
28 Author interview, Prozor, 24 June 2009.
29 The author has previously discussed this issue with a specific focus on Brčko District (see Clark 2010d: 71–73).

across BiH, respondents were asked how often they initiated a conversation about the past with members of other ethnic groups. Only 4.1 per cent of respondents answered 'whenever I get a chance', and 28.2 per cent answered 'sometimes'. In contrast, 26.2 per cent of respondents claimed that they never initiate such a conversation, and a further 30.8 per cent maintained that they only rarely do so (Pajić and Popović 2011: 19). Respondents did, however, recognize the importance of dialogue; 39.3 per cent fully agreed with the statement that people should speak about all aspects of the past in order to overcome competing versions of the war (although there were some important ethnic differences),[30] while 39.0 per cent mainly agreed (Pajić and Popović 2011: 20).

Dialogue and discussion are a critical part of any reconciliation process (Abu-Nimer, Said and Prelis 2001: 341). Quintessentially, people need to be able to reconcile their differing narratives of the war in order to be able to reconcile with each other. In BiH, 'There is still a long way to go before people can talk about the past. Instead, the issue is cloaked in silence, creating an oppressive atmosphere without trust or confidence' (Kleck 2006: 118). Interviewees consistently maintained that they avoid speaking about the past with members of other ethnic groups due to fear of provoking arguments and creating new problems and tensions. A camp survivor, for example, explained that when she returned to Prijedor, it was initially very difficult and she did not know how she would ever be able to live there again. None of her Serb neighbours spoke to her, and when she ventured into town she often encountered Serbs who had beaten and tortured detainees in the camp in which she was held. Pointing out that she now greets most of her Serb neighbours in passing, she recounted how Bosniaks and Serbs in Prijedor communicate with each other, sit together and sometimes even drink coffee together – and these are important signs of progress.[31] But when it comes to the subject of the war, she stressed, it is there that the conversation ends.[32] For interviewees on all three sides, in short, the war remains a taboo topic; and the fact that people feel unable to broach the subject with members of another ethnic group necessarily restricts the possibilities for deep contact to occur. A further critical obstacle in this regard is the prevalence of inter-ethnic mistrust, which interviewees cited as the primary reason why they no longer visited people from another ethnic group in their homes – even if they socialized with them on some level.

---

30 For example, while 43.3 per cent of Bosniaks agreed that people should speak about the past, only 38.6 per cent of Bosnian Serbs and 24.9 per cent of Bosnian Croats shared this view (Pajić and Popović 2011: 20).

31 Based on her research with women's NGOs in BiH, for example, Helms argues that, '… the coffee-drinking relationship among women was crucial, embedded as it was in wider patterns of neighborly relations and mutual aid, those relationships most violently and physically disrupted by ethnic cleansing' (2010: 24).

32 Author interview, Priedor, 30 March 2013.

Trust

In societies that have experienced intra-state war, 'one of the most basic obstacles to reconciliation is a lack of trust on the part of citizens between each other...' (Scharf and Williams 2003: 177). This is certainly the case in BiH, where levels of inter-ethnic mistrust are high among Bosnian Muslims, Bosnian Serbs and Bosnian Croats alike. The particularly 'intimate' nature of the Bosnian war, moreover, wherein people betrayed, and even committed crimes against, their neighbours and former friends, has contributed to the existence of widespread mistrust. As Arcel remarks,

> When neighbours, friends or even relatives, people that speak the same language and live in the same town and country as yourself, can commit such violent acts against you and your family, your trust and confidence in human beings and the world is shaken and will take many years to be restored.
>
> (2003: 21)

Indeed, interviewees were often very explicit about their lack of trust towards members of another ethnic group. In Bratunac, a Bosniak interviewee whose husband was killed during the war explained that she finds it extremely difficult to trust local Serbs, based on her conviction that the latter knew what was going to happen to the town's Bosnian Muslims. Arguing that there will always be boundaries between people, she disclosed that while she can communicate with Serbs, converse with them and even socialize with them in some instances, she always asks herself whether they are genuine.[33] Similarly, a Bosnian Serb interviewee in Bratunac maintained that people have yet to reach the point where they can believe in each other. Claiming that life will never return to how it was prior to the war, she was deeply sceptical about the prospects for reconciliation and highlighted the loss of trust as the biggest problem. This particular interviewee had spent four years interned in the Silos camp near Sarajevo and described how a former Bosniak friend who saw her in the camp did nothing to help her. Repeating that this man simply turned away, she identified this as a major reason why she now finds it so difficult to trust Bosnian Muslims.[34] In Goražde, an IDP from Višegrad whose two brothers were killed during the war disclosed that while she greets Serbs and sometimes drinks coffee with them, she will never be able to trust them, owing to the fact that her Serb neighbours in Višegrad never warned her of the violence to come.[35]

---

33 Author interview, Bratunac, 30 June 2008.
34 Author interview, Bratunac, 27 March 2013.
35 Author interview, Goražde, 12 June 2008. The interviewee, however, who left BiH during the war, explained that she also experienced problems with fellow Bosniaks when she returned to the country in 2002. Some people, she claimed, initially resented her for

While lack of trust is thus a serious issue in BiH, deeper insights into the problem can be gained by applying the three trust indicators which are part of the Reconciliation Matrix developed in Chapter 2 – namely levels of social distance, perceptions of the 'other' and trust inducing/trust impeding behaviour. More specifically, it is necessary to analyze whether levels of social distance are high, whether members of one ethnic group perceive the members of another ethnic group in a primarily negative and generalized way, and whether individuals are engaging in behaviour that is hindering rather than facilitating the development of trust.

Levels of social distance

The concept of social distance is quintessentially about social attitudes, and specifically the extent to which individuals either accept or reject particular situations and social interactions. High levels of acceptance indicate low social distance, while conversely high levels of rejection are indicative of significant social difference. Social distance is traditionally measured by the Bogardus Scale, developed in 1924 by Emory Bogardus (Wark and Galliher 2007). On this issue, BiH presents a rather mixed picture. Most interviewees did not object to the idea of multi-ethnic communities, and many expressed the belief that people have to live – or find a way to live – together. In November 2010, Prism Research likewise found low levels of social distance in this regard. For example, 87.0 per cent of Bosnian Croat respondents and 69.6 per cent of Bosnian Serbs said yes to having Bosnian Muslims in their community; 98.1 per cent of Bosnian Muslim respondents and 73.9 per cent of Serb respondents were disposed to having Croats in their community; and 96.3 per cent of Bosnian Muslim respondents and 90.2 per cent of Croats were in support of having Serbs in their community (Duraković et al. 2010: 136–137). Similarly on the issue of schooling, levels of social distance were relatively low; 72.4 per cent of Croat respondents and 70.5 per cent of Serb respondents did not oppose the idea of Bosnian Muslim children attending the same schools as their own children; 98.1 per cent of Bosnian Muslims and 72.4 per cent of Serbs were ready to accept Croat children in the same schools as their own offspring; and 96.5 per cent of Bosnian Muslim respondents and 78.1 per cent of Croat respondents were open to the idea of Serb children being schooled together with their own children (Duraković et al. 2010: 136–137).

On the more personal issue of marriage, however, respondents on all sides expressed higher levels of social distance. When asked whether they would

---

leaving BiH and viewed her as a traitor. Author interview, Goražde, 12 June 2008. In her own research, Pickering similarly found that, 'Urbanites who stayed in the towns during the war…told stories that conveyed the significant distance they felt from those who fled' (2007: 77).

agree to a family member marrying a Bosniak, only 25.0 per cent of Croats and 35.3 per cent of Serbs answered yes; only 37.1 per cent of Bosnian Muslims and 39.0 per cent of Serbs claimed that they would consent to a family member marrying a Croat; and 34.6 per cent of Bosnian Muslims and a somewhat higher 43.7 per cent of Croats expressed no opposition to the idea of a family member marrying a Serb (Duraković et al. 2010: 136–137). That respondents displayed higher social distance in relation to inter-ethnic marriage is consistent with the fact that during the author's fieldwork in BiH, interviewees frequently maintained that there were limits to the types of relationship that they could countenance with members of another ethnic group, due to lack of trust and the existence of barriers between people. Moreover, some interviewees explicitly expressed social distance on the subject of personal relationships, most commonly maintaining that they would disown their sons if the latter ever decided to marry someone from another ethnic group. It was Bosniak interviewees who most frequently voiced such views, specifically vis-à-vis Bosnian Serbs.

The results of the aforementioned survey by Prism Research further show that although respondents manifested generally low levels of social distance in respect of living with members of other ethnic groups, they were nevertheless most comfortable living with members of their own group. Notwithstanding the stagnant economic situation and lack of jobs in BiH, when respondents were asked whether, for job purposes, they would move to a town in which their ethnic group was not the majority, only 28.9 per cent of Bosnian Croats answered yes (compared to 30.4 per cent the previous year). The percentage of Bosnian Serbs answering yes was also low at 37.0 per cent (although slightly higher than the previous year, when the percentage was 28.0 per cent). While 45.3 per cent of Bosnian Muslims answered in the affirmative, this was nevertheless a significantly lower percentage than the previous year (61.5 per cent) (Duraković et al. 2010: 133). The data thus suggest that there exists a strong sense of safety in numbers. Hence, although many respondents were not averse to members of another ethnic group living in their community, they were far less disposed to leave their own community and live as part of a minority with members of another ethnic group.

Perceptions of the other

According to Staub, '...human beings tend to create "us" – "them" differentiations and stereotypes. Contrasting ourselves with others is a way to define the self' (1989: 274). This is particularly true in situations of war and conflict, when the psychological process of dividing people into 'in-groups' and 'out-groups' becomes a central part of the antagonistic dynamics. The contact hypothesis, first articulated after WWII (Allport 1954), posits that contact between former enemy groups can facilitate the overcoming of prejudice and negative stereotypes. In BiH, the lack of deep contact may help to explain why Bosnian Muslims, Bosnian

Serbs and Bosnian Croats alike are still prone to generalize about members of other ethnic groups and to attribute to them an array of disagreeable characteristics. Rather than regarding them as individuals, interviewees instead tended to view people simply as part of a collective and thus to ascribe to everyone in that collective the same negative traits. A Bosniak IDP from Višegrad, for example, warned the author to be very careful during any visit to the town. Maintaining that the worst Serbs are those living closest to the River Drina, she claimed that Serbs in Višegrad are real 'Četniks' and are best avoided.[36] Similarly embracing sweeping stereotypes, a Bosniak interviewee in Sarajevo who had been forced during the war to leave her home in RS declared that Serbs are naturally aggressive people who cut open the stomachs of pregnant women;[37] and in Prijedor, the Serb president of a local veterans' association was sceptical about the prospects for inter-ethnic reconciliation in the area, insisting that Bosnian Muslims are aggressive, deceitful and ill-intentioned people.[38]

That interviewees so often viewed all members of another ethnic group through the same distorting lens meant that they were strongly inclined to collectivize guilt. An oft-cited justification for criminal trials is precisely that they individualize guilt (see, for example, Akhavan 2013: 534; Kritz 1996: 128; Moghalu 2004: 216). The shift from collective to individual guilt is, in turn, a critical prerequisite for reconciliation; an all-encompassing, expansive conception of culpability that incriminates entire groups, rather than individual group members, is deeply divisive and fundamentally inimical to any meaningful rebuilding of relationships. In the words of Sir Hartley Shawcross, Britain's chief prosecutor at Nuremberg, 'There can be no reconciliation unless individual guilt for the appalling crimes replaces the pernicious theory of collective guilt on which so much racial hatred hangs' (cited in Nice 2006: 44). Although the ICTY is prosecuting individuals rather than groups, the fact that it has indicted and tried only a relatively small number of accused paradoxically means that its work has indirectly contributed to a collectivization of guilt.[39] To cite Scharf and Williams,

...where the norms and institutions do not attach individual liability to a significant number of the individuals responsible for the commission of war crimes, they run the risk that they will be unable to perform the function of

---

36 Author interview, Sarajevo, 21 March 2013. During the civil war that engulfed Yugoslavia during WWII, the Četniks, led by Draža Mihailović, fought against Tito's Partisans. Today, the term 'Četnik' is typically used in a derogatory way to refer to Serb extremists.
37 Author interview, Sarajevo, 7 May 2008.
38 Author interview, Prijedor, 2 April 2013.
39 Bass argues that, 'Tribunal justice is inevitably symbolic: a few war criminals stand for a much larger group of guilty individuals. Thus, what is billed as individual justice actually becomes a *de facto* way of exonerating many of the guilty' (2000: 300).

denying collective guilt, as many victims and observers will still believe that large or important sections of the group associated with the atrocities are still at large and will thus tend to blame the entire group rather than risk inadvertent impunity.

(2003: 171)

This is exactly what has happened in BiH; the widespread sense of incomplete or half-finished justice to which the ICTY's work has given rise has led people to reach their own conclusions about who is guilty. The prevalent tendency in BiH for people to collectivize guilt, in other words, is at least in part a reaction to the belief that the ICTY has cast the net of culpability too narrowly. This fundamentally problematizes the claim that the Tribunal 'has been essential in the promotion of reconciliation by individualising the guilt of hateful leaders and disabusing people of the myth that adversary ethnic groups bear collective responsibility for crimes' (Booth 2003: 185). Given the number and scale of crimes committed against Bosnian Muslims during the war – which is not of course to deny or downplay the fact that Bosnian Serbs and Bosnian Croats also suffered[40] – it is perhaps unsurprising that the tendency to collectivize guilt was by far the most pronounced among Bosniak interlocutors. A widow in Potočari, for example, explained that while she no longer views all Serbs as guilty like she did in 1995, she still believes that the majority of them are culpable. Insisting that many Serbs are criminals, extremists and nationalists, she stressed that it is not possible to kill thousands of people in just a few days without mass participation.[41] Echoing this, an IDP from Srebrenica who was living in Sarajevo maintained that all Serbs in Srebrenica were involved in the genocide in some way and are therefore guilty. Adding that she will never be able to forgive them, she emphasized that she will warn her young grandson to be careful of Serbs as they are not good people.[42]

If trust has an 'essentially emotional core' (Barbalet 2005: 7), so too does mistrust. This is why the latter is so difficult to overcome. In BiH, moreover, an additional factor further complicates the task of reducing inter-ethnic mistrust. Specifically, although the mistrust which so many interviewees expressed had its roots in the Bosnian war, more recent developments in the form of various (perceived) trust-impeding behaviours were clearly sustaining and fuelling it.

Trust-inducing/trust-impeding behaviour

The ultimate example of trust-impeding behaviour in BiH centres on the outstanding issue of missing persons. Some 10,000 people remain missing in BiH

---

40 The former BBC war correspondent, Martin Bell, has stressed that, '...there was no monopoly of evil or of suffering in the course of this war' (2012: 5).
41 Author interview, Potočari, 24 March 2013.
42 Author interview, Sarajevo, 29 May 2008.

and a significant number of interviewees in various locations – including Ahmići, Bratunac, Kozarac, Mostar, Prijedor and Srebrenica – were still seeking information regarding the fates of missing family members. To cite Hodžić, 'To find a person means giving him importance, it means that he existed and is not simply a number among others. It means to return his dignity' (cited in Bloch 2005a: 20).[43] More than anything, interviewees wanted to be able to give their loved-ones a dignified burial and lay them to rest; and the fact that they had been prevented from doing so was in their eyes the fault of the other ethnic group within their community. In the village of Ahmići, a Bosniak interviewee was adamant that his Croat neighbours had vital knowledge – which they were deliberately withholding – regarding the whereabouts of his missing mother and father; and stressed that he will always harbour deep mistrust towards his neighbours as long as they refuse to disclose the truth.[44] In the village of Trnopolje, a Bosniak interviewee was likewise convinced that local Serbs know where the bodies of his two missing sons are buried. Emphasizing that Serbs remained in Trnopolje during the war, he argued that they could not have failed to see everything that was happening. The interviewee was especially incredulous that a neighbour who worked in the Serb police during the war had denied having any knowledge about the fate or whereabouts of his missing sons.[45] In keeping with the above examples, an interviewee in Potočari recalled how when she first returned to the area, she sought information from local Serbs regarding her missing brother, but was always met with a wall of silence. They know everything, she asserted, but always say nothing, adding that Serbs have to protect and defend war criminals for the sake of future generations.[46]

More generally, interviewees repeatedly underlined the importance of truth as a prerequisite for trust-building. As one illustration, Bosniak interviewees in Ahmići almost always referred to Vlatko Kupreškić, a local Bosnian Croat who was convicted at the ICTY in January 2000 but acquitted a year later. While interviewees were generally of the opinion that Kupreškić, who fought in the HVO, was probably not directly involved in the attack on the village, they persistently claimed that Bosnian Croats were shooting from his house (located in the centre of Ahmići).[47] In their eyes, therefore, Kupreškić had to have known what was going to happen – and was therefore complicit in the attack. While most interviewees shopped at Kupreškić's local store, which had seemingly closed when the author returned to Ahmići in 2009, they repeatedly insisted that Kupreškić needed to tell the truth and further articulated that the village would

43 Author's translation from Bosnian.
44 Author interview, Ahmići, 10 July 2008.
45 Author interview, Trnopolje, 30 July 2008.
46 Author interview, Potočari, 24 March 2013.
47 This is consistent with witness testimony in the trial of Vlatko Kupreškić (see, for example, Prosecutor v. Josipović et al. 2000: §240).

always remain divided as long as Croats remained taciturn and refused to face the facts of what happened.

In Bratunac, Bosniak interviewees similarly called for their Serb neighbours to tell the truth and to acknowledge the crimes committed in the town during the war. In the view of a local camp survivor, it is not the case that all Serbs are culpable, but those who are not guilty are afraid of those who are – and hence the former remain quiet and persist in denial. He underlined that those Serbs who are innocent and have nothing to hide need to stand up and speak the truth, which would thereby send an important and positive signal to local Bosniaks.[48] Strong 'group think' exists among all sides in BiH, however, with people tending to express the 'Serb', 'Croat' or 'Bosniak' viewpoint rather than their own personal opinions. Hence, getting individuals to voice ideas and thoughts that contradict and radically depart from the group narrative is extremely difficult. Part of showing one's loyalty to the group seemingly entails remaining loyal to the group's own version of truth. Furthermore, in a society where 'truth' is such a deeply contested concept, the apparently straightforward claim that people need to 'speak the truth' critically misses the point; interviewees on all sides sought to convince and reassure the author that they were telling the 'real truth'.

Some more explicit behaviours are also provoking negative feeling and nourishing mistrust. Bosnian Muslims in the town of Stolac, for example, have been angered and offended by the display of Catholic religious symbols. In 2001, 14 Catholic crosses were erected in the town, an act which one interviewee described as 'a total misuse of religious symbols designed to humiliate and dominate the Bosniaks'.[49] In 2005, the foundations for 14 new crosses were laid and when both the Commission to Preserve National Monuments of BiH and the Council for Implementation of Peace ordered that the foundations for these concrete crosses be removed, the local Catholic priest organized a demonstration against this. According to members of the local Youth Forum, 'Having in mind that hundreds of citizens of Stolac were killed precisely because they were not Christian, erection of these crosses can be compared to a well-known attempt to erect a cross in Auschwitz...' (Youth Forum of Stolac 2008: 19). To take a second example, during the author's fieldwork in Prijedor in July 2008, the local SOC organized a protest against Radovan Karadžić's recent arrest. A group of around 300 local Serbs, many of them carrying pictures of Karadžić, gathered in the centre of the town, before slowly making their way to the church to pray for the former Bosnian Serb leader. Although the number of people taking part in this event was not large (the participants included teenagers and children), Bosniak interviewees demanded to know how they could trust or re-build relations with local Serbs when the latter are openly supporting men such as Karadžić.

---

48 Author interview, Bratunac, 23 March 2013.
49 Author interview, 25 August 2008.

While Mearsheimer, expressing a quintessentially Realist view of International Relations, has argued that there exists 'little room for trust among states' (1990: 12), there is similarly little room for trust among members of war-divided ethnic groups in the absence of positive behaviour that creates a basis for the re-building of relationships. Unfortunately, the behaviour that interviewees sought from members of other ethnic groups – such as admissions of guilt and the disclosure of information regarding the whereabouts of missing persons – is unrealistic in the current climate of BiH.

Mutual acceptance

While this research understands the term reconciliation to mean more than simply 'mutual acceptance by two groups of each other' (Staub 2011: 290), mutual acceptance is an important component of reconciliation. In BiH, although there is a general acceptance that people have to live together, regardless of ethnicity, there is far less sense of mutual acceptance. Interviewees frequently claimed that they were not accepted by the majority group within their community and often complained that they were victims of discrimination. Such grievances were particularly common in Prijedor. The Bosnian Muslim population of Prijedor was subjected to extreme discrimination during, and in the run-up to, the war.[50] The ICTY has noted, for example, that, 'Immediately preceding the attacks and takeover of towns and villages in Prijedor, Muslims were called upon to surrender their weapons and identify themselves, by wearing a white band on their arms and by displaying a white sheet as a flag of surrender on the windows of their homes' (Prosecutor v. Stanišić and Župljanin 2013: §658). Moreover, Bosniak interviewees always underlined that they continue to face discrimination, and particularly emphasized ongoing discrimination in respect of memorials (see Subašić and Ćurak 2014). In the centre of Prijedor, although there are a number of imposing memorials erected in honour of fallen Serbs, there is a striking absence of any memorials to commemorate the many Bosnian Muslims who were killed during the war. This has engendered deep bitterness among local Bosniaks. As Hodžić notes,

> The systematic refusal of municipal authorities to allow the creation of memorials for non-Serb victims of war crimes in any public spaces in Prijedor, as well as the erection of a monument to Serb soldiers at the location of one of the most notorious camps, Trnopolje [discussed in chapter 4], discrimination of non-Serb victims in recognizing their status and providing material assistance available to Serb victims have all contributed to reinforcing a sense of further victimization within the non-Serb communities of Prijedor.
>
> (2010: 129–130)

---

50 Bosnian Croats also suffered discrimination (see, for example, Prosecutor v. Stanišić and Župljanin 2013: §517).

If Bosnian Muslims in Prijedor have been refused the right to erect their own memorials in public places, they have also been prevented on many occasions from publicly paying respect to their dead. In May 2012, for example, a local victims' group helped to organize a small commemoration in memory of 266 women and girls who were killed or went missing in Prijedor during the war. On the orders of the local mayor, however, the police intervened to stop this event and claimed that it would disturb the peace. A camp survivor who took part in this event explained that some of the participants were wearing t-shirts adorned with the words '*Ja neću odgojiti svoje dijete da ubije tvoje dijete*' (I will not raise my child to kill your child). Once again, however, the police stepped in, claiming that these t-shirts were provocative.[51]

Beyond discrimination in respect of memorials and commemorative events, Bosniak interviewees in Prijedor also maintained that they were victims of discrimination in the job market, highlighting that there are very few Bosnian Muslims working in the town hall or in local public firms.[52] Outside of Prijedor, the theme of employment-based discrimination was similarly emphasized (notably by Bosniak interviewees). A member of the UNDP in Srebrenica, for example, explained that it is very difficult to find an ethnic balance in private companies in the area, with the exception of international firms like Cimos (a Slovene car factory in Potočari), and pointed out that public companies only employ Serbs.[53] In Mostar, Bosniak interviewees frequently argued that they do not have the same rights as local Croats, and maintained that the latter enjoy a superior standard of living as it is much easier for them to find employment; and in the nearby town of Stolac, Bosniak interviewees repeatedly emphasized that there is no place for them in many companies and institutions. Employment in local government should reflect the pre-war ethnic composition of any given municipality, in accordance with the DPA; and in the case of Stolac, Bosniaks constituted 43.4 per cent of the pre-war population, while Bosnian Croats made up 33.1 per cent and Bosnian Serbs accounted for 21.0 per cent (Kolind 2006: 123). In practice, however, the distribution of jobs within the municipality does not reflect these percentages. Discrimination exists, according to a member of the Norwegian Helsinki Committee, because, 'Post offices, hospitals and schools are also public institutions, but are not recognized as such, so there is no obligation to give [Bosniaks] jobs [in them]' (cited in Jennings and Džidžić 2008).

---

51 Author interview, Kozarac, 31 March 2013.
52 Employment-related ethnic discrimination is a widespread problem in BiH (see, for example, Amnesty International 2006; European Commission against Racism and Intolerance 2011).
53 Author interview, Srebrenica, 26 June 2008. Bosnian Serb interviewees in Srebrenica, however, always insisted that they are not treated equally, and in particular claimed that international assistance and donations have only benefitted Bosnian Muslims in the municipality.

Discrimination, whether actual or perceived, is a serious problem in BiH (Kleck 2006: 117–118) and fundamentally impedes the development of any sense of mutual acceptance. Providing further insights into the problem, which does not exclusively affect Bosnian Muslims, a 2011 report by the US Department of State found that,

> Minority returnees often faced intimidation and complained of discrimination in hiring. In returnee areas throughout the country, the percentage of minorities holding municipal employment was neither representative of current populations, nor consistent with legally mandated percentages based on the 1991 census, indicating local government failures to implement and enforce the provisions of the law....Minority returnees also faced obstructions in their access to education, health care and pension benefits, as well as poor infrastructure.
>
> (2011: 19)

An important part of feeling accepted by others is feeling that one is welcome in a particular community or society, and this is where positive gestures and signals have a critical role to play. However, there is little evidence of progress in this regard. In some ethnically-mixed areas of BiH, for example, there is almost nothing to acknowledge the existence of the other ethnic group. The town of Čapljina in Hercegovina is particularly striking in this regard. Notwithstanding the presence of a significant Bosniak community, the town has an overwhelmingly Croat-centric character. The Croatian flag is omnipresent, the town is accessed via the Dr Franjo Tuđman bridge and streets are named after Croatian and Bosnian Croat politicians and public figures – including the late Gojko Šušak (Croatia's Minister of Defence during the 1990s), Ante Starčević (a Croatian politician who founded the right-wing Croatian Party of Rights during the nineteenth century) and Mate Boban (the former head of the self-proclaimed HRHB).

If Bosniak interviewees felt neither accepted nor welcome in Čapljina, which is part of the BiH Federation, interviewees living in RS maintained that they can never feel welcome in a republic for Serbs that came into being as a result of bloodshed and genocide. This, in turn, highlights a fundamental constitutional issue that is necessarily obstructing reconciliation. If people are to fully accept each other, they need to accept and respect the state in which they live; but while Bosnian Muslims desire a unified BiH and the abolition of RS, many Bosnian Serbs favour the secession of RS. According to a 2009 survey by Gallup Balkan Monitor, 'While majorities of both Bosnian Croats and Bosniaks (63% and 80% respectively) did not agree with a potential secession of Republika Srpska in the case of a referendum in that entity, 87% of interviewees in the Serb entity supported the creation of an independent state if a majority of its citizens voted that way' (2010: 4). In the same way that Bosnian Serbs have a strong affinity to Serbia, Bosnian Croats often express their allegiance to the Republic of Croatia rather than to the state of BiH. In the aforementioned Gallup survey, for example, respondents were asked which team they would support in international sporting events, and whereas 94 per cent of Bosniaks maintained that they generally always champion their own country, in contrast 'almost three-quarters (72%) of Bosnian Croats declared their support for Croatia and 88% of Bosnian Serbs said they would get behind the Serbian national team' (2010: 5). Any constitutional changes in BiH could potentially reignite the conflict, and this is one of the major reasons why the current status quo has remained unchanged since the war ended in 1995. Moreover, it is likely to remain unchanged precisely because there are no simple or straightforward alternatives. As long as the country remains divided into two entities, however, and as long as the different ethnic groups diverge in their loyalties and hold fundamentally polarized views regarding the optimum constitutional design of BiH, this will surely restrict the space for inter-ethnic reconciliation.

To conclude this chapter, based on the four key factors of human security, deep contact, trust and mutual acceptance, there is little inter-ethnic reconciliation in post-war BiH. Hence, this finding further problematizes the argument that the ICTY's trials are contributing to reconciliation. Moreover, there is some evidence to suggest that the Tribunal's work has in certain cases created or facilitated intra-ethnic divides. The following three examples are particularly illustrative in this regard. Firstly, some Bosniak interviewees in Bratunac expressed resentment towards both the ICTY and the Mothers of Srebrenica. Maintaining that the ICTY has accorded the latter a voice and a platform which it has denied to victims in Bratunac, they further argued that the Mothers have contributed to the marginalization of Bratunac.[54] A camp survivor, for example, heavily criticized Munira Subašić, the high-profile president of the Mothers of Srebrenica and Žepa. Asserting that her rhetoric has harmed Bratunac, he stressed that Subašić only talks about Srebrenica and does not speak about victims in any comprehensive sense.[55] An interviewee whose husband was killed during the war expressed similar views. Emphasizing that victims in Bratunac have been ignored, she blamed the ICTY for this but also the Mothers, asserting that the latter have kept Srebrenica in the spotlight – thus leaving Bratunac critically overshadowed.[56]

Secondly, interviewees in Prijedor and Kozarac, as highlighted in the previous chapter, were insistent that genocide occurred in Prijedor municipality, and were thus deeply critical of the ICTY for failing to acknowledge this. As Delpla points out, 'The category of genocide particularly crystallizes such a struggle

---

54 Eight mass graves have been found in Bratunac municipality. The first were exhumed in 2002; there were 18 bodies in the Suha grave and 21 bodies in the Redžići grave. In one of the graves, the exhumation of which was completed on 11 May 2005, there were 38 bodies, of which 30 were women and children (Pargan 2012: 25).

55 Author interview, Bratunac, 23 March 2013.

56 Author interview, 28 March 2013.

[for recognition of victimhood]' (2007: 232). While interviewees' anger and bitterness were primarily directed at the Tribunal, some also appeared to harbour a degree of resentment towards the victims of Srebrenica. A camp survivor, for example, suggested that whereas those in Srebrenica died a relatively painless death as many of them were shot, those interned in camps such as Omarska and Keraterm died in agony.[57] Echoing this, another camp survivor maintained that a bullet was a gift in Omarska, because being shot was a far quicker and easier way to die than being systematically tortured and beaten day after day.[58] Not only is such moral relativism deeply problematic, but so too is the simplistic notion that victims in Srebrenica somehow suffered less than those detained in camps in Prijedor.[59]

Thirdly, in the village of Ahmići, the ICTY's work has also contributed to intra-ethnic divides among Bosnian Muslims. Problems began after a local Bosniak, who will be referred to simply as X, testified in several trials at the ICTY, including the trial of Drago Josipović – a member of HVO forces in the village of Šantići. Despite the fact that X was not actually in Ahmići when the HVO attacked the village, he told the Tribunal that Josipović – who was ultimately sentenced to 12 years' imprisonment – was innocent. X's testimony at the Tribunal thus caused considerable anger and bitterness among his Bosnian Muslim neighbours, who accused him of taking the side of the Croats. Certainly, X was on very good terms with the Bosnian Croat mayor of nearby Vitez; the author interviewed both men while they were dining together in a restaurant in the town. X claimed that few of his Bosniak neighbours now speak to him and described how someone had smeared excrement on his house.[60] The fact that the sister of a local Bosniak man in Ahmići had testified against Josipović had further contributed to intra-ethnic divisions in the village. X accused this woman, Y, of giving false testimony against Josipović; while one of Josipović's Bosniak neighbours made similar allegations and warned the author to be very careful of Y and her brother.[61]

That the ICTY has not contributed to inter-ethnic reconciliation between Bosnian Muslims, Bosnian Serbs and Bosnian Croats, however, is not the end of the story. BiH has not been the sole focus of the ICTY's work and hence no analysis of whether the ICTY's trials have had a positive effect on inter-ethnic relations would be sufficiently comprehensive without the inclusion of additional case studies. The following chapter thus turns to Croatia.

---

57 Author interview, Prijedor, 1 April 2013.
58 Author interview, 30 March 2013.
59 In its judgement against Radislav Krstić, for example, the Trial Chamber noted that it 'heard reliable evidence concerning the severe beatings and other cruel treatments suffered by the Bosnian Muslim men after they had been separated from their relatives in Potočari' (Prosecutor v. Krstić 2001: §517).
60 Author interview, Vitez, 11 July 2008.
61 Author interview, Ahmići, 12 July 2008.

Chapter 6

A Case Study of Croatia

Existing scholarly research on Croatia and the ICTY, which is limited, typically adopts a top-down approach, focusing on Croatia's fluctuating political relations with the Tribunal (see, for example, Del Ponte 2008; Peskin 2008; Peskin and Boduszyński 2003; Subotić 2009). What remains critically under-utilized, in contrast, is a bottom-up approach centred on ordinary people's views and attitudes towards the ICTY and on the impact that the Tribunal's work is having at this grassroots level. Focusing on this neglected 'view from below' and using Vukovar and Knin as case studies, this chapter argues that far from contributing to reconciliation in Croatia, the ICTY's trials have had a polarizing effect and created new ethnic grievances. The chapter begins, like the previous chapter, by exploring how local communities perceive the ICTY and whether the 'justice' that is being done in The Hague is viewed and received as such on the ground.

Reconciliation via justice?

During a conference in November 2012 on the ICTY's legacy in Croatia, the Tribunal's vice-President, Judge Carmel Agius, emphasized that, 'There is no peace without justice and justice means justice to everyone: perpetrators and victims' (ICTY 2012b). This is an idealized view; justice is a divisive concept which does not easily lend itself to shared understandings. People may have a common desire for justice (Audergon and Arye 2005: 118), but hold fundamentally divergent viewpoints on what *constitutes* justice. Croatia is a case in point. Among Serbs and Croats alike, there are strong demands for justice. Both sides, however, want justice for their own victims first and foremost, rather than a broader, inclusive justice for all victims. That people's understandings and expectations in respect of justice are coloured by ethnicity thus works against the development of a common, joint understanding of justice. What nevertheless transcends these ethnic divides is the widespread perception on both sides that the ICTY has failed to deliver justice.

Serb viewpoints, grievances and a sense of justice denied

Hirsh associates the ICTY with what he calls cosmopolitan law – 'the emerging body of law that aims to protect the human rights of individuals and groups, primarily from serious threats that may be posed to them by their "own" states, by invading states, or by other state-like social formations' (2003: xv). Among Serb interviewees in Vukovar and Knin, however, there was a strong and deep-felt sense that the ICTY accords little importance to the violation of Serbs' human rights, thus allowing crimes against Serbs to remain largely unpunished. In Vukovar, for example, 'Many Serbs see themselves as victims of crackdowns, dismissals from work, arrests and physical abuse perpetrated by Croats immediately before the war or during the siege' (Kosić and Tauber 2010: 4). Serb interviewees repeatedly emphasized that prior to the start of the war in Vukovar in May 1991, Serb homes and businesses were increasingly attacked and Serbs began to disappear (see Association of Families of Missing and Violently Abducted Persons 1999: 11–40). They further claimed that during this pre-war period, Serbs were subjected to growing pressure and threats – including silent telephone calls in the middle of the night and beatings – from local Croats who wanted to force them to leave Vukovar. The ICTY is obviously not the appropriate institution to deal with these crimes; they fall outside its temporal and substantive mandate. Ordinary people on the ground, however, are typically unfamiliar with such details, and for them it is incomprehensible that nobody has been prosecuted for these pre-war crimes. As they see it, the only explanation is that Serb victims matter less than other victims.

Interviewees further opined that the lack of prosecutions has helped to entrench the notion that all Serbs are collectively guilty for the war and siege of Vukovar, despite the fact that Serbs also suffered during this period (see Tanner 2010: 264). They maintained, for example, that they endure frequent discrimination in Croatia in part because the Croatian authorities regard all Serbs as guilty for the events of 1991. The most commonly-cited instance of discrimination was in the job market. While the economic and employment situation in Vukovar is bad for everyone,[1] Serbs insisted that they are disproportionately affected.[2] One interviewee, for example, claimed that during a job interview, the employer asked her whether she was from Borovo Naselje (a mixed area) or Borovo Selo (a Serb village). When she informed him that she was from Borovo Selo, his response was to tell her that Serbs killed two of his friends in the village in 1991. The interviewee,

---

1 The Borovo shoe factory, for example, employed between 20,000 and 22,000 people before the war. Today, it is in a state of serious disrepair and employs only a fraction of that number.
2 Minority Rights Group International (MRGI) has emphasized that, '...unemployment among the Serbs [in Croatia] is particularly high, with severe under-representation in public sector jobs amid many allegations of discrimination' (2008).

who was just four years old in 1991, was adamant that her ethnicity was the reason that she did not get the job.[3] Another interviewee claimed that whereas people once referred simply to 'Borovo', today it makes a fundamental difference whether a person is from Borovo Naselje or Borovo Selo.[4]

Serb interviewees thereby felt an acute sense of injustice vis-à-vis the ICTY. For them, it is not only a political court which has turned a blind eye to crimes committed against Serbs, but also a court which, by collectivizing Serb guilt, has contributed to quotidian injustices and discrimination against Serbs in Vukovar today. According to Simpson, war crimes trials are almost always political; they typically entail 'the performance of political contestation within the confines of a somewhat constraining legal procedure' (2007: 14). When Serb interviewees accused the ICTY of being a political court, in contrast, it was precisely to highlight the fact that the Tribunal, as they see it, adopts an ethnically-biased approach to victimhood, which has by extension encouraged Croatian authorities to do the same.

Serb interviewees in Knin similarly accused the Tribunal of failing to treat Serbs and Croats equally, highlighting in particular the lack of prosecutions in relation to Operation Storm in August 1995. Interviewees expressed anger, for example, that crimes committed in the aftermath of Operation Storm, in Serb villages such as Grubori[5] and Varivode,[6] have gone unpunished at the ICTY. For them, this was yet further evidence of the Tribunal's anti-Serb bias. A key case for Serbs in Croatia was thus the trial of the Croatian generals Ante Gotovina, Ivan Čermak and Mladen Markač.

The author first visited Knin in April 2012, exactly one year after the Trial Chamber convicted Gotovina, the commander of the Split Military District of the HV, and Markač, the commander of the Special Police of the Ministry of the Interior of the Republic of Croatia, of crimes against humanity and violations of the laws or customs of war in connection with Operation Storm (Čermak, the commander of the Knin Garrison, was acquitted). Finding that both men had significantly contributed to a JCE, the common purpose of which was 'the permanent removal of the Serb civilian population from the Krajina by force or threat of force' (Prosecutor v. Gotovina, Čermak and Markač 2011: §2314), the

3 Author interview, Borovo Naselje, 30 July 2011.
4 Author interview, Borovo Selo, 1 August 2011.
5 Five elderly Serbs were killed in the village of Grubori on 25 and 26 August 1995 (SENSE 2008). Two men, both former members of the Croatian special police, are currently on trial for these murders at the Zagreb County Court. The trial of Franjo Drlja and Božo Krajina began in November 2011.
6 Nine elderly Serbs were killed in Varivode in September 1995 (Human Rights Watch 1996), and to date nobody has been convicted for this crime. In a landmark ruling in January 2013, however, a local court held the Croatian state responsible for these murders and ordered it to pay compensation to the children of two of the victims. The Supreme Court had previously ruled, in July 2012, that 'a terrorist act was perpetrated in Varivode, for which the Republic of Croatia was responsible' (Pavelić 2013a).

Trial Chamber sentenced Gotovina and Markač to prison terms of 24 and 18 years respectively. While a handful of Serb interviewees in Knin expressed the view, contrary to the author's expectations, that Gotovina was a 'good soldier' and should not have been found guilty, the majority were satisfied with the Trial Chamber's verdicts against him and Markač. Just seven months after the interviews took place, however, the Appeals Chamber – by a majority of three to two – acquitted both defendants.

Central to the rather brief, 56-page appeal judgement[7] was the Trial Chamber's use of a so-called '200 metre margin of error' to determine the lawfulness of Croatian artillery attacks on the four key towns of Knin, Benkovac, Obrovac and Gračač (the 'Four Towns'). Ascertaining the legality or otherwise of the artillery attacks was, in turn, critical for establishing, *inter alia*, whether the HV had committed persecution as a crime against humanity through unlawful attacks on civilians and civilian objects. After hearing the testimony of an expert witness and two further witnesses with significant experience in artillery, the Trial Chamber in 2011 reached the conclusion that, '...those artillery projectiles which impacted within a distance of 200 metres of an identified target were deliberately fired at that artillery target' (Prosecutor v. Gotovina, Čermak and Markač 2011: §1898). By extension, it adjudged that artillery attacks in which the projectiles fell within 200 metres of their intended target were lawful, on the basis that such attacks could reasonably be interpreted as having offered the HV a definite military advantage (2011: §1899). Inevitably, however, some projectiles impacted more than 200 metres from their intended target and according to the Trial Chamber, the legality of such attacks needed to be assessed on a case-by-case basis.[8] Ultimately, the Trial Chamber unanimously reached the conclusion that all of the Four Towns were subjected to unlawful artillery fire (Prosecutor v. Gotovina, Čermak and Markač 2011: §1913, 1925, 1937, 1945). This finding, in turn, significantly contributed to the guilty verdicts against Gotovina and Markač in respect of the crime of persecution. According to the Trial Chamber, the shelling of the Four Towns represented an indiscriminate attack on the towns, and hence an unlawful attack on civilians and civilian objects within those towns (2011: §1911, 1923, 1935, 1943). The Trial Chamber further opined that these

---

7 In addition, both Judge Theodor Meron and Judge Patrick Robison issued brief separate opinions, and Judge Carmel Agius and Judge Fausto Pocar provided significant dissenting opinions.

8 The appeal judgement erroneously claims that, 'Using the 200 Metre Standard as a yardstick, the Trial Chamber found that all impact sites located more than 200 metres from a target it deemed legitimate served as evidence of an unlawful artillery attack' (Prosecutor v. Gotovina and Markač 2012a: §25). At the end of the above passage, a footnote in the appeal judgement refers to paragraphs 1903–1906, 1919–1921, 1932–1933 and 1940–1941 of the trial judgement. These paragraphs do not, however, substantiate the above claim; and if any part of the trial judgement did specifically support it, the Appeals Chamber would have surely cited it directly.

unlawful attacks on civilians and civilian objects in the Four Towns discriminated against the Krajina Serbs (2011: §1912, 1924, 1936, 1944), and thereby constituted persecution as a crime against humanity.

All five appeal judges regarded the Trial Chamber's use of this 200 metre margin of error as problematic (although it is crucial to underline that the Trial Chamber did not determine the unlawfulness of the artillery attacks on the Four Towns solely on the basis of the 200 metre margin of error).[9] Specifically, the Appeals Chamber opined that the Trial Chamber: '...adopted a margin of error that was not linked to any evidence received', and it provided 'no explanation as to the basis for the margin of error it adopted...' (Prosecutor v. Gotovina and Markač 2012a: §61). While the two dissenting judges, Judge Agius and Judge Pocar, did not regard these errors as fatal to the overall trial judgement, the Majority judges (Judge Meron, Judge Robinson and Judge Güney) disagreed. For them, the errors were so serious that the Trial Chamber's finding of unlawful artillery attacks on the Four Towns could not be sustained. By reductively viewing the more than 1,300 pages of the Trial Chamber's judgement through the narrow prism of the 200 metre margin of error, the Majority were able, according to Judge Agius, to effectively 'discard the Trial Judgement in one fell swoop' (Prosecutor v. Gotovina and Markač 2012b: §17).

In a statement issued in 2005, the then (and current) President of the ICTY declared, 'Let me say it again, loud and clear, the Tribunal will not close before trying Karadžić, Mladić and Gotovina' (Meron 2005). Seven years later, Judge Meron presided over a divided Appeals Chamber which ultimately overturned the Trial Chamber's guilty verdicts against Gotovina and his co-defendant. While the Majority judges' reasoning was fundamentally flawed (see Clark 2013b) and prompted strong criticisms not only from the two dissenting judges[10] but also from the Tribunal's Prosecutor,[11] it was the ultimate outcome – the acquittal of two high-profile Croatian generals – which generated strong reactions among

---

9 In addition to its impact analysis, the Trial Chamber reached the conclusion that the artillery attacks on the Four Towns were unlawful based on the following information: an order that Gotovina had issued on 2 August 1995, instructing the HV to shell the Four Towns; evidence relating to the implementation of that order; the transcript of the Brioni meeting in July 1995, which provided important insights into the intentions of the Croatian leadership; evidence from witnesses in Knin; and evidence regarding the proportionality of artillery attacks aimed at the home of the then leader of the Krajina Serbs, Milan Martić. In the Appeals Chamber, however, the Majority dealt with – and dismissed – this evidence in just seven paragraphs.

10 Judge Agius, for example, impugned the Majority's reasoning and approach as, *inter alia*, 'confusing and extremely problematic' (Prosecutor v. Gotovina and Markač 2012b: §5); and Judge Pocar insisted that the appeal judgement 'contradicts any sense of justice' (Prosecutor v. Gotovina and Markač 2012c: §39).

11 In a public statement released shortly after the Appeals Chamber delivered its verdict, for example, Serge Brammertz disclosed that, 'My Office [the OTP] is disappointed by the outcome of the Judgement' (SENSE 2012b).

Serbs, both in Croatia and Serbia. When the author returned to Knin for five days in March 2013, the dominant feeling among local Serbs was that the acquittal verdicts were a fundamental injustice and further exposed the Tribunal as a deeply politicized and biased institution. They thus shared the sentiments of Serbia's deputy Prime Minister, Rasim Ljajić, who condemned the appeal judgement as 'proof of selective justice which is worse than any injustice' (BBC 2012). Others expressed a deep sense of resignation; it was no surprise to them that a blatantly anti-Serb institution would acquit the generals, particularly in the run-up to Croatia entering the EU in July 2013. Even those interviewees who had previously defended Gotovina expressed deep concern regarding the implications of the appeal judgement, claiming that the acquittal of Gotovina and Markač will simply reinforce a culture of impunity for crimes against Serbs and help to further diminish the gravity of these crimes. Sharing such concerns, Nakarada maintains that as a result of the acquittal verdicts, '...one of the biggest ethnic cleansings since the Second World War was legitimized as a defensive military action, tainted by only a few isolated criminal incidences' (2013: 105).

Croat viewpoints, incredulity and claims of misdirected justice

While Croat interviewees were less likely than Serb interviewees to accuse the ICTY of bias, they too harboured a deep sense of injustice. In Vukovar, they particularly demanded an explanation for the absence of ICTY prosecutions in connection with the siege of the town in 1991. The relentless shelling and artillery attacks reduced this once-beautiful town on the River Danube to a desolate and scorched wasteland littered with corpses, war detritus and the broken fragments of citizens' pre-war lives. Interviewees recalled how, during the siege, they lived underground like animals, huddled together in cold dark basements, only emerging from this subterranean world when a lull in the fighting made it safe for them to do so. For them, it was therefore unfathomable that nobody has stood trial in The Hague for wreaking such devastation on a town and its people. After the fall of Vukovar on 18 November 1991, large numbers of Croats were sent to Serb-run camps, both in Vukovar and in Serbia itself (Rehak 2008). That no one has been prosecuted at the ICTY for the numerous crimes committed in these camps has further compounded acute feelings of injustice among Croats in Vukovar. According to the co-president of the Croatian Association of Camp Inmates of Serbian Concentration Camps (HDLSKL), 300 people died in these camps.[12]

The largest atrocity of the war in Croatia occurred in the vicinity of one of these camps. On the evening of 20 and 21 November 1991, at least 200 people were taken to Ovčara, located five kilometres south-east of Vukovar, and executed.

12 Author interview, Borovo Naselje, 2 August 2011.

Their bodies were thrown into a mass grave.[13] While the ICTY has prosecuted three individuals in connection with this crime – namely Mile Mrkšić, Veselin Šljivančanin and Miroslav Radić – the verdicts in this case did nothing to assuage Croat grievances vis-à-vis the Tribunal. The trial of the so-called 'Vukovar Three', which focused specifically on the Ovčara massacre, resulted in two convictions. Mrkšić, a colonel in the JNA and commander of the Guards Motorised Brigade and Operational Group South, was found guilty of murder, torture and cruel treatment and sentenced in September 2007 to 20 years' imprisonment. Šljivančanin, a major in the JNA and security officer of the Guards Motorised Brigade and Operational Group South, was found guilty of torture and sentenced to five years' imprisonment. The third defendant, Radić, a captain in the JNA, was acquitted. Unsurprisingly, these sentences generated deep anger and shock in Vukovar; they made little sense in the context of such a heinous crime. According to a local paramedic, 'If you stole a car today you would get a harsher sentence than what they [the Vukovar Three] got for the biggest crime committed here in the past 50 years' (BBC 2007). During the author's fieldwork in Vukovar four years later, not a single Croat interviewee mentioned Mrkšić or Radić. Almost all of them, however, referred to Šljivančanin, whose recent release from prison had left them struggling to fathom how a convicted war criminal could now be a free man. Their perceptions of the ICTY were inextricably bound up with the fate of this particular defendant.

Following the fall of Vukovar, Šljivančanin had been put in charge of evacuating the sick and wounded from the local hospital. Instead of being taken to a place of safety, however, the men were separated from the women and children and driven, via the JNA barracks in Vukovar, to Ovčara. When they arrived there, paramilitary soldiers and members of the Vukovar Territorial Defence (TO) beat and subsequently executed them, 'at least 194 of them' (Prosecutor v. Mrkšić, Radić and Šljivančanin 2007: §252). In 2007, the ICTY Trial Chamber held that Šljivančanin had breached his duty of care towards the prisoners of war by failing to ensure that there were enough JNA guards at Ovčara to protect them and/or by failing to prevent TO and paramilitary forces from beating them. Accordingly, it sentenced him to five years' imprisonment for aiding and abetting the crime of torture and cruel treatment.

What had sealed the fate of the victims of Ovčara was a decision taken by Mile Mrkšić to withdraw the JNA military police, thus leaving the prisoners at the mercy of the TO and paramilitary groups. In 2009, the Appeals Chamber reached the conclusion that Šljivančanin must have learnt of this withdrawal order during a meeting with Mrkšić on 20 November 1991 – and hence must have appreciated that the killing of the prisoners was now a probability (Prosecutor v. Mrkšić and

---

13 In the trial of Mrkšić, Radić and Šljivančanin, the Trial Chamber noted that, 'The remains of 200 human bodies were exhumed from this mass grave at Ovčara. There were 198 males and two females. The age range of those exhumed was between 16 and 72' (2007: §494).

Šljivančanin 2009: §101). Hence, the Appeals Chamber additionally found Šljivančanin guilty of aiding and abetting the crime of murder and accordingly increased his sentence to 17 years (Prosecutor v. Mrkšić and Šljivančanin 2009: §63). On 28 January 2010, however, Šljivančanin requested a review of the appeal judgement, maintaining that he had not been cognizant of Mrkšić's decision to withdraw the military police from Ovčara. The Appeals Chamber ultimately accepted this argument and in a review judgement delivered in 2010, it vacated the additional conviction of aiding and abetting murder (Prosecutor v. Šljivančanin 2010: §32) and imposed a new sentence of ten years. Just a year later, on 5 July 2011, Šljivančanin – who had been in custody since 2003 – was controversially granted early release.

Croat interviewees overwhelmingly seized upon the example of Šljivančanin to highlight the absence of justice at the ICTY. Nevertheless, it is important to underline that their knowledge of the case was limited. For example, they did not know why the 17-year sentence imposed by the Appeals Chamber in 2009 was substantially reduced the following year; and some of them were not aware of the Trial Chamber's finding that it was paramilitaries and members of the TO – over whom Šljivančanin had no control – and not JNA forces who committed the killings at Ovčara (Prosecutor v. Mrkšić, Radić and Šljivančanin 2007: §252). That many people remain poorly-informed about such judgements is the result of several factors, in particular the Tribunal's lack of insufficient investment in grassroots outreach activities (Parker 2009: 88) and the very negative, one-sided way in which local media typically portray the ICTY's trials. According to an interviewee from the Centre for Peace, Non-Violence and Human Rights in Osijek, 'The ICTY's work in Croatia is often reported in a way that completely lacks objectivity. Because of this, a wrong picture of the court has been created'.[14] Popular prejudice towards the ICTY, in turn, discourages people from taking an interest in its work; interviewees frequently insisted that they already know everything that they need to know about the Tribunal.

While their sense of injustice was not necessarily well-informed, it was clear that they felt a strong need to affix guilt – they needed someone to blame and to hold responsible for what happened in Ovčara. This, combined with the fact that the ICTY has conducted so few prosecutions in relation to the crime,[15] helps to explain why interviewees were so insistent on Šljivančanin's guilt and his central

---

14 Author interview, Osijek, 27 July 2011.
15 Aside from Mrkšić and Šljivančanin, no one has been convicted at the ICTY in relation to the Ovčara massacre. The proceedings against Slavko Dokmanović, the former president of Vukovar municipality, were terminated after he committed suicide in his cell on 29 June 1998 while awaiting the ICTY's verdict in his case. The former Serbian President, Slobodan Milošević, was indicted, *inter alia*, for crimes committed in Vukovar, but his trial was brought to an abrupt end when he died on 11 March 2006. The ICTY's initial indictment in 2003 against Jovica Stanišić and Franko Simatović, who as discussed in Chapter 3 were recently acquitted, included charges relating to the Ovčara massacre, but these were subsequently

Figure 6.1 Ovčara memorial near Vukovar.

role in the massacre. Hence, even those who were aware of the Tribunal's finding that Ovčara was not the work of JNA forces refused to accept it. Expressing a common viewpoint, the leader of a local veterans' group maintained that Šljivančanin, as a high-ranking military man, must have known what was going to happen at Ovčara, and that to suggest otherwise is completely implausible.[16] Interviewees' conviction that Šljivančanin must have known what lay in store for the prisoners made them unwilling and/or unable to comprehend his early release; for them, it could only be understood as a gross and flagrant injustice that dishonoured the memory and suffering of the victims.

What made the situation even harder to bear was that Šljivančanin was now a free man while Gotovina – whom interviewees unanimously described as a hero who had liberated his country – was serving (at the time of the interviews in 2011) a 24-year prison sentence. Interviewees had little knowledge of why Gotovina had been found guilty and only mentioned Knin (although Gotovina was in fact convicted of unlawful artillery attacks on the aforementioned Four Towns). They

dropped in 2006. Goran Hadžić, the former leader of the RSK, and Vojislav Šešelj, the leader of the SRS, are both currently on trial for crimes committed, *inter alia*, in Vukovar.
16   Author interview, Vukovar, 29 July 2011.

repeatedly insisted, for example, that no grenades were fired at Knin[17] and that the town remained unscathed. Interviewees thus evinced total incredulity that Gotovina could be convicted as a war criminal while nobody has been prosecuted or held accountable at the ICTY for the total destruction of Vukovar.

Unlike Bosniak interviewees in BiH, however, Croats in Vukovar seldom demanded that all war criminals must be tried. It seemed that they had wearily resigned themselves to the fact that only a small number of perpetrators would ever stand trial. In this context, even the arrest of Goran Hadžić in Serbia on 20 July 2011 – during the author's fieldwork in Vukovar – elicited only muted reactions. For interviewees, Hadžić, the erstwhile leader of the RSK, was just one individual and his capture, coming 20 years after the war in Vukovar ended, was simply too little, too late. The only hope was that Hadžić's trial would yield important information regarding the ultimate fate and whereabouts of Vukovar's remaining missing persons.[18]

Among Croat interviewees in Knin, perceptions of the ICTY were similarly negative. The overwhelming feeling was that it was absurd for the Tribunal to expend its resources putting Croats on trial; they were simply defending themselves and their country. The prosecution of Croats, and in particular Gotovina, had thereby fuelled and entrenched allegations that the ICTY is a political court with an anti-Croat bias. While interviewees did not know how many Croats had been tried at the ICTY, they always asserted that the number was very large. Indeed, one interviewee, the president of a local veterans' association, was adamant – despite being unable to cite any statistics – that the Tribunal has prosecuted more Croats than Serbs.[19] Unsurprisingly, it was the ICTY's guilty verdicts against Gotovina and Markač which had aroused a particularly deep sense of injustice. If, as Minow argues, '...selectivity in prosecution risks creating martyrs out of the few who are subject to trial and punishment' (1998: 45), nothing better illustrates this than the trial and conviction of the Croatian generals. Both in Knin and in Croatia as a whole, Croats reacted to the verdicts by expressing and manifesting their unwavering support for these men. On 5 August 2011, for example, during the annual celebrations in Knin to mark and celebrate Croatia's victory in Operation

---

17 In the trial of Gotovina, Čermak and Markač, however, the Trial Chamber found that, '... the HV fired at least 600 projectiles into Knin on 4 August 1995 and at least 300 projectiles into Knin on 5 August 1995' (2011: §1898). Heavy weaponry was also deployed, including multiple-barrel rocket launchers (Prosecutor v. Gotovina, Čermak and Markač 2011: §1898).

18 According to the ICMP, an estimated 5,500 persons were missing in Croatia at the end of the war, and approximately 2,000 are still missing today (ICMP 2013). Statistics on the number of missing persons in Vukovar are far less accessible. However, in November 2011, during the commemorations (which the author attended) to mark the twentieth anniversary of the fall of Vukovar, it was widely stated that 306 persons from the municipality of Vukovar remain missing.

19 Author interview, Knin, 12 April 2012.

Figure 6.2 A poster in central Knin.

Storm, many people were wearing t-shirts emblazoned with the words *'Gotovina – Heroj'*.[20] A year later, during fieldwork in Knin in April 2012, the author photographed a large poster of Gotovina and Markač on the side of a building. The poster declared: *'Generali, junaci, Hrvatskog domovinskog rata – Knin je uz vas!'* (Generals, heroes, of the Croatian Homeland War – Knin is with you). Moreover, across Croatia, from Vukovar to Zadar, pro-Gotovina graffiti could (and still can) frequently be seen. In short, the proceedings against Gotovina and Markač – which the media seldom covered in an objective and informative way (Stojanović and Kruhonja 2011: 5) – had become much more than simply the trial of two individuals. At stake was the legitimacy of Croatia's *'Domovinski rat'* (Homeland War).[21] In this context,

20 Vukušić notes that, 'There are many reasons that Croatians were overwhelmingly convinced of Gotovina's innocence, but one of the most compelling is that there is a video showing him yelling at his subordinates to be disciplined, organised and behave according to rules' (2014: 164). Indeed, some interviewees referred to this video, including those Serbs in Knin who opined that Gotovina is not a war criminal.
21 To cite Peskin and Boduszyński, the ICTY's indictments against the two generals raised 'the uncomfortable question that the Homeland War was not the cleanly fought, honorable battle portrayed by government leaders' (2003: 1135).

the conviction of the generals became synonymous with an attack on Croatia's war effort, thereby engendering a double sense of injustice.

There were widespread celebrations across Croatia, therefore, when, in November 2012, the Appeals Chamber overturned the Trial Chamber's verdicts against Gotovina and Markač. Reacting to the news, Croatia's Prime Minister, Zoran Milanović, exclaimed, 'We are relieved' (cited in Zebić et al. 2012); while President Ivo Josipović was quick to declare that, 'The verdict confirms everything that we believe in Croatia: that generals Gotovina and Markač are innocent' (BBC 2012). In Knin, Croat interviewees were similarly delighted; for them, justice had at last been done. However, the appeal judgement had seemingly done little to alter either their very negative views of the Tribunal or their conviction that its work is politically-driven. In March 2013, interviewees insisted, for example, that the generals – whom they repeatedly described as 'professional soldiers' who were simply doing their job – should never have been indicted and prosecuted. They also emphasized that as a result of these legal proceedings, Gotovina and Markač have effectively lost several years of their lives which they can never get back. As interviewees saw it, in other words, the justness of the acquittal verdicts did not make up for the wrongs and injustices which the ICTY had committed against the two men.

Reconciliation via truth?

According to Bassiouni, 'The ICTY represents an attempt to deal with the truth, although it is not ideal' (2003: 200). There are of course limits to how much 'truth' the ICTY can document, but a more significant problem is the fact that it has little control over how its truths are *received* by local communities on the ground. It is precisely the extent to which these communities accept and embrace the Tribunal's findings that is critical to determining the validity of the frequently posited truth-reconciliation nexus.

Serb responses to ICTY truths

Serb interviewees, whether in Vukovar or in Knin, seldom referred to specific ICTY judgements. By extension, they did not explicitly reject any of its judgements – with the notable exception of the appeal judgement against Gotovina and Markač. The key point, however, is that popular reactions to the Tribunal's judgements, and to the truths therein contained, do not take place within a vacuum. They occur within, and are influenced by, a particular hermeneutical framework which shapes how the war is viewed and understood. Serb interviewees in Vukovar, for example, vigorously rejected the claim that Serbs were the aggressors in 1991, repeatedly underscoring that Serbs could not commit aggression in their own country (an argument which overlooks the fact that the JNA entered Vukovar from Serbia). While some interviewees explicitly stated that the war did not need to happen, they also insisted that the JNA was merely trying to gain control of the situation but was prevented from doing so by Croat soldiers shooting at them from inside houses and buildings. Serb interviewees were therefore unequivocal that the war in Vukovar was a 'civil war' – started by Croats – which resulted in significant suffering and loss of life on *both* sides. Interviewees in Knin were similarly dogmatic that Serbs did not attack Croatia (how could they when they have lived in Croatia for hundreds of years?), and that Serbs and Croats alike committed crimes in what was a civil war. The erection of barricades in Knin and the establishment of the RSK, they claimed, were not acts of provocation and aggression but simply defensive measures.

Such narratives have limited explanatory value. They cannot explicate, for example, why the JNA laid siege to Vukovar, why it destroyed almost everything in sight – including Serb homes – or why Serbian paramilitaries, such as Arkan's Tigers, were active in the town (Stewart 2007: 159–160). The theme of defence is similarly at odds with the perpetration of Serb crimes in the Krajina area, like the attack on the Croat village of Kijevo.[22] The theme of reciprocal suffering which Serb narratives emphasize, however, may have contributed to a process of aversive acknowledgement; Serb interviewees were overall more willing than Croat interviewees to concede that their own side had committed crimes. It could be argued that because Serb forces and paramilitaries overall committed the largest number of crimes in Croatia, these crimes cannot easily be denied, but this fails to account for the high levels of denial that exist among Serbs in BiH. Biro et al. have identified a very pragmatic explanation for the existence of significant aversive acknowledgement in Vukovar; 'The Vukovar Serbs lost their primacy and have chosen to remain in Croatia; they must admit to the existence of war criminals on their side if they wish to remain as accepted citizens of the state' (2004: 195). This argument, which is similarly applicable to Serbs in Knin, can also help to account for the much lower levels of aversive acknowledgment in BiH, where Serbs are not a minority and have their own entity. To further build upon Biro et al.'s reasoning, the civil war narrative which Serbian interviewees so readily embraced seemingly serves a dual purpose; it allows Serbs to acknowledge the crimes committed by their own side, while also drawing attention to the fact that war crimes were likewise perpetrated by members of the other side.

The tension between, on one hand, an acutely-felt desire and need for recognition of Serb victimhood and, on the other hand, a widespread perception that the ICTY has neglected crimes against Serbs, has created a keen sense of injustice, and this is the biggest obstacle to popular acceptance and internalization of ICTY truths. Serb rejection of the appeal judgement against Gotovina

---

22 Tanner writes that Kijevo, whose inhabitants were mainly elderly, '…had been surrounded for weeks, as the road from Kijevo to the coast passed through Serb villages. It offered no threat to the Krajina authorities. In spite of that, the Knin police and the local army base razed the village to its foundations on 26 August [1991]' (2010: 255).

and Markač particularly illustrates this point. For interviewees, the acquittals trivialized and downplayed Serb suffering, by effectively creating an account-ability gap. Interviewees' rejection of the verdicts can thus be interpreted as a refusal to be complicit in this diminishing (from their perspective) of Serb vic-timhood. To cite Subotić, '...the *Gotovina* verdict was fundamentally unaccept-able because it effectively changed the entire Serbian construct of Operation Storm and delegitimized Serbian claims to victimhood at the hand of the Croats' (2013b: 21).

Croat responses to ICTY truths

Every year, on 18 November, thousands of people gather in Vukovar to remember and honour the town's victims, the hundreds of combatants and civilians whose lives were abruptly ended in 1991. In freezing, biting tempera-tures, the vast crowds slowly weave their way from the local hospital – from where the victims of Ovčara began their final journey – to the memorial centre on the outskirts of Vukovar where the beautifully-maintained graves of fallen *branitelji* (defenders) stand in neat symmetrical rows. Events such as these, coupled with the complete absence of any Serb memorials in Vukovar (Clark 2013a), have helped to reinforce and entrench a particular war narrative focused exclusively on Croat victimhood. Croat interviewees viewed and explained wartime events in Vukovar and Knin through the hermeneutical prism of the 'Homeland War', a meta-framing device constructed around the dual leitmotifs of aggression and defence: Serbs were the aggressors, driven by their desire to create an all-encompassing 'Greater Serbia', while Croats were merely defending their *dom* (home) and protecting what was theirs. It is similarly within the context of this interpretative framework that the ICTY's work is viewed. Hence, what critically determines popular reactions to the ICTY's judgements, and in particular communities' readiness to accept the truths therein contained, is the extent to which these judgements either support or challenge the discourse of the Homeland War.

When the Tribunal was first created, it garnered strong support in Croatia precisely because its trials were expected to uphold the Homeland War narrative and confirm Croatia's victim status (Peskin 2008: 95, 99). Hence, when the ICTY confounded expectations by indicting Croats, including Bosnian Croat 'defenders' such as Tihomir Blaškić, initial enthusiasm for the institution quickly waned, as did Croatia's willingness to co-operate with the Tribunal. As Subotić remarks, 'The very character of the Croatian war as understood locally has made accepting international justice demands difficult...' (2009: 108). The dominance of the Homeland War narrative, in turn, means that levels of aversive acknowl-edgement are low (Teršelić 2013: 39). How could Croats commit crimes in the context of a war in which they were simply defending themselves? In Vukovar, for example, an ex-combatant acknowledged that some Serbs were killed during the three-month siege of the town. However, he was emphatic that Serbs themselves were responsible for these deaths, not Croats.[23] For her part, a rape victim explained that if some crimes did occur on the Croat side – a possibility which she did not completely rule out – they could not be compared to Serb crimes. The latter, she maintained, were carefully planned; Serbs had names of people whom they wanted to kill. In contrast, any Croat crimes committed were simply the work of a few local 'idiots'.[24]

In Knin, where aversive acknowledgment was similarly lacking, denial served the specific function of protecting the glorified image of Operation Storm as a legitimate and valiant military campaign to liberate occupied Croatian territory. Hence, although some interviewees accepted that crimes did occur during Operation Storm, they vehemently rejected any suggestion that the HV was involved. Responsibility lay with rogue individuals and criminal groups, they underlined.[25] Some interviewees sought to further diminish these crimes by denying the civilian status of Serb victims. The deputy president of a local veterans' association, for example, claimed that in the Serb villages surrounding Knin, everyone was armed.[26] The reality, however, is that the majority of Serb victims killed during and after Operation Storm were elderly and infirm, people who remained in their villages because they were not strong enough to leave (Peskin 2008: 103; Subotić 2009: 84). Such denials, moreover, are not confined to the residents of Knin. In 2001, for example, the airing of *Storm over Croatia*, a documentary which reported on crimes against Serbs committed in the aftermath of Operation Storm, caused widespread public outrage across Croatia. As Subotić describes, 'What followed the broadcast was a series of attacks against the filmmakers, including death threats and public condemnation by all major political parties and political figures such as then prime minister Račan, as well as a debate in the parliament' (2009: 110).

The appeal judgement against Gotovina and Markač, moreover, is likely to further entrench long-standing Croat denial regarding Operation Storm. The acquittal verdict does not change the fact that significant crimes were perpetrated in the context of this military operation. During the trial of Gotovina, Čermak and Markač, for example, the Trial Chamber found that,

> ...members of Croatian military forces and the Special Police committed more than 40 acts of murders and acts of inhumane treatment and cruel treatment as crimes against humanity and violations of the laws or customs of war against Krajina Serbs and were responsible for a large number of

---

23 Author interview, Vukovar, 14 July 2011.
24 Author interview, Vukovar, 18 July 2011.
25 Certainly, there is some evidence to suggest that criminals did play a part in the perpetration of crimes against Serbs (Prosecutor v. Gotovina, Čermak and Markač 2011: §1715).
26 Author interview, Knin, 10 April 2012.

incidents of destruction and plunder as violations of the laws or customs of war, of property owned or inhabited by Krajina Serbs.

(2011: §1710)

On the ground, however, the judgement has been popularly interpreted as exonerating the HV. It has thus reinforced the common viewpoint that any crimes that occurred during and after Operation Storm were the work of a few local thugs and lone individuals. The seriousness of these crimes is thus diminished. The very complexity of the Tribunal's judgements, moreover, further facilitates denial. Interviewees, for example, were unaware that the Appeals Chamber effectively overturned the guilty verdicts against Gotovina and Markač on a technicality – the Trial Chamber's use of the 200 metre margin of error. To them, the acquittal verdicts merely verified what was already blatantly obvious, namely that the generals are innocent men who, like the entire HV, were simply defending their people and country.

Croatia is now conducting its own domestic war crimes prosecutions. However, the pace of progress has been slow, and Amnesty International has expressed concern that, 'the number of investigations conducted by the Croatian authorities is low compared to the scale of war crimes allegedly committed during and after "Operation Storm"' (2011). Indeed, the European Commission (EC) has emphasized that, 'Efforts to address impunity for war crimes should be intensified, as the majority of cases [not only those relating to Operation Storm] have yet to be successfully prosecuted' (2012a: 4). Critical issues regarding impartiality have also arisen. According to Vesna Teršelić, the head of the NGO *Documenta* in Zagreb, Serbs are far more likely to be indicted than Croats; and if Croats are indicted for crimes against a member of another ethnic group, there is a high probability that they will be acquitted or that the proceedings will drag on indefinitely (Bloch 2005b: 10). Furthermore, Serbs are more likely to be tried in absentia. For example, 'In the first eight months of 2011, 20 of the 33 active war crimes trials took place at least partially in absentia, and of the 20 newly-indicted individuals in 2011, 10 were indicted in absentia, primarily Serbs' (Human Rights Watch 2012: 2). Although Serb interviewees never referred to these domestic trials, several Croat interviewees strongly objected to the prosecution of Croatian 'heroes' such as Tomislav Merčep, the former commander of the Reserve Unit of the Ministry of the Interior. Merčep is currently on trial in Zagreb County Court, charged with war crimes committed in Vukovar municipality.

According to Ljiljana Alvir, the president of the Vukovar Mothers, '...we need to know the truth in order to be able to move forward' (cited in Bloch 2005a: 20).[27] In a similar vein, interviewees repeatedly emphasized the importance

---

27 Author's translation from Croatian.

of truth; it must be found and it must be accepted. However, in Croatia, as in BiH and Kosovo, people's memories of the war have undergone a process of 'ethnization', wherein '...a memory itself and interpretation of the past become ethnically exclusive, creating subjective, psychological realities and different symbolic meanings of common events in people who belong to different ethnic groups' (Corkalo et al. 2004: 157–158). In this context, 'truth' has become similarly 'ethnicized', with the result that any ICTY truths that undermine or contradict dominant ethno-national narratives are ignored and rejected. Hence, contrary to the Tribunal's claim that its work is helping to combat denial, the reality is that truth and denial in fact co-exist, the former reinforcing the latter.

Inter-ethnic relations

According to Corkalo et al., '...a community will never be the same in the wake of war and communal violence' (2004: 149), and interviewees frequently shared this viewpoint. Both in Vukovar and in Knin, three main arguments were repeatedly articulated: that people are already living together and do not need to reconcile; that reconciliation may be possible (although difficult) for some people but impossible for those who have lost close loved-ones; and that reconciliation cannot be forced and will take generations. Consistent with such claims, and using the Reconciliation Matrix developed in Chapter 2, the final part of this chapter demonstrates that there is little inter-ethnic reconciliation in either Vukovar or Knin.

Human security

Despite its bloody recent past and the ever-present physical reminders of the war – including battle-scarred buildings and memorials honouring the dead (but only on the Croat side) – Vukovar has a peaceful feel. Some Serb interviewees recounted experiences which had made them feel uncomfortable, such as asking for a loaf of '*hljeb*' (the Serbian word for bread) and being told that the correct (Croatian) word is '*kruh*'; or being shunned by former Croat friends. However, only a handful of interviewees claimed to feel physically insecure. Such feelings, moreover, tended to be strongest among elderly Serbs. A sexagenarian interviewee in Borovo Selo, for instance, described his fears of another war.[28] For the majority of interviewees, however, whether Serb or Croat, physical security was seemingly not an issue. Nevertheless, it is essential to note that interviewees on both sides frequently claimed that many people in Vukovar – and in particular Croat ex-combatants – are armed. Those interviewees who had fought in the war

---

28 Author interview, Borovo Selo, 10 August 2011.

themselves confirmed this. Explaining how they had struggled to acquire weapons in 1991, Croat veterans believed that they still needed their arms – just in case. It is impossible to know how many households in Vukovar have equipped themselves with guns and other light weapons; this information is simply not available. The important point is that while very few interviewees professed to feelings of insecurity, the possession of arms exposes an important 'hidden transcript' (Scott 1990).

Expressions of economic insecurity, on the other hand, were commonplace. Serb and Croat interviewees alike consistently emphasized the lack of jobs and the quotidian struggle to make ends meet. While some interviewees accepted that Serbs and Croats faced the same problems and challenges, more often than not they asserted that their own group was the most affected and disadvantaged. This is consistent with Corkalo et al.'s research in Vukovar and Mostar (2000–2002), which found that, 'Both unemployment and low incomes contribute to the feeling of being disadvantaged because of national origin. All national groups feel that their group is discriminated against in employment and realization of their rights; all feel that the other group is privileged' (2004: 157). Serb interviewees most frequently argued that they have a lower quality of life than local Croats. Croat interviewees, however, always rubbished such claims, insisting that it is in fact Croats in Vukovar who suffer the most. The economic situation, in other words, is helping to encourage inter-ethnic resentment and mutual recriminations. By extension, interviewees repeatedly maintained, like those in BiH, that if the economy were stronger[29] and if people had regular incomes, inter-ethnic relations would significantly improve. Echoing such arguments, the former head of the psychiatric ward of the local hospital, Dr Nikola Drobnjak, has pertinently suggested that, 'Enough monuments have been put up in Vukovar. Let the next monument to the town be a new factory' (cited in Matejčić 2012).

In 1998, during the surprisingly smooth process of 'peaceful reintegration', Croats began returning to Vukovar. In the same year, on the other side of the country, Serbs who had left Croatia during Operation Storm were slowly returning to Knin and the Krajina area. These Serb returnees often faced significant hostility from local Croats (Koska 2008: 192), and in particular from Croat settlers from BiH (Mesić and Bagić 2011: 30). This hostility variously manifested itself in verbal abuse, acts of vandalism and, in extreme cases, physical violence. Such problems, moreover, have persisted in certain areas. According to a 2006 report by Human Rights Watch, for example, which highlighted an 'upsurge of violence and intimidation against members of the Serb minority in Croatia' (2006: 10), parts of western Croatia were particularly affected. The report observed that, 'Most allegedly ethnically motivated incidents in 2006 have

---

29 According to the EC, 'Unemployment, public deficit and debt continued to increase in 2011 from already high levels. The high external indebtedness remains a key vulnerability of the economy' (2012a: 5).

occurred in Zadar county, especially in the villages around the town of Benkovac'. Part of the explanation, it suggested, was that, 'During the war, Serb forces killed dozens of civilians in Croat villages in the area...The crimes remain largely unpunished, which may account for the continuing tensions in the area' (Human Rights Watch 2006: 12).

In Knin, however, both Serb and Croat interviewees – like their counterparts in Vukovar – maintained that there are no inter-ethnic incidents or problems in the town. Serb interviewees in the nearby village of Golubić explained that when they first returned to their homes in 1997/1998, they did not feel entirely secure. One interviewee, for example, claimed that her new neighbours – Croats from BiH – tried to provoke Serbs by, *inter alia*, singing Četnik songs and shouting abuse. Today, however, she assessed that the principal problem in Golubić is the shortage of jobs, coupled with the relative lack of children and young people in the village.[30] Sharing this view, a second interviewee explained that while the situation was tense when he and his family returned to Golubić, they never experienced any real problems.[31]

In Knin, as in Vukovar, what interviewees did express were strong feelings of economic insecurity. More than any other issue, they wanted to underscore and discuss the bleak economic situation and lack of prospects. Knin is part of Šibensko-Kninska county, one of the least developed counties in Croatia (Serbian Democratic Forum 2007: 43). Nevertheless, 'Knin used to be a very important traffic junction with well developed industry' (Glamuzina, Šiljković and Glamuzina 2005: 85). The railway, for example, was once a major employer, repairing trains from all over Croatia, and numerous factories employed thousands of people. Due to a combination of factors, however – including the legacy of war, the onset of an economic crisis and 'a disastrous programme of privatisation' in Croatia (Tanner 2010: 303) – economic stagnation has become deeply entrenched and most of the pre-war industries in Knin have largely ground to a halt. A notable exception is the nuts and bolts factory TVIK, although it now employs significantly fewer workers than it once did. The vast majority of interviewees were unemployed, and those who had jobs were often their family's sole breadwinner.

As in Vukovar, this depressed economic situation is helping to fuel inter-ethnic tension. Serb interviewees always maintained that it is far easier for Croats to find work in Knin because the majority of businesses are Croat-owned. One of the few Serb-owned businesses is the *Tri Lovca* (The Three Hunters), a small restaurant with simple guest rooms upstairs. Croat interviewees, however, frequently claimed that Serbs have a better standard of living than Croats because they have received far more financial support and assistance. What particularly angered Croat interviewees was the fact that although not all Serbs have returned to live

---

30 Author interview, Golubić, 7 April 2012.
31 Author interview, Golubić, 8 April 2012.

in Knin on a permanent basis, they nevertheless receive a pension from the Republic of Croatia. Serb interviewees who divided their time between Croatia and Serbia, however, stressed that it was not feasible for them to permanently live in Knin and its environs, due to the difficulties and discrimination they faced in securing employment.

Deep contact

As Croats began to return to Vukovar in the late 1990s, 'Social life "doubled": new shops and coffee bars, opened by Croats, attracted exclusively Croat customers. Parallel institutions, such as local radio stations, sports clubs, and citizens' associations, were created. Children in schools[32] and kindergartens were separated into different buildings or shifts...' (Kosić and Tauber 2010: 2). Within this polarized context, however, the frequency and depth of inter-ethnic contact varies considerably and there is no 'standard' pattern. Croat ex-combatants were the least likely to have contact with Serbs. They tended to primarily spend time with fellow *branitelji*, playing cards together in their veterans' associations, drinking and socializing in particular cafes – like the café Mostar in the (predominantly Croat) Mitnica area of Vukovar – and fishing on the banks of the Danube. Few of them expressed any interest in having contact with Serbs. While some acknowledged that Serbs and Croats must communicate with each other, all of them shunned the prospect of anything more than superficial contact with Serbs. Deeper contact was impossible, ex-combatants maintained, because Serbs will not disclose the truth, in particular regarding the whereabouts of missing persons.

Nevertheless, some ex-combatants were less hard-line than others. Expressing a more moderate viewpoint, for example, the head of one veterans' association opined that while Croats and Serbs have distanced themselves from each other, they do not bother or threaten each other – and for the time being this is enough. Twenty years after the war ended, he added, Vukovar is a peaceful place and this is the most that can be expected at the present time.[33] The interviewee's colleague, a fellow ex-combatant, claimed that he still communicates with Serbs, including with those who were his friends before the war. He also emphasized, however, that these relations are not the same as they were pre-war and that something has been lost, and hence he and his former friends no longer visit each other's homes like they once did.[34] Indeed, almost all interviewees in Vukovar

---

32 As in parts of BiH, schools in Vukovar are divided, which severely limits the opportunities for inter-ethnic contact, let alone deep contact, among young people. The existence of divided schools, moreover, has significantly, and negatively, impacted on how young Serbs and Croats perceive each other (see, for example, Warshauer Freedman et al. 2004: 233–234).

33 Author interview, Vukovar, 29 July 2011.

34 Author interview, Vukovar, 29 July 2011.

underlined that inter-ethnic relations have fundamentally changed as a result of the war. Most frequently, they spoke of walls, barriers and distances between people which did not previously exist. Some Serb interviewees, moreover, believed that Croats are under pressure – from local authorities and especially ex-combatants – to refrain from more than minimal contact with Serbs.[35] While Croat interviewees typically rejected such claims, some nevertheless opined that it would not be prudent for them to be seen to be socializing with Serbs as it might arouse suspicion.

Some interviewees did spend time with members of the other ethnic group. These relations, however, were often confusing and exposed a significant disconnect between public behaviour and private beliefs. The following two examples vividly illustrate this. During the summer months, small boats repeatedly zigzag across the Danube, transporting the citizens of Vukovar to and from the small wooded island of Mala Ada. While visiting the island during a scorching Sunday afternoon in July, the author met two middle-aged Croat men, Z and B (the latter a former ex-combatant), who invited her to join their small gathering. The two men were eating and drinking with a group of eight other men, three of whom were former Serb soldiers. Relations between them seemed perfectly cordial. When the author later spoke to Z alone, however, he bitterly complained that 'Serbs' will not apologize for their actions during the war. He further explained that he did not know the three Serb men well and that whenever he is in the company of Serbs, there is always a distance between them. When asked why he socializes with people whom he does not fully trust, he sat and thought about this for several minutes, as though the question had previously never occurred to him. Ultimately, his simple answer was that human beings need to socialize and that without human interaction, life is worthless. He added that while he does not hate Serbs, he is not ready to re-build relations with them in any deep sense.[36]

Turning to the second example, during the summer months, Vukovar's elderly residents are most visible during the late afternoon and early evening, when the sun is comfortable rather than oppressive. Between 5p.m. and 7p.m. in particular, small groups of pensioners can be seen bunched together on wooden benches, sometimes deep in conversation, at other times silently observing the world around them. On one occasion, a balmy summer's evening in July, the author struck up a conversation with two sexagenarian gentlemen sitting together in the centre of the town. They explained that one of them was a Serb while the other was a Croat, and that they always sat together during the evenings. Soon after, a third man joined them, and the Serb man turned to talk to the newcomer, also a Serb. While they were engrossed in conversation, the Croat man moved to face the author and made a gesture with his hand, as if he were slitting his throat. The

---

35 Author interview, Vukovar, 18 July 2011.
36 Author interview, Vukovar, 13 July 2011.

following day, the author interviewed this man, who resolutely asserted that Serbs have always made war and cannot be trusted. After the war, this interviewee had spent three-and-a-half months in a Serb-run camp, and he repeatedly underlined that he will never forget what happened in Vukovar. He also emphasized, however, that it is a human need for people to socialize and to talk, although he was at pains to point out that he only speaks to Serbs about the weather, rising food prices and similar neutral topics – and never about the war.[37]

In Knin, as in Vukovar, ex-combatants often expressed the most extreme and intransigent views on the subject of contact. When asked about his relations with local Serbs, for example, a former combatant who was just 18 years old when he took up weapons against the enemy wryly asserted that the only good Serb is a dead Serb.[38] The deputy president of a local veterans' association similarly underscored his predilection not to have contact with Serbs, maintaining that the latter did far better out of the war than Croats did. When asked to provide an example, he claimed that Serbs have larger and more comfortable houses, although he also admitted that he had not visited any Serb homes since the war.[39] Within the total interview sample, in contrast, the majority of interviewees claimed to have some contact with members of the other ethnic group, even socializing with them on a regular or more *ad hoc* basis. The dominant theme that once again emerged, however, was that inter-ethnic relations have significantly changed. Serbs and Croats can drink coffee and play cards together, according to interviewees, but there are no real friendships.

Interestingly, one factor that has seemingly contributed to an improvement in inter-ethnic relations in Knin, however small, is the presence of Croats from BiH. The latter arrived in Knin in the aftermath of Operation Storm, at the invitation of the Croatian government.[40] Despite this, they have not been made to feel welcome. According to a Bosnian Croat interviewee from Travnik in central BiH, Bosnian Croat settlers are disliked because local people accuse them of taking their homes and jobs.[41] What also clearly emerged from fieldwork in Knin is that both Croats and Serbs look down on the settlers. Interviewees frequently described them, for example, as illiterate and backward people. Furthermore, they always maintained that the settlers are culturally different, although they could never expand on this claim or explain the precise nature of these alleged differences. Interestingly, both Serb and Croat interviewees frequently suggested that they have more in common with each other than with the settlers from BiH,

---

37 Author interview, Vukovar, 12 July 2011.
38 Author interview, Knin, 13 April 2012.
39 Author interview, Knin, 12 April 2012.
40 According to an associate protection officer at the UNHCR in Knin, 130,000 Bosnian Croats arrived in Croatia following the end of Operation Storm. Author interview, Knin, 10 April 2012.
41 Author interview, Knin, 14 April 2012.

and this belief has, in turn, facilitated at least a rudimentary sense of cross-ethnic unity against the Bosnian Croat 'outsiders'.

What is clear from the above discussion is that on the issue of contact, both Vukovar and Knin present a very mixed picture. There is essentially a spectrum of contact, in which an absence of contact co-exists with superficial contact and more extended forms of contact that involve socializing with members of the other ethnic group. The repeated references to the existence of barriers, walls and distance, however, poignantly highlight an absence of deep contact. A major factor that is fundamentally inhibiting the development of deeper bonds, as in BiH, is the critical absence of inter-ethnic trust.

Trust

In Vukovar, trust is in short supply, particularly on the Croat side. The main source of the deep mistrust that Croat interviewees habitually expressed was the widespread conviction that local Serbs are deliberately withholding vital information regarding war crimes and the whereabouts of missing persons, a prime example of trust-impeding behaviour. Serb interviewees were always emphatic that they did not possess such information. They pointed out that during the siege of Vukovar, they were living underground with Croat neighbours and hence did not see what was going on around them. They further emphasized that following the town's 'liberation'[42] on 18 November 1991, Vukovar was not a nice place to be, even for Serbs. The town was full of unsavoury characters and Četniks from Serbia, they claimed, who looted and plundered at will and whose unwelcome presence intimidated local Serbs. Croat interviewees, however, readily dismissed such arguments; how could local Serbs not be privy to vital information and facts when they remained in Vukovar after the 'fall' of the town? The problem is that as long as people's questions remain unanswered, they will continue to blame and harbour mistrust towards the other ethnic group. The ongoing search for answers is further inimical to the development of trust in the sense that it is helping to keep people locked in the past, particularly the families of missing persons.

Another indicator of the lack of trust in Vukovar is the popular tendency, on both sides, to make sweeping generalizations about members of the other ethnic group. While interviewees consistently voiced the view that it matters only whether a person is good or bad and not whether s/he is Croat or Serb, the manner in which they spoke about members of the other ethnic group manifestly belied such claims. Again and again, interviewees spoke in terms of 'us' and 'them' and readily embraced a range of stereotypes about the other group. A Serb interviewee in the village of Borovo Selo, for example, alleged that the problem

---

42 Highlighting the persistence of competing war narratives, Serbs refer to 18 November 1991 as the *oslobođenje* (liberation) of Vukovar, while for Croats this date signifies the tragic *pad* (fall) of the town.

with Croats is their reverence and admiration for Ante Pavelić and the Ustaše; while Croat interviewees often referred to Serbs as Četniks. Linked to this latter point, during a visit to the HDLSKL in Borovo Naselje, the author was given a small booklet in English about the massacre at Ovčara in November 1991.[43] Entitled *Ovčara: Scream in the Night*, the booklet is written from the fictional perspective of one of the victims and each page contains very graphic, cartoon-type images depicting the massacre itself and the brutality which preceded it. The killers are drawn as wild savages, red-eyed Četniks sporting beards and wielding long, blood-splattered knives. Written in extremely poor English, and fundamentally dehumanizing the killers, the first page describes how, in violation of the Geneva Conventions and international law, 'the members of the aggressor paramilitary had as a blood thirsty vampires attacked the wounded, civilians and defenders, were insolently robbing them, humiliating, butchering and killing on various painful ways'. On page seven, a fictive victim who narrates the events thinks about his family and in his head he says to them, 'I am happy you're not here and you won't experience this, what these weird people with bloody eyes, stinking of alcohol and sweat, are doing to us'. Such materials strongly encourage dangerous generalizations and prejudices. When learning that the author was renting a house in the Serb village of Borovo Selo, for example, Croat interviewees routinely advised great caution and warned: 'Look after yourself'.

When people look at each other not as individuals but simply as part of a wider group, they may similarly collectivize guilt. Although most Croat interviewees, when asked, acknowledged that not all Serbs are guilty, they frequently spoke about Serbs in a way that contradicted this. One interviewee, for example, explained that while she knows that not every Serb in Vukovar is guilty, she cannot trust them and has little contact with them. She repeatedly emphasized that Croats had no idea what *the Serbs* were going to do in Vukovar.[44] Another interviewee, who lost her father and husband during the war, was emphatic that Serbs cannot be trusted because of what *they* did and because *they* are not willing to apologize.[45] A third interviewee, whose mother spent three days in the Velepromet camp in Vukovar, confidently asserted that Serbs in the town remain tight-lipped because *they* know what *they* did and have something to hide.[46]

---

43 The booklet was written by Danijel Rehak, the co-president of the HDLSKL, whom the author interviewed.
44 Author interview, Borovo Naselje, 12 July 2011.
45 Author interview, Vukovar, 18 July 2011.
46 Author interview, Vukovar, 10 July 2011. The head of a local NGO, the only organization in Vukovar whose work is exclusively focused on psychosocial issues and healing, opined that generalization and collectivization of guilt can be seen as symptoms of unresolved trauma, which is being allowed to fester. Highlighting the prevalence of trauma in Vukovar, particularly among ex-combatants, he claimed that there is little political will to tackle the problem because a traumatized citizenry is easier to manipulate. Author interview, Vukovar, 10 August 2011.

Vukovar thus further problematizes the oft-made claim that criminal trials individualize guilt (see, for example, Cassese 1998: 6; Goldstone 1996: 488). Instead, what the interview data strongly indicates is that, '...the rhetorical attention international criminal lawyers devote to individual responsibility is ill-matched to the mood of the general public when it comes to questions of responsibility' (Simpson 2007: 66).

In Knin, expressions of mistrust were similarly strongest and most frequent on the Croat side. While interviewees did not accuse local Serbs of withholding information, there was a widespread consensus among them that Serbs need to face up to what *they* did and to admit that *they* were the aggressors (in both Knin and Croatia as a whole). From the interviewees' viewpoint, such an admission was a fundamental prerequisite for the (re-) building of trust. Serb interviewees, however, argued that it is Croats who must accept the truth and acknowledge that crimes occurred on both sides. Trust will remain lacking, they averred, as long as Croats persist in celebrating Operation Storm, denying the crimes therein committed and supporting war criminals like Gotovina (many interviewees continued to make this last point even after Gotovina's acquittal). Some interviewees, moreover, cited specific incidents which had further fuelled mistrust. For Serbs in Golubić, for example, one such incident was the banning of a monument to honour the 34 victims who died in the village after Operation Storm. Shortly before it was due to be unveiled on 2 October 2011, Croatia's then Minister of the Interior, Tomislav Karamarko, put a stop to the ceremony, claiming that the monument would incite ethnic incidents and disturbances in the area (B92 2011; US Department of State 2012).

Serb and Croat interviewees alike were prone to generalize about members of the other ethnic group. Serb interviewees, for example, commonly harboured a view of Croats as avid nationalists; while Croat interviewees variously claimed, *inter alia*, that Serbs are warmongers who distort history, fail to respect borders and are never satisfied with what they have. In contrast to Vukovar, however, Croat interviewees were less inclined to collectivize guilt. One possible explanation is that because Knin was not under siege, did not experience the same intensity of fighting as Vukovar and consequently suffered less war damage and loss of lives, there is not the same need/desire to affix widespread guilt. Only Croat ex-combatants, who were typically more radical in their views than other Croats in Knin, embraced the concept of collective guilt. One *branitelj*, for example, was adamant that all Serbs are guilty, since all of them were committed to the realization of a 'Greater Serbia';[47] while a second ex-combatant asserted that because few Serbs opposed Milošević,[48] whose politics led to war, it is thereby appropriate to hold all of them guilty.[49]

---

47 Author interview, Knin, 10 April 2012.
48 This is not, in fact, the case (see, for example, Clark 2008: 21–22).
49 Author interview, Knin, 12 April 2012.

Mutual acceptance

Key indicators of mutual acceptance include respect, empathy and positive gestures and signals, all of which are generally lacking in Vukovar and Knin. In both locations, Croat interviewees (with the exception of a small number of ex-combatants) frequently explained that while they do not strongly object to living alongside Serbs, the latter must respect the country in which they reside, accept the fact that they are a minority in Croatia and appreciate the rights and freedoms that they have. The overall feeling was that Serbs need to earn respect by behaving in an appropriate way that reflects their status as a minority. Among Serb interviewees, on the other hand, and especially among those living in Vukovar, there was often a strong sense that local Croats do not accept them and merely tolerate their presence because they have to. 'Everyone would be happier if we were not here', a young woman opined.[50]

The EC has underlined that, 'Croatia needs to foster a spirit of tolerance towards minorities, in particular Croatian Serbs, and to take measures to protect those who may still be subjected to threats or acts of discrimination, violence or hostility' (2012b: 7). Particularly in Vukovar, however, the scope for fostering this 'spirit of tolerance' is limited, as Croat reactions to the proposed introduction of the Cyrillic script (which only Serbs use) have graphically illustrated. At the beginning of 2013, the Croatian government, led by Zoran Milanović, announced plans to implement a constitutional law on the rights of national minorities, whereby Cyrillic would become an official script in municipalities where Serbs constitute more than one-third of the population. In such a fragile post-conflict environment as Vukovar, which is one such municipality,[51] it was not unforeseeable that the prospect of signs jointly written in both the Latin and Cyrillic scripts would provoke angry demonstrations. On 2 February 2013, for example, 20,000 Croats participated in a protest to make their views on the issue known. Local veterans' associations organized the mass protest, using the rallying cry: 'For a Croatian Vukovar, No to Cyrillic' (Reuters 2013). While Croats in Vukovar have so far expressed their opposition in a peaceful way, rather ominously groups of veterans have vowed to prevent the introduction of Cyrillic 'by any means necessary' (Pavelić 2013b). Whatever ultimately happens,[52] the key

---

50 Author interview, Borovo Naselje, 30 July 2011.
51 According to the last census in 2011, Serbs constitute 34.87 per cent of the population of Vukovar (Pavelić 2013d).
52 In the small town of Udbina in central Croatia, where the local government is a coalition between the Serbian Independent Democratic Party and the HDZ, the Cyrillic script has been in official use (alongside the Latin script) since August 2013. The local mayor, however, Ivan Pešut, who is from the HDZ, has made it clear that Udbina is a completely different case from Vukovar. In his words, 'Vukovar is a special symbol. Wounds there are still open. We have to be extremely cautious with Vukovar' (cited in Pavelić 2013c). The Croatian government will revisit the issue of introducing the Cyrillic script in Vukovar in 2014.

point is that such a controversial issue has triggered new tensions in an already volatile society; and as the president of the local Independent Democratic Serb Party, Srdjan Milaković, has rightly pointed out, 'This does not contribute to the quality of life in Vukovar, let alone coexistence and the improvement of inter-ethnic relations. All that resistance, all those protests, they are taking us a step back. Both Croats and Serbs' (cited in Hedl 2013).

Lack of empathy is a salient issue in both Vukovar and Knin. In Vukovar, Croat interviewees evinced little readiness to acknowledge the existence of Serb victims and any expressions of empathy towards Serbs were extremely rare. Even when interviewees conceded that Serbs also suffered, any potential for the development of empathy was always quickly eroded through the repeated and impassioned insistence that Serb and Croat experiences could never be compared. An interviewee in Vukovar who was still searching for information about her missing husband, for example, acknowledged the pain and trauma of any woman, whether Croat or Serb, who has lost a loved-one. For her, however, Serbs were primarily aggressors, not victims, and they needed to face this fact.[53] Indeed, the demand for Serbs to confront the past and admit the wrongs committed on their side was voiced *ad infinitum*. Croats were looking for a positive gesture from the Serbs – an apology, an avowal of wrongdoing and guilt. Yet Serbs, who rightly underscored that they are not collectively guilty, always maintained that it is Croats who need to face the fact that both sides suffered; after all, it was a war situation.

In Knin, the absence of empathy takes a more tangible form. In the centre of Knin, an imposing rectangular-shaped war monument stands in memory of the fallen heroes of Operation Storm. The main street which leads down to the memorial bears the name *Trg Oluje, 5 kolovoza 1995* (Square of the Storm, 5 August 1995). As in Vukovar, nowhere are there any memorials dedicated to Serb victims. Inclusive memorials and memorial events would constitute important positive gestures and signals. In Knin and Vukovar, however, every memorial and commemoration assumes an exclusionary form that attests to and reflects ongoing divisions regarding the past. These divisions, in turn, and the irreconcilable demands to which they have given rise critically impede the development of mutual acceptance.

In an address to the UN General Assembly on 15 October 2012, the President of the ICTY confidently asserted that the achievements of the Tribunal have 'contributed to bringing peace and reconciliation to the countries of the former Yugoslavia...' (Meron 2012). Just as this claim is deeply problematic in the case of BiH, it is no less questionable when applied to Croatia. While Judge Meron does not specify precisely how the ICTY's work has contributed to reconciliation, this chapter fundamentally challenges the argument that it has done so through

---

53 Author interview, Vukovar, 22 July 2011.

Figure 6.3 Operation Storm memorial in Knin.

the delivery of justice and truth. Justice can potentially foster reconciliation only when it is perceived as such by relevant local communities on the ground, and truth can potentially aid reconciliation only when it is accepted as such by these same local communities. Neither condition exists in Vukovar and Knin. In both locations, perceptions of injustice among Serbs and Croats alike have fused with competing ethnic narratives to severely limit the grassroots impact of the ICTY's work. The absence of reconciliation, as measured against the Reconciliation Matrix, further highlights this. In both Vukovar and Knin, Serbs and Croats co-exist in relative peace and there are few inter-ethnic incidents. While this is a step forward, coexistence is primarily the result of pragmatic, practical and personal factors, rather than the result of the ICTY's work.

Chapter 7

A Case Study of Kosovo

To date, discussion of the ICTY's achievements and impact has overwhelmingly centred on BiH. In contrast, Kosovo has been heavily neglected, and indeed this was highlighted during the ICTY legacy conference in The Hague in 2010. Reflecting on this event, the then President of the Tribunal recalled that,

> One issue that was noted in the conference as a failing was the absence of Kosovo, resulting from a variety of factors, including the low turnout of Kosovo-based participants invited to the conference. This absence was pointed out by international participants on more than one occasion.... Many asked how the Tribunal could consider its legacy vision in the region without hearing the voice of Kosovo. The Tribunal shares the concern... .
>
> (Robinson 2011: 83)

Although Kosovo[1] has not been the main focus of the Tribunal's work, it is nevertheless an important case study which completes this book's comparative analysis of the ICTY's impact on inter-ethnic reconciliation in the former Yugoslavia.

Reconciliation via justice?

Like the different ethnic groups in BiH and Croatia, Kosovo Serbs and Kosovo Albanians have their own preconceived ideas of justice and what it should look like, and these ideas have fundamentally influenced popular perceptions of the ICTY and its work. Both communities, in effect, are seeking a confirmative justice that validates and corroborates their own ethnic narratives and versions of events. Hence, notwithstanding the deep divisions between Serbs and Albanians in Kosovo, interviewees from both sides were in agreement that there is no justice at the Hague Tribunal.

---

1 While Kosovo Albanians refer to Kosovo as 'Kosova' and Kosovo Serbs refer to it as 'Kosovo-Metohija', for the sake of simplicity this chapter, consistent with international usage, calls it simply 'Kosovo'.

Serb viewpoints and allegations of bias

In Kosovo, as in BiH and Croatia, the ICTY is highly unpopular among Serbs. Without exception, Kosovo Serb interviewees insisted that the ICTY is a blatantly anti-Serb institution which lacks any impartiality. An interviewee from Fushë Kosovë/Kosovo Polje, for example, maintained that the ICTY is openly biased against Serbs because the West holds the Serbs responsible for the break-up of Yugoslavia and its descent into bloodshed;[2] and an interviewee from the Serb village of Kmetovce/Kmetoc, in the municipality of Gjilan/Gnjilane, was adamant that the Tribunal was established with the sole purpose of prosecuting and punishing Serbs.[3] These examples further highlight how 'the way in which an affected population perceives a court can be driven primarily by whom the court indicts and prosecutes' (Ford 2012: 412). By extension, it fundamentally matters not only who the Tribunal indicts and prosecutes, but also who it does not – and the very small number of prosecutions against former members of the KLA has engendered a profound and bitter sense of injustice among Serbs in Kosovo. Interviewees repeatedly accused the ICTY of allowing war crimes committed by the KLA to go unpunished, although they rarely referred to specific war crimes and did not mention places or dates.[4] Over and over again, however, they emphasized that the conflict in Kosovo was not one-sided, that crimes were perpetrated on both sides and that the Tribunal's work must reflect this reality. In a particularly impassioned attack on the ICTY, one interviewee questioned why, on one hand, the ICTY has indicted and prosecuted the majority of the key political and military figures from the Milošević era, while on the other hand it has adopted a very different approach to today's Kosovo Albanian politicians, many of whom are former members of the KLA. Maintaining that this is unjust and insulting, the interviewee dismissed the ICTY as a political game.[5]

The ICTY has conducted only two KLA-related trials. In 2003, it indicted three Kosovo Albanians: Fatmir Limaj, alleged to have been a KLA commander responsible for the KLA prison in Llapushnik/Lapušnik in western Kosovo; Isak Musliu, also alleged to have been a KLA commander and to have acted on occasion as a guard at the camp; and Haradin Bala, a guard at the camp. The indictment

---

2 Author interview, Gračanica/Graçanicë, 15 August 2012.
3 Author interview, Gjilan/Gnjilane, 23 August 2012.
4 One interviewee highlighted events in Goraždevac/Gorazhdevc, a Serb village in the municipality of Pejë/Peć. On 13 July 2003, two Serbs, aged 19 and 13, were shot and killed by a group of Kosovo Albanians as they swam in the local river. Four other Serbs, ranging in age from 12 to 20, were seriously injured. The interviewee claimed that the ICTY has never investigated this crime because it is not a neutral court. Author interview, Leposavić/q, 13 August 2012. Interviewed in January 2013, interlocutors in Goraždevac/Gorazhdevc similarly expressed deep anger that no one has been brought to justice for the deaths of the Serb youths. As the crime was committed after the war ended, however, it does not fall within the ICTY's jurisdiction.
5 Author interview, Gračanica/Graçanicë, 15 August 2012.

charged all three defendants with crimes against humanity and violations of the laws or customs of war. In November 2005, the Trial Chamber found Limaj and Musliu not guilty and released them. This verdict was confirmed on appeal two years later. However, the Trial Chamber found Bala guilty of violations of the laws or customs of war and sentenced him to 13 years' imprisonment. This too was confirmed on appeal. This case will be discussed further in the next section.

Turning to the second ICTY trial involving former members of the KLA, the Tribunal issued an indictment in March 2005 against Ramush Haradinaj, the former KLA commander in the Dukagjin operational zone in western Kosovo. The indictment charged him, on the basis of individual criminal responsibility, with crimes against humanity (specifically persecutions) and violations of the laws or customs of war in the Dukagjin operational zone (and specifically in Gjakovë/ Đakovica municipality). The indictment alleged that Haradinaj, together with his two co-defendants, was part of a JCE aimed at consolidating KLA control over the operational zone through the unlawful removal and mistreatment of Serb civilians and any other civilians – including Kosovo Albanians – who were, or were believed to be, collaborating with Serb military forces. The indictment was made public on 10 March 2005 and Haradinaj, who at that time was Kosovo's Prime Minister, resigned the following day. On 6 June 2005, he was granted provisional release. Controversially, the Tribunal also allowed him to continue to appear in public and to engage in political activities. Haradinaj returned to The Hague on 26 February 2007 and his trial began on 5 March 2007. Delivering its judgement on 3 April 2008, the Trial Chamber found Haradinaj not guilty, due to lack of evidence, and immediately released him. His co-defendant, Idriz Balaj, a fellow KLA member and the commander of the 'Black Eagles' special unit, was also found not guilty. The third defendant, Lahi Brahimaj, a member of the KLA General Staff, was sentenced to six years' imprisonment for violations of the laws or customs of war.

Both the Prosecution and Brahimaj appealed against the judgement and on 21 July 2010, the Appeals Chamber ordered a partial re-trial in the case of all three defendants. The Prosecution's first and most important ground of appeal was that the Trial Chamber had made a fundamental error when it denied the Prosecution's request for extra time to secure the testimony of two vital witnesses. The judgement of the Trial Chamber makes it clear that witness intimidation was a serious issue in this particular trial; 'Many witnesses cited fear as a prominent reason for not wishing to appear before the Trial Chamber to give evidence. The Trial Chamber gained a strong impression that the trial was being held in an atmosphere where witnesses felt unsafe' (Prosecutor v. Haradinaj, Balaj and Brahimaj 2008: §6). While the trial judgement highlights the problem more than once, the Appeals Chamber nevertheless found that the Trial Chamber:

> ...appeared to place undue emphasis on ensuring that the Prosecution took no more than its pre-allotted time to present its case, and that the Trial Chamber's deadlines for presenting evidence were respected, irrespective of

the possibility of securing the testimony of two key witnesses. This misplaced priority demonstrates that the Trial Chamber failed to appreciate the gravity of the threat that witness intimidation posed to the trial's integrity.

(Prosecutor v. Haradinaj, Balaj and Brahimaj 2010: §40)

Further finding that the Trial Chamber had 'failed to take sufficient steps to counter the witness intimidation that permeated the trial' (Prosecutor v. Haradinaj, Balaj and Brahimaj 2010: §49), which, in turn, had critically undermined the fairness of the proceedings and thus caused a miscarriage of justice to occur, the Appeals Chamber upheld the Prosecution's first ground of appeal. Quashing most of the Trial Chamber's judgement, including its decision to fully acquit Haradinaj and Balaj, the Appeals Chamber ordered a partial re-trial of all three defendants.

On 29 November 2012, 15 months after the re-trial commenced, the new Trial Chamber delivered its judgement and acquitted all three defendants. The judgement offers a detailed picture of the brutal treatment that the KLA meted out to those deemed to be collaborators and traitors (see, for example, Prosecutor v. Haradinaj, Balaj and Brahimaj 2012: §492–493, 513, 568, 576–580, 633). Moreover, the Chamber found that counts three to six of the indictment, involving various acts of murder, cruel treatment and torture, were proven. However, it also adjudged that some witnesses were unreliable (2012: §448, 451–452, 460, 554), and ultimately concluded that the evidence did not prove beyond reasonable doubt the existence of a common plan to consolidate KLA control over the Dukagjin operational zone through the mistreatment of civilians (2012: §635, 667–668). Accordingly, it found that, 'Ramush Haradinaj…is not criminally responsible for participating in a JCE in relation to the crimes charged in the Indictment under Counts 3, 4, 5 and 6' (Prosecutor v. Haradinaj, Balaj and Brahimaj 2012: §670). Although the indictment charged Haradinaj in the alternative with ordering, instigating or aiding and abetting the crimes charged in count six, relating to the abduction and mistreatment of two Kosovo Albanians, the Chamber deemed that there was no evidence 'that suggests, let alone proves beyond reasonable doubt, that Ramush Haradinaj prompted or instructed the KLA soldiers who forcefully removed Naser Lika and Fadil Fazliu from Zhabel/Žabelj to commit these acts' (2012: §572).

When asked to give their opinions on the ICTY, Serb interviewees were always quick to refer to Haradinaj's case, invoking this as a supreme example of injustice. They expressed anger and incredulity that he had been released for a second time, and often conflated this with an acquittal. In July and August 2012, however, when the majority of the interviews for this research were conducted, Haradinaj – who was granted provisional release for a second time in May 2012 – was in fact awaiting the verdict in his partial re-trial. His actual acquittal in November 2012 thus came as no surprise. It was, an interviewee in Goraždevac/Gorazhdevc explained, a deeply unjust verdict delivered by a deeply political court from which no justice can be expected.[6] To a lesser extent, interviewees cited Limaj's acquittal as a further example of failed justice, although when encouraged to expand further on their arguments, they appeared to have little information or knowledge about the case. Interestingly, they never made reference to either Haradinaj's or Limaj's co-defendants. Of particular significance, not a single interviewee mentioned the guilty verdicts against Lahi Brahimaj and Haradin Bala, sentenced to six years' and 13 years' imprisonment respectively (although the former was subsequently acquitted). Some interviewees were seemingly unaware of the verdicts against these two defendants, while others attached little significance to them; Haradinaj was seen as the 'big fish' and his case thus attracted the most interest, attention and criticism.

What has further fuelled and exacerbated the strong sense of injustice among Serbs in Kosovo is the fact that former members of the KLA are now running the country. In the words of one interviewee, 'The crazy situation exists whereby warlords and those who orchestrated war crimes are now in the government and are being supported by those who are supposed to be supporting justice'.[7] In particular, there was a widespread consensus that Kosovo's Prime Minister, Hashim Thaçi – the political head of the KLA during the war in Kosovo – should be in The Hague. Articulating this viewpoint, an IDP from Pejë/Peć, who now lives in north Mitrovica/ë, insisted that as long as 'dirty people' like Thaçi remain in power, there will never be reconciliation.[8] Thaçi has been the subject of extremely serious accusations relating to his alleged involvement in organized crime. In December 2010, Dick Marty, a Swiss senator, issued a report entitled *Inhuman Treatment of People and Illicit Trafficking in Human Organs in Kosovo* (the Marty Report). In this report, which the Council of Europe adopted in January 2011, Marty claims that, '...a small but inestimably powerful group of KLA personalities apparently wrested control of most of the illicit criminal enterprises in which Kosovar Albanians were involved in the Republic of Albania, beginning at the latest in 1998' (2010: 14). Thaçi, according to the Marty Report, was the chief of this so-called 'Drenica Group', which 'built a formidable power base in the organised criminal enterprises that were flourishing in Kosovo and Albania at the time' (2010: 14). The most serious allegation that the Report makes against the Drenica Group, and KLA members more generally, is that they were involved in 'an organised criminal conspiracy to source human organs for illicit transplant...' (Marty 2010: 25). Interviewees made frequent reference to these shocking allegations of human organ trafficking (but without ever mentioning the Marty Report), which they unquestioningly accepted. For them, the ultimate proof of the allegations' veracity was the infamous 'Yellow House'.

6 Author interview, Goraždevac/Gorazhdevc, 12 January 2013.
7 Author interview, Gračanica/Graçanicë, 15 August 2012.
8 Author interview, north Mitrovica/ë, 1 August 2012.

Information about the Yellow House, near Burrel in northern Albania, first came to light in 2004, following the publication of Carla Del Ponte's book, *Madame Prosecutor*, in which she recounts how,

> The Office of the Prosecutor would eventually receive information, which UNMIK investigators and officials had acquired from a team of credible journalists, about how, during the summer months of 1999, Kosovo Albanians had trucked one hundred to three hundred abducted persons across the border from Kosovo into northern Albania…According to the journalists' sources, some of the younger, fitter captives, who were kept well fed, examined by doctors and never beaten, were transferred to other holding facilities in and around Burrel, including a shack behind a yellow house about twenty kilometers south of the town. A room inside this yellow house, the journalists reported, had been set up as a makeshift surgical clinic; and there, doctors extracted the captives' internal organs. These organs were then smuggled through Rinas airport near Tirana for transplant into paying patients in surgical wards abroad… .
>
> (Del Ponte 2008: 277)

Investigators from both the ICTY and UNMIK subsequently visited the Yellow House, together with an Albanian prosecutor. The house had been painted white, although traces of yellow were still visible, and investigators found various medical items – including a gauze, a used syringe and two empty plastic drip bags. Inside the house, Del Ponte recalls, 'A forensic chemical spray revealed blood splatters along the walls and floor of a room inside the house, except for a clear area of the floor about six feet in length and two feet wide' (2008: 285). Seeking to explain the presence of blood, the owner initially claimed that his wife had given birth in the room several years earlier. When she herself contradicted this, however, the owner changed his story and maintained that animals had been slaughtered in the room as part of a Muslim holiday (Del Ponte 2008: 285). According to Del Ponte, 'The investigators' findings, combined with the anecdotal information the journalists had provided, were tantalizing…The syringes, the drip bags, and the other medical paraphernalia were clearly corroborative evidence…' (2008: 285). Despite this, however, the investigation was ultimately abandoned due to lack of evidence; there were no bodies, it was not possible to determine whether the traces of blood that had been found were from humans or animals and the journalists refused to disclose their sources.

The lack of prosecutions relating to crimes allegedly committed in the Yellow House and, more generally, the small number of ICTY trials involving former KLA members, have together reinforced very negative popular perceptions of the ICTY among Kosovo Serbs. However, the latter's claims that the Tribunal is biased and selective critically neglect the importance of context. Fundamentally, the possible reasons for the low number of ICTY prosecutions against ex-KLA combatants extend beyond the Tribunal itself and two in particular can be highlighted. Firstly, NATO intervened in Kosovo on the side of the Kosovo Albanians and the KLA; and the US in particular strongly championed and supported the KLA's fight for 'freedom'. In this political context, therefore, a large number of ICTY indictments against former KLA members would have been deeply problematic – and indeed embarrassing. As a policy advisor at EULEX explained, voicing his own personal opinion, 'Kosovo was supposed to be a "clean" conflict, and hence nobody wants to do anything that could undermine the morality of the NATO intervention'.[9]

Secondly, the prosecution of ex-KLA members has presented the ICTY with significant practical difficulties and challenges. In her book *Madame Prosecutor*, for example, Del Ponte recalls that very few Albanians were willing to come forward and testify against KLA suspects. Those who were prepared to do so required protection, and in some cases this meant 'resettling entire families in third countries at a time when most states were reluctant to accept such people' (Del Ponte 2008: 279). Witness protection, as previously noted, was a particular issue in the original Haradinaj trial, and indeed 34 Prosecution witnesses in the case were ultimately granted the status of protected witnesses. On this issue, the Trial Chamber remarked upon, '...Kosovo/Kosova's small communities and tight family and community networks which made guaranteeing anonymity difficult' (Prosecutor v. Haradinaj, Balaj and Brahimaj 2008: §6).

Details such as these are extremely important, but Serb interviewees were generally unaware of them. The broader point is that, as in BiH and Croatia, the strength of interviewees' opinions about the ICTY was often disproportionate to their knowledge about its work. This is not unsurprising; 'Given the complexity of both international criminal courts and international criminal law, and the nature of human decision making, it is virtually a foregone conclusion that most people in an affected population will have opinions about such courts without understanding them in any detail' (Ford 2012: 426). A lack of information about the ICTY's trials, however, has undoubtedly facilitated (although it is by no means the only contributing factor) the formation and persistence of highly negative popular opinions of the Tribunal.

Albanian viewpoints, incomplete justice and claims of false balancing

While Serb interviewees widely accused the Hague Tribunal of dispensing selective justice, Kosovo Albanian interviewees strongly emphasized the incompleteness of ICTY justice. According to Amnesty International, 'There is no accurate estimate of the number of incidents involving crimes under international law

---

9 Author interview, Prishtinë/Priština, 14 August 2012.

which took place in Kosovo. However, it is acknowledged that more than 13,000 people were killed; more than 3,600 people were disappeared or abducted; an unknown number of women were raped' (2012: 16). While no court, especially not an *ad hoc* tribunal, could prosecute all of these crimes, Kosovo Albanian interviewees repeatedly insisted that more Serbs must stand trial for war crimes, to reflect the fact that – in their estimation – an entire system was guilty. Some of them also claimed, erroneously, that no Serbs have been convicted at the ICTY for crimes committed in Kosovo.

Interestingly, not a single interviewee referred to the trial of Nikola Šainović et al., which resulted in guilty verdicts against five key Serbian political and military figures for crimes against humanity and/or violations of the laws or customs of war in Kosovo. On 26 February 2009, the ICTY Trial Chamber imposed 22-year prison sentences on three of the defendants in this case – namely Nikola Šainović, the former deputy Prime Minister of the FRY; Sreten Lukić, the former head of the MUP Staff for Kosovo; and Nebojša Pavković, the former commander of the Third Army of the JNA. Dragoljub Ojdanić, the former chief of the General Staff of the JNA, and Vladimir Lazarević, the former commander of the Prishtinë/Priština Corps of the JNA, were each sentenced to 15 years' imprisonment. The sixth defendant in the case, Milan Milutinović, the former President of Serbia, was acquitted (Prosecutor v. Šainović et al. 2009). On 23 January 2014, the ICTY Appeals Chamber upheld these convictions, while also reducing Šainovic's sentence to 18 years, Lazarević's sentence to 14 years and Lukić's sentence to 20 years (Ojdanić was granted early release on 10 July 2013) (Prosecutor v. Sainovic et al. 2014). Similarly, none of the interviewees mentioned the trial of Vlastimir Đorđević, the former Assistant Minister of the MUP and the chief of the Public Security Department of the MUP. On 23 February 2011, the Trial Chamber found Đorđević guilty of crimes against humanity and violations of the laws or customs of war and sentenced him to 27 years' imprisonment (Prosecutor v. Đorđević 2011). On 27 January 2014, the Appeals Chamber upheld these convictions but reduced Đorđević's sentence to 18 years, after reversing some of the first-instance findings and Đorđević's convictions for aiding and abetting crimes in Kosovo. The Appeals Chamber found that, '... the totality of Đorđević's criminal conduct is fully reflected in a conviction based solely on his participation in the JCE [to modify the ethnic balance in Kosovo and thus ensure Serb control over the province]' (Prosecutor v. Đorđević 2014: §833). Interviewees only referred to the trial of the late Slobodan Milošević. This was the trial that mattered most to them, and hence Milošević's untimely death in 2006 was widely viewed as the ultimate injustice (although some interviewees were convinced that the former Serbian leader is still alive).

While interviewees were consistently emphatic that the ICTY has not indicted and prosecuted enough Serbs in relation to war crimes perpetrated in Kosovo, a public opinion poll by UBO Consulting in April and May 2007 – conducted as part of the UNDP's TJ Project – revealed that the ICTY is considerably more popular among Kosovo Albanians than it is among Kosovo Serbs. According to the poll, 70 per cent of Kosovo Albanian respondents expressed high levels of satisfaction with the ICTY, in contrast to just 36 per cent of Kosovo Serb respondents (UNDP 2007: 14). Arguably, a key reason for this significant differential is that, in contrast to Kosovo Serbs, Kosovo Albanians do not regard the ICTY as a biased institution; no interviewees accused the Tribunal of being anti-Albanian. They frequently described it, however, as a political court, insisting that it is trying to equalize crimes. An ex-KLA combatant who testified for the defence in the Limaj trial, for example, alleged that the ICTY has a policy of 'balancing' crimes in the region and thereby creates a distorted version of events. Everyone knows, he vigorously asserted, that the Kosovo Albanians were victims of the Serbs.[10]

This latter point was repeated over and over again during the author's fieldwork in Kosovo. Interviewees unanimously maintained that the Kosovo Albanians were merely defending themselves against the Serb aggressors, and thus expressed anger and sheer disbelief that men such as Haradinaj and Limaj had been put on trial.[11] A shop keeper in Gjilan/Gnjilane explained that for him, the biggest disgrace is the fact that Haradinaj was sent to The Hague on two occasions.[12] Glossing over the fact that witness intimidation was a major issue in the Haradinaj case, this particular interviewee – like so many others – appeared to assume that the ICTY (Appeals Chamber) had ordered a re-trial in order to prove Haradinaj's guilt. Unsurprisingly, former members of the KLA were especially insistent that their erstwhile commanders should never have been sent to The Hague. A former KLA commander in the village of Raçak/Račak, for example, described as completely 'absurd' the fact that Haradinaj and Limaj were sent to The Hague and made to sit in the same seats as men such as Milošević and Šainović.[13] Kosovo Albanians interviewed in January 2013 thus described how they celebrated and felt vindicated when Haradinaj was ultimately acquitted in November 2012. For many of them, however, the verdict was too little, too late. Voicing a common grievance (which was similarly made in Croatia apropos of Gotovina and Markač), a former member of the KLA in Pejë/Peć stressed that Haradinaj – whom he described as a hero – lost several years of his life because of the ICTY.[14]

The biggest problem in Kosovo is that ICTY justice chafes and collides with local communities' ethnically-shaped conceptions and expectations of justice. Based on their research in the deeply-divided community of Ruhororo in Burundi, Nee and Uvin point out that, 'For many people, to the extent that they desire justice, they see it through a politicized lens' (2010: 181); and this is absolutely the case in Kosovo. Kosovo Serbs want a 'balanced justice' which recognizes the commission of war crimes on both sides, while Kosovo Albanians are seeking a 'differentiating justice' which focuses on Serb crimes and acknowledges the KLA's actions as purely defensive. Not only are the two forms of justice fundamentally

10 Author interview, Prishtinë/Priština, 15 August 2012.
11 Hayden notes that when Haradinaj was indicted, '...the Albanian population staged mass demonstrations and at least one bomb was thrown at the UN Kosovo mission' (2006: 398).
12 Author interview, Gjilan/Gnjilane, 23 August 2012.
13 Author interview, Raçak/Račak, 27 August 2012.
14 Author interview, Pejë/Peć, 11 January 2013.

incompatible, but they are also unrealistic; on one hand, KLA war crimes were not on the same scale as Serb war crimes, and on the other hand, to reiterate, Kosovo was not the one-sided conflict that it was so often portrayed as. All of this powerfully highlights, once again, the fundamental difficulties and challenges of dispensing any semblance of justice in complex post-conflict societies.

Reconciliation via truth?

One commentator has underlined that, 'If public opinion in all parts of the former Yugoslavia largely accepted the facts and findings as established by the ICTY, we could be optimistic about the future' (Ivanišević 2011a: 131). The small number of ICTY trials relating to Kosovo, however, coupled with the small number of convictions – which neither Kosovo Serb nor Kosovo Albanian interviewees actually referred to – meant that it was often impossible to assess whether and to what extent interviewees had accepted particular ICTY judgements. This section therefore focuses on gauging levels of aversive acknowledgement and denial.

Serb responses to ICTY truths

According to Andrighetto et al., '...people often interpret the impact of the conflict subjectively, viewing their own group as the only legitimate victim and the rivals as the illegitimate perpetrators of unjust and immoral misdeeds' (2012: 513). Certainly, Kosovo Serb interviewees were keen to underline that the conflict in Kosovo was not black and white and that Serbs had also suffered significantly, particularly in the aftermath of the NATO bombing when Kosovo Albanians began returning to their homes. Judah, for example, notes that, 'In the general euphoria that followed [the NATO bombing], many did not see, or overlooked, the dreadful reprisals that took place against Serbs in particular but also against Roma and other non-Albanians' (2008: 91). Dr Denis MacShane, Britain's former (and pro-Albanian) Balkans Minister (2001–2005), has himself stressed that, '...Kosovans should accept that cruel and unacceptable acts of hate and vengeful violence against Serbs did take place in the months after the liberation of Kosovo in 1999' (2011: 58).

There was, nevertheless, a general willingness of varying degrees among Kosovo Serb interviewees to acknowledge that members of their own ethnic group did commit crimes against Kosovo Albanians. Some interviewees placed the blame squarely on the shoulders of paramilitaries. For example, an IDP from Prishtinë/Priština, now living in north Mitrovica/ë, insisted that while Serb forces in Kosovo was simply defending their people and the Serbian Constitution, the formation of paramilitary groups caused problems because the latter were under no control.[15] Similarly, according to a 2007 public opinion poll by UBO Consulting, although 37 per cent of Kosovo Serb respondents identified the KLA

---

15 Author interview, north Mitrovica/ë, 1 August 2012.

as the main perpetrator of war crimes in Kosovo and 27 per cent identified NATO, 15 per cent were ready to acknowledge that Serbian paramilitary formations had committed war crimes in Kosovo (UNDP 2007: 9). Some interviewees were also willing to accept that it was not only paramilitaries who committed crimes. They were emphatic, however, that Kosovo Albanians must acknowledge the crimes committed against Serbs. Exemplifying this viewpoint, an interviewee in Gračanica/Graçanicë asserted that as long as Kosovo Albanians continue to maintain a wall of silence and fail to speak out about what happened, the situation will never improve.[16]

Aversive acknowledgement among Kosovo Serb interviewees, however, was selective. Interviewees continued, for example, to defend those Serbs who are currently on trial at the ICTY – and in particular Vojislav Šešelj, Radovan Karadžić and Ratko Mladić. They were deeply indignant that Šešelj, the leader of the SRS, has been on trial for war crimes in BiH, Croatia and Serbia (Vojvodina) since 2007, and insisted that he is an innocent man. They also expressed widespread conviction that Karadžić and Mladić were simply defending their people and thus should not be in The Hague. This latter view was particularly strong among Serbs in the north of Kosovo. In the centre of north Mitrovica/ë, for example, close to the popular *Bi Bop* café, the words '*Naš predsednik, Radovan Karadžić*' (Our president, Radovan Karadžić) are written in chunky letters on the side of a wall; and various examples of pro-Mladić graffiti can be found. In the centre of nearby Zvečan/Zveçan, on a wall directly opposite the municipality building, Mladić's name is written in large red Cyrillic letters. Just a few metres away, an imposing black and white painting of Mladić fills the entire side wall of a local shop. These examples are visual manifestations of powerful ethnic narratives which, as the previous chapters have demonstrated, the ICTY cannot easily penetrate and challenge. Men such as Šešelj, Karadžić and Mladić will thus retain their hero status, regardless of the ICTY's ultimate verdicts against them.

It is the name Raçak/Račak that evokes the strongest expressions of denial among Kosovo Serbs. On 15 January 1999, during a Serb military operation in the small village of Raçak/Račak in the municipality of Shtime/Štimlje, 45 Kosovo Albanians were massacred. In delivering its judgement in the aforementioned trial of Vlastimir Đorđević, the Trial Chamber noted that, 'During the operation, there was no outgoing fire from the village, although prior to the operation there had been a KLA presence in Račak/Raçak, including, it was thought, a KLA headquarters' (Prosecutor v. Đorđević 2011: §401). The day after the massacre, the members of the Kosovo Verification Mission (KVM)[17] began their investigations in Raçak/Račak, whereupon they were informed by representatives of the MUP that the casualties in the village (which occurred on

---

16 Author interview, Gračanica/Graçanicë, 15 August 2012.
17 The KVM was an OSCE mission headed by William Walker. It was established in October 1998 to verify that both parties to the conflict in Kosovo were complying with various agreements and UN Security Council resolutions.

Figure 7.1 Mladić street mural in Zvečan/Zvečan.

both sides) were the result of a fire-fight between Serb forces and the KLA. What the investigators found, however, contradicted this;

> In a gully or a trail, they discovered over 20 dead bodies lying in a line. The bodies appeared to have been shot at close range in the head. 10 of the bodies appeared to have been mown down. The victims were all male, and were about 50–60 years old, some had traditional Albanian caps. They did not have uniforms.
>
> (Prosecutor v. Ðorđević 2011: §407)

Two days later, on 18 January 1999, an investigative judge from the District Court in Prishtinë/Priština travelled to Raçak/Račak to conduct an on-sight investigation, having previously been unable to do so for security reasons. By this stage, all of the bodies had been taken to the local mosque, and inside the investigative judge saw 40 bodies, all but one of which were male. According to the Trial Chamber, 'The bodies she was shown had shoes which looked like military boots, some had dark grey, others navy blue, military trousers, and they had military belts on...' (Prosecutor v. Ðorđević 2011: §412). The investigative judge maintained that the bodies in the mosque bore no resemblance to the bodies in the video footage recorded by the KMV; in the Ðorđević Trial, she testified that none of the bodies that she was shown in the mosque had bullet wounds to the head and that none of them had been decapitated.

Fundamentally differing accounts of the events in Raçak/Račak immediately planted seeds of denial, and hence the massacre has always been heavily disputed – and not only among Serbs (see, for example, Gowans 2001; Johnstone 1999; Worthington 2001). In the Đorđević trial, however, the Trial Chamber ultimately accepted the accounts proffered by international observers and found that, 'not less than 45 Kosovo Albanians were killed', many of whom appeared to have been shot in the head at close range. The dead, all of whom were wearing civilian clothes, included a woman and child (Prosecutor v. Đorđević 2011: §416). Concluding that the investigative judge had been deliberately deceived (2011: §415), the Trial Chamber held Đorđević responsible for 'the staged misrepresentation of bodies and other circumstances...' (2011: §425). The Appeals Chamber similarly found that, 'following the Račak/Raçak operation he [Đorđević] took a leading role in the efforts to conceal the excessive use of force by the Serbian forces during joint operations' (Prosecutor v. Đorđević 2014: §349). When Serb interviewees in Kosovo referred to Raçak/Račak, however, they always emphatically argued that it was a set-up designed to give NATO a pretext for bombing Serbia. Interestingly, none of them mentioned the Đorđević judgement; and when the author drew attention to the Trial Chamber's conclusions, (the interviews were conducted before the Đorđević Appeals Chamber delivered its verdict on 27 January 2014), interviewees simply dismissed these as the biased and slanted findings of a political court.

The Raçak/Račak memorial complex stands atop a wind-swept hill in the centre of the village. Visitors enter the complex through a large white arch, adorned with the red Albanian flag (which is far more widely used in Kosovo than the country's official blue and yellow flag). Immediately to the right, the names and faces of the dead are imprinted into black marble squares which, positioned in two neat lines, fill the length of a long grey stone memorial wall. Adjacent to this are the bodies of the dead, buried in symmetrical rows. Each grave is marked with a short, grey triangular-shaped pillar and bears the image of a black two-headed eagle, the symbol of Albania. A short walk away, up several flights of steps, one reaches the 'gully or trail' that is mentioned in the aforementioned Đorđević Trial Chamber judgement. Along the trail, patches of red paint, symbolizing the victims' blood, mark the positions where human lives were brought to an abrupt end on 15 January 1999. Visiting the memorial complex and the 'Trail of Death' was a moving experience. If it were possible to create the conditions whereby Kosovo Serbs and Kosovo Albanians could visit each other's memorials, and thus have the opportunity to learn and see for themselves what happened in particular areas, this could potentially help to tackle the problem of denial – almost certainly in a more effective way than a distant court could ever do. It is clear, however, that for the people of Raçak/Račak at least, such visits would be both inconceivable and unwelcome. In the memorial complex, a black marble plaque bears the following words (written in poor English): 'Here rest the remains of martyrs of the nation, massacred by Serb barbarian atrocities. This tragedy occurred on the morning of 15 January 1999 when serbo-çetnik's rabid beasts of paramilitary forces attacked the innocent and vulnerable people...'.

Figure 7.2 Raçak/Račak memorial.

Albanian responses to ICTY truths

According to Oberschall, '...there is no final arbiter for truth and falsehood, no judges or jury whose decision is binding...Ordinary people select what they want to hear and what they already agree with, what is accepted in their social milieu, and what presents their group in a favorable light' (2010: 59). In Kosovo, the responses of Kosovo Albanian interviewees were particularly illustrative in this regard. What notably stood out from the interviews was a complete lack of any aversive acknowledgement, evidenced by interviewees' entrenched resistance to the very possibility that war crimes were committed on both sides. Public opinion poll research has similarly highlighted this. For example, according to the afore-mentioned 2007 public opinion poll conducted by UBO Consulting, 'Some 84% of K-Albanians categorically deny the possibility that members of their own ethnic community may have committed war crimes' (UNDP 2007: 7). The respective percentage for Kosovo Serb respondents was 37 per cent (UNDP 2007: 7). The poll further revealed that when the survey participants were asked whether members of their ethnic group *had* committed war crimes, 78 per cent of Kosovo Albanian respondents – in contrast to 27 per cent of Kosovo Serb respondents – answered negatively (UNDP 2007: 16). At the same time, more than 80 per cent of Kosovo Albanian respondents denied having any information about human rights violations committed against Kosovo Serbs after 1999 (UNDP 2007: 14).

The lack of aversive acknowledgement among Kosovo Albanians critically stems from, and is sustained by, two key factors. The first is the widely-held conviction that the war in Kosovo was entirely one-sided, a conflict in which Kosovo Albanians were legitimately and rightfully defending themselves against the Serb aggressor. This particular interpretation, moreover, has received widespread international endorsement, as the Marty Report underlines (2010: 2). Few conflicts, however, are straightforwardly black and white. In delivering its judgement in the Šainović et al. case, for example, the Trial Chamber remarked that during the second half of November and December 1998, NATO had 'observed an increasing number of incidents in Kosovo, most of them instigated by the KLA which was trying to fill the vacuum left by the withdrawing FRY [Federal Republic of Yugoslavia]/Serbian forces' (2009: §351). Four years earlier, in the trial of Limaj, Bala and Musliu, the Trial Chamber emphasized that,

> While the evidence indicates that the KLA forces were less numerous than the Serbian forces, less organised and less prepared, and were not as well trained or armed, the evidence does not suggest that the conflict was purely one-sided. KLA attacks were carried out against a variety of Serbian military, community and commercial targets over a widespread and expanding area of Kosovo.
>
> (2005: §169)

In its judgement, the Trial Chamber also rejected the Defence's submission that the militarily-superior Serb forces primarily sought not to defeat the KLA but rather to ethnically cleanse Kosovo of its majority Albanian population. The Trial Chamber found that, 'While it is true that civilians were driven out of their homes and forced to leave Kosovo as a result of military operations, the evidence discloses this to be true for both sides' (Prosecutor v. Limaj, Bala and Musliu 2005: §170).

The second key factor that is critically obstructing any process of aversive acknowledgement is the persistent assertion, which all Kosovo Albanian interviewees (and particularly ex-combatants) dogmatically embraced, that the KLA, unlike the Serbs, fought a clean war and never targeted or harmed civilians. An ex-KLA commander in Gjakovë/Đakovica, for example, averred that the KLA did not kill any civilians and only fought against other soldiers.[18] One of the KLA's founders, for his part, repeatedly emphasized that he feels deeply proud to have belonged to a liberation army which fought a just and correct war.[19] Another interviewee, who was formerly part of a female KLA unit in Drenica in western Kosovo, underlined that she and her fellow combatants were fully informed

---

18 Author interview, Gjakovë/Đakovica, 8 January 2013.
19 Author interview, Prishtinë/Priština, 17 August 2012.

about the Geneva Conventions. Stressing that, 'We truly tried to respect the rules that any soldier should respect', she was emphatic that the KLA never committed crimes against civilians.[20] Kosovo's politicians, moreover, are encouraging these expressions of denial. In an interview with the BBC in August 2010, for example, Prime Minister Hashim Thaçi was asked to comment on Haradinaj's detention in The Hague. Thaçi explained that the news came as a shock because, 'The KLA and the people of Kosovo have not committed war crimes' (cited in Radio Deutsche Welle 2012).

The reality, however, is that Kosovo Albanians did not have a monopoly on suffering in Kosovo. Human Rights Watch, for example, has noted that, 'Four hundred and seventy people went missing after the 1999 war ended and NATO troops had entered Kosovo. Ninety-five of these people are ethnic Albanians; the rest are non-ethnic Albanians, mostly Serbs' (2010); and Amnesty International has drawn attention to the fact that, 'Kosovo Serb civilians were also abducted, and subjected to torture and other ill-treatment and deliberate killings by armed Albanian groups including the KLA' (2012: 7). On this point, moreover, the Trial Chamber's judgement in the trial of Limaj, Bala and Musliu is particularly important. Kosovo Albanian interviewees only referred to this case in the context of arguing that there can be no justice at the ICTY when men such as Limaj are put on trial. The judgement in this case, however, fundamentally problematizes the interviewees' repeated assertions that the KLA always spared civilians.

While the Trial Chamber assessed that the KLA did not have a policy of specifically targeting civilians *per se* (Prosecutor v. Limaj, Bala and Musliu 2005: §215), it found that suspected Kosovo Albanian collaborators suffered harassment and abuse, while those believed to have links with the Serb military or police 'were singled out for especially severe treatment in detention' and labelled as 'traitors' (Prosecutor v. Limaj, Bala and Musliu 2005: §208). Although the Defence had attempted to argue that the KLA drew a critical distinction between civilians and collaborators, treating the latter as combatants, the Trial Chamber rejected this, satisfied that, '...the KLA definition of "collaborators" encompassed civilians as well as perceived combatants' (2005: §223). The judgement in this case further highlights that KLA crimes included the abduction of Serb civilians (Prosecutor v. Limaj, Bala and Musliu 2005: §206). In most cases, the abduction of Serb civilians 'occurred when an individual in a community or village was suspected of specific conduct adverse to the KLA or Kosovo Albanian interests...' (Prosecutor v. Limaj, Bala and Musliu 2005: §206). As for crimes committed in the Llapushnik/Lapušnik camp, although the Trial Chamber found that, 'it cannot be established with sufficient certainty that these crimes were in fact committed in pursuance of any KLA policy or plan of targeting Serbian civilians and perceived Albanian collaborators' (2005: §688; see also Prosecutor v. Limaj, Bala and Musliu 2007: §115), this does not detract from the

---

20 Author interview, Prishtinë/Priština, 17 August 2012.

fact that the KLA *did* commit crimes against civilians. (Prosecutor v. Limaj, Bala and Musliu 2005: §206).[21]

Interviewees, however, only rarely accepted that some Kosovo Albanians did commit crimes, and it was striking that they always did so in a way that avoided tarnishing the KLA's heroic image. The former KLA commander in Raçak/ Račak, for example, claimed that when the war in Kosovo ended, some individuals purchased KLA uniforms on the black market and went on to carry out a small number of crimes against Serbs. He was insistent, however, that the perpetrators were not members of the KLA. He further argued that in 1999, some Kosovo Albanians who had not fought in the war returned to Kosovo wanting to be heroes. It is possible, he explained, that these people carried out crimes.[22] Again, politicians have encouraged such arguments. In 2002, for example, Del Ponte had a meeting with Bajram Rexhepi, Kosovo's then Prime Minister. The latter 'maintained that the crimes committed by Albanians in Kosovo were the misdeeds of individuals and were, therefore, on a different plane than the crimes committed by Serbs' (Del Ponte 2008: 283).

Such denials are extremely difficult to combat; they are essential for preserving the myth that the KLA fought an honourable and righteous war to liberate Kosovo and the Kosovo Albanians. For politicians to publicly acknowledge that members of the KLA also committed crimes would critically undermine the moral foundations of the young Kosovo state. In a similar vein, Bosnian Serb denial of crimes such as Srebrenica can be understood in part as an attempt to defend the existence of the RS, while Croat denial of war crimes committed against Serbs in the Krajina area of Croatia serves to preserve the legitimacy of Operation Storm. That denial fulfils such an important function critically exposes the extreme simplicity and naïveté inherent in the claim that the ICTY can overcome the problem of denial by establishing the truth. Fundamentally, contested justice and disputed/rejected truths simply fuel ethnic grievances and sustain the persistence of competing binary narratives, whereby '...both communities compete for the status of the "real" and only victim...' (Burema 2012: 16).

Inter-ethnic relations in Kosovo

Before exploring whether inter-ethnic reconciliation exists in Kosovo, two important preliminary points should be highlighted. The first is that, as in BiH and Croatia, some interviewees had very strong, negative reactions to the word 'reconciliation'. The term was particularly contentious among Serbs in the north of Kosovo. When asked about reconciliation, it was interesting how frequently interviewees seemed surprised by the question. Their immediate reaction was often to seek clarification, by asking: 'Reconciliation between whom?' This in

---

21 The Trial Chamber also found that in some cases, these abductions 'were undertaken by independent elements of the KLA not acting pursuant to a general KLA policy or direction' (Prosecutor v. Limaj, Bala and Musliu 2005: §206).

22 Author interview, Raçak/Račak, 27 August 2012.

turn was typically followed by the emphatic assertion that, 'There is no reconciliation!' How can there be reconciliation, a taxi driver in Zvečan/Zveçan demanded to know, when he is unable to return to his home – which he claimed that Kosovo Albanians had destroyed – in south Mitrovicë/a.[23] Another interviewee, in Leposavić/q, explained that he vehemently objects to 'foreigners' turning up and talking to people about reconciliation. Opining that reconciliation is virtually impossible, he maintained that it is better for Serbs and Albanians to live apart from each other and to have only business-related contact.[24]

The second point is that there was widespread pessimism among interviewees as a whole regarding the prospects for reconciliation between Serbs and Albanians in Kosovo. A Kosovo Albanian interviewee in Prishtinë/Priština, for example, argued that Albanians have nothing in common with Serbs; they have their own languages, they have different religions and they are culturally dissimilar. Claiming that the hatred between them runs deep, he considered that although some form of reconciliation may be possible over time, the problem is that Serbs and Albanians will no longer be able to communicate with each other due to language barriers.[25] A Serb interviewee from the village of Koretište/Koretishta, in the municipality of Gjilan/Gnjilane – who emphasized that he would disown his daughters if any of them every married a Kosovo Albanian – similarly stressed that while there is much to divide Serbs and Albanians, there is little to unite them.[26] Some internationals in Kosovo themselves questioned whether reconciliation is achievable. A representative of EULEX, for example, highlighted four key reasons why, in his view, reconciliation is nigh impossible: the conflict between Serbs and Albanians is deeply engrained; Kosovo Albanians are no longer learning the Serbian language; criminals are running the government in Prishtinë/Priština; and the two communities embrace fundamentally divergent, incompatible narratives about the war. In his judgement, therefore, coexistence is the best that can be hoped for.[27]

Human security

Inter-ethnic incidents remain a regular occurrence in Kosovo, and Serbs and other minorities are the main targets.[28] According to a 2011 report by the OSCE, 'Non-majority communities in Kosovo continue to be negatively affected by

---

23 Author interview, north Mitrovica/ë, 6 August 2012.
24 Author interview, Leposavić/q, 13 August 2012.
25 Author interview, Prishtinë/Priština, 22 August 2012. When Kosovo was an autonomous province of Serbia, Albanians learnt Serbian in schools and many Serbs were able to speak at least some Albanian. Today, however, Serbs and Albanians are no longer learning each other's languages.
26 Author interview, Gjilan/Gnjilane, 23 August 2012.
27 Author interview, north Mitrovica/ë, 7 August 2012.
28 On occasion, so too are internationals. In September 2013, for example, a police officer from Lithuania was killed in north Kosovo. He was the first member of EULEX to die in Kosovo (BBC 2013e).

serious security incidents targeting persons, private property and sites of cultural and religious significance' (2011c: 26). Such incidents, moreover, are not confined to any one particular area. The report documents, *inter alia*, the desecration of Orthodox graves in Gjilan/Gnjilane town, the village of Dobri Dub/Lismir (in Fushë Kosovë/ Kosovo Polje municipality) and the village of Laplje Selo/ Llapllaselle (in the municipality of Gračanica/Graçanicë) in early 2010 (OSCE 2011c: 6, 13); attacks against the small Serb community in Prishtinë/Priština (OSCE 2011c: 13); and various security incidents against Serb returnees in western Kosovo. For example,

> Throughout 2010, security incidents targeting Kosovo Serb returnees were frequently reported in the ethnically-mixed village of Zallq/Žać in Istog/ Istok municipality. On 17 August, a returnee house under construction was damaged, while on 18 August a field of dry grass close to returnee tents was set on fire. The most significant [incident] took place on 20 February 2010, when a Kosovo Serb returnee was attacked while he was walking from Zallq/ Žać to the Kosovo Serb village of Osojane/Osojan, Istog/Istok municipality, suffering bodily injuries.
>
> (OSCE 2011c: 11)

More recently, a 2012 report by the UN Secretary-General notes that, 'On May 14 [2012], threatening letters signed by a group calling itself the "Albanian National Army" and demanding that Kosovo Serbs leave were found in eight Kosovo Serb villages in the Klinë/Klina Municipality' (UN Security Council 2012: §28). Eight days later, in the same municipality, two Kosovo Serb-owned houses in the village of Drenovac/Drenovc were set on fire (UN Security Council 2012: §28).

One factor that is significantly contributing to, and fuelling, the prevalence of inter-ethnic attacks is the large number of unresolved property issues. The International Crisis Group (ICG) has underlined this point, highlighting how 'Property disputes are a major cause of violence' (2012: 20). The Kosovo Property Agency (KPA), which has replaced the Housing and Property Directorate set up by UNMIK in 1999, is dealing with outstanding property issues, but the process is a complex and protracted one. According to the Internal Displacement Monitoring Centre, 'The KPA-led restitution process has been very slow, and it is still to adjudicate on a significant number of the 42,064 claims lodged by December 2007' (2012: 9). Property issues can lead to inter-ethnic incidents, thus undermining human security. At the same time, low rates of physical repossession of property are testament to the low levels of human insecurity that currently exist in Kosovo, particularly among Serbs. The OSCE, for example, underlines that, '…the actual repossession of property by claimants who are displaced and their return to Kosovo remains largely un-realized. This is mostly due to [the] high number of claimants who perceived that they were not yet able to return due to security or other reasons…' (2011a: 5). Certainly, Serb interviewees who remained internally displaced felt strongly that it would be unwise for them to return to their former homes. An IDP from Pejë/Peć, for example, explained that returning to his former village would be a risk that he was not prepared to take, on account of his wife and children.[29]

This interviewee expressed a deep sense of uncertainty that Serb interviewees as a whole typically shared; the ongoing reality of inter-ethnic incidents in Kosovo, combined with the popular belief that Albanian crimes against Serbs routinely go unpunished, has contributed to feelings of insecurity and vulnerability. No interviewees, even the small number who professed to enjoy good relations with their Albanian neighbours, claimed to feel completely secure. The overwhelming sense among them was that in Kosovo, you never know what might happen. This sentiment was especially strong among Serbs in north Mitrovica/ë. Although Serbs in the north are less vulnerable than Serbs in the enclaves, by virtue of being grouped together in one area rather than spread out across Kosovo, the physical division of Mitrovicë/a into its Albanian and Serb parts inevitably creates a sense of unease and uncertainty – on both sides (UNDP 2011: 52).

Issues of physical security and inter-ethnic incidents primarily affect Serbs in Kosovo. Human security, however, also has an economic component, and the poor economic situation in Kosovo affects Serbs and Albanians alike. According to the Bertelsmann Stiftung's Transformation Index (BTI), 'Kosovo remains the poorest country in the region, with 45% of the population living below the poverty line and 15% in extreme poverty. The country needs to double its economic growth in order to achieve an income level similar to neighbouring countries' (2012: 2–3). While it is beyond the scope of this chapter to explore Kosovo's economic situation in depth, the crucial point is that the latter should be recognized as an important obstacle to reconciliation. As in BiH and Croatia, interviewees in Kosovo – on both sides – opined that as long as people are without jobs[30] and without financial security, they will always dwell on the past and continually blame the other side for their own misfortunes. Interviewees repeatedly asserted that if people lived well and were able to find employment, they would have less time to think about the past, they would feel generally more positive about the future and they would have more opportunities for inter-ethnic contact.

Deep contact

According to Andrighetto et al., 'Considerable evidence demonstrates that intergroup contact is a powerful strategy for ameliorating intergroup relations' (2012: 514). In Kosovo, however, there is minimal inter-ethnic contact, and there are four key reasons for this. The first is the demographic structure

---

29 Author interview, north Mitrovica/ë, 1 August 2012.
30 According to the BTI, 'The unemployment rate in Kosovo is approximately 45%... Unemployment continues to be the country's biggest problem' (2012: 15; see also BTI 2014: 13).

of Kosovo. Serbs largely live in their own enclaves, which inevitably creates a separation between Serb and Albanian areas. In Gjilan/Gnjilane, for example, there are very few Serbs now living in the town itself. Instead, they mainly live in surrounding villages within the municipality. Due to the unresolved situation in the north of Kosovo, moreover, there is an even greater separation between Kosovo Albanians and those Serbs who live in the northern municipalities of Leposavić/q, Mitrovica/ë, Zubin Potok and Zvečan/Zveçan. A report by the Kosovar Institute for Policy Research and Development, for example, highlights that, 'For the vast majority of Kosovo Albanians living in the south, and the vast majority of Serbs living north of the Ibër/Ibar, there is no need and no coincidental possibility to meet' (Brand and Idrizi 2012: 10). Although there are a small number of Albanian villages and settlements in the north of Kosovo, their physical remoteness 'does not facilitate direct dialogue between the communities' (OSCE 2010: 22). The fact that Serbs have not returned to certain parts of Kosovo, such as Gjakovë/Đakovica,[31] or have returned in only small numbers, as in the town of Istog/k,[32] further restricts opportunities for inter-ethnic contact.

The second reason is that inter-ethnic contact is often seen as unnecessary and/or undesirable. Both Kosovo Albanian and Kosovo Serb interviewees frequently argued that there is no reason for them to have contact with members of the other ethnic group, other than for the purposes of business and trade. Every Tuesday and Thursday, for example, Serb villagers go to Gjilan/Gnjilane to sell their vegetables and produce. Although there is a large green market in Gjilan/Gnjilane, the Serb villagers (many of whom are elderly) sell at the side of the main road that runs through the town and in a small adjacent street close to the local SOC. They claimed that they do not sell at the green market as it is not safe for them to do so, and that in any case Albanians would not buy from them.[33] During the several hours that these Kosovo Serbs sat at the side of the road in the blistering heat, some Albanians did stop by to make small purchases, but there was little communication – other than a discussion of prices. An Albanian

---

31 According to the Kosovo Agency of Statistics, there are only 17 Kosovo Serbs living in the municipality of Gjakovë/Đakovica today, compared to 87,672 Kosovo Albanians (OSCE 2013a). Prior to the war, Kosovo Serbs constituted approximately 4 per cent of the municipality.
32 There are 194 Kosovo Serbs (and 36,154 Kosovo Albanians) in Istog/k today (OSCE 2013b). This makes them less than one per cent of the municipality's total population. Before the war, in contrast, they made up between 15 and 20 per cent of the municipality (Human Rights Watch 2001: 243).
33 It is impossible to know whether this is actually true, given that none of these Serbs had ever attempted to sell at the green market. The very fact that they *believe* it would be unsafe for them to do so, however, is significant; it is not only objective threats that undermine a person's human security but also *perceived* threats. Albanian interviewees, in contrast, argued that Serbs are welcome at the green market but do not have enough items to sell there.

Figure 7.3 North Mitrovica/ë.

interviewee in Gjilan/Gnjilane initially claimed that relations between local Serbs and Albanians are good. There are no problems, he underlined, and referred to the aforementioned villagers to illustrate his argument that nobody bothers the Serbs. Yet, when asked to elaborate on the nature of inter-ethnic relations in Gjilan/Gnjilane, he revealed that the predominant form of contact between Albanians and Serbs is business-related; people trade with each other because it is in their interests to do so.[34]

In the town of Gjakovë/Đakovica in western Kosovo, there are no longer any Serbs – with the exception of five women (four of them elderly) who live in the grounds of the SOC – and local residents made it clear that they wanted the situation to remain that way. Expressing a viewpoint which was consistently repeated, an interviewee who lost five members of her family during the war maintained that there is no place for Serbs in Gjakovë/Đakovica and that they have no reason to come back.[35] Gjakovë/Đakovica was very badly affected during the war – the Çarshia/Čaršija area of the town was destroyed by fire, large numbers of people

34 Author interview, Gjilan/Gnjilane, 23 August 2012.
35 Author interview, Gjakovë/Đakovica, 10 January 2013.

went missing[36] and more than 300 Albanians from Mejë/a, Orizë/a and other villages in the Reka/Caragoj Valley within the municipality were massacred on 27 April 1999[37] – and this has fundamentally affected popular attitudes towards Serbs. Quintessentially, there is a widespread belief that all of the Serbs who once lived in Gjakovë/Đakovica are guilty, directly or indirectly. Interviewees thus had little or no contact with Serbs, they did not want any and they were confident that Serbs will never return to Gjakovë/Đakovica. 'They know what they did' was an oft-repeated phrase.

The third reason for generally low levels of inter-ethnic contact, outside of business and trade, is that among interviewees on both sides, contact avoidance was often seen as a conflict prevention measure. Interviewees unanimously stressed a strong desire to live in peace and feared that increased contact – beyond politely greeting each other and trading with each other – could create new problems and tensions, including within their own communities. Several interviewees made the point that if they were seen to be on friendly terms with someone from the other ethnic group, members of their own group might become suspicious. In northern Mitrovica/ë, for example, 'Whoever crosses the barricades...breaches the unwritten but powerful "rule of the game" to not interact, and has to fear sanctions' (Brand and Idrizi 2012: 30). Indeed, in the northern part of Kosovo, limited contact is much more than a way of avoiding conflict. It is part of an existential strategy to ensure that Serbs retain their control of the north. As one of the 'bridge-watchers' in north Mitrovica/ë explained, the fear among Serbs is that increased inter-ethnic contact and interaction could allow Kosovo Albanians to steadily infiltrate the north and thus drive the Serbs out.[38] The fourth and final reason for the absence of deep contact in Kosovo is the fact that levels of trust between Kosovo Serbs and Kosovo Albanians remain low.

Trust

Trust is a rare commodity in Kosovo, and its absence fuels social distance. Kosovo Serb and Kosovo Albanian interviewees alike were very clear about the types of inter-ethnic relations that they found acceptable and felt comfortable with, and the general consensus was that some degree of distance was necessary. Interviewees were happy to trade and do business with members of the other ethnic group, but generally felt uneasy developing more personal relationships. Some Serb interviewees drew an important distinction between, on one hand, the domiciled Albanian population and, on the other hand, the so-called 'došljaci' (newcomers) who have moved into a particular area from elsewhere. An interviewee from

---

36 As of February 2000, for example, approximately 1,200 people from the municipality were missing (Human Rights Watch 2001: 212).
37 EULEX is investigating this massacre.
38 Author interview, north Mitrovica/ë, 9 August 2012.

Babin Most/Babimoc, for example, claimed that there are no problems between Serbs and those Albanians who have always lived in the village, located between Mitrovicë/a and Prishtinë/Priština. She described, however, how an influx of new Albanians from outside of Babin Most/Babimoc has made her feel insecure and uneasy; she does not know who these Albanians are or where they are from, and she instinctively distrusts them.[39]

It was the enormous difficulties of re-building trust, however, that emerged as a particularly recurrent overall theme. A Kosovo Albanian interview in Vushtrri/Vučitrn, for example, who recounted how he was forced out of his flat in July 1998, claimed that a Serb friend and neighbour had been trying to kill him and that when he returned to his home in June 1999, everything had been stolen. That is what *they* are like, he exclaimed, underlining that he will never be able to trust Serbs again.[40] For his part, a Serb IDP from Gjilan/Gnjilane emphasized that history has taught the Serbs never to trust the Albanians. Describing how Serbs and Albanians in Gjilan/Gnjilane had enjoyed good relations prior to 1999, he had expected the situation to remain peaceful when the war ended, but this did not happen. The crimes that were committed against Serbs, the interviewee explained, have forever destroyed his trust in Albanians.[41]

Although readily acknowledging that there are good and bad people in every nation, interviewees typically spoke about members of the other ethnic group in very generalized and often negative terms, evincing high levels of prejudice and binary 'us'/'them' thinking. Regularly advising the author to be very careful when visiting Albanian areas, and commonly portraying Kosovo as an unruly and mafia-ridden society from the top down, Kosovo Serb interviewees routinely implicated Kosovo Albanians in, prostitution, drug smuggling and the trafficking of human organs. They are all barbarians, a Serb taxi driver in Zvečan/Zveçan insisted.[42] Albanian interviewees, for their part, harboured strong prejudices about the north of Kosovo, maintaining that it is run by criminal gangs and the Serb mafia. They thus cautioned the author to take great care when visiting the north. They also frequently asserted that although not all Serbs are bad, the majority of them cannot be trusted; they turned on neighbours once before and they could do so again. Interviewees unanimously held Serbs responsible for the wars in the former Yugoslavia and often portrayed them as a dangerous and belligerent people. According to an interviewee in Vushtrri/Vučitrn, the Serbs are 'a pyromaniacal and genocidal nation';[43] and an interviewee in Gjakovë/Đakovica claimed that Serbs have 'dirty blood' and are naturally aggressive.[44]

---

39 Author interview, north Mitrovica/ë, 20 August 2012.
40 Author interview, Vushtrri/Vučitrn, 21 August 2012.
41 Author interview, north Mitrovica/ë, 20 August 2012.
42 Author interview, Zvečan/Zveçan, 12 August 2012.
43 Author interview, Vushtrri/Vučitrn, 21 August 2012.
44 Author interview, Gjakovë/Đakovica, 10 January 2013.

One particular issue that is helping to fuel and sustain inter-ethnic mistrust in Kosovo is the unknown fate of large numbers of missing persons (Burema 2012: 14). The International Committee of the Red Cross (ICRC), for example, reports that, 'Well over 10 years after the events in Kosovo, out of the total of 6,019 persons reported to the ICRC as missing by their families, 1,799 remain unaccounted for' (2011). Interviewees on both sides – and in particular Kosovo Albanians in Gjakovë/Đakovica – underlined the critical importance of resolving this issue, often identifying it as a key prerequisite for achieving justice (see also UNDP 2007: 13). The pace of progress, however, has been slow. According to Amnesty International, 'Cases of enforced disappearances and abductions have not yet been investigated, while the bodies of some 1,800 missing persons have still not been exhumed, identified and returned to their relatives' (2012: 5). Although there are more missing Kosovo Albanians than Kosovo Serbs, it is an issue which nevertheless affects both communities[45] and feeds a deep sense of injustice. The latter is rendered more acute in the context of popular dissatisfaction with the ICTY.

Mutual acceptance

There is little evidence to suggest that mutual acceptance exists in Kosovo, or indeed that it is something that can easily develop. On the Serb side, interviewees expressed the opinion that they are not welcome in Kosovo and that Kosovo Albanians, far from accepting the presence of a Serb minority, ultimately want to drive the Serbs out. They claimed, for example, that Kosovo Albanians are exerting subtle pressure on them to leave by, *inter alia*, purchasing homes and setting up businesses in Serb areas. When asked why Serbs are agreeing to sell their properties, an interviewee in Gračanica/Graçanicë stressed that it was almost impossible to resist Kosovo Albanians because they have money and will pay good prices.[46] Indeed, many interviewees admitted that they themselves would sell their homes for the right price, believing that they have no future in Kosovo. Interviewees living in enclaves such as Gračanica/Graçanicë and Štrpce/Shtërpcë, for example, expressed a strong sense of defeatism. 'We have lost everything' was a common refrain. Regular inter-ethnic incidents, attacks on Serb cultural heritage,[47] the widespread

45 Amnesty International, for example, notes that while the bodies of 428 Kosovo Albanians have not been accounted for, 'A much larger percentage of missing Serbs, Roma and other minorities remain unaccounted for: the whereabouts of some 450 out of 499 are still to be established' (2012: 27–28).

46 Author interview, Gračanica/Graçanicë, 15 August 2012.

47 According to an OSCE report, 'During the assessment conducted in June and July 2010, the OSCE found more than 200 Orthodox graveyards and more than 500 tombstones damaged and/or vandalized' (2011b: 4).

Figure 7.4 A road sign in Gjakovë/Đakovica.

conviction that crimes against Serbs are not properly investigated and even the simple fact that Serbian place names are often incorrectly spelt on road signs (for example, Obiljić rather than Obilić, Peč rather than Peć) – and more frequently completely blacked out – have all contributed to the entrenchment of a deep-seated feeling among Serbs that they are neither wanted nor accepted in Kosovo.

On the Albanian side, some interviewees did express the view that Kosovo would be a better place without Serbs. The majority, however, claimed that they do not have a problem with Serbs, provided that the latter do not make trouble; by this they meant that Serbs must recognize the independence of Kosovo and assimilate. Frequently claiming that Serbs have extensive rights in Kosovo (indeed more rights, insisted some, than any other minority in Europe), but overlooking the fact that these rights are not necessarily respected in practice, they completely dismissed Serb fears and concerns. In the western Kosovo town of Istog/k, for example, where large numbers of homes remain destroyed, Albanian interviewees always rejected any suggestion that security issues may have deterred Serbs from returning in large numbers (those who have returned are primarily elderly). Instead, they attributed the low number of returns to the economic situation, and one interviewee offered the explanation that Serbs prefer to live in large cities like Belgrade.[48] When asked whether Serbs would be welcome if they returned, interviewees simply stressed that Serbs would not have any problems as long as they themselves did not create problems.

Kosovo Albanian interviewees throughout Kosovo were similarly unwilling to understand the concerns of Serbs in the north, repeatedly maintaining that the latter persist in their refusal to accept Kosovo's independence only because they are controlled and manipulated by criminal gangs and the Serbian government in Belgrade. This 'theory', however, critically overlooks the fact that no Kosovo Serbs recognize Kosovo's independence. The only difference is that unlike Serbs in the north, Serbs living south of the River Ibër/Ibar have had to co-operate with Kosovo institutions and to accept Kosovo identity cards, driving licenses and so on, in order to live their lives.

This chapter, like the two previous chapters, has once again exposed as both over-simplistic and deeply problematic the idea that the ICTY can contribute to reconciliation by delivering justice and establishing the truth. In Kosovo, as in BiH and Croatia, the ICTY is rarely associated with justice; that its work consistently collides and jars with deeply-entrenched ethnic preconceptions of justice inevitably fuels widespread allegations of injustice. This, combined with the small number of ICTY trials relating to Kosovo – and the Tribunal's physical remoteness – has generated a strong sense of 'justice unseen'. None of this creates a propitious environment for the embedding and acceptance of Tribunal truths. The very fact that reconciliation – measured against human security, deep contact, trust and mutual acceptance – does not exist in Kosovo both reinforces the arguments made in this chapter and excludes the possibility that the ICTY might have contributed to reconciliation in other ways. Once again, however, this does not mean that the Tribunal should be viewed as a failure. While there is no doubt that it should have done far more to reach out to and communicate with local communities on the ground,[49] the ICTY is not operating in a vacuum; and as Hodžić underscores, 'Any discussion of the Tribunal's legacy in the former Yugoslavia that ignores the political and social context in which it is operating can be likened to squabbling over minor issues when the house is on fire' (2011: 119). In Kosovo, the unresolved political situation regarding the north, the frequency of inter-ethnic incidents and the high levels of mistrust are just some of the many hindrances to reconciliation. Ultimately, therefore, this chapter casts further doubt on the idea that the ICTY can aid reconciliation.

48 Author interview, Istog/k, 14 January 2013.
49 In 2012, for example, only 15 of the ICTY's 98 outreach activities (which overwhelmingly centred on young people and included presentations in schools and the use of documentaries) focused on Kosovo (ICTY 2012a). In 2005, moreover, the year that Haradinaj's indictment was made public, the ICTY's Outreach Unit completely neglected Kosovo (ICTY 2005).

Chapter 8

Beyond the ICTY, Beyond Courts, Beyond Transitional Justice

If the ICTY has not contributed to inter-ethnic reconciliation in BiH, Croatia and Kosovo, this raises the broader question of whether any international court can facilitate reconciliation. While this research is specifically concerned with international courts,[1] many of the arguments made in this chapter are also applicable to national courts. When the idea for this book first began to take shape, the author intended to call it *Remote Justice*, in order to highlight how the ICTY's distance from the former Yugoslavia has critically undermined its ability to aid reconciliation. Yet, while there is no doubt that a more creative and sustained outreach programme specifically focused on the grassroots level could have helped to bridge the gap between the Tribunal and local communities in the former Yugoslavia, it is clear from the foregoing chapters that there are multiple reasons why the ICTY has not contributed to inter-ethnic reconciliation, of which the inadequacies of its outreach work are only one factor. As to whether other courts have fostered reconciliation in post-conflict societies, it must be emphasized that there is a distinct lack of empirical research on this specific issue. It is therefore hoped that scholars working in the field of TJ will utilize and expand the measurement model that underpins this research to explore the social impact of other courts. Based on existing academic studies, however, it is submitted that judicial institutions operating in a post-conflict context face generic problems which significantly impact on their oft-cited capacity to encourage reconciliation. In short, international courts, it is argued, are not well-equipped to promote reconciliation, and hence it is unrealistic to expect them to contribute to this complex process. To develop this thesis further, the first part of this chapter moves the focus beyond the former Yugoslavia and draws upon examples from the ICTR, the SCSL, the ECCC and the ICC. Although all of these courts are very different,[2] the

---

1 In this chapter, all references to international courts include hybrid courts.
2 The ICTR, like the ICTY, is an *ad hoc* tribunal; both the SCSL and the ECCC are hybrid courts which apply a mixture of international and domestic law and employ both international and local staff; and the ICC is the world's first ever permanent international criminal court.

problems that they face are not. Three common problems in particular can be highlighted: the difficulty of satisfying victims that 'justice' has been done; the fact that contested justice is often divisive justice; and the frequent existence of a court–community disconnect.

Can courts help reconciliation?

The previous chapters have demonstrated that 'justice' is a profoundly contested concept within the former Yugoslavia. When we adopt a broader comparative framework, moreover, it is clear that all international criminal courts face immense challenges in satisfying communities that justice has been done, and this necessarily raises important questions about the actual and anticipated on-the-ground achievements of these judicial bodies. As Nash underlines, 'A problem with retributive justice is that it is only as good as the community or system it intends to serve, i.e., justice is only as good as society perceives it to be' (2007: 62). The fact that deeply-disputed justice can encourage and foster new societal and community divides further calls into question the extent to which criminal courts can actually aid reconciliation. Finally, international courts necessarily face an uphill struggle in engaging local communities and bridging the divide between the esoteric complexities of the legal process and the difficulties and challenges of everyday life in fragile post-conflict societies. It is, therefore, questionable whether institutions that are often heavily disconnected from local communities, poorly understood and perceived as remote can bring about the positive societal effects that their supporters claim.

Justice that fails to satisfy

Widely associating the ICTY with injustice, interviewees in the former Yugoslavia accused it, *inter alia*, of indicting and processing too few people, of undertaking politically-motivated prosecutions and of failing to sufficiently punish war criminals. When we broaden the purview beyond the former Yugoslavia, moreover, we see that such grievances and criticisms have similarly been levelled at other international courts. The number of persons indicted and prosecuted, for example, is often a profoundly contentious issue because in societies where mass atrocities have occurred, there will always be a huge discrepancy between the number of suspected/actual perpetrators and the number of persons who ultimately stand trial. This, in turn, easily foments strong sentiments of injustice. In Sierra Leone, for example, the SCSL[3] is mandated to prosecute persons bearing the 'greatest responsibility' for serious violations of international humanitarian law and Sierra Leonean law. The

3 The SCSL was established in January 2002, pursuant to an agreement between the Sierra Leonean government and the UN.

problem is that in a situation where all sides committed war crimes – a fact which the SCSL's work clearly reflects – identifying those with 'greatest responsibility' is extremely difficult. Furthermore, the Court's judges have not been consistent in how they interpret the term (Jalloh 2011: 414), and the rationale for prosecuting certain individuals over others has never been explained to local people. Not only has the Court indicted just 13 individuals,[4] but in keeping with its mandate it has pursued only 'leaders with overall command responsibility, and not the foot soldiers or the actual rapists' (Graybill 2011: 104). The problem is that this exclusive focus on the so-called 'big fish' does not necessarily deliver the justice that victims expect. According to House's research, for example, '...in the view of Sierra Leoneans, perpetrators were those who actually committed the atrocities irrespective of their levels in the chain of command' (2013: 15). Kelsall, moreover, maintains that because the armed factions fighting in Sierra Leone were often loosely organized and hence extremely fluid, 'prosecuting those at the top of notional military pyramids' is not necessarily tantamount to prosecuting those with greatest responsibility for war crimes (2013: 260).

Taken together with the fact that the Court has prosecuted men who were 'relatively unknown' to the majority of ordinary Sierra Leoneans (Mieth 2013: 14), all of this highlights a critical and common disconnect between legal justice and its reception in affected local communities. As we saw in the former Yugoslavia, 'Prosecutions at the international level may...facilitate "justice" in an abstract sense, but still fail miserably to resonate in the societies in which human rights violations occurred' (Putnam 2002: 251). The fact that international justice is inevitably *limited* justice – whether due to circumstances, political decision-making or a combination of both – necessarily restricts the scope for 'resonance'. In Cambodia, for example, more than 30 years after the genocide occurred, the

4 In 2003, the SCSL indicted five leading members of the Revolutionary United Front (RUF), although two of the indictments were subsequently withdrawn following the deaths of Foday Sankoh and Sam Bockarie. In March 2009, the remaining three defendants – Issa Sesay, Morris Kallon and Augustine Gbao – were sentenced to prison terms of 52, 40 and 25 years respectively. The SCSL has also prosecuted three members of the Armed Forces Revolutionary Council (AFRC). In 2008, Alex Brima, Ibrahim Kamara and Santigie Borbor Kanu received prison sentences of 50, 45 and 50 years respectively. The fate and whereabouts of Johnny Paul Koroma, however, the AFRC'S former leader whom the Court indicted in 2003, remain unknown. Most controversially, the Court indicted and prosecuted three members of the Civil Defence Forces (CDF), including the CDF leader Sam Hinga Norman. Norman died in February 2007, but later that year the Court sentenced his co-defendants, Moinina Fofana and Allieu Kondewa, to prison terms of six years (increased on appeal to 15 years) and eight years (increased on appeal to 20 years) respectively. The most significant 'big fish' prosecuted at the SCSL is the former President of Liberia, Charles Taylor, who provided substantial assistance to the RUF. On 26 April 2012, the SCSL convicted Taylor of 11 counts of war crimes and crimes against humanity and sentenced him to 50 years' imprisonment. This was upheld on appeal a year later.

ECCC[5] is prosecuting just five senior leaders of the former Democratic Kampuchea. While it is easy to criticize the Court for taking such a cautious approach (Bockers, Stammel and Knaevelsrud 2011: 77), it is arguably more constructive to ask what can realistically be expected from an institution that is dealing with so few cases. Underscoring this point, Dicklitch and Malik maintain that, 'Trying a handful of "those most responsible" is not enough to heal a trau-matized nation – especially when the government still contains members of the Khmer Rouge, and low-level perpetrators live freely in villages and urban areas' (2010: 519).

The 'justice' that criminal trials are able to deliver, in short, will almost never be enough to satisfy those on the ground – and in particular victims. In such circumstances, it is difficult to envisage how international courts can contribute to reconciliation. Indeed, as the previous chapters have demonstrated, the work of an international court and the contested nature of the justice that it delivers may reinforce existing divisions and further help to polarize communities.

Contested justice, divisive justice

If certain ICTY judgements – including Gotovina, Haradinaj, Orić and Perišić – have proven especially contentious and unpopular among particular ethnic groups in BiH, Croatia and Kosovo, in Sierra Leone significant controversy has similarly surrounded some of the SCSL's work, notably the Civil Defence Forces (CDF) trial and the prosecution of Sam Hinga Norman (for a detailed analysis of the CDF trial, see Kelsall 2013). The former deputy Defence Minister and the head of the CDF, Norman was highly popular among many Sierra Leoneans; 'Many were grateful to him for the sacrifice he had made in leading the CDF that had defended the public during the RUF [Revolutionary United Front] onslaught and when the national army had abandoned them' (Tejan-Cole 2009: 240). The fact that Sierra Leone's President Kabbah, from whom Norman took his orders, was never indicted further fuelled the sense of injustice which Norman's trial provoked (Jalloh 2011: 425). Although Norman died (following a hip operation in Senegal) before the Court delivered its verdict, experts on Sierra Leone have variously claimed that by prosecuting a man whom many regarded as a hero (Kelsall 2013: 49), the SCSL exacerbated divisions in the country (Tejan-Cole 2009: 240), alienated large numbers of victims (Lamin 2009: 250) and 'appears to have hurt efforts at national reconciliation...' (Jalloh 2011: 459).

If a court can antagonize local communities by prosecuting all sides in a con-flict, the example of the ICTR highlights some of the problems that can ensue when a court prosecutes only one side. It will be recalled from Chapter 1 that

---

5 Some 1.7 million people were killed during the Cambodian genocide between 1975 and 1979. Following ten years of negotiations between the UN and the Cambodian government, the ECCC began its work on 1 July 2006 and issued its first indictment a year later.

reconciliation is an explicit part of the ICTR's mandate, and Tribunal officials have consistently argued that its work is having a positive effect in this regard. According to Moghalu, for example, a former spokesperson and legal advisor to the ICTR, '...the conviction of senior figures by the ICTR has contributed to reconciliation in Rwanda by individualizing guilt, in contrast to the tendency to assign guilt to groups' (2002: 33); and in an address to the UN Security Council on 12 June 2013, the ICTR Registrar, Bongani Majola, emphasized that, 'Since its inception, the ICTR has sought to contribute to the process of reconciliation in Rwanda by helping to restore a sense of justice and playing a role in the development of a lasting peace in the Great Lakes region' (Majola 2013). In the aftermath of a genocide in which up to one million people were killed, the ICTR was always going to struggle to deliver 'justice'. However, the lack of any concerted attempt to prosecute crimes committed by the Rwandan Patriotic Front (RPF) (Haskell and Waldorf 2011: 50) – due to persistent obstruction from President Paul Kagame (the former military leader of the RPF) and the Rwandan government[6] – means that the ICTR is delivering a very one-sided justice focused exclusively on Hutu perpetrators. This, in turn, necessarily sends a highly controversial message; '...that Tutsi leaders enjoyed impunity, that they were above the law, that the innocent victims of their violence did not count' (Del Ponte 2008: 179). Hence, ICTR justice is particularly open to challenge, and the contested nature of its work strongly problematizes the argument that its trials are contributing to reconciliation. Haskell and Waldorf, for example, maintain that while it may be too soon to conclusively judge whether the ICTR and ICTY have fostered reconciliation, 'One can nevertheless conclude that the ICTR's failure to prosecute RPF crimes has not promoted reconciliation in Rwanda, as impunity for these crimes remains a divisive issue' (2011: 78).

The extent to which the ICC[7] is fully committed to fighting impunity has likewise been called into question. In northern Uganda, for example, the Court has only indicted members of Joseph Kony's Lord's Resistance Army (LRA), despite the fact that both the LRA and the United People's Defence Force (UPDF) have committed war crimes (Branch 2007: 182). Although the ICC's former Prosecutor, Luis Moreno-Ocampo, has sought to argue that LRA and UPDF crimes are qualitatively different in terms of their gravity (2006: 501), such assertions are unlikely to resonate with victims of UPDF crimes, thus impacting on how the Court is viewed. To cite Clark, '...the ICC's investigations

6 According to Lyons, a criminal defence attorney at the ICTR, '...what I did not realize until I actually worked on a case, and especially after I was working in the prisons of Rwanda, was how much overt State political intervention goes on, how much the Rwandan government tries to influence and control the ICTR, to intimidate witnesses, to disregard its co-operation obligations, etc.' (2010: 4).
7 The ICC came into being with the adoption of the Rome Statute in 1998, which entered into force on 1 July 2002.

into LRA and not UPDF crimes create a perception of the ICC as one-sided and heavily politicised' (2008: 42). Similarly, questions have been raised as to why, in the Ivory Coast, the ICC has only indicted the country's former President, Laurent Gbagbo (whose case is currently at the pre-trial stage), and not any members of forces loyal to the new President, Alassane Ouattara (Amann 2013: 26). According to one commentator, 'The fact that Gbagbo is in prison looks very hypocritical to Gbagbo supporters', not least because Ouattara 'seems to be very reluctant to scrutinize his own troops, his own supporters and their conduct during the recent civil war' (Joseph Hellweg, cited in Scully 2012).

What further increases the scope for contested justice is the fact that courts are judged not only on an internal, national basis (who are they prosecuting and not prosecuting within the affected country/countries themselves), but also on an external, international basis (who are they prosecuting and not prosecuting at the global level). In short, if communities perceive so-called 'global justice' as in fact a highly discriminating phenomenon which selectively targets only certain countries or geographic areas, this will necessarily influence how they respond to a court's work and the 'justice' it administers. In 2008, for example, President Abdoulaye Wade of Senegal 'questioned why the Court [ICC] was only target-ing Africa after the indictment of the Sudanese President Omar al-Bashir...' (Nyawo 2012: 136); and in 2011, the chief executive of the African Union (AU) denounced the ICC as 'discriminatory', maintaining that its African-centric focus[8] was myopic in the context of Western interventions in Iraq and Afghanistan (Amann 2013: 27). Two years earlier, in 2009, during a visit to Ituri in the Democratic Republic of Congo (DRC) to speak to local people about the work of the ICC and the trial of Thomas Lubanga Dyilo,[9] the President of the Court, Song Sang-Hyun, was asked 'why the ICC was not prosecuting cases concerning Israel and Europe instead of focusing on Lubanga' (Richardson 2012: 116). Audience members further sought to know why the Court has failed to prose-cute any of the foreign trading companies whose activities have fuelled the fight-ing in the DRC (N'Sapu 2010). More recently, in September 2013, Kenya's parliament voted to withdraw from the ICC after the latter charged the coun-try's President and deputy President, Uhuru Kenyatta and William Ruto respec-tively, with crimes against humanity. Maintaining that the charges against Kenyatta and Ruto are a step too far, politicians from Kenya's Jubilee Coalition have called upon their citizens to defend the country's sovereignty (BBC 2013c).

8 The ICC's current caseload centres on war crimes committed in the following countries: the Central African Republic, Darfur, the DRC, Ivory Coast, Kenya, Libya, Mali and Uganda.
9 Indicted by the ICC in 2006, Lubanga was the leader of the Union of Congolese Patriots (UPC) in Ituri. In 2012, the Trial Chamber found him guilty of war crimes, including enlisting and conscripting children under the age of 15 into the military wing of the UPC and using them to participate actively in hostilities. On 10 July 2012, the Court sentenced Lubanga to 14 years' imprisonment.

Furthermore, there is considerable support for Kenya's position within the AU, which has called for Kenyatta and Ruto to be tried in Kenya under local jurisdiction.[10] According to the Rwandan ambassador to the AU, 'It is not only the case of Kenya. We have seen international justice becoming more and more a political matter' (BBC 2013f).[11]

War crimes investigations and trials are always highly sensitive and 'politically controversial' (Goldstone 2000: 132). International courts operate in extremely difficult environments and this, coupled with the enormous challenges of satisfying communities that justice has been done, means that they are often more likely to entrench (or in some cases even exacerbate) existing divides than to bridge them. Indeed, by their very nature, criminal trials are ill-suited to promoting reconciliation. Firstly, they are adversarial, and '"[a]dversarial" has an inimical connotation of hostility, detrimental to reconciliation' (Eser 2011: 145). Secondly, unlike restorative justice processes, criminal trials do not encourage perpetrators to make amends and 'put things right'. Hence, the guilty may continue to maintain their innocence while their victims are left with many unanswered questions. To cite Kohen, Zanchelli and Drake, 'Because the retributive system either discourages or prevents victims and offenders from interacting with one another, stereotypes are maintained on both sides, offenders need not take responsibility for the harm they have caused, and victims cannot gain access to information that only offenders can provide' (2011: 6). Thirdly, criminal trials are potentially disempowering (Westberg 2011: 360), and hence they may not deliver what people need to be able to contemplate reconciliation. Highlighting this, Zehr argues that, 'The justice process...requires dependence upon proxy professionals who represent offender and the state. This, in turn, removes the process of justice from the individuals and communities which are affected' (2005: 79–80). To build upon Zehr's argument, what further removes the process from affected individuals and communities is the sheer complexity of criminal trials, and this complexity critically contributes to the common problem of court-community disconnects.

The court–community disconnect

In BiH, Croatia and Kosovo, it is clear that local communities are not well-informed about the ICTY and that there is little sense of local ownership of the judicial process. Other international courts have similarly struggled to connect with and engage local communities. The ICTR, for example, based in Arusha in

---

10 African nations, led by Rwanda, recently presented the UN Security Council with a resolution calling for the trials of Kenyatta and Ruto to be suspended. Only seven members of the Security Council, however, voted in favour of the motion while nine abstained (BBC 2013g).

11 Moreover, it is not only local actors and African leaders who have questioned whether 'international' criminal justice is genuinely international (see, for example, Fawthrop and Jarvis 2004: 6; Schabas 2013: 551).

Tanzania, is geographically remote from the people of Rwanda. This necessarily creates a crucial disconnect between the Tribunal and its intended beneficiaries – and by extension makes it more difficult for the Tribunal to achieve a positive local impact. Highlighting this point, Kohen, Zanchelli and Drake remark that, '...the ICTR is little more than a distant mirage of a judicial process for many Rwandans...In fact, many Rwandans refer to the proceedings as "the Arusha trials", showing a clear lack of ownership or familiarity with the ICTR' (2011: 10). The challenges to fostering a sense of local ownership, moreover, are substantial. As Mukherjee points out, 'The tribunal's inaccessibility and the fact that the proceedings are concluded in English and French (only in 2000 did the ICTR also include Kinyarwanda) make it difficult for the Rwandan people to attend court proceedings or hear news of it' (2011: 336).

These examples reinforce the importance of creative, sustained and grassroots-focused outreach work (Clark 2009). If people do not fully understand the work of a court, and if they view it as a distant and externally-owned institution that has little direct relevance to their own everyday lives, it is difficult to envisage how that institution can positively impact on internal processes within the affected society. To cite Stromseth, '...the tribunals must work harder to engage local populations who will often be deeply sceptical of justice institutions based on bitter domestic experience' (2009: 93). Notwithstanding the importance of outreach, it is certainly not a panacea because court-community disconnects are not solely the result of a court's geographic remoteness. Quintessentially, the problem of remote justice highlights deeper and more fundamental issues regarding the relationship between international courts and local communities.

Firstly, the intricacies of international criminal law and the complexities and length of the judicial process mean that even when courts are based in-country, there will always be a gap between the institution and the local population. A survey by Pham et al., for example, found that in Cambodia, people's knowledge of the ECCC was at best very limited (2009: 36–37). The authors note that, 'Nationally, when we include those who were unable to say how many [people] had been arrested, this means that only 3 percent of respondents were able to identify the five individuals currently awaiting trial without any errors' (Pham et al. 2009: 37). Based on interviews with young people in Cambodia, Dicklitch and Malik similarly found that: 'Most of our respondents were not well acquainted with the intricacies of the tribunal, and only 36.6% stated that they were interested in attending the trials' (2010: 522). Similar issues have arisen in relation to the SCSL. According to House's research, for example, 'With regard to the people it came out that the SCSL did not largely enjoy local support and Sierra Leoneans did not show much interest in it...They would not understand the complexity of such a mechanism and its mandate to prosecute those who bear the "greatest responsibility"' (2013: 19). In other words, outreach work can only do so much; the challenge is not only to inform local communities, but also to spark and sustain their interest in a slow and protracted legal process which will often fall short of their expectations.

Secondly, when people are struggling to make ends meet – as is often the case in fragile post-conflict societies – they are unlikely to closely follow the work of courts. In Cambodia, for example, Pham et al. found that, 'While respondents viewed accountability as important and wanted to see former Khmer Rouge tried and punished for past crimes, justice was not a priority for most respondents. Rather, respondents said their priorities were jobs (83%), services to meet basic needs including health (20%), and food (17%)' (Pham et al. 2009: 34). During eight months of ethnographic fieldwork in October 2010 and April 2012, Mieth encountered parallel attitudes in Sierra Leone. She recalls that, '...many of the people I talked to were struggling to secure their livelihood, and consequently lacked interest in the work of the Court' (Mieth 2013: 16). Fundamentally, regardless of where courts are located, their trials and their promises of delivering justice can seem highly abstract and peripheral in communities where people face quotidian existential and security challenges.

Thirdly, justice has multiple meanings and formal retributive justice will not resonate in every society. In societies which have their own forms of justice, for example, and which adhere to a more restorative, needs-based idea of justice,[12] retributive justice and its inherently punitive ethos may fail to strike a chord (Theidon 2006: 436), thus bringing to the fore another dimension of remoteness. According to Mieth, for example, 'With their notions of justice as a restorative action, it was difficult for the majority of Sierra Leoneans I spoke with to understand how the work of the Special Court was to bring them justice if it did not have any direct influence on their situation' (2013: 16); and during ethnographic fieldwork with indigenous Maya Q'eqchi survivors in Guatemala,[13] Viaene found that,

> Survivors almost never spontaneously demand prosecution of the perpetrators during the focus group discussions and interviews. Once they start speaking about justice, they almost never express a wish to sue the responsible national or local authorities...Survivors raise the question: what benefit would a prosecution bring for them? If the intellectual perpetrators are in prison they cannot help victims.
>
> (2010: 296)

---

12 Restorative justice 'is widely understood as a series of theoretical and practical discourses which attempt to facilitate dialogue and reconciliation among victims, offenders and the community' (McEvoy and Eriksson 2008: 321).
13 Between 1960 and 1996, Guatemala experienced a protracted civil war. Shortly after the war ended, the government established a TRC, the Historical Clarification Commission, and in 1999 the latter issued its report. The Commission found that during the country's civil war, the state's military forces committed genocide against some indigenous groups, and in 2004 the Guatemalan state itself admitted that a policy of genocide existed. A National Reparations Programme was implemented almost ten years after the war ended, with relative success, but there have been very few criminal prosecutions.

As these two examples demonstrate, there is significant scope for deep disappointment with the trial process in societies where justice is primarily understood in a restorative sense. Criminal trials focus on the offender, not on the victim; and the emphasis is on punishing those who are found guilty, not on 'problem solving and on repairing harm' (Eriksson 2009: 1). Even in societies where justice is primarily associated with criminal trials, victims often want – and expect – more than retributive justice alone. During his research with ICTY witnesses, for example, Stover found that most of them eschewed a definition of justice focused exclusively on punishment. Rather, they favoured a more holistic definition of justice encompassing a wide range of social and economic rights for victims, 'including the right to live where they wanted and to move about freely and without fear; the right to have the bodies of loved ones returned for proper burial; the right to meaningful and secure jobs; and the right to receive adequate treatment for... psychological trauma...' (Stover 2007: 120). The crucial point is that if there is a serious disjuncture between the 'justice' that people on the ground expect and the 'justice' that a court is delivering, this will help to foster and exacerbate court–community disconnects.

To conclude this section, further empirical research is needed to explore and assess whether international courts can contribute to reconciliation in post-conflict societies, and the measurement model developed in this monograph provides an important point of departure. What the foregoing analysis has sought to demonstrate, however, by adopting a broader comparative framework, is that the relationship between criminal trials and reconciliation is problematic not only in the case of the ICTY and the former Yugoslavia. Rather, there are a number of more general and generic issues arising from the work of international courts which raise wider questions about the extent to which these complex judicial institutions are able, and should be expected, to facilitate reconciliation. The latter requires more than criminal trials alone (Boraine 2006: 27; Mwangi 2009: 272–273; Villa-Vicencio 2009b: 45), and hence different parts of the 'transitional justice spectrum' should be explored (Grodsky 2009: 824). Shifting the focus back to the former Yugoslavia, the second part of this chapter considers whether and how a TRC – and specifically a regional TRC – could potentially encourage reconciliation in the former Yugoslavia.

Restorative justice and reconciliation in the former Yugoslavia

Many post-conflict societies have experimented with TRCs of various types, including Argentina, Guatemala, Haiti, Liberia, Morocco, Sierra Leone, South Africa, Sri Lanka and Timor-Leste (see Hayner 2011). Despite the widespread use of such commissions, scholars have frequently pointed out that our knowledge of their effects remains limited (Brahm 2007: 17; Fletcher, Weinstein and Rowen 2009: 167; Mendeloff 2009: 600). As in the case of criminal courts, these information gaps reflect and highlight the enormous challenges inherent in measuring impact. As Hirsch, MacKenzie and Sesay underscore, '...there are virtually no established mechanisms...for assessing the overall success of the commissions in achieving their stated objectives' (2012: 387). Notwithstanding the fact that many unanswered questions remain surrounding TRCs and their effects, there is a growing consensus among scholars and policy-makers that both retributive justice and restorative justice have a fundamental role to play in societies recovering from conflict and gross human rights violations (Commissioner for Human Rights 2012: 9; Jelačić 2006; Robinson 2011: 25; Teršelić 2013: 43).

In the former Yugoslavia, in keeping with this broader trend, widespread disappointment with the ICTY has contributed to a developing appreciation – particularly within the NGO sector – of the limitations of criminal trials and of the consequent need to explore other, complementary ways of dealing with the past. Such awareness has helped to generate significant interest in the TRC concept and its potential application in the Western Balkans, and this in turn has allowed the idea of establishing a regional TRC to take root. While both Serbia and BiH have previously experimented with various forms of truth commission,[14] with little success, the Coalition for RECOM is the most serious – and most ambitious – attempt to date to initiate and implement a genuine TRC process.

The coalition for RECOM

Composed of more than 250 NGOs and victims' associations throughout the former Yugoslavia, the Coalition for RECOM was launched in Podgorica, Montenegro, on 9 May 2008. Three years later, on 26 March 2011, the Coalition

---

14 In 2001, the then Yugoslav President, Vojislav Koštunica, established a national TRC in Serbia. However, the commission consisted only of Serbs and never issued a report. Most problematically, its main aim was 'to look into the causes and course of the armed conflicts that took place in the former Yugoslavia, and not into the unspeakable violations of international humanitarian law that were perpetrated as those conflicts were unfolding...' (Pejić 2001: 12). In BiH, the Commission for Investigating the Truth Regarding Suffering of the Serbs, Croats, Bosniaks, Jews and Others in Sarajevo in the period between 1992 and 1995 was established in 2006, followed two years later by the TRC of the Municipal Assembly of Bijeljina. From the start, however, both commissions were mired in controversy and failed to deliver. The commission that attracted the most interest was the Srebrenica Commission, established by the RS government on 15 December 2003 to report on events in and around Srebrenica between 10 and 19 July 1995. The Commission found that 7,793 people were killed during this ten-day period and a further 938 people were killed after 19 July 1995. While it fell short of acknowledging that genocide occurred, its findings prompted the RS government to issue a formal public apology on its official website. Noting, however, that the then RS President, Dragan Čavić, 'subsequently declined to attend a burial ceremony for hundreds of Srebrenica victims...', Subotić remarks that, 'This behavior has only confirmed what Bosniac victims and many international observers suspected – that the sole impetus for this about-face in the Republika Srpska came from international actors...who put increasing pressure on the RS to face up to its past or else meet with further international isolation' (2009: 152).

adopted a draft statute which, *inter alia*, outlines RECOM's six objectives (RECOM 2011b). These include establishing the facts about the war crimes and other gross violations of human rights committed on the territory of the former Yugoslavia; assisting political elites and members of society to accept these facts; contributing to the fulfilment of victims' rights;[15] and helping to clarify the fate of missing persons. According to the draft statute, RECOM will have 20 commissioners, who must be both citizens of a Party to the Agreement and persons 'of integrity and respect, upholding high ethical standards, dedicated to fostering a culture of tolerance and constructive dialogue in solving disputes, and capable of enjoying the trust of the people in all Parties to the Agreement' (article 24). There will be five commissioners from BiH, three from Croatia and a further three from both Serbia and Kosovo; while Montenegro, Macedonia and Slovenia will each have two commissioners (article 23). RECOM's temporal mandate will extend from 1 January 1991 until 31 December 2001 (article 15). Underscoring that the idea of creating a regional TRC emerged and developed in response to popular dissatisfaction with the ICTY (Rowen 2012: 701), the preamble to RECOM's draft statute explicitly remarks that trials at the Tribunal and in national courts 'do not fully satisfy victims' needs for justice and are insufficient for the creation of the conditions necessary to achieve a lasting peace in the region' (RECOM 2011b).

The adoption of the draft statute was followed by a six-week campaign to collect as many signatures as possible in support of RECOM. While the goal of one million signatures was not achieved, Golčevski maintains that, 'The campaign showed unprecedented backing of the people of the region for the Initiative, given that in that short period over 542,000 signatures of support for the establishment of the regional Commission have been collected' (2013: 99). In a similar vein, the Commissioner for Human Rights of the Council of Europe has underlined that, 'The RECOM initiative is the only regional initiative that has gathered such wide support from a significant number of representatives of civil society, victims' associations and individuals from all countries in the former Yugoslavia' (2012: 36). While this is true, it is also the case that RECOM has strong detractors on all sides. An interviewee from the Centre for Peace, Non-Violence and Human Rights in Osijek, for example, who was involved in the campaign to collect one million signatures, emphasized that RECOM has many critics in Croatia. 'People in Croatia', he

---

15 According to article 1 of RECOM's statute, victims are 'persons who individually or collectively suffered harm, including physical and mental injury, emotional suffering, economic loss or substantial impairment of their fundamental rights, through acts or omissions that constitute gross violations of international human rights law or serious violations of international humanitarian law. The term "victim" also includes the immediate family of dependents of the direct victim and persons who have suffered harm in intervening to assist victims or to prevent victimization' (RECOM 2011b).

reflected, 'are very disappointed with the ICTY and with the decisions of local courts, and this is one of the reasons why there is relatively little support for RECOM in Croatia; people do not expect anything positive to come from it'. He further underlined that there remains a widespread tendency for people to differentiate between victims, recalling that when he speaks to members of the public about RECOM and explains that its aim is to compile a comprehensive list of victims, he is often asked: 'Which victims?'[16] The media has been particularly instrumental in generating popular resistance to RECOM. Highlighting this point, Mekina notes that, 'An especially popular thesis in the Croatian media is that the aim of RECOM is to "even out the guilt"...' (2011). RECOM is thus framed as a threat to the memory and honour of the 'Homeland War'.

The arguments put forward by opponents of RECOM in Croatia, however, are by no means unique. In BiH, one of the concerns in RS is that RECOM's work will serve to marginalize Serb victims. According to Slaviša Đukić, the president of the Association of Prisoners in RS,

> Serbian patriots know very well that the director of the Humanitarian Law Center, Nataša Kandić, the greatest Serb hater, is behind this project which aims to minimize the number of Serb victims in the recent Homeland War and to declare Serbs the sole perpetrators of the war, designating Republika Srpska as a genocidal creation.
>
> (cited in Mekina 2011)

Branislav Đukić, the head of the Union of Former Prisoners of RS, has similarly alleged that RECOM is part of a campaign to 'cement the ongoing marginalization of Serb victims' (cited in Mekina 2011). A common grievance among Bosnian Muslims, for their part, is that any attempt to treat all victims equally is deeply problematic – because not all victims are in fact equal. Vigorously insisting that Bosnian Muslims suffered the most, a rape victim maintained that there are even critical differences between Bosnian Muslim mothers and Bosnian Serb mothers. The latter lost sons who died fighting, she stressed, while the former lost sons who were killed as civilians.[17] Echoing this, a camp survivor was at pains to point out that although the Serb side sustained many casualties during the war, the loss of soldiers cannot be equated with the loss of civilians. He further questioned the wisdom of allowing all victims to tell their stories. In the absence of any checks and balances to ensure that people are telling the truth, he claimed, individuals will be able to say whatever they like and such 'empty stories' will not help anyone.[18]

16 Author interview, Osijek, 27 July 2011.
17 Author interview, Sarajevo, 21 March 2013.
18 Author interview, Sarajevo, 22 March 2013.

In Kosovo, the fact that RECOM will treat all victims equally has also proven highly controversial. Di Lellio and McCurn underscore that victims in Kosovo are seeking recognition: 'For Albanians, this means the official acknowledgement of a state-led policy of expulsion from their country and/or extermination during the Milošević era. For Serbs, it requires the recognition of their continuing role as victims of an embattled demographic minority in their "usurped" ancestral land' (2013: 131–132). On both sides, however, there is deep scepticism that the desired recognition will come from any commission that is focused on all victims; and this 'poses a serious complication to the [RECOM] project... ' (Di Lellio and McCurn 2013: 132).

The potential significance of RECOM – and the need for realistic expectations

The fact that RECOM has its fair share of critics does not, however, detract from its significance as a regional experiment in restorative justice. Moreover, RECOM has two particular strengths when compared to the ICTY (or indeed national courts). The first is that public consultations have been a fundamental part of the RECOM process. Between May 2006 and the end of 2009, for example, 79 debates took place at the local, national and regional levels (RECOM 2011a: 263). This strong public engagement, which was critically lacking vis-à-vis the ICTY, is in turn conducive to developing a sense of local ownership of the RECOM process. According to Golčevski, for example, 'The specific value of RECOM is that it is an entirely "home grown" process, based on the bottom-up approach. The whole process has hitherto been conceived and implemented by local actors responding to local needs' (2013: 101). While some scholars have questioned RECOM's 'local' credentials (see, for example, Di Lellio and McCurn 2013: 137), it is at least a *partly* home-grown process and one that arguably has greater possibilities to engage and connect with local people than any criminal court.

RECOM's second main strength is that because it is a victim-centred and non-adversarial process, there is greater potential for it to make an impact. In a court of law, victims' testimony is only one part of the trial process and it serves the specific purpose of enabling the judges to decide whether the accused is guilty. RECOM, in contrast, is about giving all victims an opportunity to tell their stories, because of the latter's intrinsic value, and exposing members of the public to those stories in a non-confrontational way. As this research has shown, 'The lack of a widely accepted narrative of the war is one of the major points of contention within the region' (Kirk McDonald 2011: 93–94), and RECOM will necessarily struggle to overcome the problem of competing ethnic truths. It is potentially more difficult, however, for people to deny and dispute information that is directly relayed to them by victims themselves. In South Africa, for example, the TRC's 'public airing of the country's dark past made it difficult – if not impossible – for white South Africans to cling to a narrative that failed to include the daily injustices and horrors experienced by their black countrymen' (Kohen, Zanchelli and Drake 2013: 11; see also Gibson 2004c: 150).

Nevertheless, it is also essential to reiterate that the RECOM project is extremely ambitious; and it remains to be seen whether it is in fact too ambitious. What is certain is that if the idea of creating a regional commission does ultimately come to fruition – and this will critically depend on the will and support of the region's political leaders (Džidić 2013c; Golčevski 2013: 98; Subotić 2013b: 29) – RECOM will face enormous challenges. It is therefore essential that those involved in this project learn key lessons from previous TRC experiments in other parts of the world, and three such lessons are especially important – and the minimum prerequisites for the success of any future commission. Firstly, governments and political leaders in the former Yugoslavia must fully support RECOM and its objectives. Without a genuine state-led commitment to fostering an open and public discussion about the past, which is crucial (Fletcher et al. 2009: 215), any TRC process necessarily risks becoming a simple act of political subterfuge. The example of Sri Lanka's Lessons Learnt and Reconciliation Commission (2010–2011), established by the government following the end of its 26-year civil war with the Liberation Tigers of Tamil Eelam (LTTE), powerfully illustrates this point. To cite Robertson QC, this Commission 'had no distinguished figures among its members and was over-concerned in its report to find that all the human rights abuses against the Tamils – which it could hardly deny – were committed by rogue elements of the army, and not by any senior officer or government figure' (2012: 394). The Commission's report, in short, effectively endorsed and corroborated the government's own version of 'truth', a one-sided and 'Potemkin-like pretence at bloodlessness' (Weiss 2012: 240) focused on the culpability and criminality of the LTTE.

Secondly, it is essential to be realistic about what RECOM – and indeed any TRC process – can potentially achieve. Golčevski, for example, notes that the RECOM process is 'expected to generate a positive change in how the various ethnic groups of the Western Balkans perceive and conceptualize each other' (2013: 104); and the European Parliament recently described RECOM as 'an important mechanism for the reconciliation process' (cited in Džidić 2013b). It should be noted, however, that the aforementioned draft statute does not explicitly refer to reconciliation as one of RECOM's official aims. It is also necessary to underline that aside from Gibson's excellent research on South Africa's TRC (discussed in Chapter 2), which yielded evidence of a positive correlation between truth and reconciliation (2004a; 2004b; 2004c), there have been few attempts to systematically and empirically explore the relationship between TRCs and reconciliation. Hence, there should be no automatic expectation that RECOM will contribute to reconciliation. As the example of the ICTY poignantly illustrates, any TJ process that generates high expectations also risks giving rise to deep disappointments when these expectations are not fulfilled. The argument submitted here is that RECOM will have the potential to contribute to the removal of certain obstacles to reconciliation. Any progress on the issue of missing persons, for example, will help to bring a degree of closure to many families, particularly in BiH. Equally, the creation of a space in which victims' stories can be told and heard will be important for enabling and encouraging 'perspective-taking' – defined as the 'willingness to listen to the adversary's story' (Bilali and Vollhardt 2013: 145) – and the development of more inclusive, non-ethnic understandings of victimhood.

Thirdly, victims themselves must have realistic expectations of RECOM. They need to be clear from the outset about their role in the process and about what they can and cannot expect to gain from telling their stories. Victims in Sierra Leone, for example, assumed that they would receive financial and material assistance from the country's TRC (Millar 2010: 491), and their unmet expectations impacted on the Commission's ultimate legacy. Based on his research in Makeni, for example, a city north-east of the Sierra Leonean capital Freetown, Millar maintains that, 'Within both the sociocultural context and the everyday poverty and dislocation of the non-elite's post-war lives, the TRC was expected to provide resources, not talk. As a result, truth telling failed to have the impact western scholars and practitioners expected of it' (2010: 492). In Peru, the creation of a TRC in 2001 generated similar expectations within victim communities, and the hope of financial redress was an important factor in many victims' decision to participate in the process (Laplante and Theidon 2007: 240). Questioning whether truth is in fact enough for victims, Laplante and Theidon posit that, 'To fulfill the expectation that truth can be the bridge to a future that does not repeat the past...the expectations of those who provided testimony to the violence they suffered and endured must inform post-conflict policies. Thus, reparations may be essential to constructing that bridge' (2007: 250). RECOM's draft statute makes reference to reparations; article 14(f) describes one of RECOM's functions as 'recommending measures to help prevent the recurrence of human rights abuses and to ensure reparations to the victims' (RECOM 2011b). If reparations are ultimately paid to victims, this will be a positive development. Nevertheless, victims should be strongly discouraged from automatically associating any future participation in the RECOM process with reparations and monetary redress.

Fletcher et al. question 'whether the emergence of criminal accountability for mass atrocities has dislodged or obscured the importance of other processes and interventions needed to create an enduring platform for social stability in countries that have experienced protracted, state-sponsored violence' (2009: 166–167). The ICTY's work, however, and in particular the growing awareness that it has fostered regarding the limitations of criminal trials, has paved the way for societies in the former Yugoslavia to consider other ways of dealing with the past. The creation of the Coalition for RECOM can thus be viewed as an indirect part of the ICTY's legacy. It is to be hoped that RECOM will ultimately become a reality. Yet, neither RECOM nor any other TRC process should be regarded as the key to fostering reconciliation in the former Yugoslavia. The challenges of reconciling individuals and communities in any post-conflict society call for a 'thick' and holistic approach encompassing more than retributive and restorative justice elements. Quintessentially, 'totalizing experiences necessitate totalizing responses' (Fletcher and Weinstein 2002: 639).

Exploring wider paths to reconciliation as part of a holistic approach

Emphasizing the importance of holism, the 'ecological' model for social reconstruction developed by Fletcher and Weinstein identifies six particular interventions – including criminal trials, TRCs, psychosocial interventions and community interventions – as 'critical components of a carefully orchestrated attempt at social repair' (2002: 625). According to this multi-level model, TJ interventions are only one part of a holistic approach to reconciliation, and it is on this particular point that the final part of this chapter builds. The aim is not to formulate an exhaustive list of factors necessary for reconciliation in BiH, Croatia and Kosovo, but rather to highlight possible additional paths to reconciliation outside of formal TJ processes. This final section focuses specifically on media (in its widest sense) and education.

Media pathways

In 2009, a British filmmaker, Rob Lemkin, made a documentary about the Cambodian genocide. Entitled *Enemies of the People*, the film features two former members of the Khmer Rouge who speak about their reasons for participating in the genocide. The two men, together with a third former member of the Khmer Rouge, subsequently took part in a dialogue, via video-conferencing, with several survivors of the genocide who now live in California. According to the organizers, both the film and the video-conference were very successful in allowing victims and perpetrators to gain new insights into the genocide and to learn how the events unfolded from the other's perspective. The film, for example, 'gave people an opportunity to see and hear former KR [Khmer Rouge] admit their guilt and express remorse at a safe distance…' (Quintiliani et al. 2011: 512), and the video-conference enabled both genuine dialogue and truth-seeking. Moreover, the organizers report that, 'Some survivors were deeply moved by the perpetrators' genuine desire to account for their actions and willingness to answer difficult questions' (Quintiliani et al. 2011: 512–513). Although the video-conference was only a small event involving just eight survivors of the genocide, this does not detract from its significance. In a holistic approach to reconciliation, each level of society is important – as Fletcher and Weinstein's ecological model highlights – and hence smaller-scale projects should not be regarded as any less valuable than large-scale, national projects.

However, one of the reasons why the media is potentially such an important peace-building tool is precisely because it can reach a wide audience. In Rwanda, for example, the most popular and accessible media source, the radio, is no longer being utilized to incite ethnic hatred and fear as it was during the genocide

(Thompson 2007), but instead to promote tolerance and perspective-taking. In 2004, as one illustration, *Radio La Benevolencija*,[19] a Dutch NGO, began broadcasting a fictional drama about an inter-village conflict. The idea is that listeners will be able to relate to aspects of the conflict, to empathize with the characters and to thus learn both how to resist incitements to violence and how to heal trauma. Research by Bilali and Vollhardt, moreover, suggests that the radio drama is having some positive effects. Dividing the respondents into two groups, they surveyed 842 Rwandans using an audio-based priming technique and an audio-questionnaire. In the first group, the questionnaire was read out by one of the main positive characters from the radio drama and preceded by a jingle from the programme. In the second group, in contrast, both the jingle played and the actor delivering the questionnaire had no connection with the programme. Ultimately, the researchers found that, '...participants who were primed with the radio drama were less likely than participants in the control condition to agree that the history they had learned from close others is the only true history. They were also more tolerant toward expressing different views of history in Rwanda' (Bilali and Vollhardt 2013: 147). Those who were primed with the voice of a character from the radio drama also 'reported greater perceived similarity between the in-group's and other groups' suffering in Rwanda (i.e., more inclusive victim consciousness)' (Bilali and Vollhardt 2013: 147). This particular example thus suggests that media can be used to encourage and facilitate perspective-taking, the absence of which is a serious obstacle to the development of empathy and trust – both core elements of reconciliation.

To reiterate, every post-conflict society is unique, and accordingly the challenges that reconciliation poses are, at least in part, context-specific. Hence, it is not the author's intention to suggest that we can simply transpose ideas from societies such as Cambodia and Rwanda and straightforwardly apply them to BiH, Croatia and Kosovo. The point, rather, is to show that the media should be creatively explored and utilized as part of a holistic approach to reconciliation. In the former Yugoslavia, media has a particularly important role to play in helping to publicize and promote some of the important work which various NGOs are undertaking. In 2011, for example, the Humanitarian Law Centre (HLC), a Belgrade-based NGO, launched the first volume of *The Kosovo Memory Book*,[20] which provides factual information about all those who lost their lives in Kosovo between 1998 and 2000. A year later, the HLC and the RDC in Sarajevo jointly published *The Bosnian Book of the Dead*. Based on, *inter alia*, witness statements, archive material from 725 organizations and data from the State Commission for Missing Persons of BiH, this book lists the names of 95,940 victims of the war and the names of a further 5,100 victims whose fate still remains unknown.

19   See http://www.labenevolencija.org/
20   A further three volumes of the *Kosovo Memory Book* are due to follow by 2015.

According to Nataša Kandić, the director of the HLC, *The Bosnian Book of the Dead* 'will prevent public silence about the victims and their being treated as mere statistics' (cited in RECOM 2013). Mirsad Tokača, the RDC's director, has similarly claimed that, 'This list will hopefully stop the number games which politicians are fond of. We are maintaining the memory and trying to free the daily political narrative of mythical ideologies and national interests' (cited in Džidić 2013a).

In order for the Kosovo and BiH books to potentially make such an impact, however, it is imperative that they reach a mass audience. It is also essential for people to understand how the lists of the dead were compiled, in order to minimize claims that the information is inaccurate and skewed. Milivoje Ivanišević, the director of the RS Institute for Research on Suffering of the Serbs, for example, has dismissed *The Bosnian Book of the Dead* as unreliable and described it as 'immoral' that Serb victims 'were recorded by the same people who killed them' (cited in Alec 2013). This is precisely where the media becomes relevant. A television documentary, for example, would not only allow *The Kosovo Memory Book* and *The Bosnian Book of the Dead* to reach a wide audience, but it would also be able to provide the public with critical background and methodological information.

Education pathways

Ethnically-segregated schools continue to exist in the former Yugoslavia. In BiH, for example, the so-called 'two schools under one roof' system, which operates in parts of the Federation, means that Croat and Bosniak children have their classrooms in different parts of the school building, or that they use the same classrooms at separate times (Clark 2010e). In this way, not only are many children being denied the opportunity to learn and socialize with peers from outside of their own ethnic group, but they are also being taught different 'ethnic' curricula. Interestingly, interviewees always emphasized that reconciliation needs time and maintained that future generations will move the process forward. As long as young people are divided and segregated in schools, however, and as long as they are learning different histories and geographies, the notion that future generations hold the key to reconciliation seems unduly optimistic. To cite Pickering, 'Separating students by ethnicity and language and preventing interaction in the classroom...clearly harms reintegration efforts' (2007: 39). All of this further highlights the importance of a holistic approach to reconciliation. To heavily invest in TJ processes which seek to establish 'the facts', for example, makes little sense when children and young people are being taught completely different versions of events depending on their ethnicity. The Commissioner for Human Rights of the Council of Europe has thus emphasized that, 'All countries concerned [in the former Yugoslavia] should realise the vital need to teach history without resorting to one single interpretation of events' (2012: 41).

More should therefore be done to explore possible educational reforms as part of a comprehensive approach to reconciliation (Jones 2012). In its Recommendation 1880 (2009), for example, the Parliamentary Assembly of the Council of Europe emphasized that, '...history teaching can be a tool to support peace and reconciliation in conflict and post-conflict areas...' (2009: §1). Schools should thus be encouraged to promote and teach inclusive histories that recognize and respect different viewpoints and perspectives. It is precisely this multi-perspective approach which the Joint History Project (JHP) seeks to foster. Initiated in 2005 by the Greece-based Centre for Democracy and Reconciliation in Southeast Europe (CDRSSE), the JHP aims in the long term 'to revise ethno-centric school history teaching by avoiding stereotypes, by identifying attitudes that encourage conflict, by suggesting alternative teaching methods and by encouraging the idea of multiple interpretations of one event' (CDRSSE n.d.). To this end, the JHP has created history textbook supplements, designed to change the way in which the subject is taught through an emphasis on multilateral viewpoints. Unfortunately, such endeavours have to date met with limited success in the former Yugoslavia. That the textbook industry is under strong state control, for example, means that, 'History teachers...see no clear benefit to adopting textbook supplements that are not sanctioned or approved by the state and would, presumably, require them to do more work than if they only relied on official textbook materials' (Subotić 2013a: 277–278). While educational reform in the former Yugoslavia is a hugely contentious subject and poses enormous challenges, it is an important part of the reconciliation process and small changes in the way that subjects such as History are taught would be an important step forward. Indeed, the fact that a major part of the ICTY's outreach activities are now directly focused on young people in the former Yugoslavia (through, *inter alia*, school visits and presentations) is a welcome development.

This chapter does not lend itself to any neat, definitive conclusions because there is no magic formula for reconciliation; and certainly this research is not about trying to identify the key 'ingredients' for inter-ethnic reconciliation in the former Yugoslavia. Nevertheless, by virtue of arguing that the ICTY has not contributed to reconciliation in BiH, Croatia and Kosovo, and by further questioning whether any court can facilitate the process, this research necessarily requires that we think about other possible ways of aiding reconciliation in the former Yugoslavia. While this chapter has stressed the potential of restorative justice, through a focus on RECOM, it has also emphasized that post-conflict reconciliation requires a comprehensive and holistic approach which extends beyond the recourse to TJ processes. The need for such an approach is based in significant part on the fact that we still do not know enough about the effects of courts and TRCs, and hence the imperative of further empirically-driven impact research cannot be over-emphasized. This chapter has examined only two possible pathways to reconciliation as part of a holistic approach, namely media and education. However, it is important to refrain from making strong assumptions about what it is that local communities need in order to reconcile (Prieto 2012: 546).

Ultimately, therefore, the key to developing a holistic approach to reconciliation is to listen to local people themselves, in order to understand what they themselves need in order to move forward. As Pickering underscores, 'Paying attention to ordinary people as they go about their everyday lives in real postconflict landscapes...is a great way to understand the conditions necessary for reconstructing more inclusive urban communities' (2007: 166).

Conclusion

In an address to the UN General Assembly on 14 October 2013, the ICTY President declared: '...we may rest assured that the Tribunal will leave behind it a world transformed: a world in which ...expectations of principled accountability for those who stand accused of atrocities will remain the norm, and the rule of law will continue to prevail' (Meron 2013c). It is true that when we look at the macro level, the world today is in many ways a different place: political power and leadership no longer necessarily afford the protection that they once did; the steady growth of war crimes courts and tribunals has institutionalized the fight against impunity (although this fight remains selective); and the jurisprudence of these bodies has hugely enriched and advanced international criminal law. Furthermore, so much has changed since I began this research in 2008: Karadžić and Mladić are now on trial, Gotovina has been convicted and subsequently acquitted, Haradinaj has had a re-trial which ended in a not-guilty verdict. At the micro level, however, there has been far less change. Victims continue to wait for justice, for information about missing loved-ones, for much-needed answers. People continue to reject uncomfortable truths and to take refuge in denial; and significant obstacles to reconciliation persist, not least an absence of inter-ethnic trust. It is precisely these continuities which have always contributed to and reinforced my deep scepticism that the ICTY can assist reconciliation. This research is the product of that scepticism and of my curiosity to establish whether, empirically, there is any evidence to support claims that the Tribunal is aiding reconciliation in the former Yugoslavia.

Summary of findings

Focused on BiH, Croatia and Kosovo, based on over 350 semi-structured interviews conducted over a five-year period and underpinned by a measurement model constituted by the three key prongs of justice, truth and inter-ethnic relations, this research has categorically argued that the ICTY has not had any positive impact on reconciliation. The 'justice' that it dispenses is deeply contested and has thereby generated significant grievances on all sides. The foregoing chapters thus lend at least some support to the claim that, '...the objective of justice, while purporting to aid reconciliation by acknowledging the heinous nature of the crimes, creates a roadblock to mutual harmony and peace' (Mukherjee 2011: 341). While it is true that interviewees commonly identified justice as a necessary prerequisite for reconciliation, they seldom associated the ICTY itself with justice. It is also the case that interviewees widely underscored the importance of truth. Truth in itself, however, is not enough. Fundamentally, interviewees also wanted acknowledgement from members of other ethnic groups of their own group's suffering, but such acknowledgement is rare. The Tribunal has established a multitude of facts, but too often these facts have failed to penetrate and gain local acceptance. In short, facts that challenge a group's war narrative are strongly resisted and frequently denied, and in this way the ICTY's work has helped to harden rather than to dilute rival ethnic narratives. Campbell suggests that the ICTY can be understood as 'a site where competing discourses of transitional justice and memory intersect...' (2013: 249), and local responses to its judgements similarly manifest this intersection of competing discourses and memories. Finally, it is impossible to make any claims about the ICTY's impact without exploring what is happening at the grassroots level and analyzing quotidian inter-ethnic relations. Operationalizing and measuring the concept of reconciliation using a Reconciliation Matrix and the four key variables of human security, deep contact, trust and mutual acceptance, this research has endeavoured to show that reconciliation does not exist in BiH, Croatia or Kosovo. At best there is peaceful coexistence, but this has resulted less from the ICTY's work than from simple pragmatism (people generally accept, even if begrudgingly, that they have to live together) and the practical demands of everyday life.

This work is by no means the first to contest the notion that a court can contribute to reconciliation (see, for example, Fletcher, et al. 2009: 169; McMahon and Forsythe 2008: 435; Sadat 2012: 17; Stover and Weinstein 2004b: 323; Tolbert 2013). It is, however, the first to develop a clear model for assessing a court's impact on reconciliation and the first to comprehensively demonstrate – based on extensive empirical data – that the ICTY has not aided reconciliation in the former Yugoslavia. Dancy suggests that, 'Justice, reconciliation and peace are notions that, rather than being conceived as discrete goals, would be more properly understood as "epiphenomenal" conditions that "supervene" on life once other social prerequisites are met' (2010: 368). Specifically with regards to reconciliation, the social prerequisites in the case of BiH, Croatia and Kosovo include major progress on the fundamental issue of missing persons, the commitment of those in power to advancing reconciliation and the creation of a space for 'bridging dialogue' which 'allows parties to a past conflict to become more cognisant of its underlying issues and consequences' (Ireton and Kovras 2012: 73). Fundamentally, the ability of the ICTY to contribute to the fulfilment of these social prerequisites, which are testament to the fact that multiple obstacles to reconciliation still exist, is necessarily limited. If the Tribunal is not well-positioned to aid reconciliation in the former Yugoslavia, the broader argument of this research is that reconciliation is not a realistic goal for any criminal court, it should not be part of a court's mandate and it should not be something that we expect these complex institutions to deliver or facilitate.

Lessons to be learnt

There are at least four key lessons to be learnt from this research. The first and most obvious is that our expectations of courts should be more modest and measured. In 2011, a regional consultation report on the ICC suggested that, 'Even though the ICC does not have the mandate to pursue peace and reconciliation, the Court should consider these initiatives as it engages in countries affected by armed conflict...' (Murithi and Ngari 2011: 2). In the absence of any positive empirical data, however, the persistence of this posited nexus between trials and reconciliation is deeply problematic and symptomatic of a widespread tendency to expect far more of these institutions than they can often in fact accomplish (Moghalu 2002: 33). This, in turn, can detract from their real successes. The focus of research on international criminal courts should thus be on their actual achievements, which are significant, and not on their anticipated and hypothesized achievements. Fundamentally, there is no place for 'the projection of exaggerated normative fantasies on to this seeming panacea' (Akhavan 2013: 529). Judge Patrick Robinson has acknowledged that 'overly ambitious expectations' can be deeply detrimental to a court and ultimately contribute to a decline in public support when these expectations are not met (2011: 25). The crucial point about the ICTY, however, is that it has often encouraged these high expectations (Vukušić 2013: 623); we saw in Chapter 1, for example, that high-profile figures within the Tribunal have consistently associated its work with reconciliation. In the process of reining in our expectations of criminal courts, the latter themselves thus have a fundamental role to play. They have an especially important part to play in tempering the expectations of victims, which once again highlights – to return to a critical theme of this research – the imperative of creative and sustained outreach work aimed particularly at the grassroots of society. Victims are the ultimate stake-holders and judges of international justice, and they will always remain deeply disappointed as long as their initial expectations are unduly high and beyond the realistic capabilities of institutions with limited resources and typically finite mandates (Mendeloff 2009: 621). Perhaps the most obvious way to keep expectations (and not only those of victims) in check is simply to remind ourselves that, as Akhavan argues, 'The need for international tribunals is itself a failure. Prevention may not always be possible, but in many cases it is a feasible option' (2013: 531). To view courts in this way is to immediately appreciate their limitations and challenges.

The second key lesson, linked to the above, is that it may be neither appropriate nor constructive to speak about reconciliation in the immediate aftermath of war and large-scale atrocities. Even several years after a conflict has ended, the use of the term can continue to generate significant resentment and resistance, particularly among victims who may feel that they are *expected* to reconcile,[1] and it can detract attention from the more immediate needs of post-conflict societies. Weinstein thus suggests that rather than focusing on reconciliation, we should instead 'consider the idea that, as a starting point, living together peacefully without overt violence may be enough; that anything more than that is years, perhaps generations, away' (2011: 7). Ultimately, therefore, reconciliation is not only an unrealistic goal for a court, but it is also an inappropriate goal. Individuals, communities and societies must be left to approach and discuss the issue of reconciliation in their own time. It is not for courts or any other external actors to set the agenda and to decide when people are ready for reconciliation.

The third lesson to be learnt is that the mandates of these courts should not be broadly generic, but rather contextually-specific and tailored to the particular circumstances and needs of individual post-conflict societies. When a court's official goals are discordant with the wider operational societal context, it will always struggle to fulfil its mandate. Highlighting this point apropos of the SCSL, for example, Mieth maintains that,

> ...Special Court officials can be criticized for their ignorance of the context they operated in, which led them to such bold promises of "justice" and "peace"...[T]hese claims are for a large part based on assumptions, and as soon as the everyday situation of Sierra Leoneans is taken into consideration, such promises seem out of place.
>
> (2013: 21)

In a similar vein, the fact that the ICTY was established at a time when the war in BiH was still raging necessarily raises questions about the appropriateness of the Security Council's decision to mandate the Tribunal with, *inter alia*, 'contributing to the restoration and maintenance of peace'. Although reconciliation is not an official part of the ICTY's mandate, claims that the Tribunal can contribute to this process are similarly contextually frictional and overlook the critical fact that there are few local actors working on the process of improving inter-ethnic relations. The imperative of crafting contextually-sensitive court mandates, in turn, illuminates an important role for local communities and especially victims. While it is often the case that 'local communities are rarely consulted to inform the design, implementation and evaluation' of TJ policies (Pham and Vinck 2007: 232), these communities can provide fundamental insights into individual post-conflict societies and the problems, challenges and needs that exist therein. The example of community restorative justice in Northern Ireland is just one illustration (Eriksson 2009: 61). Hence, communities must be given

---

1 According to a survivor of the 1994 Rwandan genocide, for example, 'People come to Rwanda and talk of reconciliation...It's offensive. Imagine talking to Jews of reconciliation in 1946. Maybe in a long time, but it's a private matter' (cited in Gourevitch 1998: 240).

a voice; this is a prerequisite for the development of inclusive and tailor-made TJ mechanisms that reflect local realities rather than simply the priorities and policies of their creators.

The fourth and final main lesson is that we should not rush to create courts in the immediate aftermath of conflicts (and even less so during these conflicts). Justice should of course be timely, but we should not equate timeliness with hastiness. Fletcher, et al. point out that, 'The rush to select and implement transitional justice in the immediate aftermath of violence or repression appears to lead to hasty decisions about which of the dominant transitional justice models should be imposed' (2009: 216). More importantly, the sense of urgency that has underpinned the creation of courts like the ICTY can mean that these institutions are established prematurely – i.e. before the societies that they are set up to benefit are in fact ready for them. Of course, in the aftermath of war crimes and widespread human rights violations, justice is often an immediate demand, and justice delayed may be viewed on the ground as justice denied. Nevertheless, if courts are established before the societies in question have begun to deal with what happened, before they have begun to tackle some of the legacies of war and conflict – such as denial, nationalism and economic malaise – and before citizens have been properly informed about the purpose of courts and their limitations, these judicial bodies may not realize their full potential. To reiterate, courts are not a panacea and they cannot fix a society's problems. Hence, the extent to which courts are able to assist post-conflict societies will arguably depend, at least to some degree, on the extent to which these societies have begun to help themselves and to deal with some of their internal problems. Left unaddressed, these problems can severely constrain and blunt a court's impact.

Moving forward

Where do we go from here? While this work maintains that the posited linkage between courts and reconciliation is deeply problematic and must be re-thought, further empirical research on this issue is needed. Have other international courts had a more positive impact on inter-ethnic/community relations than the ICTY has had? If they have not, to what extent are the reasons for this contextually specific? To what extent do other case studies support the argument that there are generic issues which render international criminal courts fundamentally ill-suited to aiding reconciliation? Is there any evidence to suggest that local courts, which are significantly under-researched within the TJ literature, can contribute to reconciliation and improved inter-ethnic relations in a way that international courts cannot? These are some of the key questions which remain to be answered – and which need to be answered. This research has addressed a significant empirical gap within existing literature on international courts, and it is hoped that other scholars will now build on it and further utilize/expand the measurement model developed in Chapter 2.

It is also clear that in order to truly gauge and understand the impact of courts, longitudinal research is immensely valuable. As Sikkink and Booth Walling underline, '...when we evaluate the impact of trials, we need to look at their impact over the longer term, not just in the fragile moment of transition' (2007: 442). To what extent do popular perceptions of these courts positively change over time? Does the passage of time allow for a greater appreciation of courts and their achievements? Is it the case that, '[j]udgments about whether justice has been done are likely to change, not just in response to what was done to deliver justice but in reaction to other changes in the social context, such as one's attitude toward the group to which the perpetrator belongs...' (van der Merwe 2009: 137)? Can courts have a positive effect on inter-ethnic relations in the long term? These too are important questions that require further investigation, and it would thus be extremely interesting to repeat this research in ten or 20 years' time. If time is a healer, it might also dilute the disappointments, grievances and widespread sense of injustice that the ICTY's work has generated in BiH, Croatia and Kosovo. It would also be intriguing to explore whether the International Residual Mechanism for Criminal Tribunals (the Mechanism), which is another creation of the UN Security Council and is tasked with carrying out the residual functions of the ICTY and ICTR,[2] will have any impact on popular perceptions of the ICTY within the former Yugoslavia (and of the ICTR in Rwanda).

The Mechanism, which has a branch for the ICTY and another branch for the ICTR,[3] is responsible, *inter alia*, for preserving and maintaining the Tribunals' voluminous archives (UN 2010: §27). These archives constitute a fundamental documentary and historical record (Adami and Hunt 2005: 111), and some scholars are already lauding their potential benefits. Frisso, for example, claims that, 'For the victims, this information might help to contextualize their experiences and, as a consequence, alleviate their suffering' (2011: 1118); and Vukušić suggests that, 'this material [the ICTY's archives] provides the means to combat some denial and narrow the space where that denial can exist' (2013: 625). In a 2009 report, the UN Secretary-General even went as far as to refer to the Tribunals' archives as 'tools for fostering reconciliation and memory' (Ban 2009: 46). These archives should not become the new focus for our high expectations, but they are an important topic for future research. According to the Registrar of both the ICTY and the Mechanism, 'The toil of the Tribunals is not, and must not be, just a momentous achievement, obtained through the labour of their

---

2 The functions of the Mechanism include the protection of victims and witnesses, appellate proceedings and providing assistance to national jurisdictions. According to Resolution 1966 (22 December 2010), '...the Mechanism shall operate for an initial period of four years...and for subsequent periods of two years...' (UN 2010: §17). As yet, there is little scholarly work on the Mechanism (but see McIntyre 2011; Pittman 2011).

3 These ICTY and ICTR branches of the Mechanism began functioning on 1 July 2013 and 1 July 2012 respectively.

hundreds of staff. It is in the hands of the archivists to ensure that this endeavour is preserved and, equally importantly, made accessible to the world...' (Hocking 2012). It is also imperative, however, that the archives are made accessible to people in the former Yugoslavia (and Rwanda). Unfortunately, given that these archives will be 'co-located with the respective branches of the Mechanism' (UN 2010: annex, §27(2)), their local impact is likely to be minimal.

******

More than 300 years ago, in *A Critical Essay upon the Faculties of the* Mind (1709), the Irish author Jonathan Swift remarked that, 'Laws are like cobwebs, which may catch small flies but let wasps and hornets break through' (cited in Weiss 2011: 777). The purpose of international courts is precisely not to allow the wasps and hornets to break through – although many of them do when it is politically convenient for the international community to allow them to do so. Sri Lanka's Mahinda Rajapaksa and Zimbabwe's Robert Mugabe are just two examples. Yet, unlike cobwebs, we cannot simply sweep these courts aside. They are extremely important and this research should not be read in any way as an attempt to detract from the ICTY's successes and achievements. The ICTY was a necessary creation and so too were the courts established after it, not least the ICC. In order to do justice to these courts, however, it is imperative to understand and appreciate their limitations; and it is hoped that this research has succeeded in convincing readers – and that it will ultimately convince policy-makers – that international courts should not be associated with reconciliation.

Bibliography

ICTY Judgements

Prosecutor v. Banović (2003). *Case No. IT-02-65/1-T,* Trial Chamber Judgement, 28 October 2003.

Prosecutor v. Blaškić (2000). *Case No. IT-95-14-T,* Trial Chamber Judgement, 3 March 2000.

—— (2004). *Case No. IT-95-14-A,* Appeals Chamber Judgment, 29 July 2004.

Prosecutor v. Bralo (2005). *Case No. IT-95-17-S,* Trial Chamber Sentencing Judgement, 7 December 2005.

Prosecutor v. Deronjić (2004). *Case No. IT-02-61-S,* Trial Chamber Sentencing Judgement, 30 March 2004.

Prosecutor v. Đorđević (2011). *Case No. IT-05-87/1,* Trial Chamber Judgement, 23 February 2011.

Prosecutor v. Đorđević (2014). *Case No IT-05-87/I-A,* Appeals Chamber Judgement, 27 January 2014.

Prosecutor v. Erdemović (1996). *Case No. IT-96-22-T,* Trial Chamber Sentencing Judgement, 29 November 1996.

—— (1997). *Case No. IT-96-22-A,* Appeals Chamber Judgement, 7 October 1997.

—— (1998). *Case No. IT-96-22-Tbis,* Trial Chamber Second Sentencing Judgement, 5 March 1998.

Prosecutor v. Gotovina, Čermak and Markač (2011a). *Case No. IT-06-90-T,* Trial Chamber Judgement, 15 April 2011.

—— (2011b). *Case No. IT-06-90-T,* Trial Chamber Judgement, Volume II, 15 April 2011.

Prosecutor v. Gotovina and Markač (2012a). *Case No. IT-06-90-A,* Appeals Chamber Judgement, 16 November 2012.

—— (2012b). *Case No. IT-06-90-A,* Dissenting Opinion of Judge Agius, 16 November 2012.

—— (2012bc). *Case No. IT-06-90-A,* Dissenting Opinion of Judge Pocar, 16 November 2012.

Prosecutor v. Hadžihasanović and Kubura (2006). *Case No. IT-01-47-T,* Trial Chamber Judgement, 15 March 2006.

—— (2008). *Case No. IT-01-47-A,* Appeals Chamber Judgement, 22 April 2008.

Prosecutor v. Haradinaj, Balaj and Brahimaj (2008). *Case No. IT-04-84-T,* Trial Chamber Judgement, 3 April 2008.

—— (2010). *Case No. IT-04-84-A*, Appeals Chamber Judgement, 21 July 2010.

—— (2012). *Case No. IT-04-84bis-T*, Retrial Judgement, 29 November 2012.

Prosecutor v. Josipović et al. (2000). *Case No. IT-95-16-T*, Trial Chamber Judgement, 14 January 2000.

—— (2001). *Case No. IT-95-16-A*, Appeals Chamber Judgement, 23 October 2001.

Prosecutor v. Karadžić (2013). *Case No. IT-9S-SI18-AR98bis.l*, Appeals Chamber Judgement (98*bis*), 11 July 2013.

Prosecutor v. Kordić and Čerkez (2001). *Case No. IT-95-14/2-T*, Trial Chamber Judgement, 26 February 2001.

Prosecutor v. Krstić (2001). *Case No. IT-98-33-T*, Trial Chamber Judgement, 2 August 2001.

—— (2004). *Case No. IT-98-33-A*, Appeals Chamber Judgement, 19 April 2004.

Prosecutor v. Kvočka et al. (2001). *Case No. IT-98-30/1-T*, Trial Chamber Judgement, 2 November 2001.

Prosecutor v. Limaj, Bala and Musliu (2005). *Case No. IT-03-66-T*, Trial Chamber Judgement, 30 November 2005.

—— (2007). *Case No IT-03-66-A*. Appeals Chamber Judgement, 27 September 2007.

Prosecutor v. Mrđa (2004). *Case No. IT-02-59-S*, Trial Chamber Sentencing Judgement, 31 March 2004.

Prosecutor v. Mrkšić, Radić and Šljivančanin (2007). *Case No. IT-95-13/1*, Trial Chamber Judgement, 27 December 2007.

Prosecutor v. Mrkšić and Šljivančanin (2009). *Case No. IT-95-13/1-A*, Appeals Chamber Judgement, 5 May 2009.

Prosecutor v. Mucić et al. (1998). *Case No. IT-96-21-T*, Trial Chamber Judgement, 16 November 1998.

Prosecutor v. Mucić, Delić and Landžo (2001). *Case No. IT-96-21-Tbis-R117*, Trial Chamber Second Sentencing Judgement, 9 October 2001.

Prosecutor v. (Dragan) Nikolić (2003a). *Case No. IT-94-2-S*, Trial Chamber Sentencing Judgement, 18 December 2003.

—— (2005). *Case No. IT-94-2-A*, Judgement on Sentencing Appeal, 4 February 2005.

Prosecutor v. (Momir) Nikolić (2003b). *Case No. IT-02-60/1-S*, Trial Chamber Sentencing Judgement, 2 December 2003.

—— (2006). *Case No. IT-02-60/1-A*, Judgement on Sentencing Appeal, 8 March 2006.

Prosecutor v. Obrenović (2003). *Case No. IT-02-60/2-S*, Trial Chamber Sentencing Judgement, 10 December 2003.

Prosecutor v. Orić (2006). *Case No. IT-03-68-T*, Trial Chamber Judgement, 30 June 2006.

—— (2008). *Case No. IT-03-68-A*, Appeals Chamber Judgement, 3 July 2008.

Prosecutor v. Perišić (2011). *Case No. IT-O4-81-T*, Trial Chamber Judgement, 29 July 2011.

—— (2013a). *Case No. IT-O4-81-A*, Appeals Chamber Judgement, 28 February 2013.

—— (2013b). *Case No. IT-O4-81-A*, Partially Dissenting Opinion of Judge Liu, 28 February 2013.

Prosecutor v. Plavšić (2003). *Case No. IT-00-39&40/1-S*, Trial Chamber Sentencing Judgement, 27 February 2003.

Prosecutor v. Popović et al. (2010). *Case No. IT-05-88-T*, Trial Chamber Judgement, 10 June 2010.

Prosecutor v. Prlić et al. (2013). *Case No. IT-04-74*, Judgement Summary, 29 May 2013.
Prosecutor v. Šainović et al. (2009). *Case No. IT-05-87*, Trial Chamber Judgement, 26 February 2009.
—— (2014). *Case No. IT-05-87-A*, Appeals Chamber Judgement, 23 Janurary 2014.
Prosecutor v. Šešelj (2013). *Case No. IT-03-67-T*, Decision on Defence Motion for Disqualification of Judge Fredrik Harhoff and Report to the Vice-President, 28 August 2013.
Prosecutor v. Sikirica, Došen and Kolundžija (2001). *Case No. IT-95-8-T*, Trial Chamber Judgement, 13 November 2001.
Prosecutor v. Šljivančanin (2010). *Case No. IT-95-13/1-R.1*, Appeals Chamber Review Judgement, 8 December 2010.
Prosecutor v. Stakić (2003). *Case No. IT-97-24-T*, Trial Chamber Judgement, 31 July 2003.
—— (2006). *Case No. IT-97-24-A*, Appeals Chamber Judgement, 22 March 2006.
Prosecutor v. Stanišić and Simatović (2013a). *Case No. IT-03-69-T*, Trial Chamber Judgement, Volume I, 30 May 2013.
—— (2013b). *Case No. IT-03-69-T*, Trial Chamber Judgement, Volume II, 30 May 2013.
—— (2013c). *Case No. IT-03-69-T*, Dissenting Opinion of Judge Picard, 30 May 2013.
Prosecutor v. Stanišić and Župljanin (2013). *Case No. IT-08-91-T*, Trial Chamber Judgement, 27 March 2013.
Prosecutor v. Tadić (1997). *Case No. IT-94-1-T*, Trial Chamber Opinion and Judgement, 7 May 1997.
—— (1999). *Case No. IT-94-1-A*, Appeals Chamber Judgement, 15 July 1999.
Prosecutor v. Tolimir (2012). *Case No. IT-05-88/2-T*, Trial Chamber Judgement, 12 December 2012.

UN Security Council Resolutions

UN (1992a). Security Council Resolution 764, *S/Res/764 (1992)*, 13 July 1992.
UN (1992b). Security Council Resolution 771, *S/RES/771(1992)*, 13 August 1992.
UN (1992c). Security Council Resolution 780, *S/RES/780 (1992)*, 6 October 1992.
UN (1993a). Security Council Resolution 808, *S/RES/808 (1993)*, 22 February 1993.
UN (1993b). Security Council Resolution 827, *S/RES/827 (1993)*, 25 May 1993.
UN (1994). Security Council Resolution 955, *S/RES/955 (1994)*, 8 November 1994.
UN (1998a). Security Council Resolution 1160, *S/RES/1160 (1998)*, 31 March 1998.
UN (1998b). Security Council Resolution 1166, *S/RES/1166 (1998)*, 13 May 1998.
UN (2000). Security Council Resolution 1329, *S/RES/1329 (2000)*, 30 November 2000.
UN (2003). Security Council Resolution 1503, *S/RES/1503 (2003)*, 28 August 2003.
UN (2004). Security Council Resolution 1534, *S/RES/1534 (2004)*, 26 March 2004.
UN (2010). Security Council Resolution 1966, *S/RES/1966 (2010)*, 22 December 2010.

Books and journal articles

Abu-Nimer, Mohammed; Abdul Aziz Said and Lakshitha S. Prelis (2001). 'Conclusion: The Long Road to Reconciliation', in Mohammed Abu-Nimer (ed.) *Reconciliation, Justice and Coexistence: Theory and Practice* (Lanham, MD: Lexington Books), pp. 339–348.

Adami, Tom A. (2007). '"Who Will Be Left to Tell the Tale?" Recordkeeping and International Criminal Jurisprudence', *Archival Science* 7(3): 213–221.

Adami, Tom A. and Martha Hunt (2005). 'Genocidal Archives: The African Context – Genocide in Rwanda', *Journal of the Society of Archivists* 26(1): 105–121.

Akhavan, Payam (1998). 'Justice in The Hague, Peace in the former Yugoslavia? A Commentary on the United Nations War Crimes Tribunal', *Human Rights Quarterly* 20(4): 737–816.

—— (2013). 'The Rise, and Fall, and Rise, of International Criminal Justice', *Journal of International Criminal Justice* 11(3): 527–536.

Allport, Gordon W. (1954). *The Nature of Prejudice* (Reading, MA: Addison-Wesley).

Amann, Diane Marie (2013). 'A Janus Look at International Criminal Justice', *Northwestern Journal of International Human Rights* 11(1): 5–29.

Amir, Yehuda (1969). 'Contact Thesis in Ethnic Relations', *Psychological Bulletin* 71: 319–342.

Amstutz, Mark R. (2005). *The Healing of Nations: The Promise and Limits of Political Forgiveness* (Lanham, MD: Rowman and Littlefield).

Andrieu, Kora (2009). '"Sorry for the Genocide": How Public Apologies Can Help Promote National Reconciliation', *Millennium: Journal of International Studies* 38(1): 3–23.

Andrighetto, Luca; Silvia Mari, Chiara Volpato and Burim Behluli (2012). 'Reducing Competitive Victimhood in Kosovo: The Role of Extended Contact and Common Ingroup Identity', *Political Psychology* 33(4): 513–529.

Arbour, Louise (2004). 'The Crucial Years', *Journal of International Criminal Justice* 2(2): 396–402.

Arcel, Libby Tata (2003). 'Introduction', in Libby Tata Arcel, Sabina Popović, Adbulah Kučukalić and Alma Bravo-Mehmedbašić (eds) *Treatment of Torture Survivors in a Post-War Society* (Sarajevo: Centre for Torture Victims), pp.17–28.

Arcel, Libby Tata; Sabina Popović, Abdulah Kučukalić, Alma Bravo-Mehmedbašić, Damir Ljubotina, Jasmina Pušina and Lejla Šaraba (2003). 'The Social and Psychological Impact of Traumatic Events and Torture in a Bosnian Civilian Population', in Libby Tata Arcel, Sabina Popović, Adbulah Kučukalić and Alma Bravo-Mehmedbašić (eds) *Treatment of Torture Survivors in a Post-War Society* (Sarajevo: Centre for Torture Victims), pp.40–69.

Arriaza, Laura, and Naomi Roht-Arriaza (2008). 'Social Reconstruction as a Local Process', *International Journal of Transitional Justice* 2(2): 152–172.

Arzt, Donna E. (2006). 'Views on the Ground: The Local Perception of International Criminal Tribunals in the former Yugoslavia and Sierra Leone', *The ANNALS of the American Academy of Political and Social Science* 603(1): 226–239.

Askin, Kelly D. (2003). 'Reflections on Some of the Most Significant Achievements of the ICTY', *New England Law Review* 37(4): 903–914.

Association of Families of Missing and Violently Abducted Persons (1999). *Vaš Lik, Naš Put* (Vukovar: Association of Families of Missing and Violently Abducted Persons).

Atashi, Elham (2009). 'Challenges to Conflict Transformation from the Streets', in Bruce W. Dayton and Louis Kriesberg (eds) *Conflict Transformation and Peacebuilding: Moving from Violence to Sustainable Peace* (New York: Routledge), pp.45–60.

Audergon, Arlene and Lane Arye (2005). 'Transforming Conflict into Community: Post-War Reconciliation in Croatia', *Psychotherapy and Politics International* 3(2): 112–121.

Auerbach, Yehudith (2005). 'Forgiveness and Reconciliation: The Religious Dimension', *Terrorism and Political Violence* 17(3): 469–485.

Axboe Nielsen, Christian (2013). 'Surmounting the Myopic Focus on Genocide: The Case of War in Bosnia and Herzegovina', *Journal of Genocide Research* 15(1): 21–39.

Babbitt, Eileen F. (2003). 'Evaluating Coexistence: Insights and Challenges', in Antonia Chayes and Martha Minow (eds) *Imagine Coexistence: Restoring Humanity after Violent Ethnic Conflict* (San Francisco, CA: Jossey-Bass), pp.102–127.

Barkan, Elazar (2003). 'Restitution and Amending Historical Injustices in International Morality', in John Torpey (ed.) *Politics and the Past: On Repairing Historical Injustices* (Lanham, ML: Rowman & Littlefield Publishers Inc.), pp.91–102.

Bar-On, Dan (2007). 'Reconciliation Revisited for More Conceptual and Empirical Clarity', in Janja Beč-Neumann (ed.) *Darkness at Noon: War Crimes, Genocide and Memories* (Sarajevo: University of Sarajevo), pp.63–84.

Barria, Liliam A. and Steven D. Roper (2005). 'How Effective are International Criminal Tribunals? An Analysis of the ICTY and ICTR', *International Journal of Human Rights* 9(3): 349–368.

Bass, Gary Jonathan (2000). *Stay the Hand of Vengeance: The Politics of War Crimes Tribunals* (Princeton, NJ: Princeton University Press).

Bassiouni, M. Cherif (2003). 'Justice and Peace: The Importance of Choosing Accountability over *Realpolitik*', *Case Western Reserve Journal of International Law* 35(2): 191–204.

Bassiouni, M. Cherif and Marcia McCormick (1996). *Sexual Violence: An Invisible Weapon of War in the former Yugoslavia*, Occasional Paper No. 1 (Chicago: De Paul University College of Law).

Baum, Steven K. (2008). *The Psychology of Genocide: Perpetrators, Bystanders and Rescuers* (Cambridge: Cambridge University Press).

Bell, Martin (2012). *In Harm's Way: Bosnia – A War Reporter's Story*, revised and updated edition (London: Icon Books).

Bijedić, Suzdina; Milena Savić, Milena Timanović, Murat Tahirović, Anđelko Kvesić, Fadil Redžić, Mujo Čerkezović, Jasmin Mešković and Senad Jusufbegović (2013). '"Yesterday's Torture Victims, Today's System Victims. What Shall We Be Tomorrow?"', in Mima Dahić (ed.) *Vive Žene: Centre for Therapy and Torture, Journal of Articles: Rehabilitation of Torture Victims* 4: 43–58.

Bilali, Rezarta and Johanna Ray Vollhardt (2013). 'Priming Effects of a Reconciliation Radio Drama on Historical Perspective-Taking in the Aftermath of Mass Violence in Rwanda', *Journal of Experimental Social Psychology* 49(1): 144–151.

Biro, Miklos; Dean Ajduković, Dinka Corkalo, Dino Djipa, Petar Milin and Harvey M. Weinstein (2004). 'Attitudes toward Justice and Social Reconstruction in Bosnia Herzegovina and Croatia', in Eric Stover and Harvey M. Weinstein (eds) *My Neighbor, My Enemy: Justice and Community in the Aftermath of Mass Atrocity* (Cambridge: Cambridge University Press), pp.183–205.

Bloch, Corinne (2005a). '*Za nas, rat je danas*', in Katarina Kruhonja (ed.) *Kultura Mira: Suočavanje s prološću* (Osijek: Centre for Peace, Non-Violence and Human Rights), pp.20–22.

——(2005b). '"*Očekujem da će sudstvo poboljšati svoju praksu*" – *Vesnu Teršelić intervjuirala je Corinne Bloch*', in Katarina Kruhonja (ed.) *Kultura Mira: Suočavanje s prološću* (Osijek: Centre for Peace, Non-Violence and Human Rights), pp.10–12.

Bloomfield, David (2003). 'Reconciliation: An Introduction', in David Bloomfield, Teresa Barnes and Luc Huyse (eds) *Reconciliation after Violent Conflict: A Handbook* (Stockholm: International Institute for Democracy and Electoral Assistance), pp.10–18.

—— (2006). 'On Good Terms: Clarifying Reconciliation', *Berghof Report* 14: 1–35.

Bockers, Estelle; Nadine Stammel and Christine Knaevelsrud (2011). 'Reconciliation in Cambodia: Thirty Years after the Terror of the Khmer Rouge Regime', *Torture* 11(2): 71–83.

Booth, Cherie (2003). 'Prospects and Issues for the International Criminal Court: Lessons from Yugoslavia and Rwanda', in Philippe Sands (ed.) *From Nuremberg to The Hague: The Future of International Criminal Justice* (Cambridge: Cambridge University Press), pp.157–192.

Boraine, Alex (2006). 'Defining Transitional Justice: Tolerance in the Search for Justice and Peace', in Alex Boraine and Sue Valentine (eds) *Transitional Justice and Human Security* (Cape Town: International Centre for Transitional Justice), pp.22–37.

Borneman, John (2002). 'Reconciliation after Ethnic Cleansing: Listening, Retribution, Affiliation', *Public Culture* 14(2): 281–304.

Brahm, Eric (2007). 'Uncovering the Truth: Examining Truth Commission Success and Impact', *International Studies Perspectives* 8(1): 16–35.

Branch, Adam (2007). 'Uganda's Civil War and the Politics of ICC Intervention', *Ethics and International Affairs* 21(2): 179–198.

Burema, Lars (2012). 'Reconciliation in Kosovo: A Few Steps Taken, A Long Road Ahead', *Journal on Ethnopolitics and Minority Issues in Europe* 11(4): 7–27.

Burg, Steven L. and Paul S. Shoup (1999). *The War in Bosnia-Herzegovina: Ethnic Conflict and International Intervention* (New York: M.E. Sharpe).

Campbell, Kirsten (2013). 'The Laws of Memory: The ICTY, the Archive and Transitional Justice', *Social and Legal Studies* 22(2): 247–269.

Carolan, Robert (2008). 'An Examination of the Role of Hybrid International Tribunals in Prosecuting War Crimes and Developing Independent Court Systems: The Kosovo Experiment', *Transnational Law and Contemporary Problems* 17(9): 9–29.

Cassese, Antonio (1998). 'Reflections on International Criminal Justice', *The Modern Law Review* 61(1): 1–10.

Chapman, Audrey R. (2009). 'Approaches to Studying Reconciliation', in Hugo van der Merwe, Victoria Baxter and Audrey R. Chapman (eds) *Assessing the Impact of Transitional Justice: Challenges for Empirical Research* (Washington, DC: United States Institute of Peace Press), pp.143–172.

Cherry, Janet (2009). 'Truth and Transitional Justice in South Africa', in Hugo van der Merwe, Victoria Baxter and Audrey R. Chapman (eds) *Assessing the Impact of Transitional Justice: Challenges for Empirical Research* (Washington, DC: United States Institute of Peace Press), pp.249–264.

Clark, Janine Natalya (2008). *Serbia in the Shadow of Milošević: The Legacy of Conflict in the Balkans* (London: IB Tauris).

—— (2009). 'International War Crimes Tribunals and the Challenge of Outreach', *International Criminal Law Review* 9(1): 99–116.

—— (2010a). 'The State Court of Bosnia and Hercegovina: A Path to Reconciliation?' *Contemporary Justice Review* 13(4): 371–390.

—— (2010b). 'Missing Persons, Reconciliation and the View from Below: A Case-Study of Bosnia-Hercegovina', *Southeast European and Black Sea Studies* 10(4): 425–442.

—— (2010c). 'Religion and Reconciliation in Bosnia and Hercegovina: Are Religious Actors Doing Enough?' *Europe-Asia Studies* 62(4): 371–394.

—— (2010d). 'Bosnia's Success Story? Brčko District and the "View from Below"', *International Peacekeeping* 17(1): 67–79.

—— (2010e). 'Education in Bosnia-Hercegovina: The Case for Root-and-Branch Reform', *Journal of Human Rights* 9(3): 344–362.

—— (2011). 'The Impact Question: The ICTY and the Restoration and Maintenance of Peace', in Bert Swart, Alexander Zahar and Göran Sluiter (eds) *The Legacy of the International Criminal Tribunal for the Former Yugoslavia* (Oxford: Oxford University Press), pp.55–80.

—— (2012a). 'Fieldwork and its Ethical Challenges: Reflections from Research in Bosnia', *Human Rights Quarterly* 34(3): 823–839.

—— (2012b). 'Reflections on Trust and Reconciliation: A Case-Study of a Central Bosnian Village', *International Journal of Human Rights* 16(2): 239–256.

—— (2013a). 'Reconciliation through Remembrance? War Memorials and the Victims of Vukovar', *International Journal of Transitional Justice* 7(1): 116–135.

—— (2013b). 'Courting Controversy: The ICTY's Acquittal of Croatian Generals Gotovina and Markač', *Journal of International Criminal Justice* 11(2): 399–423.

Clark, Phil (2008). 'Law, Politics and Pragmatism: The ICC and Case Selection in Uganda and the Democratic Republic of Congo', in Nicholas Waddell and Phil Clark (eds) *Courting Conflict? Justice, Peace and the ICC in Africa* (London: Royal Africa Society), pp.37–45.

Cohen, Leonard (1993). *Broken Bonds: The Disintegration of Yugoslavia* (Boulder, CO: Westview Press).

Cohen, Roger (1998). *Hearts Grown Brutal: Sagas of Sarajevo* (New York: Random House).

Cohen, Stanley (2001). *States of Denial: Knowing About Atrocities and Suffering* (Cambridge: Polity Press).

Combs, Nancy Amoury (2002). 'Copping a Plea to Genocide: The Plea Bargaining of International Courts', *University of Pennsylvania Law Review* 151(1): 1–157.

Cook, Stuart W. (1985). 'Experimenting on Social Issues: The Case of School Desegregation', *American Psychologist* 40(4): 452–460.

Cords, Marina (1993). 'On Operationally Defining Reconciliation', *American Journal of Primatology* 29(4): 255–267.

Corkalo, Dinka; Dean Ajduković, Harvey M. Weinstein, Eric Stover, Dino Djipa and Miklos Biro (2004). 'Neighbors Again? Intercommunity Relations after Ethnic Cleansing', in Eric Stover and Harvey M. Weinstein (eds) *My Neighbor, My Enemy* (Cambridge: Cambridge University Press), pp.143–161.

Crocker, David A. (2002). 'Punishment, Reconciliation, and Democratic Deliberation', *Buffalo Criminal Law Review* 5(2): 509–549.

Dabić, Vojin S. and Ksenija M. Lukić (1997). *Crimes without Punishment: Vukovar, Sarvaš and Paulin Dvor* (Vukovar: Women's Association of Vukovar Community, 1997).

Dancy, Geoff (2010). 'Impact Assessment, Not Evaluation: Defining a Limited Role for Positivism in the Study of Transitional Justice', *International Journal of Transitional Justice* 4(3): 355–376.

De Grieff, Pablo (2007). 'The Role of Apologies in National Reconciliation Processes: On Making Trustworthy Institutions Trusted', in Mark Gibney (ed.) *The Age of Apology: Facing Up to the Past* (Philadelphia: University of Pennsylvania Press), pp.120–136.

Del Ponte, Carla (2008). *Madame Prosecutor: Confrontations with Humanity's Worst Criminals and the Culture of Impunity* (New York: Other Press).

Delpla, Isabelle (2007). 'In the Midst of Injustice: The ICTY from the Perspective of Some Victims Associations', in Xavier Bougarel, Elissa Helms and Ger Duijzings (eds) *The New Bosnian Mosaic: Identities, Memories, and Moral Claims in a Post-War Society* (Aldershot: Ashgate), pp.211–234.

Di Lellio, Anna and Caitlin McCurn (2013). 'Engineering Grassroots Transitional Justice in the Balkans: The Case of Kosovo', *East European Politics and Societies* 27(1): 129–148.

Dickinson, Laura A. (2003). 'The Relationship Between Hybrid Court and International Courts: The Case of Kosovo', *New England Law Review* 37(4): 1059–1072.

Dicklitch, Susan and Aditi Malik (2010). 'Justice, Human Rights and Reconciliation in Postconflict Cambodia', *Human Rights Review* 11(4): 515–530.

Doder, Dusko (1993). 'Yugoslavia: New War, Old Hatreds', *Foreign Policy* 91: 3–23.

Donnais, Timothy (2002). 'The Politics of Privatization in Post-Dayton Bosnia', *Southeast European Politics* 3(1): 3–19.

Donnelly, Caitlin and Joanne Hughes (2009). 'Contact and Culture: Mechanisms of Reconciliation in Schools in Northern Ireland and Israel', in Joanna R. Quinn (ed.) *Reconciliation(s): Transitional Justice in Postconflict Societies* (Montreal: McGill University Press), pp.147–173.

Drumbl, Mark (2004). 'Prosecutor v. Radislav Krstić: ICTY Authenticates Genocide at Srebrenica and Convicts for Aiding and Abetting', *Melbourne Journal of International Law* 5(2): 434–449.

Dwyer, Susan (2003). 'Reconciliation for Realists', in Judith Rodin and Stephen P. Steinberg (eds). *Dilemmas of Reconciliation: Cases and Concepts* (Waterloo, ON: Wilfrid Laurier University Press), pp.91–110.

Enns, Diane (2013). 'Justice after Violence: Critical Perspectives from the Western Balkans', *Studies in Social Justice* 7(2): 181–187.

Eriksson, Anna (2009). *Justice in Transition: Community Restorative Justice in Northern Ireland* (Devon: Willan Publishing).

Eser, Albin (2011). 'Procedural Structure and Features of International Criminal Justice: Lessons from the ICTY', in Bert Swart, Alexander Zahar and Göran Sluiter (eds) *The Legacy of the International Criminal Tribunal for the Former Yugoslavia* (Oxford: Oxford University Press), pp.108–148.

Fara-Andrianarijaona, Lorène (2013). 'International Criminal Justice: The EU's Strategy for Reconciliation and Peace', *European Security Review* 68: 2–16.

Fatić, Alexander (2000). *Reconciliation via the War Crimes Tribunal?* (Aldershot: Ashgate).

Fawthrop, Tom and Helen Jarvis (2004). *Getting Away With Genocide? Elusive Justice and the Khmer Rouge Tribunal* (London: Pluto Press).

Feierstein, Daniel (2012). 'The Concept of "Genocidal Social Practices"', in Adam Jones (ed.) *New Directions in Genocide Research* (London: Routledge), pp.18–36.

Fletcher, Laurel E. and Harvey M. Weinstein (2002). 'Violence and Social Repair: Rethinking the Contribution of Justice to Reconciliation', *Human Rights Quarterly* 24(3): 573–639.

—— (2004). 'A World unto Itself? The Application of International Justice in the former Yugoslavia', in Eric Stover and Harvey M. Weinstein (eds) *My Neighbor, My Enemy* (Cambridge: Cambridge University Press), pp.29–48.

Fletcher, Laurel F; Harvey M. Weinstein and Jamie Rowen (2009). 'Context, Timing and the Dynamics of Transitional Justice: A Historical Perspective', *Human Rights Quarterly* 31(1): 163–220.

Ford, Stuart (2012). 'A Social Psychology Model of the Perceived Legitimacy of International Criminal Courts: Implications for the Success of Transitional Justice Mechanisms', *Vanderbilt Journal of Transnational Law* 45(2): 405–476.

Frisso, Giovanna M. (2011). 'The Winding Down of the ICTY: The Impact of the Completion Strategy and the Residual Mechanism on Victims', *Goettingen Journal of International Law* 3(3): 1093–1121.

Fukuyama, Francis (1992). *The End of History and the Last Man* (London: Penguin Books).

Gallagher, Tom (2003). *The Balkans after the Cold War: From Tyranny to Tragedy* (Abingdon: Routledge).

Galtung, Johan (1969). 'Violence, Peace and Peace Research', *Journal of Peace Research* 6(3): 167–191.

Gibson, James L. (2004a). *Overcoming Apartheid: Can Truth Reconcile a Divided Nation?* (New York: Russell Sage Foundation).

—— (2004b). 'Does Truth Lead to Reconciliation? Testing the Causal Assumptions of the South African Truth and Reconciliation Process', *American Journal of Political Science* 48(2): 201–217.

—— (2004c). 'Overcoming Apartheid: Can Truth Reconcile a Divided Nation?' *Politikon* 31(2): 129–155.

—— (2009). 'Taking Stock of Truth and Reconciliation in South Africa: Assessing Citizen Attitudes through Surveys', in Hugo van der Merwe, Victoria Baxter and Audrey R. Chapman (eds) *Assessing the Impact of Transitional Justice: Challenges for Empirical Research* (Washington, DC: United States Institute of Peace Press), pp.173–190.

Gibson, James and Christopher Claassen (2010). 'Racial Reconciliation in South Africa: Interracial Contact and Changes over Time', *Journal of Social Issues* 66(2): 255–272.

Glamuzina, Martin; Željka Šiljković and Nikola Glamuzina (2005). 'Demographic Developments in the Town of Knin in 1991/2001 Intercensal Period', *Geoadria* 10(1): 69–89.

Glenny, Misha (1996). *The Fall of Yugoslavia: The Third Balkan War*, 3rd edition (London: Penguin Books).

Goldstone, Richard J. (1996). 'Justice as a Tool for Peace-Making: Truth Commissions and International Criminal Tribunals', *New York University Journal of International Law and Politics* 28(3): 485–503.

—— (2000). *For Humanity: Reflections of a War Crimes Investigator* (New Haven, CT: Yale University Press).

—— (2002). 'Prosecuting Rape as a War Crime', *Case Western Reserve Journal of International Law* 34: 277–285.

Gourevitch, Philip (1998). *We Wish to Inform You that Tomorrow We will be Killed with Our Families: Stories from Rwanda* (New York: Picador).

Govier, Trudy (2009). 'A Dialectic of Acknowledgement', in Joanna R. Quinn (ed.) *Reconciliation(s): Transitional Justice in Postconflict Societies* (Montreal: McGill University Press), pp.36–50.

Gow, James; Rachel Kerr and Zoran Pajić (eds) (2014). *Prosecuting War Crimes: Lessons and Legacies of the International Criminal Tribunal for the former Yugoslavia* (Abingdon: Routledge).

Graybill, Lyn S. (2011). 'Partial Justice and Reconciliation for Sierra Leone Women but Reparations and Reform Remain Elusive', *Research in Social Movements Conflicts and Change* 32: 101–120.

Gready, Paul (2011). *The Era of Transitional Justice: The Aftermath of the Truth and Reconciliation Commission in South Africa and Beyond* (Abingdon: Routledge).

Grodsky, Brian (2009). 'Re-Ordering Justice: Towards a New Methodological Approach to Studying Transitional Justice', *Journal of Peace Research* 46(6): 819–837.

Hagan, John and Sanja Kutnjak Ivković (2006). 'War Crimes, Democracy and the Rule of Law in Belgrade, the former Yugoslavia and Beyond', *The ANNALS of the American Academy of Political and Social Science* 605: 129–151.

Halpern, Jodi and Harvey M. Weinstein (2004). 'Empathy and Rehumanization after Mass Violence', in Eric Stover and Harvey M. Weinstein (eds) *My Neighbor, My Enemy: Justice and Community in the Aftermath of Mass Atrocity* (Cambridge: Cambridge University Press), pp.303–322.

Hamber, Brandon and Gráinne Kelly (2009). 'Too Deep, Too Threatening: Understandings of Reconciliation in Northern Ireland', in Hugo van der Merwe, Victoria Baxter and Audrey R. Chapman (eds) *Assessing the Impact of Transitional Justice: Challenges for Empirical Research* (Washington, DC: United States Institute of Peace Press), pp.265–293.

Harmon, Mark (2005). 'Questions and Answers Session', in Liam McDowall (ed.) *Bridging the Gap between the ICTY and Communities in Bosnian and Herzegovina: Conference Proceedings, Srebrenica, 21 May 2005* (The Hague: ICTY Registry), pp.66–70.

Haskell, Leslie and Lars Waldorf (2011). 'The Impunity Gap of the International Criminal Tribunal for Rwanda: Causes and Consequences', *Hastings International and Comparative Law Review* 34(1): 49–85.

Hayden, Robert M. (2000). *Blueprints for a House Divided: The Constitutional Logic of the Yugoslav Conflicts* (Michigan: The University of Michigan Press).

—— (2006). 'Justice Presumed and Assistance Denied: The Yugoslav Tribunal as Obstruction to Economic Recovery', *International Journal for the Semiotics of Law* 19(4): 389–408.

—— (2011). 'What's Reconciliation got to do with it? The International Criminal Tribunal for the former Yugoslavia (ICTY) as Antiwar Profiteer', *Journal of Intervention and Statebuilding* 5(3): 313–330.

Hayner, Priscilla B. (2011). *Unspeakable Truths: Transitional Justice and the Challenge of Truth Commissions*, 2nd edition. (New York: Routledge).

Helms, Elissa (2010). 'The Gender of Coffee: Women and Reconciliation Initiatives in Post-War Bosnia and Herzegovina', *Focaal – Journal of Global and Historical Anthropology* 57: 17–32.

—— (2012). '"Bosnian Girl": Nationalism and Innocence Through Images of Women', in Daniel Šuber and Slobodan Karamanić (eds) *Retracing Images: Visual Culture after Yugoslavia* (Leiden: Brill), pp.195–222.

Henham, Ralph and Mark Drumbl (2005). 'Plea Bargaining at the International Criminal Tribunal for the former Yugoslavia', *Criminal Law Forum* 16(1): 49–87.

Hewstone, Miles; Ed Cairns, Alberto Voci, Juergen Hamberger and Ulrike Niens (2006). 'Intergroup Contact, Forgiveness and Experience of "the Troubles" in Northern Ireland', *Journal of Social Issues* 62(1): 99–120.

Hirsh, David (2003). *Law against Genocide: Cosmopolitan Trials* (London: The GlassHouse Press).

Hirsch, Michal Ben-Josef; Megan MacKenzie and Mohamed Sesay (2012). 'Measuring the Impacts of Truth and Reconciliation Commissions: Placing the Global "Success" of TRCs in Local Perspective', *Cooperation and Conflict* 47(3): 386–403.

Hodžić, Refik (2010). 'Living the Legacy of Mass Atrocities: Victims' Perspectives on War Crimes Trials', *Journal of International Criminal Justice* 8(1): 113–136.

—— (2011). 'A Long Road Yet to Reconciliation: The Impact of the ICTY on Reconciliation and Victims' Perceptions of Criminal Justice', in Richard H. Steinberg (ed.) *Assessing the Legacy of the ICTY* (Leiden: Martinus Nijhoff Publishers), pp.115–119.

Holá, Barbora; Alette Smeulers and Catrien Bijleveld (2009). 'Is ICTY Sentencing Predictable? An Empirical Analysis of ICTY Sentencing Practice', *Leiden Journal of International Law* 22(1): 79–97.

House, Matthew (2013). 'Justice Within the Arrangement of the Special Court for Sierra Leone Versus Local Perceptions of Justice: A Contradiction or Harmonious?' *European Journal of Science and Public Policy* 10: 13–23.

Humphrey, Michael (2003). 'International Intervention, Justice, and National Reconciliation: The Role of the ICTY and ICTR in Bosnia and Rwanda', *Journal of Human Rights* 2(4): 495–505.

Huyse, Luc (2003). 'The Process of Reconciliation', in David Bloomfield, Teresa Barnes and Luc Huyse (eds) *Reconciliation after Violent Conflict: A Handbook* (Stockholm: International Institute for Democracy and Electoral Assistance), pp.19–33.

Ignatieff, Michael (1998). *The Warrior's Honor: Ethnic War and the Modern Conscience* (New York: Metropolitan Books).

Ireton, Kathleen and Iosif Kovras (2012). 'Non-Apologies and Prolonged Silences in Post-Conflict Settings: The Case of Post-Colonial Cyprus', *Time Society* 21(1): 71–88.

Ivanisević, Bogdan (2011a). 'The Archives as a Means of Confronting the Past', in Richard H. Steinberg (ed.) *Assessing the Legacy of the ICTY* (Leiden: Martinus Nijhoff Publishers), pp.129–132.

Ivanišević, Milivoje (2011b). *Srpska zagarišta: Serbian Ruins of Srebrenica* (Belgrade: Institute for Research on Suffering of Serbs in the Twentieth Century).

Jalloh, Charles Chernor (2011). 'Special Court for Sierra Leone: Achieving Justice?' *Michigan Journal of International Law* 32(3): 395–459.

Jallow, Hassan Bubacar (2008). 'The Contribution of the United Nations International Criminal Tribunal for Rwanda to the Development of International Criminal Law', in Phil Clark and Zachary D. Kaufman (eds) *After Genocide: Transitional Justice, Post-Conflict Reconstruction, and Reconciliation in Rwanda and Beyond* (London: Hurst & Company), pp. 261–279.

Jansen, Stef (2013). 'If Reconciliation is the Answer, Are We Asking the Right Questions?' *Studies in Social Justice* 7(2): 229–243.

Jeong, Ho-Won (2005). *Peacebuilding in Postconflict Societies: Strategy and Process* (Boulder, CO: Lynne Rienner).

Jones, Briony (2012). 'Exploring the Politics of Reconciliation through Education Reform: The Case of Brčko District, Bosnia and Herzegovina', *International Journal of Transitional Justice* 6(1): 126–148.

Judah, Tim (2000). *The Serbs: History, Myth and the Destruction of Yugoslavia*, 2nd edition (New Haven, CT: Yale Nota Bene).

—— (2008). *Kosovo: What Everyone Needs to Know* (Oxford: Oxford University Press).

Kamatali, Jean Marie (2003). 'The Challenge of Linking International Criminal Justice and National Reconciliation: The Case of the ICTR', *Leiden Journal of International Law* 16(1): 115–133.

Kelman, Herbert C. (2008). 'Reconciliation from a Social-Psychological Perspective', in Arie Nadler, Thomas Malloy and Jeffrey D. Fisher (eds) *The Social Psychology of Intergroup Reconciliation* (Oxford: Oxford University Press), pp.15–32.

Kelsall, Tim (2005). 'Truth, Lies, Ritual: Preliminary Reflections on the Truth and Reconciliation Commission [in Sierra Leone]', *Human Rights Quarterly* 27(2): 361–391.

—— (2013). *Culture under Cross-Examination: International Justice and the Special Court for Sierra Leone* (Cambridge: Cambridge University Press).

Ker-Lindsay, James (2012). *Kosovo: The Path to Contested Statehood* (London: IB Tauris).

Kerr, Rachel (2005). 'The Road from Dayton to Brussels? The International Criminal Tribunal for the Former Yugoslavia and the Politics of War Crimes in Bosnia', *European Security* 14(3): 319–337.

—— (2007). 'Peace through Justice? The International Criminal Tribunal for the Former Yugoslavia', *Southeast European and Black Sea Studies* 7(3): 373–385.

Kerr, Rachel and Eirin Mobekk (2007). *Peace and Justice: Seeking Accountability after War* (Cambridge: Polity Press).

Khan, Madiha Inara (2014). 'Historical Record and the Legacy of the International Criminal Tribunal for the former Yugoslavia', in James Gow, Rachel Kerr and Zoran Pajić (eds) *Prosecuting War Crimes: Lessons and Legacies of the International Criminal Tribunal for the former Yugoslavia* (Abingdon: Routledge), pp.88–102.

King, Gary; Robert Keohane and Sidney Verba (1994). *Designing Social Inquiry: Scientific Inference in Qualitative Research* (Princeton, NJ: Princeton University Press).

King, Kimi L. and James D. Meernik (2011). 'Assessing the Impact of the International Criminal Tribunal for the former Yugoslavia: Balancing International and Local Interests While Doing Justice', in Bert Swart, Alexander Zahar and Göran Sluiter (eds) *The Legacy of the International Criminal Tribunal for the Former Yugoslavia* (Oxford: Oxford University Press), pp.7–54.

Kirk McDonald, Gabrielle (2004). 'Problems, Obstacles and Achievements of the ICTY', *Journal of International Criminal Justice* 2(2): 558–571.

—— (2011). 'Everything to Everyone: Debate over the Final Location of the ICTY Archives', in Richard H. Steinberg (ed.) *Assessing the Legacy of the ICTY* (Leiden: Martinus Nijhoff Publishers), pp.93–94.

Klarin, Mirko (2001). '*Nirnberg Sada!*' in ICTY, *The Path to The Hague: Selected Documents on the Origins of the ICTY* (The Hague: ICTY), pp.96–97.

—— (2004). 'The Tribunal's Four Battles', *Journal of International Criminal Justice* 2(2): 546–557.

—— (2009). 'The Impact of ICTY Trials on Public Opinion in the former Yugoslavia', *Journal of International Criminal Justice* 7(1): 89–96.

—— (2011). 'Building the ICTY Legacy for Local Communities', in Richard H. Steinberg (ed.) *Assessing the Legacy of the ICTY* (Leiden: Martinus Nijhoff Publishers), pp.111–114.

Kleck, Monika (2006). 'Refugee Return: Success Story or Bad Dream? A Review from Eastern Bosnia', in Martina Fischer (ed.) *Peacebuilding and Civil Society in Bosnia-Hercegovina: Ten Years After Dayton* (Münster: Lit-Verlag), pp.107–122.

Kohen, Ari; Michael Zanchelli and Levi Drake (2011). 'Personal and Political Reconciliation in Post-Genocide Rwanda', *Faculty Publications: Political Science, Paper 44*: 1–22.

Kolind, Torsten (2006), 'In Search of "Decent People": Resistance to the Ethnicization of Everyday Life among the Muslims of Stolac', in Xavier Bougarel, Elissa Helms and Ger Duijzings (eds) *The New Bosnian Mosaic: Identities, Memories, and Moral Claims in a Post-War Society* (Aldershot: Ashgate), pp.123–139.

Kontsevaia, Diana B. (2013). 'Mass Graves and the Politics of Reconciliation: Construction of Memorial Sites after the Srebrenica Massacre', *Totem: The University of Western Ontario Journal of Anthropology* 21(1): 15–31.

Kosić, Ankica and Charles Tauber (2010). 'Promoting Reconciliation through Youth: Cross-Community Initiatives in Vukovar, Croatia', *Peace and Conflict* 16(1): 1–14.

Koska, Viktor (2008). 'Return and Reintegration of Minority Returnees: The Complexity of the Serbian Returnees' Experiences in the Town of Glina', *Politička misao* 16(5): 191–217.

Kostić, Roland (2012). 'Transitional Justice and Reconciliation in Bosnia-Herzegovina: Whose Memories, Whose Justice?' *Sociologija* 55(4): 649–666.

Kriesberg, Louis (1998). *Constructive Conflicts: From Escalation to Resolution* (Lanham, MD: Rowman & Littlefield).

—— (2007). 'External Contributions to Post-Mass-Crime Rehabilitation', in Béatrice Pouligny, Simon Chesterman and Albrecht Schnabel (eds) *After Mass Crime: Rebuilding States and Communities* (Tokyo: United Nations University Press, pp.243–270).

Kritz, Neil J. (1996). 'Coming to Terms with Atrocities: A Review of Accountability Mechanisms for Mass Violations of Human Rights', *Law and Contemporary Problems* 59(4): 127–152.

Kubai, Anne N. (2007). 'Between Justice and Reconciliation: The Survivors of Rwanda', *African Security Review* 16(1): 53–66.

Kučukalić, Abdulah; Libby T. Arcel, Sabina Popović, Alma Bravo-Mehmedbašić, Jasmina Pušina and Lejla Šaraba (2003). 'Socio-Demographic Characteristics of Torture Survivors in B&H', in Libby Tata Arcel, Sabina Popović, Adbulah Kučukalić and Alma Bravo-Mehmedbašić (eds) *Treatment of Torture Survivors in a Post-War Society* (Sarajevo: Centre for Torture Victims), pp.29–39.

Lambourne, Wendy (2009). 'Transitional Justice and Peacebuilding after Mass Violence', *International Journal of Transitional Justice* 3(1): 28–48.

Lamin, Abdul Rahman (2009). 'Charles Taylor, the Special Court for Sierra Leone and International Politics', in Chandra Lekha Sriram and Suren Pillay (eds) *Peace Versus Justice? The Dilemma of Transitional Justice in Africa* (Scottsville: University of KwaZulu-Natal Press), pp.248–261.

Laplante, Lisa J. and Kimberly Theidon (2007). 'Truth With Consequences: Justice and Reparations in Post-Truth Commission Peru', *Human Rights Quarterly* 29(1): 228–250.

LeBor, Adam (2002). *Milošević: A Biography* (London: Bloomsbury Publishing).

Lederach, Jean Paul (1997). *Building Peace: Sustainable Reconciliation in Divided Societies* (Washington, DC: United States Institute of Peace Press).

—— (1999). *The Journey Toward Reconciliation* (Scottdale, PA: Herald Press).

—— (2001). 'Civil Society and Reconciliation', in Chester A. Crocker, Fen Osler Hampson and Pamela Aall (eds) *Turbulent Peace: The Challenges of Managing International Conflict* (Washington, DC: United States Institute of Peace Press), pp.841–854.

Leebaw, Bronwyn Anne (2008). 'The Irreconcilable Goals of Transitional Justice', *Human Rights Quarterly* 30(1): 95–118.

Lefko-Everett, Kate (2012). 'Ticking the Time Bomb or Demographic Dividend? Youth and Reconciliation in South Africa, SA Reconciliation Barometer Survey: 2012 Report' (Cape Town: Institute for Justice and Reconciliation).

Lescure, Karine and Florence Trintignac (1996). *International Justice for former Yugoslavia: The Working of the International Criminal Tribunal of The Hague* (The Hague: Kluwer Law International).

Lewicki, Roy J. and Carolyn Wiethoff (2000). 'Trust, Trust Development and Trust Despair', in Morton Deutsch and Peter T. Coleman (eds) *The Handbook of Conflict Resolution: Theory and Practice* (San Francisco, CA: Jossey Bass), pp.86–108.

Lombard, Karin (2003). 'Report of the First Round of the SA Reconciliation Barometer Survey – September 2003' (Cape Town: Institute for Justice and Reconciliation).

Long, William J. and Peter Brecke (2003). *War and Reconciliation: Reason and Emotion in Conflict Resolution* (Cambridge, MA: MIT Press).

MacShane, Denis (2011). *Why Kosovo Still Matters* (London: Haus Publishing Ltd).

Malcolm, Noel (2002). *Bosnia: A Short History* (London: Pan Books).

Mannergren Selimović, Johanna (2010). 'Perpetrators and Victims: Local Responses to the International Criminal Tribunal for the former Yugoslavia', *Focaal: Journal of Global and Historical Anthropology* 57: 50–61.

Maoz, Ifat (2011). 'Does Contact Work in Protracted Asymmetrical Conflict? Appraising 20 Years of Reconciliation-Aimed Encounters Between Israeli Jews and Palestinians', *Journal of Peace Research* 48(1): 115–125.

May, Larry (2010). *Genocide: A Normative Account* (Cambridge: Cambridge University Press).

McDonald, Gabrielle Kirk (2011). 'Everything to Everyone: Debate over the Final Location of the ICTY Archives', in Richard H. Steinberg (ed.) *Assessing the Legacy of the ICTY* (Leiden: Martinus Nijhoff Publishers), pp.93–94.

McEvoy, Kieran and Anna Eriksson (2008). 'Restorative Justice in Transition: Ownership, Leadership and "Bottom-Up" Human Rights', in Dennis Sullivan and Larry Tift (eds) *Handbook of Restorative Justice* (Abingdon: Routledge), pp.321–335.

McIntyre, Gabrielle (2011). 'The International Residual Mechanism and the Legacy of the International Criminal Tribunals for the former Yugoslavia and Rwanda', *Goettingen Journal of International Law* 3(3): 923–983.

McMahon, Patrice C. and David P. Forsythe (2008). 'The ICTY's Impact on Serbia: Judicial Romanticism Meets Network Politics', *Human Rights Quarterly* 30: 412–435.

Mearsheimer, John (1990). 'Back to the Future: Instability in Europe after the Cold War', *International Security* 15(1): 5–56.

Meernik, James (2005). 'Justice and Peace? How the International Criminal Tribunal Affects Societal Peace in BiH', *Journal of Peace Research* 42(3): 271–289.

Meernik, James D; Angela Nichols and Kimi L. King (2010). 'The Impact of International Tribunals and Domestic Trials on Peace and Human Rights after Civil War', *International Studies Perspectives* 11(4): 309–334.

Meierhenrich, Jens (2008). 'Varieties of Reconciliation', *Law and Social Inquiry* 33(1): 195–231.

Mendeloff, David (2009). 'Trauma and Vengeance: Assessing the Psychological and Emotional Effects of Post-Conflict Justice', *Human Rights Quarterly* 31(3): 592–623.

Menkel-Meadow, Carrie (2002). 'Practicing "In the Interests of Justice" in the Twenty-First Century: Pursuing Peace as Justice', *Fordham Law Review* 60: 1761–1774.

Meron, Theodor (2004a). 'Procedural Evolution in the ICTY', *Journal of International Criminal Justice* 2(2): 520–525.

Mesić, Milan and Dragan Bagić. (2011). *Manjinski Povratak u Hrvatsku: Studija Otvorenog Procesa* (Zagreb: UNHCR).

Mieth, Friederike (2013). 'Bringing Justice and Enforcing Peace? An Ethnographic Perspective on the Impact of the Special Court for Sierra Leone', *International Journal of Conflict and Violence* 7(1): 10–22.

Millar, Gearoid (2010). 'Assessing Local Experiences of Truth-Telling in Sierra Leone: Getting to "Why" Through a Qualitative Case Study Analysis', *International Journal of Transitional Justice* 4(3): 477–496.

Minow, Martha (1998). *Between Vengeance and Forgiveness: Facing History after Genocide and Mass Violence* (Boston, MA: Beacon Press).

Moghalu, Kingsley Chiedu (2002). 'Image and Reality of War Crimes Justice: External Perceptions of the International Criminal Tribunal for Rwanda', *The Fletcher Forum of World Affairs* 26(2): 21–46.

—— (2004). 'Reconciling Fractured Societies: An African Perspective on the Role of Judicial Prosecutions', in Ramesh Thakur and Peter Malcontent (eds) *From Sovereign Impunity to International Accountability: The Search for Justice in a World of States* (Tokyo: United Nations Press), pp. 197–223.

—— (2009). 'Prosecute or Pardon? Between Truth Commissions and War Crimes Trials', in Chandra Lekha Sriram and Suren Pillay (eds) *Peace Versus Justice? The Dilemma of Transitional Justice in Africa* (Scottsville: University of KwaZulu-Natal Press), pp.69–95.

Moreno-Ocampo, Luis (2006). 'Keynote Address: Integrating the Work of the ICC into Local Justice Initiatives', *American University International Law Review* 21(4): 497–503.

Morton, Adam (2004). *On Evil* (Abingdon: Routledge).

Mukherjee, Geetanjali (2011). 'Achieving Reconciliation through Prosecution in the Courts: Lessons from Rwanda', *Conflict Resolution Quarterly* 28(3): 331–348.

Mwangi, Wambui (2009). 'The International Criminal Tribunal for Rwanda: Reconciling the Acquitted', in Chandra Lekha Sriram and Suren Pillay (eds) *Peace Versus Justice? The Dilemma of Transitional Justice in Africa* (Scottsville: University of KwaZulu-Natal Press), pp.262–274.

Nadler, Arie, and Ido Leviatan (2006). 'Intergroup Reconciliation: Effects of Adversary's Expressions of Empathy, Responsibility and Recipients' Trust', *Personality and Social Psychology Bulletin* 32(4): 459–470.

Nakarada, Radmila (2013). 'Acquittal of Gotovina and Markač: A Blow to the Serbian and Croatian Reconciliation Process', *Merkourios: Utrecht Journal of International and European Law* 29(76): 102–105.

Nash, Kaley (2007). 'A Comparative Analysis of Justice in Post-Genocidal Rwanda: Fostering a Sense of Peace and Reconciliation?' *Africana* 1(1): 59–98.

Nee, Ann and Peter Uvin (2010). 'Silence and Dialogue: Burundians' Alternatives to Transitional Justice', in Rosalind Shaw and Lars Waldorf (eds) *Localizing Transitional Justice: Interventions and Priorities after Mass Violence* (Stanford, CA: Stanford University Press), pp.157–182.

Nesdale, Drew and Patrick Todd (2000). 'Effect of Contact on Intercultural Acceptance: A Field Study', *International Journal of Intercultural Relations* 24(3): 341–360.

Nettelfield, Lara J. (2010). *Courting Democracy in Bosnia and Herzegovina: The Hague Tribunal's Impact in a Postwar State* (Cambridge: Cambridge University Press).

Neuffer, Elizabeth (2003). *The Key to My Neighbour's House: Seeking Justice in Bosnia and Rwanda* (London: Bloomsbury Publishing).

Nice, Geoffrey (2006). 'Accountability: State Responsibility', in Alex Boraine and Sue Valentine (eds) *Transitional Justice and Human Security* (Cape Town: The International Centre for Transitional Justice), pp.43–52.

Noor, Masi; Rupert James Brown and Garry Prentice (2008). 'Precursors and Mediators of Intergroup Conflict in Northern Ireland: A New Model', *British Journal of Social Psychology* 47(3): 481–495.

Nuhanović, Hasan (2007). *Under the UN Flag: The International Community and the Srebrenica Genocide* (Sarajevo: DES Sarajevo).

Nyawo, James (2012). 'Historical Narrative of Mass Atrocities and Injustice in Africa: Implications for the Implementation of International Criminal Justice', in Vincent O. Nhemielle (ed.) *Africa and the Future of International Criminal Justice* (The Hague: Eleven International Publishing), pp.125–159.

Oberschall, Anthony (2000). 'The Manipulation of Ethnicity: From Ethnic Cooperation to Violence and War in Yugoslavia', *Ethnic and Racial Studies* 23(6): 982–1001.

—— (2007). *Conflict and Peace Building in Divided Societies: Responses to Ethnic Violence* (Abingdon: Routledge).

—— (2010). 'Memory, Historical Responsibility, Truth and Justice: The Balkan Wars', *Corvinus Journal of Sociology and Social Policy* 1(1): 31–60.

Obradović-Wochnik, Jelena (2014). 'Revisionism, Denial and Anti-ICTY Discourse in Serbia's Public Sphere: Beyond the "Divided Society" Debate', in James Gow, Rachel Kerr and Zoran Pajić (eds) *Prosecuting War Crimes: Lessons and Legacies of the International Criminal Tribunal for the former Yugoslavia* (Abingdon: Routledge), pp.182–203.

Oette, Lutz (2010). 'Peace and Justice, or Neither? The Repercussions of the al-Bashir Case for International Criminal Justice in Africa and Beyond', *Journal of International Criminal Justice* 8(2): 345–364.

Ogata, Sadako (2003). 'Foreword: Imagining Coexistence in Conflict Communities', in Antonia Chayes and Martha Minow (eds) *Imagine Coexistence: Restoring Humanity after Violent Ethnic Conflict* (San Francisco, CA: Jossey-Bass), pp.xi–xv.

Ohlin, Jens David (2011). 'Proportional Sentences at the ICTY', in Bert Swart, Alexander Zahar and Göran Sluiter (eds) *The Legacy of the International Criminal Tribunal for the Former Yugoslavia* (Oxford: Oxford University Press), pp.322–341.

Overy, Richard (2003). 'The Nuremberg Trials: International Law in the Making', in Philippe Sands (ed.) *From Nuremberg to The Hague: The Future of International Criminal Justice* (Cambridge: Cambridge University Press), pp.1–29.

Owen, David (1996). *Balkan Odyssey* (London: Indigo).

Owen, James (2006). *Nuremberg: Evil on Trial* (Stirlingshire: Headline Review).

Pajić, Zoran and Dragan M. Popović (2011). 'Facing the Past and Access to Justice from a Public Perspective', *Special Report*, 20 April 2011 (Sarajevo: UNDP).

Pargan, Mehmed (2012). *Bratunac: Svjedočanstvo o nekaznjenom genocidu* (Tuzla: Bosnian Media Group).

Parker, Sara (2009). 'The International Criminal Tribunal for the former Yugoslavia: The Promise and Reality of Reconciliation in Croatia', *Peace and Conflict Studies* 15(2): 81–102.

Pejić, Jelena (2001). 'The Yugoslav Truth and Reconciliation Commission: A Shaky Start', *Fordham International Law Journal* 25(1): 1–22.

Peskin, Victor (2008). *International Justice in Rwanda and the Balkans: Virtual Trials and the Struggle for State Cooperation* (Cambridge: Cambridge University Press).

Peskin, Victor and Miecysław Boduszyński (2003). 'International Justice and Domestic Politics: Post-Tudjman Croatia and the International Criminal Tribunal for the former Yugoslavia', *Europe-Asia Studies* 55(7): 1117–1142.

Pettigrew, Thomas F. (1998). 'Intergroup Contact Theory', *Annual Review of Psychology* 49(1): 65–85.

Pham, Phuong and Patrick Vinck (2007). 'Empirical Research and the Development and Assessment of Transitional Justice Mechanisms', *International Journal of Transitional Justice* 1(2): 231–248.

Pickering, Paula (2007). *Peacebuilding in the Balkans: The View from the Ground Floor* (Ithaca, NY: Cornell University Press).

Pillay, Suren (2009). 'Conclusion', in Chandra Lekha Sriram and Suren Pillay (eds) *Peace Versus Justice? The Dilemma of Transitional Justice in Africa* (Scottsville: University of KwaZulu-Natal Press), pp.347–357.

Pittman, Thomas Wayde (2011). 'The Road to the Establishment of the International Residual Mechanism for Criminal Tribunals: From Completion to Continuation', *Journal of International Criminal Justice* 9(4): 797–817.

Prieto, Juan Diego (2012). 'Together after War while the War Goes On: Victims, Ex-Combatants and Communities in Three Colombian Cities', *International Journal of Transitional Justice* 6(3): 525–546.

Putnam, Tonya L. (2002). 'Human Rights and Sustainable Peace', in Stephen John Stedman, David Rothchild and Elizabeth M. Cousens (eds) *Ending Civil Wars: The Implementation of Peace Agreements* (Boulder, CO: Lynne Rienner), pp.237–272.

Quinn, Joanna R. (2009). 'Introduction', in Joanna R. Quinn (ed.) *Reconciliation(s): Transitional Justice in Postconflict Societies* (Montreal: McGill University Press), pp.3–13.

Quintiliani, Karen; Susan Needham, Robert Lemkin and Thet Sambath (2011). 'Facilitating Dialogue Between Cambodian American Survivors and Khmer Rouge Perpetrators', *Peace Review: A Journal of Social Justice* 23(4): 506–513.

Ramet, Sabrina P. (2002). *Balkan Babel: The Disintegration of Yugoslavia from the Death of Tito to the Fall of Milošević*, 4th edition (Boulder CO: Westview Press).

Ramulić, Edin (2011). 'Victims' Perspectives', in Richard H. Steinberg (ed.) *Assessing the Legacy of the ICTY* (Leiden: Martinus Nijhoff Publishers), pp.103–106.

Ray, John (1983). 'Racial Attitudes and the Contact Thesis', *Journal of Social Psychology* 119: 3–10.

RECOM (2011a). *The Consultation Process on the Establishment of the Facts About War Crimes and Other Gross Violations of Human Rights Committed on the Territory of the Former Yugoslavia* (Belgrade: Humanitarian Law Centre).

Rehak, Danijel (2008). *Through the Roads of Hell: Through Serbian Concentration Camps 1991…Into 21st Century* (Zagreb: Croatian Association of Camp Inmates of Serbian Concentration Camps).

Richardson, Henry J. (2012). 'African Grievances and the International Criminal Court', in Vincent O. Nhemielle (ed.) *Africa and the Future of International Criminal Justice* (The Hague: Eleven International Publishing), pp.81–123.

Rigby, Andrew (2001). *Justice and Reconciliation: After the Violence* (London: Lynne Rienner).

Robertson QC, Geoffrey (2012). *Crimes against Humanity: The Struggle for Global Justice*, 4th edition (London: Penguin Books).

Robinson, Patrick L. (2011). 'The Way Forward', in Richard H. Steinberg (ed.) *Assessing the Legacy of the ICTY*, pp.267–269.

Rogel, Carole (1998). *The Breakup of Yugoslavia and the War in Bosnia* (Westport, CT: Greenwood Press).

Rohde, David (2012). *Endgame: The Betrayal and Fall of Srebrenica, Europe's Worst Massacre since World War II* (London: Penguin Books).

Rowen, Jamie (2012). 'Mobilizing Truth: Agenda Setting in a Transnational Social Movement', *Law and Social Inquiry* 37(3): 686–718.

Sarkin, Jeremy (2001). 'The Tension Between Justice and Reconciliation in Rwanda: Politics, Human Rights, Due Process and the Role of the *Gacaca* Courts in Dealing with the Genocide', *Journal of African Law* 45(2): 143–172.

Saxon, Dan (2005). 'Exporting Justice: Perceptions of the ICTY among the Serbian, Croatian and Muslim Communities in the former Yugoslavia', *Journal of Human Rights* 4(4): 559–572.

Schabas, William A. (2013). 'The Banality of International Justice', *Journal of International Criminal Justice* 11(3): 545–551.

Scharf, Michael P. (1997). *Balkan Justice: The Story Behind the First International War Crimes Trial since Nuremberg* (Durham, NC: Carolina Academic Press).

Scharf, Michael P. and William A. Schabas (2002). *Slobodan Milošević on Trial: A Companion* (New York: Continuum).

Scharf, Michael P. and Paul R. Williams (2003). 'The Functions of Justice and Anti-Justice in the Peace-Building Process', *Case Western Reserve Journal of International Law* 35(2): 161–190.

Scheffer, David J. (2004). 'Three Memories from the Year of Origin, 1993', *Journal of International Criminal Justice* 2(2): 353–360.

Schrag, Minna (1995). 'The Yugoslav Crimes Tribunal: A Prosecutor's View', *Duke Journal of Comparative and International Law* 6(1): 187–195.

Scott, James C. (1990). *Domination and the Arts of Resistance: Hidden Transcripts* (New Haven, CT: Yale University Press).

Serbian Democratic Forum (2007). *Croatia: Economic Development Program – Period 2007–2010* (Zagreb: Serbian Democratic Forum).

Shaw, Rosalind (2007). 'Memory Frictions: Localizing the Truth and Reconciliation Commission in Sierra Leone', *International Journal of Transitional Justice* 1(1): 183–207.

Shrader, Charles R. (2003). *The Muslim-Croat Civil War in Bosnia: A Military History, 1992–1994* (College Station, TX: Texas A&M University Press).

Sikkink, Kathryn and Carrie Booth Walling (2007). 'The Impact of Human Rights Trials in Latin America', *Journal of Peace Research* 44(4): 427–445.

Silber, Laura and Allan Little (1996). *The Death of Yugoslavia*, revised edition (London: Penguin Books).

Silk, Joan B. (2002). 'The Form and Function of Reconciliation in Primates', *Annual Review of Anthropology* 31: 21–44.

Simić, Olivera (2011). 'Bringing "Justice" Home? Bosnians, War Criminals and the Interaction between the Cosmopolitan and the Local', *German Law Journal* 12(7): 1388–1407.

Simpson, Gerry (2007). *Law, War and Crime* (Cambridge: Polity Press).

Skaar, Elin (2012). 'Reconciliation in a Transitional Justice Perspective', *Transitional Justice Review* 1(1): 54–103.

Sorabji, Cornelia (2006). 'Managing Memories in Post-War Sarajevo: Individuals, Bad Memories and New Wars', *Journal of the Royal Anthropological Institute* 12(1): 1–18.

Sriram, Chandra Lekha (2009). 'Transitional Justice and Peacebuilding', in Chandra Lekha Sriram and Suren Pillay (eds) *Peace Versus Justice? The Dilemma of Transitional Justice in Africa* (Scottsville: University of KwaZulu-Natal Press), pp.1–17.

Staub, Ervin. (1989) *The Roots of Evil: The Origins of Genocide and Other Group Violence* (New York: Cambridge University Press).

—— (2000). 'Genocide and Mass Killing: Origins, Prevention, Healing and Reconciliation', *Political Psychology* 21(2): 367–382.

—— (2011). *Overcoming Evil: Genocide, Violent Conflict and Terrorism* (Oxford: Oxford University Press).

Staub, Ervin; Laurie Anne Pearlman, Alexandra Gubin and Athanase Hagengimana (2005). 'Healing, Reconciliation, Forgiving and the Prevention of Violence after Genocide or Mass Killing: An Intervention and its Experimental Evaluation in Rwanda', *Journal of Social and Clinical Psychology* 24(3): 297–334.

Steinberg, Richard H. (ed.) (2011). *Assessing the Legacy of the ICTY* (Leiden: Martinus Nijhoff Publishers).

Stephen, Chris (2004). *Judgement Day: The Trial of Slobodan Milošević* (New York: Atlantic Monthly Press).

Stewart, Christopher S. (2007). *Hunting the Tiger: The Fast Life and Violent Death of the Balkans' Most Dangerous Man* (New York: Thomas Dunne Books).

Stojanović, Mladen and Katarina Kruhonja (eds) (2011). *Monitoring War Crimes – Report January/May 2011* (Osijek: Centre for Peace, Nonviolence and Human Rights).

Stover, Eric (2007). *The Witnesses: War Crimes and the Promise of Justice in The Hague* (Philadelphia, PA: University of Pennsylvania Press).

Stover, Eric and Harvey M. Weinstein (eds) (2004a). *My Neighbor, My Enemy: Justice and Community in the Aftermath of Mass Atrocity* (Cambridge: Cambridge University Press).

—— (2004b). 'Conclusion: A Common Objective, a Universe of Alternatives', in Eric Stover and Harvey M. Weinstein (eds) *My Neighbor, My Enemy* (Cambridge: Cambridge University Press), pp.323–342.

Stromseth, Jane (2009). 'Justice on the Ground: Can International Criminal Courts Strengthen Domestic Rule of Law in Post-Conflict Societies?' *Hague Journal on the Rule of Law* 1: 87–97.

Subašić, Munira (2011). 'Turning Darkness into Light: The Quest for Justice by Srebrenica's Mothers', in Richard H. Steinberg (ed.) *Assessing the Legacy of the ICTY* (Leiden: Martinus Nijhoff Publishers), pp.133–138.

Subašić, Haris and Nerzuk Ćurak (2014). 'History, the ICTY's Record and the Bosnian Serb Culture of Denial', in James Gow, Rachel Kerr and Zoran Pajić (eds) *Prosecuting War Crimes: Lessons and Legacies of the International Criminal Tribunal for the former Yugoslavia* (Abingdon: Routledge), pp.133–150.

Subotić, Jelena (2009). *Hijacked Justice: Dealing with the Past in the Balkans* (Ithaca, NY: Cornell University Press).

—— (2013a). 'Remembrance, Public Narratives and Obstacles to Justice in the Western Balkans', *Studies in Social Justice* 7(2): 265–283.

Tanner, Marcus (2010). *Croatia: A Nation Forged in War*, 3rd edition (New Haven, CT: Yale University Press).

Tejan-Cole, Abdul (2009). 'Sierra Leone's "Not So" Special Court', in Chandra Lekha Sriram and Suren Pillay (eds) *Peace Versus Justice? The Dilemma of Transitional Justice in Africa* (Scottsville: University of KwaZulu-Natal Press), pp.223–247.

Theidon, Kimberly (2006). 'Justice in Transition: The Micropolitics of Reconciliation in Postwar Peru', *Journal of Conflict Resolution* 50(3): 433–457.

Thompson, Allan (ed.) (2007). *The Media and the Rwandan Genocide* (London: Pluto Press).

Thompson, Mark (1992). *A Paper House: The Ending of Yugoslavia* (London: Vintage).

Thoms, Oskar N.T.; James Ron and Roland Paris (2010). 'State-Level Effects of Transitional Justice: What Do We Know?' *International Journal of Transitional Justice* 4(3): 329–354.

Tieger, Alan and Milbert Shin (2005). 'Plea Agreements in the ICTY: Purpose, Effects and Propriety', *Journal of International Criminal Justice* 3(3): 666–679.

Tokača, Mirsad (2005). '*Ideja da netko kontrolira moju prošlost za mene je nepodnošljiva*', in Katarina Kruhonja (ed.) *Kultura Mira: Suočavanje s prološću* (Osijek: Centre for Peace, Non-Violence and Human Rights), pp.6–8.

Trimikliniotis, Nicos (2012). 'Sociology of Reconciliation: Learning from Comparing Violent Conflicts and Reconciliation Processes', *Current Sociology* 61(2): 244–264.

Tutu, Desmond (1999). *No Future Without Forgiveness* (London: Rider).

—— (2009). 'Foreword', in Charles Villa-Vicencio, *Walk with Us and Listen: Political Reconciliation in Africa* (Washington, DC: Georgetown University Press), pp.ix–xii.

van der Merwe, Hugo (2009). 'Delivering Justice During Transition: Research Challenges', in Hugo van der Merwe, Victoria Baxter and Audrey R. Chapman (eds) *Assessing the Impact of Transitional Justice: Challenges for Empirical Research* (Washington, DC: United States Institute of Peace Press), pp.115–142.

van der Merwe, Hugo; Victoria Baxter and Audrey R. Chapman (2009). 'Introduction', in Hugo van der Merwe, Victoria Baxter and Audrey R. Chapman (eds) *Assessing the Impact of Transitional Justice: Challenges for Empirical Research* (Washington, DC: United States Institute of Peace Press), pp.1–11.

Viaene, Lieselotte (2010). 'The Internal Logic of the Cosmos as "Justice" and "Reconciliation": Micro-Level Perceptions in Post-Conflict Guatemala', *Critique of Anthropology* 30(3): 287–312.

Villa-Vicencio, Charles (2009a). *Walk with Us and Listen: Political Reconciliation in Africa* (Washington, DC: Georgetown University Press).

—— (2009b). 'Inclusive Justice: The Limitations of Trial Justice and Truth Commissions', Chandra Lekha Sriram and Suren Pillay (eds) *Peace Versus Justice? The Dilemma of Transitional Justice in Africa* (Scottsville: University of KwaZulu-Natal Press), pp.44–68.

Vladisavljević, Nebojša (2008). *Serbia's Antibureaucratic Revolution: Milošević, the Fall of Communism and Nationalist Mobilization* (Basingstoke: Palgrave MacMillan).

Volf, Miroslav (2000). 'Forgiveness, Reconciliation, and Justice: A Theological Contribution to a More Peaceful Social Environment', *Millennium: Journal of International Studies* 29(3): 861–877.

Vukušić, Iva (2013). 'The Archives of the International Criminal Tribunal for the former Yugoslavia', *History* 98(332): 623–635.

—— (2014). 'Judging Their Hero: Perceptions of the International Criminal Tribunal for the former Yugoslavia in Croatia', in James Gow, Rachel Kerr and Zoran Pajić (eds) *Prosecuting War Crimes: Lessons and Legacies of the International Criminal Tribunal for the former Yugoslavia* (Abindgon: Routledge), pp.151–181.

Vulliamy, Ed (1994). *Seasons in Hell: Understanding Bosnia's War* (London: Simon and Schuster, 1994).

Wahaj, Sofia A.; Kevin R. Guse and Kay E. Holekamp (2001). 'Reconciliation in the Spotted Hyena (*Crocuta crocuta*)', *Ethnology* 107(12): 1057–1074.

Wark, Colin and John F. Galliher (2007). 'Emory Bogardus and the Origins of the Social Distance Scale', *American Sociologist* 38(4): 383–395.

Warshauer Freedman, Sarah; Dinka Corkalo, Naomi Levy, Dino Abazović, Bronwyn Leebaw, Dean Ajduković, Dino Djipa and Harvey M. Weinstein (2004). 'Public Education and Social Reconstruction in Bosnia and Herzegovina and Croatia', in Eric Stover and Harvey M. Weinstein (eds) *My Neighbor, My Enemy: Justice and Community in the Aftermath of Mass Atrocity* (Cambridge: Cambridge University Press), pp.226–247.

Weinstein, Harvey M. (2011). 'Editorial Note: The Myth of Closure, the Illusion of Reconciliation – Final Thoughts on Five Years as Editor-in-Chief', *International Journal of Transitional Justice* 5(1): 1–10.

Weinstein, Harvey M. and Eric Stover (2004). 'Introduction: Conflict, Justice, and Reclamation', in Eric Stover and Harvey M. Weinstein (eds) *My Neighbor, My Enemy: Justice and Community in the Aftermath of Mass Atrocity* (Cambridge: Cambridge University Press), pp. 1–26.

Weinstein, Harvey M; Laurel E. Fletcher, Patrick Vinck and Phuong N. Pham (2010). 'Stay the Hand of Justice: Whose Priorities Take Priority?' in Rosalind Shaw and Lars Waldorf (eds) *Localizing Transitional Justice: Interventions and Priorities after Mass Violence* (Stanford, CA: Stanford University Press), pp.27–48.

Weiss, Gordon (2012). *The Cage: The Fight for Sri Lanka and the Last Days of the Tamil Tigers* (London: Vintage Books).

Weiss, Peter (2011). 'Taking the Law Seriously: The Imperative Need for a Nuclear Weapons Convention', *Fordham International Law Journal* 34(4): 776–787.

Westberg, Megan (2011). 'Rwanda's Use of Transitional Justice after Genocide: The *Gacaca* Courts and the ICTR', *Kansas Law Review* 59(4): 331–367.

Wiebelhaus-Brahm, Eric (2010). *Truth Commissions and Transitional Societies: The Impact on Human Rights and Democracy* (Abingdon: Routledge).

Wilson, Richard A. (2003). 'Anthropological Studies of National Reconciliation Processes', *Anthropological Theory* 3(3): 367–387.

—— (2005). 'Judging History: The Historical Record of the International Criminal Tribunal for the Former Yugoslavia', *Human Rights Quarterly* 27(3): 908–942.

Woodward, Susan (1995). *Balkan Tragedy: Chaos and Dissolution after the Cold War* (Washington DC: The Brookings Institution).

Wu, Kristen Xueqin (2013). 'Experiences that Count: A Comparative Study of the ICTY and SCSL in Shaping the Image of Justice', *Utrecht Law Review* 9(1): 60–77.

Zečević, Jasna (2013). 'Preface', in Mima Dahić (ed.) *Vive žene*: Centre for Therapy and Torture, *Journal of Articles: Rehabilitation of Torture Victims* 4: 5–6.

Zehr, Howard (2005). *Changing Lenses: A New Focus for Crimes and Justice*, 3rd edition (Scottdale, PA: Herald Press).

Zimmermann, Warren (1995). 'The Last Ambassador: A Memoir of the Collapse of Yugoslavia', *Foreign Affairs* 74(2): 2–20.

Internet articles and reports

Alec, Anes (2013). 'Book Publishers Hope for Dialogue, Reconciliation', 1 March 2013, available at: http://www.setimes.com/cocoon/setimes/xhtml/en_GB/features/setimes/features/2013/03/01/feature-02 (accessed 6 May 2013).

Alić, Enes (2013). 'Unemployment Linked to Politics in BiH', 14 March 2013, available at: http://www.isaintel.com/2013/03/14/unemployment-linked-to-politics-in-bih/ (accessed 4 June 2013).

Amnesty International (2006). *Bosnia and Herzegovina: Behind Closed Gates – Discrimination in Employment*, EUR 63/001/2006, 26 January 2006, available at: http://www.amnesty.org/en/library/info/EUR63/001/2006 (accessed 30 April 2013).

—— (2011). 'Document – Croatia: Praise for "Operation Storm" Creates Climate of Impunity', Public Statement, EUR 64/010/2011, 9 August 2011, available at: http://www.amnesty.org/en/library/asset/EUR64/010/2011/en/fa1c3d11-ce39-4537-ab13-b8b1816cc6cf/eur640102011en.html (accessed 8 January 2013).

—— (2012). *The Right to Know: Families Still in the Dark in the Balkans*, EUR 05/001/2012, 30 August 2012, available at: http://www.amnesty.org/en/library/asset/EUR05/001/2012/en/0a33c2c7-c145-4958-a8d1-b946b569c6aa/eur050012012en.pdf (accessed 3 February 2013).

Arbour, Louise (1998). 'Statement by the Prosecutor following the Withdrawal of the Charges against 14 Accused', 8 May 1998, available at: http://www.icty.org/sid/7671 (accessed 12 June 2013).

Arslanagić, Sabina (2010). 'Dodik Again Denies Srebrenica Genocide', 3 December 2010, available at: http://www.balkaninsight.com/en/article/dodik-slams-international-community-for-referring-to-srebrenica-massacre-as-genocide (accessed 2 July 2013).

B92 (2008). 'Serb Victims Remembered in Bjelovac', 14 December 2008, available at: http://www.b92.net/eng/news/region.php?yyyy=2008&mm=12&dd=14&nav_id=55727 (accessed 3 June 2013).

—— (2011). 'Croatia Bans Commemoration to Serb Victims', 2 October 2011, available at: http://www.b92.net/eng/news/region-article.php?yyyy=2011&mm=10&dd=02&nav_id=76664 (accessed 8 March 2013).

Balkan Insight (2010a). 'Dodik Wants Review of Srebrenica Numbers', 9 April 2010, available at: http://www.balkaninsight.com/en/article/dodik-wants-review-of-srebrenica-numbers (accessed 3 February 2013).

—— (2010b). 'Blaškić Apology for Crimes in Bosnian War', 15 April 2010, available at: http://www.balkaninsight.com/en/article/blaksic-apology-for-crimes-in-bosnian-war (accessed 27 May 2013).

Ban, Ki-Moon (2009). *Report of the Secretary-General on the Administrative and Budgetary Aspects of the Options for Possible Locations for the Archives of the International Criminal Tribunal for the former Yugoslavia and the International Criminal Tribunal for Rwanda and the Seat of the Residual Mechanisms for the Tribunals*, S/2009/258, 21 May 2009, available at: http://www.icty.org/x/file/About/Reports%20and%20Publications/CompletionStrategy/090521_sg_report_residual_mechanism.pdf (accessed 21 November 2013).

—— (2010). 'Address to the Review Conference on the International Criminal Court: "An Age of Accountability"', 31 May 2010, available at: http://www.un.org/sg/selected-speeches/statement_full.asp?statID=829 (accessed 13 March 2013).

Barbalet, Jack (2005). 'Trust and Uncertainty: The Emotional Basis of Rationality', Conference Paper presented at the London School of Economics, 12 December 2005, available at: http://www.kent.ac.uk/scarr/events/Barbalet%20trust%20 paper%202.pdf (accessed 2 May 2013).

BBC (2007). 'Croatian Anger at Vukovar Verdict', 28 September 2007, available at: http:// news.bbc.co.uk/1/hi/world/europe/7017758.stm (accessed 5 February 2013).

—— (2012). 'Hague War Court Acquits Croat Generals Gotovina and Markač', 17 November 2012, available at http://www.bbc.co.uk/news/world-europe-20352187 (accessed 21 November 2012).

—— (2013a). 'Bosnian Town Holds "Funeral" to Protest at Unemployment', 4 March 2013, available at: http://www.bbc.co.uk/news/world-europe-21664488 (accessed 8 June 2013).

—— (2013b). 'Serbian President Apologizes for Srebrenica "Crime"', 25 April 2013, available at: http://www.bbc.co.uk/news/world-europe-22297089 (accessed 27 June 2013).

—— (2013c). 'Kenya MPs Vote to Withdraw from ICC', 5 September 2013, available at: http://www.bbc.co.uk/news/world-africa-23969316 (accessed 30 September 2013).

—— (2013d). 'Dutch State Liable for Three Srebrenica Deaths – Court', 6 September 2013, available at: http://www.bbc.co.uk/news/world-europe-23986063 (accessed 30 September 2013).

—— (2013e). 'EU Police Officer Killed in Kosovo', 19 September 2013, available at: http://www.bbc.co.uk/news/world-europe-24158153 (accessed 30 September 2013).

—— (2013f). 'African Union Summit on ICC Pullout over Ruto Trial', 20 September 2013, available at: http://www.bbc.co.uk/news/world-africa-24173557 (accessed 30 September 2013).

—— (2013g). 'UN Rejects Africa Bid to Halt Kenya Leaders' ICC Trials', 15 November 2013, available at: http://www.bbc.co.uk/news/world-africa-24961169 (accessed 2 December 2013).

Bilefsky, Dan (2013). 'Violence Mars Election in Kosovo', 4 November 2013, available at: http://www.nytimes.com/2013/11/05/world/europe/violence-mars-election-in-kosovo.html?_r=0 (accessed 7 November 2013).

Brammertz, Serge (2013a). 'Address of Prosecutor Serge Brammertz on the Occasion of the ICTY's Twentieth Anniversary', 27 May 2013, available at: http://www.icty.org/sid/11321 (accessed 29 May 2013).

—— (2013b). 'Completion Strategy Report: Prosecutor Brammertz's Address before the Security Council', 12 June 2013, available at: http://www.icty.org/sid/11335 (accessed 18 July 2013).

Brand, Judith and Valdete Idrizi (2012). *Grass-Root Approaches to Inter-Ethnic Reconciliation in the Northern Part of Kosovo*', *Kosovar Institute for Policy Research and Development*, Policy Paper Series 2012/03, February 2012, available at: http://www.kipred.org/advCms/documents/65788_Grassroots_approaches_to_ inter-ethnic_reconciliation_in_northern_Kosovo.pdf (accessed 31 August 2012).

BTI (2012). *BTI 2012: Kosovo Country Report*, available at: http://www.bti-project. de/fileadmin/Inhalte/reports/2012/pdf/BTI%202012%20Kosovo.pdf (accessed 8 November 2012).

—— (2014). *BTI 2014: Kosovo Country Report*, available at: http://www.bti-project. de/uploads/tx_jpdownloads/BTI_2014_kosovo.pdf (accessed 7 February 2014).

CDRSEE (n.d.). 'Joint History Project', available at: http://www.cdsee.org/projects/jhp (accessed 8 September 2013).

Commissioner for Human Rights of the Council of Europe (2012). *Post-War Justice and Durable Peace in the former Yugoslavia*, February 2012, available at: http://www.coe.int/t/commissioner/source/prems/Prems14712_GBR_1700_PostwarJustice.pdf (accessed 7 May 2013).

Del Ponte, Carla (2003). 'Address by Mrs Carla Del Ponte, Chief Prosecutor of the International Criminal Tribunal for the former Yugoslavia, to the United Nations Security Council', 10 October 2003, available at: http://www.icty.org/sid/8180 (accessed 9 July 2013).

—— (2005). 'Keynote Speech by Carla Del Ponte, Prosecutor of the International Criminal Tribunal for the former Yugoslavia, Annual Conference of Political Affairs Division IV, "Civilian Peace Building and Human Rights in South-East Europe"', 1 September 2005, available at: http://www.icty.org/sid/8544/en (accessed 16 July 2012).

—— (2007). 'Address by Tribunal Prosecutor Carla Del Ponte to NATO Parliamentary Assembly in Belgrade: The ICTY and the Legacy of the Past', 26 October 2007, available at: http://www.icty.org/sid/8829/en (accessed 29 January 2014).

Drakulić, Slavenka (2009). 'The False Repentance of Biljana Plavšić', 23 October 2009, available at: http://www.eurozine.com/articles/2009-10-23-drakulic-en-html (accessed 25 July 2013).

Džidić, Denis (2013a). '"Bosnian Book of the Dead" Published', 22 January 2013, available at: http://www.balkaninsight.com/en/article/bosnian-ngo-presents-written-memorial-to-victims (accessed 3 September 2013).

—— (2013b). 'European Parliament Backs RECOM Truth Commission Initiative', 21 March 2013, available at: http://www.balkaninsight.com/en/article/european-parliament-calls-for-rekom-support (accessed 4 September 2013).

—— (2013c). 'Balkan States "Must Back Truth Commission Now"', 20 May 2013, available at: http://www.balkaninsight.com/en/article/balkan-states-must-back-truth-commission-now (accessed 29 September 2013).

—— (2013d). 'Stanišić "in Shock" After Acquittal', 30 May 2013, available at: http://www.justice-report.com/en/articles/stanisic-in-shock-after-acquittal (accessed 5 June 2013).

EC (2012a). *Communication from the Commission to the European Parliament and the Council on the Main Findings of the Comprehensive Monitoring Report in Croatia's State of Preparedness for EU Membership*, COM(2012) 601 Final, 10 October 2012, available at: http://ec.europa.eu/enlargement/pdf/key_documents/2012/package/hr_rapport_2012_en.pdf (accessed 10 June 2013).

—— (2012b). *Comprehensive Monitoring Report on Croatia – Accompanying the Document "Communicating from the Commission to the European Parliament and the Council – Comprehensive Monitoring Report on Croatia's State of Preparedness for EU Membership*, SWD(2012) 338 Final, 10 October 2012, available at: http://eur-lex.europa.eu/LexUriServ/LexUriServ.do?uri=SWD:2012:0338:FIN:EN:PDF (accessed 10 June 2013).

European Commission against Racism and Intolerance (2011). *ECRC Report on Bosnia and Herzegovina (fourth monitoring cycle)*, 8 February 2011, available at: http://www.coe.int/t/dghl/monitoring/ecri/country-by-country/bosnia_herzegovina/BIH-CBC-IV-2011-002-ENG.pdf (accessed 9 June 2013).

EU (2013). 'Serbia and Kosovo Reach Landmark Deal', 19 April 2013, available at: http://eeas.europa.eu/top_stories/2013/190413_eu-facilitated_dialogue_en.htm (accessed 22 April 2013).

Gallup Balkan Monitor (2010). *Focus on Bosnia and Herzegovina*, November 2010, available at: http://www.balkan-monitor.eu/files/Gallup_Balkan_Monitor-Focus_On_Bosnia_and_Herzegovina.pdf (accessed 15 July 2013).

Golčevski, Nenad (2013). 'RECOM – A Regional Initiative for Supporting Reconciliation', 26th workshop of the PFP Consortium Study Group 'Regional Stability in South East Europe', August 2013, available at: http://www.bmlv.gv.at/pdf_pool/publikationen/pfpc_26_rssee.pdf (accessed 7 September 2013).

Gowans, Stephen (2001). 'Sorting through the Lies of the Račak Massacre and Other Myths of Kosovo', 15 February 2001, available at: http://www.mediamonitors.net/gowans1.html (accessed 6 October 2012).

Halimović, Dženana (2010). 'Genocide Denial Concern in Bosnia', 1 October 2010, available at: http://iwpr.net/report-news/genocide-denial-concern-bosnia (accessed 9 July 2013).

Hamber, Brandon and Gráinne Kelly (2005). *A Place for Reconciliation? Conflict and Locality in Northern Ireland*, Democratic Dialogue, Report 18, September 2005, available at: http://www.healingthroughremembering.org/images/j_library/lib/A%20Place%20for%20Reconciliation.pdf (accessed 11 June 2013).

Harhoff, Frederik (2013). 'ICTY Judge Frederik Harhoff's Email to 56 Contacts', 6 June 2013, available at: http://www.bt.dk/sites/default/files-dk/node-files/511/6/6511917-letter-english.pdf (accessed 19 July 2013).

Hedl, Drago (2013). 'Dispute over Serb Symbols Unsettles Croatia's Vukovar', 5 March 2013, available at: http://www.balkaninsight.com/en/article/dispute-over-serb-symbols-unsettles-croatia-s-vukovar (accessed 7 March 2013).

Hina (2013). 'Brammertz: ICTY's New Practice Makes it Hard to Prove Accused's Guilt', 4 June 2013, available at: http://dalje.com/en-world/brammertz--ictys-new-practice-makes-it-hard-to-prove-accuseds-guilt/470784 (accessed 7 June 2013).

Hocking, John (2012). 'Remarks of John Hocking, Opening of the Arusha Branch of the Mechanism for International Criminal Tribunals', 2 July 2012, available at: http://www.unmict.org/files/statements/120702_registrar_hocking_arusha_en.pdf (accessed 4 October 2013).

Hodžić, Refik (2012). 'Mittal Suppresses Memories of Omarska', 27 May 2012, available at: http://www.bosnia.org.uk/news/news_body.cfm?newsid=2848 (accessed 11 July 2013).

Human Rights Watch (1996). *Impunity for Abuses Committed During 'Operation Storm' and the Denial of the Right of Refugees to Return to the Krajina*, 1 August 1996, available at: http://www.hrw.org/reports/1996/Croatia.htm (accessed 6 February 2013).

—— (2001). *Under Orders: War Crimes in Kosovo*, 26 October 2001, available at: http://www.hrw.org/sites/default/files/reports/Under_Orders_En_Combined.pdf (accessed 30 November 2012).

—— (2006). *Croatia: A Decade of Disappointment – Continuing Obstacles to the Reintegration of Serb Returnees*, September 2006, available at: http://www.hrw.org/sites/default/files/reports/croatia0906webwcover.pdf (accessed 3 April 2013).

—— (2010). 'Kosovo/Albania: Investigate Alleged KLA Crimes', 15 December 2010, available at: http://www.hrw.org/es/news/2010/12/15/kosovoalbania-investigate-alleged-kla-crimes (accessed 5 October 2012).

—— (2012). 'Croatia – Country Summary', January 2012, available at: http://www.hrw.org/sites/default/files/related_material/croatia_2012.pdf   (accessed   8 March 2013).

ICG (2012). *Setting Kosovo Free: Remaining Challenges*, Europe Report No.218, 10 September 2012, available at: http://www.crisisgroup.org/~/media/Files/europe/balkans/kosovo/218-setting-kosovo-free-remaining-challenges (accessed 5 November 2012).

ICMP (2012). 'Over 7,000 Srebrenica Victims Have Now Been Recovered', 11 July 2012, available at: http://www.ic-mp.org/press-releases/over-7000-srebrenica-victims-recovered/ (accessed 7 July 2013).

—— (2013). 'Southeast Europe', available at: http://www.ic-mp.org/icmp-world-wide/southeast-europe/ (accessed 1 August 2013).

ICRC (2011). 'Kosovo: Fate of Over 1700 Missing Person yet to be Clarified', 24 November 2011, available at: http://www.icrc.org/eng/resources/documents/news-release/2011/kosovo-news-2011-11-25.htm (accessed 30 October 2012).

ICTY (n.d.). 'Achievements', available at: http://www.icty.org/sid/324 (accessed 7 September 2013).

—— (2005). 'ICTY Outreach Activities – 2005', available at: http://www.icty.org/sid/10116 (accessed 22 September 2013).

—— (2012a). 'ICTY Outreach Activities – 2012', available at: http://www.icty.org/action/outreachnews/11222 (accessed 22 September 2013).

—— (2012b). 'Conference on ICTY Legacy in Croatia Concludes in Zagreb', 8 November 2012, available at: http://www.icty.org/sid/11134 (accessed 21 January 2013).

—— (2013a). 'Judgement List', available at: http://www.icty.org/sections/TheCases/JudgementList (accessed 5 December 2013).

—— (2013b). 'The Cost of Justice', available at: http://www.icty.org/sid/325 (accessed 8 October 2013).

Immigration and Refugee Board of Canada (2003). 'Bosnia-Herzegovina: Return of Muslims to Vlasenica; Ethnic Breakdown of Population; Reports of Landmines Placed on the Property of Muslims to Discourage Return; Reports of Insecurity or Instability in Vlasenica', 8 September 2003, available at: http://www.irb-cisr.gc.ca/Eng/ResRec/RirRdi/Pages/index.aspx?doc=415213 (accessed 5 June 2013).

Intellinews.com (2013). 'Bosnia's Jobless Rate Flattens at 46.1% at End-March 2013 – Employment Agency', 30 May 2013, available at: http://www.intellinews.com/bosnia-and-herzegovina-1011/bosnia-s-jobless-rate-flattens-at-46-1-at-end-march-2013-employment-agency-6765/ (accessed 5 June 2013).

Internal Displacement Monitoring Centre (2012). *Kosovo: Durable Solutions Still Elusive 13 Years after Conflict*, 10 October 2012, available at: http://reliefweb.int/sites/reliefweb.int/files/resources/kosovo-overview-oct2012.pdf   (accessed 17 November 2012).

Ipsos Strategic Marketing (2011). *Attitudes towards War Crimes Issues, ICTY and the National Judiciary*, 18 October 2011, available at: http://www.osce.org/serbia/90422 (accessed 1 June 2013).

Ivanišević, Bogdan (2013). 'Falling Out of Love With the Hague Tribunal', 11 June 2013, available at: http://www.balkaninsight.com/en/article/falling-out-of-love-with-the-hague-tribunal (accessed 28 October 2013).

Jelačić, Nerma (2006). 'Rushing Over Truth Commissions Won't Aid Justice', 31 August 2013, available at: http://www.tuzilastvorz.org.rs/html_trz/(CASOPIS)/ENG/ENG07/1622.pdf (accessed 2 September 2013).

Jennings, Simon and Denis Džidžić (2008). 'Stolac: A Town Deeply Divided', 28 July 2008, available at: http://iwpr.net/report-news/stolac-town-deeply-divided (accessed 5 July 2013).

Johnstone, Diana (1999). 'The Račak Hoax', 20 January 1999, available at: http://emperors-clothes.com/articles/Johnstone/racakhoax.htm (accessed 6 October 2012).

Jorda, Claude (2000). 'Speech by his Excellency, Judge Claude Jorda, President of the International Criminal Tribunal for the former Yugoslavia, to the UN General Assembly', 20 November 2000, available at: http://www.icty.org/sid/7806/en (accessed 11 May 2013).

Kabashaj, Safet and Ivana Jovanović (2013). 'War Crimes Apologies Could Help Reconciliation', 26 February 2013, available at: http://www.setimes.com/cocoon/setimes/xhtml/en_GB/features/setimes/features/2013/02/26/feature-02 (accessed 29 October 2013).

Karabegović, Dženana and Ognjen Zorić (2013). 'Consternation at Serbian Security Officers' Acquittal', 3 June 20013, available at: http://iwpr.net/report-news/consternation-serbian-security-officers-acquittal (accessed 5 June 2013).

Karugarama, Tharcisse (2013). 'Statement by Honourable Tharcisse Karugarama, Minister of Justice and Attorney-General of Rwanda', 10 April 2013, available at: http://rwandaun.org/site/2013/04/10/statement-by-honourable-tharcisse-karugarama-minister-of-justice-and-attorney-general-of-rwanda/ (accessed 20 April 2013).

Kerry, John (2013). 'Special Court of Sierra Leone Appeals Chamber Upholds Conviction of Charles Taylor: Press Statement, John Kerry', 26 September 2013, available at: http://www.state.gov/secretary/remarks/2013/09/214823.htm (accessed 23 October 2013).

Lesova, Polya and Sarah Turner (2011). 'EU Agrees Closer Fiscal Ties; Britain Opts Out', 9 December 2011, available at: http://www.marketwatch.com/story/europe-summit-fails-to-reach-full-agreement-2011-12-08 (accessed 31 July 2013).

Lyons, Beth S. (2010). 'The Evolution of a Partisan: Observations of a Criminal Defense Attorney at the ICTR', July 2010, available at: http://works.bepress.com/beth_lyons/1 (accessed 25 September 2013).

Majola, Bongani (2013). 'Registrar's Speech at the Town Hall Meeting, 30 January 2013', available at: http://www.unictr.org/tabid/155/Default.aspx?id=1342 (accessed 18 July 2013).

Marty, Dick (2010). *Inhuman Treatment of People and Illicit Trafficking in Human Organs in Kosovo*, AS/Jur (2010) 46, 12 December 2012, available online at: http://www.assembly.coe.int/CommitteeDocs/2010/ajdoc462010prov.pdf (accessed 15 October 2012).

Matejčić, Barbara (2012). 'Vukovar Still Imprisoned by Its Bloody Past', 21 February 2012, available at: http://www.balkaninsight.com/en/article/vukovar-still-imprisoned-by-its-bloody-past (accessed 27 February 2013).

Mekina, Igor (2011). 'Analysis of Public Criticism and Support for the Initiative for RECOM', 20 September 2011, available at: http://www.zarekom.org/documents/Analysis-of-Public-Criticism-and-Support-of-the-Initiative-for-RECOM.en.html (accessed 7 June 2013).

Meron, Theodor (2004b). 'Address of Judge Theodor Meron, President of the ICTY, to the UN General Assembly', 15 November 2004', available at: http://www.icty.org/sid/8339/en (accessed 1 February 2013).

—— (2005). 'Statement of Theodor Meron, President of the International Criminal Tribunal for the former Yugoslavia, Delivered at the Inauguration of the War Crimes Chamber of the State Court of Bosnia and Herzegovina', 9 March 2005, available at: http://www.icty.org/sid/8632/en (accessed 17 July 2013).

—— (2012). 'Address of Judge Theodor Meron, President of the International Criminal Tribunal for the former Yugoslavia, to the United Nations General Assembly', 15 October 2012, available at: http://www.icty.org/x/file/Press/Statements%20and%20Speeches/President/121015_pdt_meron_un_ga_en.pdf (accessed 20 November 2012).

—— (2013a). 'Public Redacted Version of 13 February 2012: Decision of the President on Early Release of Mlađo Radić', 9 January 2013, available at: http://www.icty.org/x/cases/kvocka/presdec/en/130109.pdf (accessed 15 July 2013).

—— (2013b). 'ICTY's 20th Anniversary – Statement by President Judge Theodor Meron', 27 May 2013, available at: http://www.icty.org/sid/11319 (accessed 29 May 2013).

—— (2013c). 'Address of Judge Theodor Meron to the United Nations General Assembly', 14 October 2013, available at: http://www.icty.org/x/file/Press/Statements%20and%20Speeches/President/131014_pdt_meron_un_ga_en.pdf (accessed 6 November 2013).

Ministry of Finance and Treasury of BiH and UN Country Team (2010). *Progress Towards the Realization of the Millennium Development Goals in Bosnia and Herzegovina*, July/August 2010, available at: http://www.undp.org/content/dam/bosnia_and_herzegovina/docs/Research&Publications/MDG/MDGs%20Progerss%20Report%202010/BiH_MDGs_BiH_Progress_Report_2010_FINAL_ENG.pdf (accessed 8 May 2013).

Mitić, Suzana (2013). 'Štrbac: Hague Verdicts Still Surprising', 31 May 2013, available at: http://voiceofserbia.org/content/strbac-hague-verdicts-still-surprising (accessed 5 June 2013).

Moratti, Massimo (2004). 'The Return Process in Prijedor: Experiences of a Human Rights Officer', available at: http://migrationeducation.org/20.1.html?&rid=30&cHash=ffea973476a4502878869d5ff10a88fb (accessed 14 July 2013).

Moreno-Ocampo, Luis (2003). 'Election of the Prosecutor, Statement by Mr Luis Moreno-Ocampo, New York', 22 April 2003, available at: http://www.iccnow.org/documents/MorenoOcampo22Apr03eng.pdf (accessed 3 May 2013).

MRGI (2008). 'Croatia Overview', July 2008, available at: http://www.minority-rights.org/?lid=2647&tmpl=printpage (accessed 6 September 2012).

Murithi, Tim, and Allan Ngari (eds) (2011). *The ICC and Community-Level Reconciliation: In-Country Perspectives – Regional Consultation Report*, February 2011, available at: http://www.iccnow.org/documents/IJR_ICC_Regional_Consultation_Report_Final_2011.pdf (accessed 31 October 2013).

N'Sapu, Prince Albert Kumwamba (2010). 'Why the ICC Should Prosecute Legal Persons', March 2010, available at: http://www.globalpolicy.org/international-justice/the-international-criminal-court/general-documents-analysis-and-articles-on-the-icc/48871.html (accessed 2 February 2013).

Office of the High Representative (1995). *The General Framework Agreement for Peace in Bosnia and Herzegovina, Annex 7: Agreement on Refugees and Displaced Persons*, 14 December 1995, available at: http://www.ohr.int/dpa/default.asp?content_id=375 (accessed 2 March 2013).

Orentlicher, Diane F. (2008). *Shrinking the Space for Denial: The Impact of the ICTY in Serbia* (Washington D.C: Open Society Justice Initiative), available at: http://www.refworld.org/pdfid/4cdcebe12.pdf (accessed 30 October 2012).

—— (2010). *That Someone Guilty Be Punished: The Impact of the ICTY in Bosnia* (New York: Open Society Institute), available at: http://www.ictj.org/sites/default/files/ICTJ-FormerYugoslavia-Someone-Guilty-2010-English.pdf (accessed 2 November 2012).

OSCE (2010). *Kosovo Communities Profiles: 2010 – Kosovo Serbs*, available at: http://www.osce.org/kosovo/75450 (accessed 30 September 2012).

—— (2011a). *Challenges in the Resolution of Conflict-Related Property Claims in Kosovo*, June 2011, available at: http://www.osce.org/kosovo/80435 (accessed 5 November 2012).

—— (2011b). *Maintenance of Orthodox Graveyards in Kosovo*, September 2011, available at: http://www.osce.org/kosovo/84399 (accessed 5 November 2012).

—— (2011c). *Municipal Responses to Security Incidents Affecting Communities in Kosovo and the Role of Municipal Safety Councils*, December 2011, available at: http://www.osce.org/kosovo/86766 (accessed 5 November 2012).

—— (2013a). 'Gjakovë/Đakovica – Municipal Profiles', January 2013, available at: http://www.osce.org/kosovo/13111 (accessed 8 November 2013).

—— (2013b). 'Istog/Istok – Municipal Profiles', January 2013, available at: http://www.osce.org/kosovo/13115 (accessed 8 November 2013).

Parliamentary Assembly of the Council of Europe (2009). *History Teaching in Conflict and Post-Conflict Areas*, Recommendation 1880, 30 March 2009, available at: http://www.assembly.coe.int/Documents/AdoptedText/ta09/EREC1880.htm (accessed 4 September 2013).

Pavelić, Boris (2013a). 'Croatian Court: State Responsible for Serbs' Murder', 24 January 2013, available at: http://www.balkaninsight.com/en/croatian-court-procclaims-state-responsible-for-killed-serbs (accessed 1 March 2013). [Note that the misspelling of 'proclaims' is correct for this web address.]

—— (2013b). 'Croatian Veterans Plan Mass Rally against Cyrillic', 5 April 2013, available at: http://www.balkaninsight.com/en/article/rally-against-cyrillic-in-zagreb-sunday (accessed 16 May 2013).

—— (2013c). 'Croatian Town Installs Cyrillic Signs for Serbs', 26 August 2013, available at: http://www.balkaninsight.com/en/article/croatian-town-of-udbina-introduces-cyrrilic-1 (accessed 5 December 2013).

—— (2013d). 'Croatia War Veterans Trash Cyrillic Signs in Vukovar', 2 September 2013, available at: http://www.balkaninsight.com/en/article/vukovar-bilingualism-introduce-faces-violent-resistance (accessed 8 September 2013).

Pham, Phuong; Patrick Vinck, Mychelle Balthazard, Sokhom Hean and Eric Stover (2009). *So We Will Never Forget: A Population-Based Survey on Attitudes about*

Social Reconstruction and the Extraordinary Chambers in the Courts of Cambodia, January 2009, available at: http://hhi.harvard.edu/sites/default/files/publications/publications%20-%20vulnerable%20-%20so%20we%20will%20never%20forget.pdf (accessed 31 August 2013).

Radio Deutsche Welle (2012). 'Interview with Kosovo Prime Minister Hashim Thaçi', 23 October 2012, available at: http://www.kryeministri-ks.net/?page=2,107,3010 (accessed 23 October 2012).

Radio.net (2013). 'Croatian President, Parl't Speaker Urge Croatia, Bosnia to Turn to Future', 29 May 2013, available at: http://daily.tportal.hr/264904/Croatian-president-parl-t-speaker-urge-Croatia-Bosnia-to-turn-to-future.html (accessed 1 July 2013).

RECOM (2011b). 'The Statute', 26 March 2011, available at: http://www.zarekom.org/uploads/documents/2011/04/i_836/f_28/f_1865_en.pdf (accessed 30 June 2013).

—— (2013). 'The Bosnian Book of the Dead', 25 January 2013, available at: http://www.zarekom.org/news/The-Bosnian-Book-of-the-Dead.en.html (accessed 23 September 2013).

Reuters (2013). 'Thousands of Vukovar Croats Rally against Serb Cyrillic Signs', 2 February 2013, available at: http://www.reuters.com/assets/print?aid=USBRE91109C20130202 (accessed 6 March 2013).

Sadat, Leila Nadya (2012). 'The Legacy of the International Criminal Tribunal for Rwanda', 3 July 2012, available at: http://law.wustl.edu/harris/documents/ICTRLecture-LegacyAd%20HocTribunals9.12.12.pdf (accessed 20 June 2013).

Scully, Simone (2012). 'Ivory Coast Ex-President's War Crimes Trial Unlikely to Help Reconciliation', 17 November 2013, available at: http://simonescully.com/2012/11/17/ivory-coast-ex-presidents-war-crimes-trial-unlikely-to-help-reconciliation/ (accessed 2 September 2013).

SENSE (2008). 'Not a Word about Grubori', 16 July 2008, available at: http://www.sense-agency.com/icty/not-a-word-about-grubori.29.html?cat_id=1&news_id=11661 (accessed 6 February 2013).

—— (2012a). 'Dutch Supreme Court Confirms "Absolute Immunity" of UN', 13 April 2012, available at: http://www.sense-agency.com/icty.29.html?news_id=13817 (accessed 8 March 2013).

—— (2012b). 'Prosecution Will Consider a Motion for a Review of Gotovina and Markač Judgement', 21 November 2012, available at: http://www.sense-agency.com/icty/prosecution-will-consider-a-motion-for-a-review-of-gotovina-and-markac-judgment.29.html?news_id=14414 (accessed 21 December 2012).

—— (2013a). 'New Figures for Srebrenica Victims', 9 July 2013, available at: http://www.sense-agency.com/icty/new-figures-for-srebrenica-victims.29.html?news_id=15152 (accessed 28 June 2013).

—— (2013b). 'Instead of Resignation, Meron Offers Victims "New Chapter"', 26 July 2013, available at: http://www.sense-agency.com/icty/instead-of-resignation-meron-offers-victims-%E2%80%98new-chapter%E2%80%99.29.html?news_id=15214 (accessed 28 October 2013).

Shaw, Rosalind (2005). *Rethinking Truth and Reconciliation Commissions: Lessons from Sierra Leone*, United States Institute of Peace, Special Report 130, February 2005, available at: http://www.usip.org/sites/default/files/sr130.pdf (accessed 2 September 2013).

Stahn, Carsten (2011). 'Between "Faith" and "Facts": By What Standards Should We Assess International Criminal Justice?' Inaugural Lecture, 31 October 2011, available at: https://openaccess.leidenuniv.nl/bitstream/handle/1887/19651/Oratie%20Stahn.pdf?sequence=2 (accessed 18 May 2013).

State Court of BiH (2012). 'Đelilović, Mustafa et al.: Case Information', available at: http://www.sudbih.gov.ba/?opcija=predmeti&id=683&jezik=e (accessed 12 June 2013).

—— (2013). 'Indictment Issued against Vehid Subotić', 7 June 2013, available at: http://www.tuzilastvobih.gov.ba/komponente/print_vijesti.php?id=1923&jezik=e (accessed 12 June 2013).

Subotić, Jelena (2013b). 'Perspectives for Transitional Justice and Reconciliation', 26th workshop of the PFP Consortium Study Group 'Regional Stability in South East Europe', August 2013, available at: http://www.bmlv.gv.at/pdf_pool/publikationen/pfpc_26_rssee.pdf (accessed 7 September 2013).

Teršelić, Vesna (2013). 'Perspectives for Normalization in Croatia and Other Post-Yugoslav Countries in the Aftermath of ICTY Verdicts', 26th workshop of the PFP Consortium Study Group 'Regional Stability in South East Europe', August 2013 available at: http://www.bmlv.gv.at/pdf_pool/publikationen/pfpc_26_rssee.pdf (accessed 7 September 2013).

Tolbert, David (2013). 'Can International Justice Foster Reconciliation?' 10 April 2013, available at: http://www.ictj.org/news/can-international-justice-foster-reconciliation (accessed 23 October 2013).

TRIAL (Swiss Association against Impunity) (2012). *Written Information for the Consideration of Bosnia and Herzegovina's Second Periodic Report by the Human Rights Committee*, (CCPR/C/BIH/2), September 2012, available at: http://www2.ohchr.org/english/bodies/hrc/docs/ngos/TRIALAlternativeReportBosnia106.pdf (accessed 3 July 2013).

UN (1948). *Convention on the Prevention and Punishment of the Crime of Genocide, 9 December 1948*, available at: http://www.hrweb.org/legal/genocide.html (accessed 23 March 2013).

UN (2013). 'Special Representative, UN Security Council Members Hail 19 April Agreement as "Decisive Step" Towards Normalizing Serbia-Kosovo Relations', 14 June 2013, available at: http://www.un.org/News/Press/docs/2013/sc11033.doc.htm (accessed 20 June 2013).

UN Commission of Experts (1994). *Annex V: The Prijedor Report*, S/1994/674/Add.2 (Vol. I), 28 December 1994, available at: http://www.ess.uwe.ac.uk/comexpert/anx/V.htm (accessed 30 April 2013).

UNDP (2007). *Public Perceptions on Transitional Justice: Report on Transitional Justice Opinion Polling Survey Conducted in April-May 2007 in Kosovo*, May 2007, available at: http://uboconsulting.com/publications/Transitional%20Justice.pdf (accessed 1 November 2013).

UNDP (2011). *Mitrovicë/a Public Opinion Survey*, March 2011, available at: http://www.unkt.org/wp-content/uploads/2012/08/Final_ENG_Mitrovica-Opinion-Poll-5.pdf (accessed 17 June 2013).

UNHCR (2000). *Minority Returnees to the Republika Srpska – Bosnia and Herzegovina*, June 2000, available at: http://www.unhcr.org/3c3b02994.pdf (accessed 7 June 2013).

UNHCR (2013). '2013 UNHCR Regional Operations Profile – South-Eastern Europe', available at: http://www.unhcr.org/pages/49e48d766.html (accessed 9 June 2013).

UN News Centre (2011). 'Interview with Serge Brammertz, Prosecutor of the International Criminal Tribunal for the former Yugoslavia', 9 June 2011, available at: http://www.un.org/apps/news/newsmakers.asp?NewsID=33 (accessed 2 March 2013).

UN Security Council (2012). *Report of the Secretary-General on the United Nations Interim Administration Mission in Kosovo*, S/2012/603, 3 August 2012, available at: http://www.un.org/en/ga/search/view_doc.asp?symbol=S/2012/603 (accessed 11 May 2013).

US Department of State (2011). *2010 Human Rights Report: BiH*, 8 April 2011, available at: http://www.state.gov/documents/organization/160181.pdf (accessed 5 May 2013).

—— (2012). *2011 Country Reports on Human Rights Practices – Croatia*, 24 May 2012, available at: http://www.unhcr.org/refworld/country,,USDOS,,HRV,,4fc75aaac,0.html (accessed 10 March 2013).

Verbica, Angelina (2013). 'Election Violence in Kosovo Hits Serbs Hardest', 5 November 2013, available at: http://www.dw.de/election-violence-in-kosovo-hits-serbs-hardest/a-17206941 (accessed 9 November 2013).

Worthington, Peter (2001). 'The Hoax that Started a War', 2 April 2001, available at: http://www.balkanpeace.org/index.php?index=article&articleid=6989 (accessed 11 October 2012).

Zebić, Enis; Ognjen Zorić, Branka Mihajlović and Ljudmila Cvetković (2012). 'Croatian Joy, Serbian Anger at Gotovina Acquittal', 19 November 2012, available at: http://iwpr.net/report-news/croatian-joy-serbian-anger-gotovina-acquittal (accessed 21 December 2012).

Other

Duraković, Dina; Adnan Efendić, Aleksandar Draganić, Đorde Čekrlija, Ivan Barbalić, Fahrudin Memić and Edin Šabanović (2007). *Early Warning System: Third Quarterly Report – July/September 2007* (Sarajevo: UNDP).

Duraković, Dina; Adnan Efendić, Nicola Nixon, Aleksandar Draganić, Senad Slatina and Edin Šabanović (2010). *Early Warning System 2010* (Sarajevo: UNDP).

Youth Forum of Stolac (2008). *Pro Memoria Against Apartheid in the Stolac Municipality: March 2008* (unpublished document on file with the author).

XY Films (2004) *Justice Unseen, Slijepa Pravda* (Sarajevo: XY Films), available at: http://www.xyfilms.net/content/view/19/31/lang,english/ (accessed 5 May 2013).

Index